POSTSCRIPT TO ADVENTURE

POSTSCRIPT TO ADVENTURE

The Autobiography of Ralph Connor

by
Charles Gordon

Introduction: Clara Thomas
General Editor: Clara Thomas

Heritage Books No. 1

McClelland and Stewart Limited

ISBN O-7710-2228-X

The Canadian Publishers
McClelland and Stewart Limited
25 Hollinger Road, Toronto

Printed and bound in Canada

CONTENTS

Introduction . . . . *by* J. KING GORDON

CONTENTS

L' Envoi

FOREWORD

Postscript to Adventure: The Autobiography of Ralph Connor was written by Charles Gordon in the months immediately preceding his death in 1937. Its introduction, written by his son, J. King Gordon, underlines and testifies to the authenticity of this story of a gifted man who lived and worked in two careers with remarkable vigour and success. The beliefs and attitudes of Charles Gordon, Presbyterian minister, were dramatized in every one of the twenty-six novels he wrote under the pseudonym of Ralph Connor. Those values exactly matched and mirrored the needs and ideals of millions of readers in the first two decades of this century. As he recalled his life and wrote it down, Charles Gordon had neither relinquished his faith in those values nor lost his power to dramatize them in prose. His autobiography is not only a colourful story of an exceptional man and an exceptional life–it is also a lively document in Canada's cultural history.

Charles Gordon was one of six sons and one daughter of a Presbyterian minister who had come to Canada from Scotland as a missionary to a Scotch settlement near Sherbrooke in the Eastern Townships of Quebec. His mother, Mary Robertson of Sherbrooke, was a woman of outstanding ability and, for her time, unusual opportunities. She had been educated at Sherbrooke Academy and then at Mount Holyoke College in Massachusetts, and as a very young woman, had refused an invitation to become Principal of Mount Holyoke in order to marry Donald Gordon. Her son, Charles, was born in the Indian Lands' Presbyterian Manse in Glengarry County, Ontario. He grew up there and in Harrington, a village near the town of St. Mary's in southwestern Ontario. He graduated from the University of Toronto, taught school for a short time, attended Knox College and began his career as a missionary in southern Manitoba and then at Banff. He was ordained in 1890 at Calgary, the centre of "the largest presbytery in the world."

From that time on Charles Gordon was a committed westerner, enthralled by the size, the beauty and the variety of western Canada and ebulliently optimistic about its growth and development. Beginning in 1894 he was centred in Winnipeg, first as a missionary on the outskirts of "a hustling city fresh from its big boom of '81-'83," and then as the first–and continuing–minister of St. Stephen's church. He continued at St. Stephen's until the end of his ministerial career. In World War I he went overseas as Chaplain to Winnipeg's 79th Cameron Highlanders. Then he became Chaplain-In-Chief to the Canadian Forces Overseas. He was Moderator of the Presbyterian

Church in 1921, and a dedicated worker for the union with the Methodist and the Congregational churches which came into being in 1925.

The phenomenal publishing career of Ralph Connor began in 1896 with the writing of a story, "Christmas Eve in a Lumber Camp," for the Presbyterian church paper, *The Westminster Magazine*. Its editor, James MacDonald, scented literary success for its author from the start. He pressed Charles Gordon into revisions and extensions of his work until the book *Black Rock: A Tale of the Selkirks* was completed. Canadian booksellers advised Mac-Donald to risk an edition of only three hundred copies, but the chapters which had been serialized for *The Westminster* had been very popular and in the end a first edition of five thousand copies was printed–a huge printing for a Canadian publisher at that time. Meanwhile, George Doran, also a Canadian, beginning his publishing career with Fleming H. Revell of Chicago, publishers of religious literature, had read the serialized chapters. He brought out an edition of five hundred copies in the United States. Its success was immediate and, as Doran reports, fantastic:

> Its success was immediately so great that many pirated editions appeared, for the book had not been printed in the United States and consequently it was not copyrighted. While the author and the authorized publisher derived no revenue from these pirated editions, the sale of millions of copies made Ralph Connor a household name in the United States and prepared a very large public for his later books. The next book, *The Sky Pilot*, a tale of the foothills, had an immediate sale of 250,000 copies which later reached well over a million copies (George Doran, *Chronicles of Barabbas, 1884-1934*).

With Ralph Connor's third book, *The Man From Glengarry*, his American sales exceeded five million copies. Ralph Connor was the great success of Doran's publishing firm, then and for many years later. Every year in the fall they published a new Connor novel with an initial run of 200,000 copies. Every year Charles Gordon struggled, and George Doran struggled, to get a completed manuscript: "Sometimes we would be printing up to page 256 while he was writing page 257 . . . And we would be obliged to cable the last 100,000 words to London for the British edition." Ralph Connor's success put Doran in the first rank of American publishers and it immeasurably extended the field of influence of Charles Gordon, Canadian Presbyterian minister.

In *Postscript To Adventure* Gordon speculates on the reasons for the phenomenal success of his first novels. In them he described the West from his own experience and out of his own boundless optimism:

[They] gave an authentic picture of life in the great and wonderful country of western Canada, rich in colour and alive with movement, the stamping ground of the buffalo and his hunters, the land of the trapper, the Mounted Police and that virile race of men and women, the first pioneers who turned the wild wilderness into civilization.

Then he continues by testifying that these pictures in his novels were taken from personal experience. He knew the country and he had ridden over it. He knew the mountain passes and he had swum his horse across the rivers. Most important of all he had met and respected the men and women who were pioneering that country.

Charles Gordon also considered that his "definitely religious motif" was a reason for the success of his fiction. In this he is corroborated by George Doran whose autobiography gives a detailed sketch of the importance of evangelical publishing in nineteenth-century America, and of its gradual expansion into the fiction field with the success of a few best-selling authors like Ralph Connor and Harold Bell Wright. Gordon accounts for his vast readership by the fact that "religion is here set forth in its true light as a synonym of all that is virile, straight, honourable and withal tender and gentle in true men and women."

It is certainly true that on this continent in the nineteenth century novels had been either considered "women's reading," romantic diversions for busy housewives, or looked upon by a puritanical, pioneer people as doubtful diversions for a truly Christian man. When Gordon says "I have received hundreds of letters expressing gratitude for a novel that presented a quality of religious life that 'red-blooded' men could read and enjoy," he is testifying to the enthusiasm with which men as well as women read his work. Theodore Roosevelt, for instance, assured Charles Gordon that he could pass an examination in *Black Rock* and *The Sky Pilot;* in England Sydney Webb professed great admiration for his work; and in fact, hosts of readers in America and Canada, England and Scotland, were for a time, familiar with his tales and with the name of Ralph Connor.

In 1913 Thomas Guthrie Marquis, writing the chapter "English-Canadian Literature" for Doughty and Shortt's *Canada and Its Provinces*, dated the beginning of the "modern school" of Canadian fiction writers at about 1908. Marquis discusses the work of Ralph Connor who is, he says, one of the new group who have moved away from provincial attitudes and techniques to be influenced by world standards. His final comment on Connor's fiction adds a penetrating and convincing extension to Charles Gordon's own assessment of his novels' appeal: "Gordon's power lies not so much in his ability as a constructive artist as in the strong, isolated passages. His gentler action is commonplace; but his incidents, such as football matches and barroom brawls, are masterly bits of work."

In fact the "red-blooded" men whom Gordon saw as being benefited by the quality of religious life in his work were also getting a large measure of action, strongly spiced with violence. Connor's first works were early, and very typically Canadian examples of the genre, long since established in American fiction and film, as the "western." They are simple, strong, moral fables, characterized by an intermixture of violent actions and set against a western frontier-background of rugged magnificence. They were exciting stories and they answered his readers' dreams of freedom, progress and a new, vigorous society. They combined all this with the attitudes, the aims, and the morality of Gordon's own unshakable religious ideals and convictions.

Furthermore, his belief in Canada and her future was so strong, and so passionately did he set up the ideal of "a Canadian" that his works could–and did–give his readers the archetypal "TRUE NORTHMAN, STRONG AND FREE." This man Gordon saw as a product of the challenges of the land itself. The magnificence of Canada and the very difficulties of its settling were to him a sublime challenge from God for the testing of man. Charles Gordon's life was grounded in his belief in a God-centered universe, and his readers responded to his sense of challenge, endurance and triumph with an enthusiasm and, sometimes, a faith that equalled his own.

In *Postscript To Adventure*, Charles Gordon speaks of Ralph Connor with the detachment of a third person: "Of all men, the most surprised at the reception of his books was Ralph Connor himself. He had not the slightest ambition to be a writer. He made little effort after polished literary style. Things just came to him and he put them down." Charles Gordon may not have had literary ambitions in any specific direction, but as every word in *Postscript To Adventure*, as well as his other works, testifies, he was a natural story-teller and dramatizer of men, women, and their lives. Once that side of his nature and his gift had become productive, had been "born" as it were under the psuedonym of Ralph Connor, it flourished in invention until his death. The moral fable of man struggling and winning over the base elements in his nature was to Gordon the groundwork of his writing: "*Black Rock* is an example of that rare thing in writing, a successful novel with a purpose." But that "purpose" was also contained in works whose energy of narrative, inventiveness of plot, and building of action to climactic incidents display the real gift of the creative storyteller as well as Gordon's own unflagging effort.

This characteristic combination of "Connor qualities" distinguishes *Postscript To Adventure*. Both the strengths of his writing and the qualities of the man that made that writing famous are evident in it. Its thirty-nine chapters are divided into five parts and though the arrangement of the book is chronological, each chapter, particularly in Parts I, II, and III, is an entity, a short story in the autobiographical mould. The early parts of the book, the recollections of youth written by an old man, incorporate an excitement, an optimism, an energy, and a quality of myth-making that make for good reading. Charles Gordon's experiences in World War I are the watershed in the book. After that horror and his efforts to engage Canada in a united war effort and then to engage America in a war effort on the side of the Allies, he was a sadder and a more skeptical man. The faith which he first had in the League of Nations was undermined by the events of the twenties and thirties. There is a shadow across the last sections of *Postscript To Adventure* which adds to the depth of its authenticity. What Gordon had hoped for, what Connor had written of with such ebullient optimism–the possibility of man's understanding of man and nation of nation through Christian charity–was eroded and undermined as time went on. But the courage and the determination of Charles Gordon himself did not fail. The very writing of *Postscript To Adventure* at the end of his life is a final testimony to the endurance and the energy of his ideals.

Clara Thomas
York University,
October, 1974.

INTRODUCTION

The Lake stretches for twelve miles. The nearest island is called Lone Tree Island. Ten or fifteen years ago the solitary dead tree fell down but the name persists. Beyond it is the Island with the Leaning Pine Tree. Then beyond farther is Bare Point and past the point the channel taken by the boats going to Long Lake or Blindfold Lake or Yellow Girl Bay.

This is the view from the Birkencraig Lookout. My father did most of his writing there in the last few years. In the morning the lake would sparkle in the sunshine. Across the lake in the boat channel the motorboats would crawl along—stubby gray fishing boats with a slow pop-pop-pop, Chris-Craft with an airplane roar racing to meet the Winnipeg train, livery boats from the Devil's Gap Camp, with a long string of canoes and rowboats cruising up the lake for a day's fishing. Sometimes a canoe would come silently close to shore immediately below the Lookout, in and out of the bays of Birkencraig. Then he would stop writing and watch the flash of the paddle and study critically the stroke of the man in the stern. At night, when the full moon rose over the Indian Reservation and climbed up into the southeastern sky, the lake would be turned into molten silver. On these nights the birches near the Lookout would appear ghostly and they whispered amongst themselves. There he would sit writing in the circle of yellow light from the oil lamp and over his shoulder and beyond him you could see the silver lake stretching for miles, silver to the horizon.

He slept up there. When he first came down from the city in July he would tell us how he lay awake listening to the lapping of the waters on the rocks below him, how the crows wakened him in the morning holding council in the spruce trees, how, when he got up and looked out in the early morning, he saw a mother duck and her six little ducks in the water just beside the Pump House.

For more than thirty years we have been coming down to the Lake of the Woods. First he came alone and pitched a tent on an island close to the mainland. He was working on a book. The publishers were calling for manuscript and it was impossible to get on with it in the midst of all the calls upon him in Winnipeg. He would cook his breakfast over an open fire, work all morning and paddle across to the boarding house at Norman for lunch. The next summer he took me down with him and I slept for the first time on a balsam bough bed and heard the sound of the wind in the pine trees at night. He gave me my first lessons in swimming and woodcraft and in handling a canoe.

Next year we acquired Birkencraig—my highland grandfather gave it its name—and built the cottage and the Lookout. We all grew up to feel more at home in the woods and in and on the water than in cities. Our friends would come down to visit us and there would be sixteen or eighteen around the dinner table on the veranda. When the numbers got down to eight or nine we had a "small camp." In those carefree days before the war, before the world had any problems, it was tennis and swimming and sailing, even woodchopping and splitting was made a game of skill, and in the evening singing round a fire. Sometimes it would be a big bonfire on the point, to which our friends would come from other islands. More often, especially as the autumn chill was felt, we would gather around the fire of pine knots in the living room. Then, beginning with plantation songs, he would gradually lead us into the rousing French-Canadian river songs— "Alouette" and "En Roulant." But when he sang Drummond's pathetic habitant ballad—"The Wreck of the Julie Plante"—we would sit hushed looking at his face in the firelight.

The war interrupted all that. But afterwards, even when we became scattered across the Dominion, Birkencraig continued to exert its powerful spell upon us. It remained a place of gathering for Clan Gordon. The summer of 1937 was a particularly happy one. We were all home for a few weeks together, with the exception of Marjorie in London, who was preparing to leave for home via the Orient. There was a new camper too, in young Peter, aged fifteen months, the first grandson. The Book was the main concern. He would sit writing in the Lookout. In the study below the typewriters were pounding out the first draft of the typescript. When dinner was called and he came down from the Lookout he would stop at Peter's window and talk to him through the screen. Peter, supposed to be sleeping, would inevitably welcome these interviews with enthusiasm. A second and a third call would go out and he would arrive apologetic but actually unrepentant and take his place at the head of the table. The talk would range all the way from the latest quirk in the outboard motor to the situation in Spain or in China. In recent years the World has invaded the sanctuary of Birkencraig. After dinner half a dozen of us would sit often for an hour or more discussing with him what was happening and what was likely to happen in Europe and Asia and in our own country.

It had taken a great deal of persuasion to get him launched on the reminiscences of his life. He seemed to think that that sort of thing should come at the end of life. And for all his seventy-six years he lived as a young man. There had been no break in the adventure of his life. It had been a natural transition from the woods of Glengarry to the playing fields of Toronto University, from the prospecting trips with his eldest brother in the northern woods to the pioneer mission field in the foothills of the Rockies, from the fight against the devil and political corruption in the boom days of Winnipeg to the Great War, from the postwar struggle for social justice to the desperate struggle for world peace. Into each conflict he carried the faith and courage and gaiety of a young man. In the later years it would often surprise me to see his persistent challenge to life in contrast with the disillusionment and cynicism of so many of my own contemporaries. No, reminiscences were the work of an old man who had laid down the burden of today's battle and who looked back upon a finished life. That was not his role—yet.

Once he began to write most of his doubts vanished. His memory was clear and vivid, of a photographic quality, as he says. He lived again his earlier days, fought again the old battles, entered into the valleys of defeat and despair, climbed the peaks of triumph. It was an exciting retracing of steps. The more recent years were not so easy. The war and postwar periods had raised so many questions and left so many unanswered. The trenches of Flanders in 1916 had taught him what war was really like. All through the twenties it remained unthinkable to him that man would ever again embark upon such tragic folly. Men had fought and died that war might never again come upon the earth. The League of Nations had arisen embodying the will to peace of the peoples of the earth. But the nations seemed held in a fate that doomed them to destruction. The consequences of Versailles worked out their disastrous conclusions in Europe. Nations and their leaders, driven by fears and hatred, led on to acts of aggression by their nationalistic or imperialistic necessities betrayed the League and entered upon feverish preparations for a new war.

He wrote faithfully of his part as the chaplain of the 43rd Cameron Highlanders and reproduced the idealism that carried him through those terrific years. At night by the fire he would stoutly defend the League, tell of its achievements, account for its failures. Day by day, the papers would arrive from town carrying the news of Spain and China, of Hitler, Franco and Mussolini. He was tired, and the writing was putting his faith to a final test. Someone would be chopping at the block. He would come down and taking up the other ax demonstrate the fine art of two-ax splitting. His eye was as true as it had been fifty years ago. Or he would go down to the dock and push off in his canoe to the next island. In half an hour he would be back with a couple of straight sticks of birch or cherry with the curve of the root to form the handle. For hours he would work with his knife and sandpaper. Then would come shellac and more sandpaper until the handle was like polished ivory. Then he would return to those war and postwar chapters.

My work took me back east late in August. I had postponed my leaving as long as possible. It is always difficult to go away from Birkencraig. This year it was especially difficult. I can see him quite clearly standing on the dock in his old gray sweater beside my mother and young Peter, who always liked to see the boats come and go. He stood there with his hand raised in good-bye until the boat rounded the point of an island and he was out of sight. Word of his illness came early in October. At first the news was not alarming and he had been in such good health all summer that we felt little anxiety. Then the reports grew worse. After an operation, he did not show his usual powers of recuperation. The day I was leaving Toronto for Winnipeg I received word from John Farrar about the manuscript. Certain work of revision was necessary and not wishing to disturb him during his illness John Farrar had asked me to take it in hand. I agreed but did so with a heavy sense of responsibility.

All next day as the train swayed around the curves in the barren country north of Lake Superior I read the manuscript, making my notes and comments. In the evening I had finished. It had been a strangely moving experience. For in that day I had lived through his life with him, not in morbid retrospect but vividly as he lived it, recapturing with him its excitement, its light and its shadow. I put down my immediate impressions on the slip of paper that is now before me.

"Here is a life whose keynote is courage and a high devotion to humanity. See him in Glengarry, his mother's spirit filling him with awe and reverence, the woods casting their spell upon him, the men of the woods, battling the elemental forces within and without, his heroes. See him at Harrington, fighting a desperate struggle with his brother as they race one another following the binder—'for ten years a pain over my heart.' See him at Varsity, 135 pounds in the scrimmage, gallantly vying with his mighty brother, Gib, the greatest half-back in Canada. See him in the struggle with the storm on Lake Nipissing, that desperate chute on the Wanapitei. There is the man, courage always pressing the limitations of the flesh. After college the sense of mission takes possession of him. He hears about the men of the West from the Great Superintendent and to the West he gives the best years of his life, struggling not against flesh and blood but against principalities and powers. He never ceased to be a Westerner. The same challenge of a great cause took him to France. He was a patriot but in his response to the war there was something much more than patriotism. He believes till today in the idealism which was at the root of the Allied cause. He hated war; but other things he hated more—greed, cowardice and hypocrisy. And after the war in his industrial work, in his struggle for justice you see the man himself. He will be remembered not as an old man but one to whom as to a youth life was an adventure."

I could not get out of my mind the thought—here is a life that is complete. The postscript has been written. So strong was this feeling upon me that when the train stopped at the railway divisional point of Armstrong I had the dispatcher telephone Winnipeg for news. The report was reassuring. He had spent a quiet day and seemed better. He was looking forward to seeing me in the morning. A great weight was off my mind. Apparently my premonition had been wrong. In his phrase, "the best of life is still ahead"—new adventure, new struggle, new joys. I thought of my mother's unwavering and cheerful courage through much anxiety and was thankful that she would have rest tonight. I wakened just as dawn was breaking over lakes and granite hills, so reminiscent of the Lake of the Woods country. It was gray and the first snow flurries were filling up the pockets in the rocks.

He died peacefully that morning just as the first light was showing. In the days and weeks that followed when it was so difficult to reconcile oneself to the end of a life that was so much of the very essence of life, the impressions of that train journey kept recurring—flashes of his debonair charm, his cool courage, his quiet faith in God and man. "The measure of a man's power to help his brother," he had written in the preface to *The Sky Pilot* forty years ago, "is the measure of the love in the heart of him and of the faith he has that at last the good will win. With this love that seeks not its own and this faith that grips the heart of things, he goes out to meet many fortunes, but not that of defeat." One day these words may be inscribed on stone in Old Kildonan close beside the memorials to those other pioneers of the West—John Black, John M. King, James Robertson. But already they are graven in the hearts and lives of thousands who journeyed with him for a while along the road.

In editing the manuscript no important alteration has been made and it stands substantially in its original form. In the interest of unity certain sections have been reduced and some have been expanded from earlier drafts. In the Glengarry chapter, for instance, certain stories, the description of the "university of the forest," additional comments on the school curriculum have been added from the pencil drafts in the original notebooks. The chapter entitled "The Coming of Ralph Connor" was in the original scheme of the book but for some reason, perhaps his own modesty, it was omitted from the final draft. We have felt that it should be included.

When first the idea of the book was projected I talked over the scheme with him. As I have indicated, he was averse to writing his "Memoirs." The book, if written at all, would be simply a running account of incidents and personalities that had played some part in his life. I have before me what are probably the first jottings on the plan of the book:

> Men women & things
> as I met them
> as they came to me
> as they touched me

Later, the autobiographical character developed. But when the book is considered as an autobiography there are many omissions, much material absent that one should like to see included. A letter from my mother dated August 22nd had said that he was "working away at his book—has got through the League of Nations. I hope it will soon be finished. Then he will have to be sure he has not left out any important period." Much more could have been written about the West —not only the story of the foothills and the ranges, but the story of the whole development of Western Canada. For half a century his work was built into its history.

While his interest in public affairs was constantly drawing him beyond the confines of his church he never ceased to regard himself primarily as a Christian minister. A stanch Presbyterian in the Calvinist tradition of his Highland forbears, he had little patience with creeds that guarded beliefs of ancient times but failed to express the new truth eternally revealing itself. He had even less patience with denominational lines that stood as barriers between the people of the church of Christ. Religion to him was what met the deepest needs of lonely men and women in prairie shacks, of boys in the mining camps and the great cities, of brave men facing wounds and death, of peoples demented by greed and hatred and the dread of war. It was natural that he should be at the very heart of the movement for church union. In Western Canada he worked out with others successful schemes of co-operation and joint missions between the various Protestant churches. As early as 1902, along with Principal Patrick and Dr. Bryce of Manitoba College, he carried the greetings of the Presbyterians to the Methodist Conference. Years afterwards he spoke of that memorable occasion in a letter to Dr. Chown, the honored leader of Canadian Methodism: "After a reference to the vast possibilities agricultural and otherwise of the West, I referred to the anomaly of one great church in Canada finding it necessary to send a deputation to another great church in Canada to bear greetings, each of which recognized the other as a true church of Christ. Never should we reap the spiritual harvest of these plains until we had found a way to unite our forces." Principal Patrick took up the suggestion and uttered the challenge to the Methodist General Conference which responded in the famous resolution. The march to church union had begun. In that march of nearly a quarter of a century we see him constantly in the vanguard. In season, out of season, in presbytery, synod and general assembly, in country schoolhouse and great city church he urged the vast opportunities that opened up before a United Church of Canada. In 1921 the General Assembly of the Presbyterian Church chose him as moderator. The union issue had reached its crisis and speaking engagements in all parts of the Dominion made continued demands upon his time. Perhaps most vividly remembered are his visits to his native county of Glengarry and to the Maritime Provinces with Dr. James Endicott of the Methodist Church. To those Highland congregations, intensely loyal to their historic faith, he carried the appeal and the challenge of a higher loyalty to a faith and to a church that were the fulfillment of the best in the Presbyterian tradition. On June 10, 1925, in the city of Toronto, he witnessed the consummation of that early vision that came to him on the western mission field, the union of the Presbyterian, Methodist and Congregational churches in the United Church of Canada.

There are many who will remember him as a great preacher. It is interesting that he reached the height of his power in the pulpit after he had retired from the active ministry in St. Stephen's, Winnipeg, and was devoting himself to preaching and lecturing missions across Canada, in the United States, and in New Zealand and Australia. The secret of his power lay in his awareness of the tremendous mission of the church in desperate times and in the imaginative quality of heart and mind which may well be the very essence of the life of the spirit. When he preached on the Shepherd Psalm you followed the shepherd with his sheep over the hillside, to the best pastures, to the quiet pool at noontide and back to the shelter of the canyon as evening fell. If it was the Good Samaritan, he took you to the mountain road where a traveler lay beaten and bleeding. You watched the busy Levite hurrying on his way, saw the Priest, preoccupied with temple duties, pass with a glance, saw the Samaritan come along on his beast, dismount and run quickly to the side of the wounded man. "The highway religion is the religion for these days!" It was more than storytelling, for there was in it much of the Highland fire of his father, a compelling, persuasive quality that drove you to seek the Kingdom of Heaven that he knew to be a present reality.

The chapter on the Council of Industry by no means exhausts the account of his struggles for social justice and industrial peace which, beginning in the mining camps in the eighties, continued until the end. The other day I came across the typescript draft of a statement he wrote in 1936 on behalf of the young unemployed men from the relief camps of Western Canada. They had organized a trek to present their grievances to the Canadian government at Ottawa. They were stopped at Regina, Saskatchewan, by the police who employed unnecessary violence so that a riot ensued. Here is a single paragraph of his plea for justice:

"We, the Trekkers, appeal to you, the Youth of Canada, to take such action as will secure to us, and to hundreds of thousands of young Canadians, like us, out of work, the right to live, by honest work as free men and not as slaves:

the right to live, as you live, in decent contacts;

the right to give help, as you do, to those who depend upon you;

the right to make homes, as you do, for those who love us and whom we love.

The Trekkers cannot bring themselves to believe that you, the Youth of Canada, so recently their comrades in the classroom and on the campus, in factory, shop and office, independent and free, in the full enjoyment of your rights in this our common country, will forget us, who are denied these rights and allow us to be quite forgotten."

Something of his intense concern for world peace and his loyalty to the League of Nations comes out in the later chapters. Just after he had finished his work on the manuscript early in September a letter arrived calling his attention to the statement of the moderator of the United Church of Canada on the appalling suffering and devastation resulting from the war in China. I am told that for days after receiving that letter he went about greatly distressed and though exhausted gave himself to hours of labor in preparing a reply. The result was a seven and a half page letter calling upon Christian people especially to rally their forces against the onward march of fascism. It was his last public writing and is included just as he wrote it as Chapter XXXVIII.

During his illness the news reached him of the death of a very dear friend, Principal Clarence MacKinnon of Pinehill Theological College in Halifax. A memorial service was to be held in Dr. MacKinnon's former church, Westminster, Winnipeg. He was asked by his friend, the incumbent pastor of the church, if he would prepare a tribute to Dr. MacKinnon to be read at the service. He was weak. Next morning was his operation. But he took his pencil and began writing. It was never finished. I came across the fragment—the last thing he wrote:

"A common sorrow, a common loss. Your minister, dearly loved and trusted, and my old-time friend, comrade and fellow worker has gone from our sight. The voice which so often charmed us is still, that smile of warm illumination that so often drew our hearts to him is . . . A comrade in the ministry of the gospel, a faithful champion of the principles of our holy religion, we remember him with gratitude and tender affection. His service to his country and to his church as a great preacher and teacher others will speak of—I think of him as you do as a dearly loved intimate friend loyal to the heart's core, true in all circumstances. We remember him and thank God for him. His friendship enriched life for us and strengthened our faith in man and in God. Now he is gone but only from our sight. He lives in our lives. For lives are like flowers . . ."

He told my mother that he wanted to include a passage from Gwen's Canyon in *The Sky Pilot*. For he was back in the canyon where the flowers grow that only those who know suffering can see. As the shadows in the canyon darkened the beauty of the flowers seemed to grow more intense. And he went on until the canyon opened out upon a great sunset.

J. KING GORDON

PART ONE
Horizons Beyond

CHAPTER I

The Chief of the Clan

HIGHLAND COLOR AND CHARACTER—SCOTTISH
LEGEND — FAMILY DISCIPLINE

In their first reaches rivers take their color from their springs.
From the glaciers of the Great Divide the Bow River leaps steel-
gray, and steel-gray it flows for a hundred miles. When the July sun
beats hot upon the mountains, a hundred rills and streamlets from
either side pour their waters into the Bow, but each little rill is
steel-gray. At the foot of Mount Rundle there is a change. There the
Bow makes a sudden turn and pours its waters down a great valley
flanked by mighty snow-capped ranges. But the tourist standing on
the lofty terrace of the Canadian Pacific Chalet notes that the water
along its right bank is no longer steel-gray. There the little Spray,
blue as the sky, pours its limpid waters into the river, and for miles
the Bow on its north bank runs blue-gray and continues blue-gray
for a hundred miles or more. But flowing through the foothill country into the mighty Saskatchewan, the Bow runs brown, watering
millions and millions of acres on its way to the sea.

So it is with lives of Highland men: they take vivid color first
from their mountain springs, but later from the softer plains of
their environment they grow dull and brown, less romantic but
just as wet.

My father was a Highlander from the misty glen of the Garry,
within sight of the Big Bens and within sound of the tumbling
Tilt. A glen glorious in the sun with the purple tints of heather and
the golden glow of the broom, and when evening falls whispering
with eerie voices from the spirit world about.

Even after the schools and the university had done their best
or worst for him, my father was never quite sure about the ghosts
and warlocks. After all, who could tell? Strange sights were seen

3

and weird voices were heard. His mystic origin never quite lost its touch upon him.

There still shivers in the psychic caverns of my soul an eerie thrill as I recall and tell my children the story of the return to the glen of the phantom regiment of Atholl Highlanders, led by their hawk-faced chief, who had died, man by man, on the far sands of India. Well do I remember how we listened with a shudder to my father telling this weird bedtime story in the old Glengarry manse. The tale runs thus: It was in one of the Indian wars. Highlanders from the glen were set to hold a little hill on the left flank till the main body should come up. Gradually the enemy stole round their flanks and threatened their rear.

"What now?" asked a young captain of his chief. "Shall we fall back?"

"Na na, my bonnie lad," said his chief cheerily. "Here we were set and here will we stand."

And stand they did, to be cut down to a man. In every shieling of the clan and in the castle hall the story was told to wives, mothers and children, while in the evenings the pipers pacing slow wailed out the "Lament of the Hill."

"One evening," continued my father, his voice dropping a tone or two, "my brother Gilbert and a neighboring lad, after the day's work, were taking the horses up the glen to the pasture. Their way led up between tall firs, past the iron gate leading into the policies of the Duke of Atholl, over a bridge that crossed a burn, and so on up the glen. It was growing dark as they neared the bridge. Suddenly their ponies stood still, ears pricked forward, shivering and refusing to proceed. As the boys tried to force them onward the horses wheeled with a snorting and shivering and finally turned and raced back down the road. A second time the boys tried to force their ponies on, but in vain. The third time my brother, shortening the grip of the reins said, 'I'll make ye go forward this time,' and forced his pony back to the bridge. At that moment they heard the sound of marching feet coming toward them. The ponies sprang off the road and stood trembling." At this point my father's voice would take on a husky tone. "Down the glen they could see the shadowy forms of marching Highlanders, and hear the tramp—

tramp—tramp—tramp of each file as they crossed the little bridge. Past the shuddering boys the column marched. As the officer in command, six feet three, marching in the rear passed my brother, sitting shivering on the pony, he turned his head and glared fiercely into my brother's eyes. On they went like marching shadows, wheeled to the right, and marched through the closed iron gate tramp—tramp—tramp—tramp right into the Duke of Atholl's policies, and were lost among the dark firs beyond. Then, mark you!"—my father would raise an admonishing finger—"the ponies, mad with terror, dashed homeward, the boys rushed into the house and in a paroxysm of tears threw themselves at our mother's feet and told their strange story." Portentous silence would hold us children for a time and then I remember Mother once saying, "Now, papa, you should not tell that story at night. You should tell it in the broad daylight."

"Huh!" said my brother Gilbert, ever a sturdy heretic. "We wouldn't believe it in daytime, and"—noting the twinkle in father's eye—"Papa doesn't believe it himself."

"Ah," replied my father, gravely shaking his head, "you never can tell what things those people would be seeing in that glen."

"Well, there are no Highlanders like that in this country whatever," said my little sister, staring with big blue eyes.

"Oh, aren't there? What about Macdonald Dhu and Big John MacGillivray?"

"Yes," said Gilbert, the stout unbeliever, "and Kenny Crupach and Soldier McRae?" mentioning two lame and undersized and altogether nonheroic Highlanders in the congregation. At the shout of laughter which greeted these two names the phantom column of Highlanders vanished into thin air. Who would be afraid of Kenny Crupach or Soldier McRae?

But nonetheless the spirit world was a very real world to my father. Neither angels from the bright heavens nor devils from the pit were to be scoffed at or despised. Belief in the spirit world put passion into his preaching. Many a time have I watched the faces of the people grow rigid and pale under his denunciation of sin and his predictions of judgment to come. His preaching, however, reached its greatest height as he pictured the "Love of the Cross," and often have I seen the tears flowing down the deep-lined cheeks of his old elders as he waxed eloquent on this theme. He was indeed a great preacher. Not one of all the great preachers I have known could ever thrill my soul as could my father when I was a little lad.

He was a passionate man and his children stood in dread of his wrath at times. He punished us seldom. He had no need to. His word was enough. One thrashing only—that is, a real thrashing—I vividly remember. I bore him no grudge for it, because my conscience at the time, however it might react today, was on his side. That was the only instance of serious chastisement at my father's hands that I can remember.

During my father's frequent absences from home the burden of discipline fell most heavily upon our mother's shoulders. We were a band of young ruffians, wild as the deer in the forests which we roved and doubtless needing discipline enough. Her punishments were fairly but contemptuously described by a French maid, Annette Bourget: "Huh, de missis lickem him notting! Nevaire hurt one skeeter." But there was a part of the punishment that never failed to bring a pang to my heart, and often tears to my eyes. After punishment she made us kneel down while she prayed with us, and no matter how filled with anger my heart might be, before the prayer was ended the love and grief in her voice and the tears in her eyes never failed to break me up. Before the prayer was over my arms would be round her neck. In spite of this, I could not help the feeling that she was taking a rather unfair advantage of me. Poor soul! Her burden was truly heavy enough at times.

CHAPTER II

My Mother

MARY ROBERTSON — MOUNT HOLYOKE — GAELIC
FORTITUDE — A SAINT IN THE BACKWOODS

I THINK first of her hazel-brown eyes with that pure light in them that babies have, swift to respond to her world with smiles or with tears. She was of the Robertson clan, the most ancient, so the Robertsons say—and who should know better?—of all the Scottish clans, being derived from Robert's son, to wit the son of Robert the Bruce. And she also carried herself with an air fitting such descent. My earliest memory of her is very vivid. I see her entering the drawing room on some great occasion. Tall she seemed, though of medium height, walking, as they were taught to walk in those days, not with the heels first clumping down, but with toes first peeping out like little mice from under her wide-sweeping hooped silk skirt. A great lady yet without an atom of pride, gentle, sweet and gracious, breeding in every line of her face, in every movement of her body. She came of cultured people. Her father's sister was the mother of Robertson Smith, that great Scottish Hebrew scholar and great heretic who was ejected by the Free Church of Scotland for his advanced view on the Old Testament literature and became the editor of the Encyclopaedia Britannica. He was a fiery little fighter, constituting with A. B. Davidson and George Adam (now Sir George Adam) Smith the dauntless three who gave leadership to the modern interpretation of Hebraistic literature in Britain. Her father, a man of fine culture and of high spiritual quality, unable to endure the chill of the old Moderate Church of Scotland, emigrated first to New England, and thence to Canada, where he found a more congenial spiritual home in the Congregational Church. Settling in the little town of Sherbrooke, Quebec, he reared and educated his large family, some of whom played a distinguished part in the history of the

7

province. The eldest son became a member of Parliament and for twelve years, under both political parties, held the office of provincial treasurer. Two other sons, Andrew and William, became distinguished members of the Montreal bar. A sister, Margaret, became a novelist, well known in her day.

Mary, my mother, the second youngest of the family, after graduating from the Sherbrooke Young Ladies' Academy went at the age of nineteen to finish her education in the Mount Holyoke Ladies' Seminary, the most famous in the United States in that day. Her brilliant intellectual powers immediately won the attention of her teachers and especially of the principal, the famous and greatly loved Mary Lyon. One day the senior class, so her sister Margaret told me, was struggling with a problem in Euclid's Sixth Book; sitting among the juniors was Mary Robertson, her eyes alight with excitement and understanding. The teacher, noticing her eager face, asked: "Mary, do you understand this problem?"

"Yes," said the young girl, "I think so."

"Come and try it."

The young junior made the necessary solution with ease.

"Would you like to join the senior class in Geometry?" asked the teacher.

"I should like to try," replied the girl.

She was enrolled among the seniors and carried on the work of both classes through the term. At the end of the second year she graduated with honors in English, Mathematics and Philosophy and returned to her home in Sherbrooke.

The following year Mary Lyon died. A few months later a deputation from the Board of Directors came to Sherbrooke to invite Mary Robertson to become the principal of Mount Holyoke. She was then about twenty-two years old. She was eager to go, but not quite sure of herself. Her father, who had noticed the frequent visits of a young Highland missionary working among the Scottish emigrants settled at Lingwick in the Lake Megantic district, advised against her going.

"I think the Lord will doubtless find you some good work to do in Canada, my lassie," he said. And the Lord did. Before a year had passed she yielded to the impetuous wooing of a fiery young Highlander and went with him to be the minister's wife among the crude crofters from the Islands and Highlands of Scotland, settled at Lingwick. The change from the life in her cultured home to that in the poorly furnished Lingwick manse among the struggling Gaelic-speaking emigrants of her husband's congregations can hardly be imagined by the people of this day.

On her first Sabbath, after the sermon the Gaelic-speaking women crowded about the minister's wife to give her welcome. Alas, she could not understand a word of their speech. Some of them burst into tears in their disappointment. She went home with her husband and demanded a Gaelic dictionary. Gaelic dictionary! He had none. What need had he of a Gaelic dictionary? But he had a Gaelic Bible. A gruesome thing in language. She sent for a dictionary and struggled with that uncanny tongue. In six months she could read the Gospels and recite the Lord's Prayer to the old ladies in their own tongue.

"Och, but you have the bonnie Gaelic," said a dear old woman, delighted with the fine Anglicized Gaelic speech of her minister's wife, but more with the courage and diligence shown in her efforts to master their native tongue.

That was the beginning. Day and night she was in and out of their poor little cabins, often evil-smelling. Herself a mere girl, she taught them—how careful she had to be—how to keep their homes clean, how to cook their food, how to care for their babies. She learned their Gaelic songs—really won them first by that—and then taught them her English hymns. She organized the women into classes for Bible study. She poured out for them the treasures of her mind and heart, and in return they lavished upon her their gratitude and devotion; and when they had learned how, they later gave her personal service and care, day and night, when she came to need it.

Two years or more she lived and worked with these people and left among them a memory that never faded. For instance, forty years later at the Presbyterian General Assembly meeting in Montreal I was invited to dinner at one of the grand homes in that city. I found myself sitting beside a handsome dark-eyed young woman who greeted me with, "I know all about your mother. I am from Lingwick."

"Then you do not know my mother, for she left Lingwick long before you were born."

"But I know her well. My mother was in her Bible class. She has often told me about her. She is seventy years old and still talks about her, almost never without tears."

"Tell me about her," I said.

"My mother lost her first baby. Your mother came on her pony and stayed with her all that night. She laid the body out. My mother can never forget what your mother did for her. All those women have never forgotten her."

"Go on," I said, "if you don't mind." The tears were running down her cheeks.

"Thirty-eight years after your mother left for Glengarry she came back with your father to visit us in Lingwick. Your father was conducting the Sacrament services. I will never forget what I saw. After the service the women, old, gray-haired grannies and younger ones too, were crowding about her, kissing her and fondling her. Those who could not kiss her cheeks and lips kissed her fingers. Yes, and the hem of her mantle. Never did I see such a sight. They had been members of her Bible classes. We who had never seen her stood looking on, crying like a lot of babies. After nearly forty years, mind you. God help you, lad, you need to be a good man, I tell you."

And in my heart I prayed that God would make me worthy of her, a prayer not yet answered.

I met my mother first in the Indian Lands Presbyterian manse, Glengarry, to which my father took her after two years or so in Lingwick. I often wonder at his nerve. Indian Lands, settled by Scotia crofters dispossessed from the Highlands and Islands by poverty-stricken lairds and dukes to make room for deer forests, poor, crude in their manner of life, passionate in their hates and loyalties, grand friends but desperate enemies. It was Lingwick over again, but more remote from civilization. The nearest railway was twenty five miles distant. There for eighteen years she lived on a glebe of twenty-four acres, cut from the bush and the deep pine forest, out of which the people had cut their little farms. How desperately lonely she was no one ever knew. She hardly knew herself, she was too busy. Her babies, arriving with biennial regularity, the women and girls of her husband's congregation, the men and boys too, all demanded her care and got it. She was far too busy for self-pity. As in Lingwick, she organized the women into Bible classes and sewing circles. She helped them to make their homes clean and beautiful. She demonstrated before their eyes how to live a saintly life. For a saint she was, if God ever made one.

As I read of the saintly women of old I smile to myself and wonder how they could have fared with their sainthood in the backwoods of Glengarry. She was a saint, but a gay and gallant saint. She had no fear of the forest. On her pony, a baby perched before her on the pommel of her saddle and another on the way, she would gallop along the trails winding through the forest, skirting bogholes, jumping logs—once she made her pony leap over a slumbering cow—with the bark of a fox or the long howl of a wolf sounding in her ears. In the spring the wolves were somewhat of a nuisance. One early November morning with the hoarfrost thick on the ground and the sun coming up over the treetops—my father being away on one of his long missionary journeys—I followed my mother through the pasture field, trying to gather up and care for the lambs torn by the wolves during the preceding night. Her pale face, wet with pitiful tears as we carried the torn lambs on my sled to the barn, is still a poignant memory. She had a courage that never flinched.

This is not the place for my mother's life story. I am simply trying to tell you something of my origins. For it is only fair to say that the inspiration for whatever small service I may have done for my fellow men came from her. Forty-six years ago I saw her lovely hazel-brown eyes close for the last time, and the faint fluttering breath leave her lips. To this very hour, as I write these words, I feel the pang of that parting and ever shall.

CHAPTER III

Glengarry

OUR GLENGARRY folk, as I have said, were mostly from the Highlands and Islands of Scotland. They were sturdy, industrious, patient, courageous. They cut their farms out of the forest, transforming the timber into houses with furniture for themselves and into stables and barns for their animals. Their only tools at first were the broadax, chopping ax, adze, saw, auger, hammer; their only nails were wooden pins. With these tools they built their very presentable and comfortable houses and steadings.

The clearing of the land was desperately hard work. I have often thought with admiration of the courage of a man who on reaching his lot of solid forest could drive his ax to the eye into the first tree of his first clearing. They learned by experience the need and the worth of co-operative work. After the standing forest had been cut down into a "slashing," the neighbors came with their axes and oxen to make a bee and clean up the slashing, piling brush and logs for the burning, leaving only the stumps which later would be cut out or burnt out. So the fields were prepared for plow and harrow. Often as a boy I watched, with unconscious admiration, Big John Bawn McRae swing across a field, scattering handfuls of oats from a sheet slung round his shoulders. The implements for planting were plow, harrow and hoe; for harvesting, scythe and cradle. I remember the first mowing machine brought into the settlement and the wonder and doubtful approval of the crowd of farmers gathered to see it work. The grain, in the early days before the wagons came in or while the fields were too rough for wagons, was hauled to the barn or the stacks on wooden sleds or stone boats drawn by oxen. Later in the winter it would be threshed on the barn floor with the flail and winnowed with the fork. It was all hard work, but the courage and endurance of these men never failed. They were building more than homes, and making more than farms. They were building and making a nation.

Their toil would be lightened with fun and frolic, for a bee drew together not only the men and boys for the work, but the women and girls as well. After the day's work games and athletic contests would follow, and later on there would be a grand supper and a dance to the fiddle or the pipes. In winter the older members of the community would be busy cutting, splitting and hauling firewood of maple, beech, elm, birch, and for the kindling pine, spruce and cedar. The younger men at the first freeze-up would be off to the shanties. The tales of the lumbermen in *The Man from Glengarry* are from real life. Often I rode to school on the big timber sticks, sixty feet long and more, which were being hauled to the Scotch River to be floated down to the Ottawa when the ice broke, and thence by the St. Lawrence to Quebec for the British navy. A wild and colorful life was the lumberman's, full of danger and adventure, making the square timber, collecting the great sticks into rafts, breaking up jams, and running the rapids.

Gay and gallant youths were these young Highlanders, quick as a wild lynx on their feet, fearless to face the boiling waters, loving a fight for river rights or for the honor of their clan, generous with their hard-won pay to new friend or to wily pimp, gambler or harlot. But the Great Revival that swept Glengarry in the early sixties changed all that. My only memory of it is that someone lifted me high to see the gleam of the swaying torches through the dark bush that lit the steps of men, women, boys and girls making their way round bogholes to the new brick church at the nineteenth concession. The mighty sweeping of that religious upheaval tamed the fighting, drinking, lusting Glengarry men into the finest rivermen that plied their adventurous trade on the Ottawa and the St. Lawrence.

But the tales of the fierce old days survived down into my time, stirring my youthful heart with profound regret that deeds so heroically splendid should all be bad. For in spite of the Great Revival we were of the same race, with ancient lust of battle in our blood. Never have I forgotten the thrill of pride in my heart the day that my elder brother, Stewart, stripped to his shirt on a winter day, stood out before the lads of the Scotch River and dared any man of them to come over. In his moments of wrath he was a terror to the whole school. He had the strength of a bull. I have seen him, when he came to manhood, stoop, lay his open hand on the floor, lift my father standing one foot on his hand and one on his wrist—lift him standing, a man of nearly two hundred pounds, and set him on the table. A wild lot— Glengarry men—as wild as the wild creatures of the forest in which they lived, fearing no man or beast or devil.

It is one of the tragedies of literature that historians fill their pages with the doings of men and leave unsung the lives of the heroines of the race. Less colorful doubtless are the lives of mothers, wives, sisters, but more truly heroic and more fruitful in the upbuilding of human character and in the shaping of a nation's history. At the very foundation of a people's greatness is the home. Splendid and hazardous as are the deeds of men in the battle of life, nothing they endure in the way of suffering can compare with what the mothers of a pioneer colony, remote from civilization, are called upon to suffer in the bearing and rearing of children. The loneliness, the dangers, the hardships of fathers and sons in the remote lumber camps or in the rafts down the river are as nothing to the appalling loneliness, the dangers, the hardships that mothers and daughters have to meet and endure in the little log houses in the clearing with children to clothe and care for in health and in sickness, and to keep regularly at school, to train and discipline, with beasts to water and feed, with fires to keep alight when snowdrifts pile round the little house to the eaves, shutting them off for days and nights from their neighbors, with no one but God available for their help. All this is a part of my experience, and at times when I begin to lose my faith in the nobler qualities of the race I let my mind wander back to the wives, mothers and sisters of the pioneer-settlers of Glengarry and find my faith revive.

Every age, every race has its trials, dangers and despairs to meet. But today things are surely easier in the care of a family. There is the not-unimportant problem of keeping the family neatly and comfortably clad. The tailor, the dressmaker, the department store, it will be conceded, play no minor role in the solution of this problem. But I think of my mother and her six sons. I never wore store clothes till

I was twelve. Tailor McRae—or Tailor Ruagh, as we called him from the definitely ruddy tint of his hair—used to come once a year in the fall with his tapes and scissors, his needles, thread and buttons and spend a week in the manse outfitting the six boys with their annual suits. There was no difficulty in the selection of the quality, color, weight of the cloth, nor the style of the garments to be made. These had all been taken care of. For there stood Tailor Ruagh, a huge web of fulled cloth made from our own wool, a serviceable gray, thick enough to stand alone and guaranteed to last through the whole year. From this web our suits were cut. There was no "fashing" about styles. There was only one style and that never went out. In the week Tailor Ruagh measured, cut and basted, while some neighbor women, coming in relays, helped to sew and shape the material into coats, vests and trousers. If the results were not quite in harmony with the lines of various limbs, well, so much the worse for the limbs. It was a busy time and hard work, but my mother always made a kind of picnic of it. There would be a rest for a cup of tea with cheese and oat cakes, and almost always doughnuts, pies and honey which the good friends had brought with them. And while they worked there would be Gaelic songs, redolent of the Hebrides, and hymns of my mother's teaching, or perhaps a story read or a bit from the Book. Oh, it was a grand time for the women. But for the boys, who had to appear in church in their new gray suits that felt and looked like coats of mail, the time was not so very grand.

Shirts of radiant and variegated hues, spun and woven by our neighbor friends, were made without Tailor Ruagh's help. These were quite beneath his dignity. Everything we wore, except our boots and moccasins was homemade, and of homespun material. I cannot halt to speak of the cleaning, the carding, the dyeing, the spinning, the weaving of the wool necessary to produce blankets, sheets, quilts for beds, or dresses for the girls. But think, will you, of the hours at the spinning wheel, the sitting little wheel and the walking big wheel, the dyeing, the weary banging and shuttling of the looms necessary to these glorious results. Compare with all the brain and back-racking effort, the mere chopping, hewing, hauling and rafting of timber sticks.

We cannot give space to the other multitudinous tasks of the women, such as the milking, the butter and cheese making, the pickling and transforming of various wild fruits into delicious jams and preserves, the curing of pork and beef, the drying of herbs. Then, outside, there was the care of hens, ducks and geese and of their wayward and wandering offspring, the safe delivery of spring calves and lambs and pigs. And always the baby to nurse or attend to, or Jimmie to keep from the fire or from falling into the well, or Maggie from the jam jar or the milk pan. Lumbering or plowing or cradling, indeed! "Tut, tut, men. Haud yer whisht!"

And in that great work of homemaking, the greatest in the world, the minister's wife held a high place, for to her it was given to show women how to make homes, not only warm, clean, tasteful and cozy, but also how to make them radiant with a spiritual glow and pure with a love "that suffereth long and is kind, that envieth not, that doth not behave itself unseemely, that hopeth all things, believeth all things, endureth all things, love that never faileth."

All that is set down in *Glengarry School Days* is true. Our education began in the little log schoolhouse of great hewn pine logs, plastered at the cracks. The plaster, strangely enough, on the boys' side somehow during the summer months, had an invariable habit of falling out. We were a destructive lot of young devils. I was going to say "creatures," but I shall substitute, for those boys were a lovable lot. The interior walls were without decoration of any kind. On the back wall beside the teacher's desk was a blackboard, on the walls were maps of the world, of Europe, Asia and America. None of Canada or the United States. These could be found in our geographies. Nothing else could be seen on the bare log walls. Three windows on each side with small panes, and one behind the teacher's desk, broke the blank space. These windows were protected by stout wooden shutters, bolted on the inside. But for these shutters the windows could not have survived a single week. An array of unprotected windowpanes often had proved too great a temptation to the destructive propensities of our time. We were indeed a wild lot. The entrance was through a porch. At the door on a bench stood a pail of water with a tin cup hanging on a nail, convenient for all to use, with a fine democratic disregard of all silly hygienic rules. In fact, we had never heard that there were such rules. The more finicky might rinse out the cup before drinking, throwing the rinsing on the floor. But this precautionary act was regarded as an indication of "pride," a grave offense in the eyes of the school. On cold winter days the large box stove stood red-hot. In summer the stove was removed.

Discipline was maintained by the "force and fear" method. An essential article in school was the "tawze," a solid leather strap split into fingers. Failing a tawze, the teacher would send one or two of the bigger boys to the bush for birch "gads" about four feet long, supple and strong. The whole school enjoyed the ironic possibility that the purveyors of the rods might themselves be the first to furnish demonstration of their efficiency.

One teacher I remember for a refinement of cruelty in his method of punishment. This was to gather in his fist the four fingers of his unhappy victim and apply vigorously to the protruding finger tips a pointer or ruler. We forgave this little eccentricity, however, because of his repertoire of comic songs, with which at recess or after school he would regale select parties of his pupils.

The Glengarry folk were a fighting people. The whole spirit of the school was permeated by the fighting motif. Every recitation was a contest. The winners went joyously to the top, the failures remained ignominiously at the foot. Medals of a quarter of a dollar for seniors, sixpences for juniors were provided. The pupil holding the head of the class for a day carried his medal home upon an inflated breast, and wore it next day till he lost his place. The pupil carrying the medal for a week could keep it. Also classes were frequently dismissed to their seats by a series of questions in mental arithmetic. Every pupil in the class was on his toes, the one first shouting the correct answer marched proudly to his seat. Good practice it was. As to the ethics and psychology let experts in modern pedagogy decide.

The gravest defect in our educational system was the emphasis laid upon feats of memory. Geography, for instance, had little to do with the "ge" in its Greek root. It was quite remote from "the earth." The boy or girl who could recite, without error, the capes, bays, peninsulas and other physical features of North or South America went to the top. In all my Glengarry school days I never drew a map.

Grammar, which was "the science and art of speaking and writing the English language with perfection," divided into orthography, etymology, syntax and prosody, whatever that may be, was largely a matter of memory. We learned lists of the various Parts of Speech. I knew all the pronouns: personal, possessive, relative, demonstrative and distributive. The climax of absurdity seems to have been reached when we were asked to recite a complete list of the prepositions in the English language, as set forth in Lennie's *Grammar* in a solid block of small print three inches by four. A similar list of conjunctions, adverbs and interjections was set down for us. The pupil, unfortunately, was often left in a horrible uncertainty as to the list to which a particular word might belong.

Even arithmetic, astonishing as it may appear to the modern schoolboy, was largely a matter of memory. Problems were solved by Rules of Proportion, simple or compound, by the Laws of Decimals or Fractions, or, most ghastly of all, by the Rules of Square or Cube Root. These rules you learned by rote, and if you could fit your sums into the framework your answer would infallibly be right. Square and cube root were at the very end of our arithmetic and were our special objects of aversion, particularly the latter. We had a rhyme that expressed this aversion:

> For Square Root I don't care a hoot
> But Cube Root, she's a brute!

and she was. The Rule of Cube Root must have consisted of at least six paragraphs of small print making up in all a solid block some five inches by four. This rule we were forced to memorize.

Spelling, which to those unfamiliar with the derivation of the English language is entirely a memory exercise, was transformed into a veritable logomachy. Spelling contests, in which the whole school participated, were frequently held during the last period on Friday. Indeed, spelling bees were frequently staged between different school sections, and made occasions of social festivity. I am quite confident that the spellers of my day were superior to those of my children's day. Looking back over half a century of experience of various systems of education I come to the conclusion that while in range and variety, and in scientific method, the modern excels, yet in thoroughness and exactitude of memory the pupils of the little log school would quite hold their own.

But of the great world in which we lived we knew almost nothing. The processes of nature did not exist for us. Of contemporary peoples, their thoughts, their manner of life, their systems of government we were entirely ignorant. They were foreigners and, therefore, unknown, more or less despicable, and even dangerous.

Our sports were simple and homemade—swimming, skating, athletic contests, and primitive versions of baseball and hockey. Shinty or shinny, as we called it, was an importation from Scotland and was usually played on the hard beaten snow of the schoolyard. There were few rules. The game was played with a hard rubber ball and homemade sticks. We would cut from the bush a good elm or hickory cudgel with a natural crook. It was a savage game which often gave rise to fights. For we went in for no such frills as umpires or referees.

Of organized sport the youth of Glengarry knew nothing. They had access, however, to the wonderful university of the forest with all the wealth of fauna and flora contained therein. In that university they developed their powers of observation, skill in action, cool courage, patient endurance. At night the forest had its terrors. My eldest brother, Robertson, who was a great hunter even as a boy, used to tell us a thrilling wolf story. It passed into the legendary lore of our family. One night in the spring, when the wolves were hungry, he was returning on his pony from the post office in company with a lumberman who was riding home from the shanties. As they left the clearing and entered the black swamp they heard the long howl of a lone wolf but paid no heed to it. In a few minutes came an answering howl far in front followed by the short, sharp barks of the she-wolf and her cubs.

"Huh! Those devils are out again, are they?" said the shantyman touching up his horse to a canter. Almost immediately they heard a chorus of quick sharp yelps coming from all sides.

"They're hunting us," said the shantyman and put his horse to the gallop, Robertson keeping pace on his pony. There was nearly a mile of forest with the going none too good. Looking back over his shoulder he could see in the light of the dim moon the pack, how many he could not tell, running flat and low.

"Is your pony surefooted?" the shantyman asked.

"She's all right," said my brother, proud of his little black mare, our mother's pony.

"For God's sake, send her along then! If only I had my gun! I hate to run from them cowards." As he spoke he took off his jacket and tied it to the end of a packing rope that hung on his saddle and waited. The leader of the pack was almost at their horses' tails. They had only a hundred yards of forest to go. The shantyman dropped his jacket and paid out the rope letting it trail on the road behind. The wolves fell upon it and tore the rope out of his hand. But the leader paid no attention to the jacket, gathering speed in swift short springs, he slipped up between the horses and leaped for the pony's throat. But the shantyman, shaking a foot clear of the stirrup, swung a heavy kick on the brute's jaw. The wolf fell with a howl under the pony's feet. A hundred yards away they saw the light of a swinging lantern and heard the loud clear call of a woman's voice. The wolves, too, saw and heard. They checked, halted, and faded away like shadows into the bush.

"Mother! Mother! Is that you?" gasped my brother, flinging himself off the pony into her arms. "Weren't you afraid?"

Her face was white, her eyes like stars in the lanternlight.

"Afraid? I never thought of it. I heard the wolves and I heard the horses' feet."

Wolves we hated. Bears we respected. A bear was a gentleman and would mind his business if you minded yours. But surprise him or press him too closely and he would give you a fight worthwhile. Unless struck in a vital spot he would carry a dozen bullets. One I know carried thirteen before he succumbed.

As a little boy I used to gaze with awe upon four deep cuts across the face of our dining room table. The story was this: Returning home late at night my father had left on the table the remnants of supper, some ham, honey, bread and butter, and had retired to bed. He was awakened out of his sleep by the sound of someone below. In his nightgown he slipped downstairs. Someone was moving about the room. He called out, "Who is there? James, bring me some matches." Immediately there was a crash of breaking dishes, a hairy something brushed against him and escaped through the door. A light revealed tablecloth, food and dishes in a heap on the floor, and on the table the marks of the four bear claws.

Encounters with bears were not uncommon. In my memory I carry a vivid picture of the Sinclair boys driving past the school at noon hour with a huge black bear dead on their sleigh, his red tongue sticking out and red splashes on his black coat. The hunters had two Minnie rifles and three black hunting dogs. I felt that the bear had hardly had a fair chance for his life.

If the forest had certain terrors for the younger boys, in the broad light of day it was a wonderland of mystery and beauty, a rare playground which they shared with all the shy things of the bush. There were squirrels, red and black, woodchucks, mink and muskrat, and the rare beaver. Above and about them in the trees were the birds— the tapping woodpecker, the shrieking blue jay, the wood pigeon, cooing and courting, all the wee twittering things, wrens, gray birds, wood sparrows, finches and, high in the treetops, the noisy crow. Low among the cedars and spruce the shy partridge hid, its variegated coloring a sure protection, while overhead the hawk soared and broke the stillness of the woods with its shrill hunting cry. On a rare occasion we saw the gray eagle, on the topmost peak of a dead pine, silent, haughty and solitary, fearful of nothing.

Through the forest flowed a little river. In springtime it was a rushing torrent filled with great cakes of ice upon which the bigger boys would cross. But in midsummer it was a softly flowing stream, shallow so that you could see bottom but here and there circling into a deep pool. One such pool made for us a swimming hole which we knew as the "dee-pole" with emphasis on the "dee." On hot summer days we would come home by the dee-pole a mile out of our way to plunge into its cool water. And we would spend most of the long Saturday afternoons, when we could get free from our weeding and hoeing, in and about that place of surpassing joy.

As I look back through the varied years, the Glengarry forest more than any other place arrests and holds my memory, fills me with the pain of longing and stirs my lingering and grateful delight.

Living twenty-five miles from the railroad in the heart of the forest we had little knowledge of the larger world.

The Fenian Raid in 1866 called out our volunteers, the Glengarry Fencibles, famous in the war of 1812. But I carry only a few memories of that invasion. One was the surprising arrival of Colin McKerracher, who was studying for the ministry, resplendent in his new uniform, to bid us farewell on his way to the front. Another was a song the boys brought back with them, which we all used to sing, a verse of which ran thus:

> Old Mahoney wanting cash,
> Maybe contemplates a dash
> With his dupes upon our tilts to make a raid.
> But he'll find to his dismay,
> That the thing will never pay,
> And he'll wish across the line he'd safely stayed.

> Chorus
> Tramp, tramp, tramp the boys are marching,
> Cheer up comrades let them come.
> For beneath the Union Jack
> We will drive the Fenians back,
> And we'll fight for our beloved Canadian home.

What the "tilts" were I know not till this day, but I remember driving the cows home of an evening and shouting the song at the top of my voice.

A third memory is of my brother, Stewart, then a lad of about fourteen, bitterly crying in the dark of the early morning, beside a wagonload of men bound for the war. He had arranged, unknown to his parents, to go off for the war with a friend. But at the last moment the friend's father interfered and forbade the adventure.

Another national event barely made a ripple on the surface of our life in the backwoods. In 1867 Canada became a Dominion. I was seven years old. I don't remember hearing a word about this great achievement, even in the manse. I do recall shouting at the top of my voice, "Hurrah for Canada!" I imagine that shout may have been an echo from some loyal and excited Canadian giving vent to his patriotic emotion.

Life in the backwoods—what a significant word that is: back-woods—of Indian Lands was immune from the influences, good and evil, of the great world outside.

CHAPTER IV

Highland Religion

THE SCOTTISH CHURCH IN CANADA—PADLOCKS
AND POLEMICS—"IFTHINE ENEMY"—THE OTHER
FAITHS—SHINING WINDOWS.

FROM THE time of Constantine, Christianity has been a polemic religion. Its early conquests were won by its spiritual powers only. By the end of the fourth century, however, after the church had made alliance with the state, it lost much of its primitive power. The Reformation in Britain was largely political and both in England and in Scotland was closely identified with political movements.

The Presbyterian Church in England, and especially in Scotland, assumed powers of state control. In Scotland the Presbyterian Church became the state church and exercised large influence and control in the temporal affairs of the people. This union of temporal and spiritual power had its natural reaction in the claim of the state to authority over the church. As a protest against this claim of state control, some six hundred ministers in what is known in Scottish ecclesiastical history as the Disruption, in 1843, walked out from their manses, and with their congregations left their churches and formed the Free Church of Scotland, which soon grew to be a vigorous and missionary church.

In the early days of Canadian history Presbyterian settlers from Scotland, Ireland, Holland and from the United States, retaining their ecclesiastical affiliations with their home churches, settled in large numbers in Eastern and Central Canada, so that at one time in the Canadian provinces, Maritime and Central, there were no fewer than ten types of Presbyterians with their separate churches.

In Glengarry the first Presbyterians were for the most part associated with the Church of Scotland—the Auld Kirk, as it was known. The Disruption in Scotland was a very real protest against the encroachment by the state upon the independence of the church, but in Canada there was no such invasion by the state and therefore no cause for division. But the Free Church in the homeland, feeling that the great principles of religious freedom were threatened wherever the Established, or Auld, Kirk was in existence, dispatched delegates to Canada under whose influence the Free Presbyterian Church was set up.

At the time of the Disruption in Scotland my father was a student in theology in Aberdeen. For conscience' sake he left the Auld Kirk College, surrendering a bursary, and became an ardent Free Churchman. He carried the memory of this experience with him to Canada, and naturally joined the Free Presbyterian Church.

In his Glengarry congregation there was at first no distinction between the Auld Kirk and the Free. But the division soon appeared and trouble ensued. The congregation was overwhelmingly Free Church. But the church building and about two hundred acres of land belonged to the Auld Kirk of whom there were half a dozen or so members in the congregation. These Auld Kirkers claimed the church building, although it had been erected almost entirely with Free Church money. The minister protested. The church ought to belong to those who had paid for it.

On a certain Sabbath morning the minister, my father, a fiery Highlander, found the church door locked with a new padlock and his congregation outside waiting admission. They had not long to wait.

"Donald McEwen, open this door," ordered the minister.

"There is a new lock on the door, sir," said the beadle.

"Give me the key!" said the minister. Donald handed him the key.

"Is this the key of this church?"

"Yes, sir, but they have put on a new lock, sir."

"I ask you, is this the key which you have always used to open this church?"

"Yes, sir, but this lock—"

"Answer my question! Is this the key of this church? Yes or no."

"Yes, sir, it is the key, but—"

"This is the key which ordinarily opens this door? Yes or no."

"It is the key."

The minister with slow and painstaking care, but with no result, tries the key.

"Donald, and you Mr. McNaughton, and all of you will notice that there is something wrong with this lock. The key will not open it. Stand clear!"

With a quick step the minister drives his foot against the door. The padlock is snapped, the door stands open. The people pass in for the public worship of God.

The minister is summoned to court in Cornwall to answer the charge of housebreaking and unlawful entry. On his black stallion, for the roads were muddy, and followed by a great cavalcade of mounted Free Kirkers, the minister rides twenty-five miles to the courts. The scene, as described in the book, *Torches Through the Bush,* is enacted.

The minister escapes jail but the Free Kirkers lose the church.

Religion in Glengarry in those days was a solemn and serious matter, a thing of life and death. An arrangement was made by the court for the use of the building by the Free Church folk, those of the Auld Kirk being too few to support a minister of their own. In a short time the Free Church people with great enthusiasm proceeded to erect a new brick church for themselves, which thereupon became the only Presbyterian church for the community, and Auld Kirkers remaining aloof from these housebreakers and seceders were without church privileges.

They tell a story, how true it is I cannot say, of how the chief champion of the Auld Kirk was won back to membership in the new church. One cold winter day the minister on his pastoral rounds, with his wife in the cutter beside him, came to the house of the leading Auld Kirker, Duncan Cameron.

"Mary," he said to his wife, "are you not cold?"

"Oh, just a little," she replied.

"Mary, you are very cold indeed," asserted the minister. "We will drive in and get warm at Duncan Cameron's."

"But, papa, Duncan Cameron—"

"Whisht, woman! Will he refuse shelter to a woman starving with the cold?" asked the minister with a twinkle in his eye.

He drove up to the door. Old Duncan himself appeared at the door, stern and forbidding.

"My wife is feeling the cold, Mr. Cameron," said the minister. "Perhaps you will not be keeping us out."

"God bless my soul, minister!" said the old man. "Is it a heathen you will be thinking that I am?"

In a few minutes they were cozily sitting in the large and comfortable kitchen before a blazing fire, with a cup of tea in their hands and Mrs. Cameron pressing oatcakes and scones upon them.

After half an hour of kindly inquiry about the family and especially about Christy's new baby, a lusty grandson, the minister in a voice of solemn authority said:

"Duncan, you will pass me the Book."

What could a man do? The Bible was brought. Family worship ended, the minister and his wife, with the eager aid of Duncan and his wife, wrapped themselves up warmly and proceeded to thank their hosts for their hospitality.

"If thine enemy hunger feed him, eh, Duncan?" said the minister with a little twinkle in his eye.

"My God! minister, don't be saying them words," said Duncan in a husky voice.

"Well, I will say no more than this, Duncan," said the minister in a voice kind but solemn. "The church is there. It is not my church nor is it your church. It is the house of God. And He Himself will give you a welcome on the Sabbath Day."

The following Sabbath the congregation was astonished beyond measure to see Duncan Cameron and his wife, followed by their daughter, Christy, with her new baby in her arms, and her husband walk down the aisle to their seats in the church. A little later Duncan Cameron explained the phenomenon to his friend Kenneth McRae.

"God pity me, could I turn them freezing from my door? And when he 'took the books' you know yourself how it was."

There was little denominational rivalry, however, in the community for the sufficient reason that there were no rival churches. There were Baptists, few in number, but very stanch. They had no settled minister, but occasionally a minister would visit the district and hold a series of meetings in the homes of his people. One I remember well, a Mr. R. Rainboth, a handsome man and very courteous in his manners. Riding by the school one day he lifted his stovepipe hat in salutation of the pupils out at recess, which act of courtesy we considered a clear indication of pride. This opinion was strengthened by the revelation that his hair was "split in the middle," an unforgivable display of pride in the opinion of the boys. Mr. Rainboth was an eloquent and ardent exponent of the Baptist faith and had the hardihood, moreover, to challenge the Presbyterian minister to public debate.

The stage was set in the Presbyterian church. The church was packed. Glengarry folk, being mostly of Highland stock, love a fight. That the fight was of a spiritual nature relieved it of all carnal elements. Even churchmen and churchwomen could enjoy it with a clear conscience.

The Presbyterian minister was to open the debate, which he did by a dissertation on the origin and nature, worship and sacraments of the Old Testament church, together with its limitations and imperfections. At the end of the second day he was still in the Old Testament and going strong. But such was the overwhelming passion of his eloquence, so furious were his denunciations of the Baptist heresies, so truly terrible was his aspect as he marched up and down the platform that his opponent failed to appear on the third day, and the debate was over. The Presbyterians were jubilant, the Baptists scornfully disgusted.

"Debate?" exclaimed a Baptist brother, "Would you call that a debate?"

"What else?" inquired a Presbyterian.

"Well, all I will say is, it was God's mercy he did not have a claymore in his fist."

No, there was little denominational rivalry within the confines of the Presbyterian area. Methodists there were none. Never as a boy did I behold a Methodist in the flesh. At Moose Creek, ten miles or so away, there were said to be Methodists. But what sort of creatures they were I knew not. To my mind they were of such a nature that I would hate to meet them in the dark.

There were, however, Congregationalists, with whom the Presbyterians were on the most friendly terms. This was doubtless due to the fact that the minister's wife had been a Congregationalist. The younger generation, however, bore towards the Congregationalists a feeling of rivalry that amounted almost to contempt. The Congregational church was a small wooden structure, unpainted and without a steeple. Its windows had little square panes like those of the school. It was altogether contemptible. Its very name was contemptible: it was known as the Little Church. And there it stood right across the road from the new Presbyterian church, grand with steeple and proper church windows and everything.

My brother and I, passing by the Little Church one day, paused to look at it. Its mere existence was an affront to our church. Unprotected the square panes of the Little Church glowed in the sunlight. Denominational zeal suddenly flamed up in my heart. By an evil chance a number of perfectly smooth stones lay in the dust at my feet. The temptation proved irresistible. I picked up a stone and flung it at a window. The stone crashed through one of the square panes. My brother with shocked but delighted admiration rocked with laughter. Excited with the success of my own daring achievement and stimulated by his glee, I sent a second stone smashing through the window. Not to be outdone, my brother tried a shot, with perfect success. The thing became a contest of skill and daring. When most of the panes were shattered a sudden conviction of the enormity of our offense dawned upon us. We dashed off homeward filled with a feeling of mingled pride and terror, but also with a dread of doom. We were undoubtedly possessed of the devil. Nothing that I can think of could be a finer testimony both to the high esteem and affection in which our parents were held by the Congregational community and to the spirit of Christian forbearance shown by the members of the Little Church than the fact that the windows were quietly repaired without a word of complaint to the parents of the offenders.

CHAPTER V

The Manse in Zorra

A NEW HOME—LIMITATIONS OF CIVILIZATION—
ADVANCES IN EDUCATION—TWO MUSICAL
GENIUSES—FATHER PLAYS A PIBROCH—FIRST
GLIMPSE INTO THE CLASSICS—EARNING MONEY
FOR COLLEGE—CONTEST WITHOUT QUARTER

In 1870, when I was ten years of age, my father was called to another congregation in Zorra, Western Ontario. A Highland people with a mixture of inferior breeds, Lowland and English.

It was a great change for us all; in things material, a decided advance. The homes of the people were more modern, more comfortable, their farms better cultivated and more productive. Farm machinery of modern type saved the people from backbreaking drudgery. Roads had been graveled and swamps drained. The forests, alas for us boys, had been reduced to little wood lots, where nothing bigger or more dangerous than a woodchuck or a skunk could be found, and where the only game were a few timid partridge. The forests had given place to great wheat crops, turnip and potato fields, magnificent orchards. Never had I seen an apple growing in Glengarry, the only apples I ever ate were out of a barrel brought by my father from Montreal on his return from Presbytery meetings, and handed out one by one, as if they had been gold. And with the orchards were lovely gardens surrounding fine stone and brick houses.

Everything seemed to be made for us by someone else and somewhere else, far away. We were "cribbed, cabined, confined" by civilization. At times we reverted to our primitive barbarism. One Saturday, armed with ax and saw, we organized an expedition for butternuts. Fine spreading butternut trees lined the road a mile away. We climbed the trees, sawed off the limbs—not all, but all we needed —and garnered our spoil. Next week a local paper spread upon its pages an indignant protest against our vandalism, destroying the beauty of the trees. Our disgust was equaled only by our amazement at this infringement of our liberties.

But the people were kind and we soon became friendly with them. The boys, too, accepted us after sundry decisive encounters in which Glengarry methods of war had worked out their natural results. Life, however, had lost much of its dash and daring, we became tame and also somewhat dull.

The schools were better. We no longer learned lists of prepositions, conjunctions and interjections. In arithmetic we used the analytic method. Then, too, we studied algebra, composition, literature, and began to read with a definite end in view—the examination for entrance to high school. This examination became at once the bête noire and the spur of our school studies. We were introduced to organized sports, to baseball, football, ice shinny, with rules and umpires which did much to eliminate the pugilistic element, a common feature of all Glengarry games. In fact, we were becoming civilized.

Near the school we had, praise be! a swimming hole, with muddy banks and turbid water, but cool and wet. Besides this there was an oatmeal mill, half a mile from the manse, with a mill dam, cool, clear and deep, a wonderful place for a real swim and dive. That mill and mill dam became a great joy in our lives. Thither we would resort in the summer evenings and on Saturdays. We liked the mill dam, not only for the swim, but more because the miller was a famous fiddler. After supper in the long summer evenings we would run up over a hill and drop down into a little vale with shading willows overhanging the dam. On a hot summer evening what a joy it was to rip off shirt and pants and plunge headlong into the cool, dark water, and then after our swim we would gather at the door of the mill and Billy Sutherland would bring out his fiddle, tip his chair against the wall, and after a few preliminary tunings was away. Scotch reels and strathspeys, jigs, schottisches and all the other kinds, quaint old laments and Negro melodies, one after another for an hour, two hours, without speaking a single word, he would play, not so much to entertain us as for the sheer joy of playing to a sympathetic audience. I have heard the finest players in the world play great music, but never has the fiddle got into my feet as when Billy Sutherland's flying elbow and fingers were manipulating the strings.

Our nearest neighbor, Sullivan Ross, was a musical genius too. He made his own violins great and small, and fine instruments they were, and he played them, not with the finish and delicacy of Billy Sutherland, but with deeper, fuller tones. His master instrument, however, was the bagpipes. Far into the night we could hear Sullivan playing up on the hill, and often have I sat out on the doorstep listening in the moonlight with an ache in my heart and tears not far away. Sullivan Ross was a great music lover. Any day in the middle of harvest he could easily be beguiled at the noon rest to take up his violin or tune up his pipes and regale us boys for an hour or two while the harvest waited in the field. Like Billy Sutherland, he was a "quiet" man of few words, but such was the eloquence of his fiddle or his pipes that we never missed his speech. He had a singular reticence in referring to his wife. Never did he name her as Margaret or Mrs. Ross, or even "the wife." He always referred to her as "she." My youngest brother, a wag in his way, once determined to force him to indicate his wife in more definite manner. Sullivan, in the course of narrating some incident, said:

"She was going out to the milkhouse and—"

"Who?" inquired my brother.

"She was going out."

"Who was going out?"

"Oh," said Sullivan with a nod of his head toward his wife, "she was going—"

"Who was going?" insisted my brother.

"Oh, she—Jack's mother." And that was the nearest he could get the husband to a definite reference to his wife.

Returning to the bagpipes. In Zorra there was a number of excellent pipers, and at many country fairs at which Caledonian games were held pipe contests were a prominent feature. My father was quite mad over the pipes. Nothing would more delight the minister's heart than to stand by and listen for an hour or more to a bagpipe competition, indicating by word and sign his approval or disapproval. In his boyhood days in his home glen of Blair Atholl he had often accompanied his brother, Gilbert, head piper to the Duke of Atholl and the winner of many prizes in his day, to the various Highland gatherings to listen to the pipe competitions.

On the occasion of his last visit to his native land he, without the knowledge of his family, secured possession of his brother's pipes and brought them with him to Canada. In the days of his youth pipe playing of reels and the like had been regarded as a somewhat doubtful amusement for a Christian man, not so much so the grand old pibrochs. After some preliminary practicing on the chanter in the privacy of his study upstairs, one day to the amazement of his wife and family he appeared in the drawing room with his pipes and in a somewhat shamefaced manner began tuning up. Then when the tones of drones and chanter were in perfect accord away he went into one of the great pibrochs. The pibroch, be it remembered, is no reel or strathspey or any such light music. The pibroch is the classic type of pipe music, being a lament or dirge played in memory of some notable national disaster, such as a defeat in war, or a clan calamity, such as the death of a chief. The pibroch, moreover, is the most intricate, the most difficult of all pipe music. In structure it consists first of a simple theme, which in the second playing is elaborated with a variation known as the "cruan luach." At the third repetition there is a further elaboration of the theme known as the "doubling" of the cruan luach—a most intricate and difficult performance. Before the eyes of his amazed wife and family the minister began to march back and forth wailing his pibroch. At length his pipe ceased and he stood waiting. We all sat speechless for some moments.

"Well," he said to his wife, "what do you think of that?"

"Oh," said Mother in surprise, "were you playing something?"

"Playing something!" he exclaimed fiercely.

"I thought you were just tuning up," said Mother, who had never heard a lament, her knowledge of pipe music being confined to reels, marches and the like.

"Tuning up, woman?" he said in mingled pity and scorn.

"I couldn't catch any tune," said Mother faintly.

"Tune? Tune? Ye poor Lowland buddie. That, let me tell you, was the grandest music on earth. It was 'The Macintosh Lament,'" he said solemnly.

"Oh," said my mother penitently. "Play it again, papa."

For a moment or two he hesitated. Would it be casting pearls before swine? Then, with gracious condescension, he proceeded to explain the structure of the pibroch. First the theme, then the various elaborations, concluding with the weird and wild doubling of the cruan luach.

"Oh, do play it again," pleaded Mother earnestly, ready to endure any suffering in her desire to heal his wounded Highland pride. Remember all this was in a parlor some fourteen feet square. People of lesser breeds reading these words, who have never heard the pipes skirl and drone indoors, cannot appreciate the heroic fortitude behind this request.

He glanced at her curiously, then throwing up the drones over his shoulder and announcing, "This is the theme," he began again his pibroch. Immediately I caught the weirdly beautiful air.

"Now comes the cruan luach."

Again he played the theme and added the elaboration.

"And now for the doubling!"

Once more came the lovely wailing theme, then the elaboration or cruan luach, and then finally the doubling.

Then and there we had our initiation into the pibroch, or lament, which made pipe music for us all a new and marvelous thing in music. Thereafter, many a night when we heard the first ring of the drones up in the study, we would all gather in "to hear the pipes." Truth demands, however, that I should say that Mother, and indeed most of the family, preferred to listen in the dining room across the hall. For my part I loved the throbbing of the drones and the wild shriek of the chanter from the vantage ground of the parlor sofa, from which I could see the gallant old Highlander pace slowly back and forth, head up, shoulders back, coattails swinging like a kilt, and his blue eyes on the far hills of Blair Atholl.

After a few weeks' familiarity with the pipes his conscience became sufficiently hardened, or enlightened, to permit him to delight his family with reels and marches, strathspeys and such pipe music as ordinary pipers play.

Our Zorra congregation was named Harrington from the village near our home. Ten miles away in the little town of St. Marys was situated the high school at which we had our training for the university. Every Monday morning, rain or shine, we drove ten miles in to our school and every Friday night we drove home again for the week end. That week end at home did a vast deal to steady us, for we needed steadying to keep us loyal to the high traditions of that home.

Our first master, the principal of the school, was a Mr. Tytler, a perfect disciplinarian. No need of cane in his case, his eye, his manner were sufficient to ensure perfect order. A quite remarkable teacher, he made us keen about our work. He was also a fine gentleman, beautifully dressed and groomed, and we all adored him. We owed much to him. But it was from a later teacher, William Dale, that I had my first suggestion of the beauty of classic literature. He was the antithesis of Tytler in manner, dress and general style. He was a clumsily dressed, farmerlike man, devoid of anything suggesting the style and manner of a gentleman. But he knew his classics. Once as I was droning out in dictionary English a translation of one of the odes of Horace, he suddenly stopped me:

"Gordon, has it occurred to you that it is poetry you are translating, not Caesar or Tacitus? It is a little song with rhythm and music in it. It goes something like this." Then in the most exquisitely beautiful words he translated for us the "Ode to Lalage."

That evening I went straight home and got at my Horace. And after my spadework with grammar and dictionary I labored at my translation. I was not content with mere poetic English. At two o'clock in the morning I had my ode done into rhyme. There was a little twinkle in Dale's eye as he said: "Quite good, Gordon. Very good indeed. Of course it is not necessary that even quite good poetry should always rhyme."

I have always been grateful to William Dale for what he did for me that day. He opened to me the gate into new and wonderful fields of beauty in human speech. From him I learned to discriminate between the delicate grace of Horace, the restrained and stately music of the *Aeneid,* the sonorous splendor of the *Iliad,* the terse and steady march of Livy, and the forensic passion of the philippics of Demosthenes. Dale later became a distinguished professor in Toronto University.

I look back upon my high school days as very happy days. English, classics, mathematics came easily to me. I was inclined to specialize in English and classics, but graduated in all three departments with first-class honors.

I was devoted to sports, but though terribly ambitious I never attained to the first rank. I became pitcher on our baseball team, but was too light for a high place in football, never weighing more than 125 pounds.

It was not easy for my father, on his meager minister's salary, to provide for us at high school. At the close of the spring term my brother and I used to hire out with the farmers to work in the fields for the months of July, August and a part of September. It was hard work and heavy work, but we became experts and were greatly in demand. Indeed, we became champion hoers and binders of grain behind the reaper. In the heavy fall wheat it took five men to keep up with the machine; in lighter grain spring wheat or oats, four men or, if specially expert, three could keep up. I remember well a day when we two won great fame throughout the district by keeping up with the machine all day. In this way we were able to help considerably in meeting the cost of our education, for we always drew the highest wages, a dollar and a half and often two dollars a day. One season we were able to make the astonishing amount of $140 each, a substantial contribution to our school expenses.

In pitching sheaves and in heavy work my brother was the better man, but in binding, the matter had never come to an issue between us. One season, however, we had been working in different sections of the country, each winning fame in his own district. In the last week of the harvest we chanced to come together for the same boss. A contest could hardly be avoided. Gilbert would have gladly been content to do a day's work and let it go at that. But I was ambitious. I had won out in contests with bigger and stronger men. He would hate to beat me. He would be glad to let me win, but this he knew I would not have. So there was nothing for it but a fight. It was the last week of harvest. We were going back to school next week. We were both hard, fit, ready to give our best. The conditions suited me perfectly. The field was spring wheat, light, straight, free from thistles. There was no open suggestion of a contest. But we knew it was unavoidable and we went at it. In keeping up with the machine we would each take two swaths at a time to save walking. This meant that the outside man would have at least one extra sheaf, sometimes two to bind. But to even up the game we would change from inside to outside at each corner. At 7:30 in the morning the machine turned into the field. We loafed along till the machine had four swaths ahead of us, which left two swaths for each; then we were off, Gilbert taking the outer and longer swaths. At the first corner I finished first and proceeded to take again the outside and longer swaths.

"Hold up! My swaths!" said Gilbert. "Take your own swaths."

"Oh, all right!" I said lightly. "It's all the same?"

"Not quite! Why should you carry the heavy end?"

By noon a record binding speed had been maintained but there had been no open break into a race.

The dinner proved more than usually enticing and after dinner we went to the orchard to rest in the shade and eat harvest apples from the trees overhead. A rather unfortunate thing it proved to me.

In the afternoon I determined to strike a racing gait. I was confident of my speed. Gilbert allowed me to maintain a lead of a sheaf, sometimes of two, never more. After two hours we were frankly and openly going at top speed, except that we did not run between sheaves. That would have been unseemly. Even yet we were not supposed to be racing. We had been six and a half hours in the field, going practically at top speed. There were still two and a half hours left us. I felt perfectly fresh. Gilbert was apparently in no trouble, so I ventured to let out a link. I began to step over my sheaf after the final shove of the band, instead of throwing it back off my knee. This gained a fraction of a second, but tended to sacrifice a certain amount of neatness in work. Another hour and a half went on at the same pace.

"Say, what's all this nonsense for?" at length said Gilbert. "You'll hurt yourself, if you don't look out."

"Hurt myself? I'm fresh as a daisy! Come on! Get a move on." It was an uncalled-for gibe.

He made no reply but in a few minutes he cut down my very slight lead and drew level with me. I had still a few links left. I let them out and hurled myself at my sheaves.

"You're a fool!" said Gilbert.

"Aw! come on! Don't be a quitter. You can stand it for another half hour."

This was an unnecessary insult. The machine had finished, we had only one clear round to go.

"I can stand it, all right. But I don't want to see you make a fool of yourself."

"Don't worry about me," I said with a laugh. "This is our ordinary gait at Orlando Reid's."

"Orlando Reid's? All right then. Let her go. I'll hang your shirt on the fence," he said angrily and let out a link or two of speed, taking definitely a lead.

Immediately I regretted my words. I had reached my utmost limit of speed unless I should scamp my raking a bit, and openly run between sheaves. Immediately I did both. One swipe with the rake was enough and between sheaves I dashed at full speed. And soon I was in the lead again, but my breath was choking me, my eyes were growing dim.

The boss, who had been watching us, came to meet us.

"Hey!" he cried, "where's the fire?" We paid no heed. I was beginning to stumble, but I kept in the lead. Gilbert was almost level with me.

"Say, Gilbert?" said the boss, coming up to us. "Did you see it?"

Gilbert stopped. "See what?"

"The rabbit? He was scairt to death! He took one look at you fellas and jumped clean over the fence."

There was a current saying that in the heart of every wheat field we should find a rabbit.

Gladly enough I stopped my mad race. Everything was black before me. I couldn't speak a word. I bent over a sheaf and slowly tied it, struggling desperately to get control of my breath. Then I turned my back on them and stood gazing at the sun dipping behind the treetops. I can see them yet. The tall elms with their magnificent crowns lit with the fires of the setting sun. Meanwhile I fought for breath control.

"Say, boy!" said Gilbert to me quietly as we were walking to the house, "you had me licked. I was going to quit at the next sheaf."

"Quit? It's a lie! Quit? You?" I turned my back on him lest he should see my tears.

"Yes! Well, perhaps not quit. But you're a better binder than I am, Charley."

I threw myself into a fit of coughing. I couldn't bear that he should see me crying.

"Darn that cough," I said. "Must have got a bit of chaff down my throat."

"Yes, Charley," he said, "you're a—"

"Darn your eyes," I burst out, blubbering outright. "I'll knock your block off."

As I spoke I leaped at him.

He wound his arms round me.

"Yes," he continued. "But I can beat you at this game!" So saying, he held me fast and finally threw me laughing heartily the while.

The fame of that day went through the land, when the two Gordon boys kept up with the machine. But for ten years following that nine-hour struggle, whenever I stooped I could always catch a dull pain on my right side.

That fight was characteristic of us both. I never had quite the weight or strength to keep up easily with the company I affected. At rugby football it was the same. I made the team playing quarter and I think kept my end up, but it was ever a desperate fight. I had to fight savagely. Gilbert, on the other hand, had a magnificent form and was acknowledged to be the finest halfback of his time in Canada. It was a glorious thing to see him go down through the whole field, swift as a hare, to make his touch. I shall have more to tell of him. He was the finest man I ever knew and I have known many fine men.

St. Mary's High School prepared us with an honors standing for Toronto University. Following high school we both taught for a year and a half, luckily in neighboring country schools, and thence proceeded to our university course.

CHAPTER VI

University Days

By the year 1879 Canada had a fairly well-organized system of education, university, college, high school and common school being coordinated into a smoothly working unity. From the common schools through high schools to the university, the upward path was clearly defined. Higher education in Ontario was afforded by Toronto University in the city of that name, and by Queen's University situated in the little city of Kingston on Lake Ontario. Between these two institutions a keen rivalry existed. Toronto affected to regard Queen's with a somewhat patronizing air, which of course Queen's resented bitterly. Toronto's real rival on something like equal terms was McGill University in the city of Montreal in the Province of Quebec, where educational and athletic records were both high. High schools in Western Ontario, for the most part, sent their boys to Toronto, those from Central Ontario generally favored Queen's, while those from Eastern Ontario and from Quebec went to McGill.

I say "boys" for up till 1882 the sacred portals of universities in Canada had not been opened to female students. While I personally voted for the extension of university privileges to women I was conscious of a secret feeling of which I was somewhat ashamed, that something of the lofty splendor of university life had departed with the advent of women.

It was a little like playing baseball with a soft ball. But the high standing in the class lists taken by Miss Margaret and Miss Edith Brown, the daughters of the Honorable George Brown, editor of Canada's greatest newspaper, the *Globe,* and one of Canada's great statesmen, as also the capturing of a scholarship in mathematics by

Miss Ralmer took all the "soft ball" feeling out of us. We patronized the female students no longer. Still, though we found the young ladies charming, if somewhat exclusive in their ways, there remained an indefinable regret at the passing of a certain virility from university life at the coming of "the skirts."

In the autumn of 1880 my brother and I began our university life, for though we had matriculated in 1879 financial stringency forced us to take our first year extramurally, while teaching in country schools.

As I look back upon our early experiences in the city I cannot escape a feeling of amazement at our immaturity, in spite of our four years in high school and our experience for a year and a half as country schoolteachers.

The city offered us a wonderful experience. Neither its bright lights, however, nor its shady resorts affected us in any degree. Fortunately our limited finances saved us from indulgence in wild or reckless living, our expenditures being limited as a rule to twenty-five cents a week. Furthermore, our time and energies were absorbed by our university activities—classwork, gymnasium, rugby, university politics—"Inside" against "Outside"—Glee Club, Y.M.C.A. We saw little of city social life with the exception of student parties. But looking back upon our university days I can see we owed much to our church connections. St. James Square Presbyterian Church, of which the minister was the Rev. Dr. J. M. King, a fine scholar and a preacher of great intellectual and spiritual power, was a popular church. Dr. King's church was always crowded with students. His great gifts as a teacher drew the students to his Sunday afternoon Bible class. He was the greatest Bible teacher I ever knew. I am not counting in this category my mother, whose gifts as a teacher in any subject she undertook to expound were far and away above those of anyone else.

University life was intensely absorbing. Our classwork held first place with us, and to it we gave our main strength. Here for the first time in our lives our paths divided. Gilbert, having chosen to be a doctor, took the science course; I, having decided for the ministry, chose classics and English. We did fairly good work and took a quite respectable honois stand in our class lists. But we were too deeply interested in other phases of university life to sacrifice them to academic standing. And I think we chose wisely. It has always been rather surprising to me to discover how many medalists in the university class lists have made a rather indifferent showing in the arena of life.

We were above everything keen for athletics. Through the winter months we spent hours every afternoon in the gymnasium where we took a respectable place in the usual lines of bar, ring and swing work.

In the gym by a sheer accident I won a great reputation as a pugilist. One day while I was going through a series of sparring exercises with a friend, there came into the gymnasium Bob McNair, a big bony Highlander, weighing 180 pounds or so, six feet two, a famous football back, a heavy hammer thrower and champion quoit player, and a great pal of mine. For some time McNair stood watching our passes with obvious contempt.

"Here! What are you monkeying about?" he cried at length to my sparring partner. "Let me have those gloves."

"No, thanks, Mac," I said. "I have no intention of being knocked out by you."

"Oh, come on! I never had them on in my life. I can't hurt you."

"You can't, eh?" I replied. "You are just the kind of brute that would kill me."

"Nonsense, I won't hurt you. I want to see how it goes."

Upon his assurance that he would only spar lightly I agreed to have a round with him.

For two or three rounds I easily blocked his wild, clumsy swings. At length, growing impatient, he exclaimed, "Oh, come on! Stop this nonsense! Let's go to it."

With a rush at me he beat down my guard and landed some quite smart blows.

"Here! Let up, McNair!" I remonstrated. "I'm not going to fight a big bull like you."

"Oh, come on! I won't hurt you," he cried, rushing in on me.

"Now, McNair, quit that or I'll hit you," I warned in desperation.

"That's the idea!" he said and rushed again, his fists swinging and his guard wide open.

As he rushed I stepped to meet him, caught him with a straight arm absolutely rigid fair on the bridge of the nose. His own 180 pounds hurled recklessly upon my straight, stiff arm wrought disaster for him. He was lifted clear off his feet, he swung round, fell upon a pair of parallel bars, clutched and hung there. They carried him into the washroom and poured water over his face. It took twenty minutes to thoroughly restore him. Then regarding my slight form with wonder and contempt, he grunted indignantly:

"Where in blazes do you get the weight for that punch?"

"You furnished the weight, Mac. You ran on to my fist. I didn't do anything."

"You didn't, eh? Well, thank the good Lord you didn't!" he said. "But it was a deevil o' a welt."

As a result my reputation as a hitter went through the college, and I was careful not to wreck it by any further boxing bouts.

In track athletics my brother took a high place as a runner, but our great passion was for rugby, to which we gave every spare moment of our time during the autumn months. I can still feel the thrill that used to run through my very soul as, immediately upon the close of our last afternoon lecture about four o'clock, we would dash off to the gym, tear out of our clothes and into our rugby kit, listening meanwhile to the echoing "thump! thump!" of the ball outside where men were practicing drop kicks and punts. At that time had I been offered the choice between a scholarship in classics and a place in the Senior Rugby Team I would without a moment's hesitation have chosen the latter. My brother soon became famous on the practice field. He was strong, quick, cool with a courage that nothing could daunt, probably the swiftest runner and certainly the best dodger on the team. He finally came to be recognized as the finest halfback of his day in Canada. As for me, I had neither his weight nor his speed nor his strength, but I became a rather skillful manipulator of the ball, and a fair average runner and passer.

My first practice hour with the Senior Rugby Team I have never been able to forget. The green players were put first into the scrimmage, and a brutal test that was in those days. We played English rugby with nine men on a side in the scrum, the biggest and heaviest in the team. Between these eighteen men the ball was laid and the word given. The game was to push your opponents back gradually, carrying the ball with you till you pushed your ball right through, or till the scrum resolved itself into a squirming, struggling mass of monsters, three or four layers deep. In such a case heaven help the man next mother earth, and all the more if he happened to weigh something less than 135 pounds! In the heart of that ton and a half weight of human flesh, driven by several ton weight of demonic energy, a slightly built chap stood a fair chance of being flattened into a pancake. Blind, gasping, choking, again and again I emerged from that maelstrom of human fury certain I should never be able to endure another go, but praying that the captain should not notice my flattened condition. The first practice was the worst. It was my brother who saved me from a complete funk.

"Say, Charley, how can you stick it?" he said on our way home from our first workout. "It almost killed me the first time."

I had intended to tell him I could not possibly stick the terrific crush of the scrimmage. Now I was jubilant to know that he had felt just as badly as I in that fearful fight for life. I resolved to stick, which I did, and to my amazement still lived. After a week or so the captain put me on as quarterback, where I really belonged and where he had always meant me to be. After that change my joy in the game was complete. I became quite a decent quarter. But Gilbert became the scintillating star of the team. Life has brought me many thrills, but nothing has ever brought me a more ecstatic delight and pride than seeing Gilbert take the ball from a pass of mine on our own quarter line and set off down the field, running, head well back, like a deer, dodging, knocking off a would-be tackler with an open hand full in the face, cutting away a gripping clutch with a swift downward swipe and making his touchdown, all the while with a pleasant smile on his face, while the crowd of Varsity followers went frantically mad, rending the air with cries of "Gib! Gib! Gib!"

The story of the football match in Ralph Connor's *Prospector* gives a true picture of a terrific struggle, not with McGill, however, but with a band of savage Irishmen from Ottawa College who played to win regardless of rules and regulations and reckless of life and limb, their own or the enemy's. In spite of their unscrupulous disregard of rules and their utterly ruthless tactics, they were a great football team. It was a joy to meet them on the field, a glorious triumph to defeat them and no shame to be beaten by them.

After the close of the rugby season we gave most of our spare time to the University Glee Club, as we were quite keen about music. During our second year under the inspiration of Professor Maurice

Hutton, the distinguished head of the classical department, and of Professor Ramsay Wright, a brilliant scientist, both Oxonians, the club with great daring undertook the production of Sophocles's play *Antigone* with music. It was the first time a Greek play set to music had been done in the original in modern times. In this production we were both fortunate enough to have a place in the first quartet, Gib in the bass, I in the tenor, and the experience afforded us special advantages in voice training.

Out of our Glee Club there developed another musical organization, which won us some fame and later exerted an important influence in our lives. Together with three other members of the University Glee Club we organized what was known as the Toronto University Student Quintet. Besides my brother and myself, who took second bass and first tenor respectively, the members were Dick Tibb, second tenor, Mac Hamilton, first bass, and Bob Haddow, who became our comedian. And a rare artist he was. Never on the professional stage or off have I seen a finer artist in the role of comic acting. To our work in the student quintet we gave a considerable portion of our spare time. For the organization held together about eight years, and during our university and college courses it was our custom to give two hours every Saturday morning to practice. The University Glee Club and more especially the Quintet not only did a great deal for our musical education, but incidentally furnished many opportunities for the cultivation of the social side of our lives, and led to many delightful and lasting friendships.

After graduation from the university my brother and I were forced to take up teaching to raise funds for our further education in our professions. I became classical master in the Chatham High School in Western Ontario, and Gilbert fortunately obtained a position as a resident master in Upper Canada College, the most famous boys' school in Canada. As master in Upper Canada he did full-time work and at the same time carried on his medical course in Trinity Medical College. It was a strenuous bit of work. Only his magnificent physique and his invincible pluck carried him through. After a year and a half of high school teaching I entered Knox College and proceeded on my theological course to graduation. Similarly my brother completed his medical training.

CHAPTER VII

Canoe Trip

FAREWELL TO ALMA MATER—INTO THE WILDS WITH
AN EXPERT WOODSMAN—PRESCRIPTION FOR THE
JOY OF LIVING—CANOE WISDOM—PROSPECTING—
CANOE AGAINST A GALE

IN 1883 WE graduated from the university. How large a place that
institution had made for itself in my heart I never knew till after
I had written my last examination. I walked out through the door
under the noble Gothic arch and made my way on to the beautiful
green in front. Then I turned and looked at the noble building, one
of the finest on the continent. It was a perfect day in early May, the
trees in Queen's Park were at their best. I was suddenly stricken
with an acute homesickness. It was a shock to remember that the
varsity was no longer mine, I was no longer of it. I belonged to the
great mob outside. I walked slowly down that green toward the
School of Science and turned once more to look at the scene before
me. There lay the campus, vividly green, the scene of many a hard
rugby battle, and beyond it the university, calm, grandly magnificent
with its fine old façade of Gothic mullioned windows, every window
tricked out with its funny-faced gargoyles, the whole now softened
with green splashes of ivy. No longer mine. I lay with my face on
the greensward, homesick and desperately lonely. For the first time
I understood the heart of the old Hebrew poet when he sang:

> Thy saints take pleasure in her stones,
> Her very dust to them is dear.

I had not dreamed, till that moment, how dear stones and dust could
be.

My last year had put a heavy physical strain on me. Classwork
had been heavy, side reading extensive. Social claims had become more
engrossing and, besides, financial stress made it necessary that I should

do a good deal of coaching. I came out of my exams more or less a wreck. Gilbert had secured a job with the *Mail* as a reporter for the summer. I was in low water every way when my eldest brother, Robertson, breezed into Toronto on his way to the north country in quest of gold. He was a mining engineer, had done a lot of exploring and now had a commission to do some prospecting in the great unknown country in the Far North beyond the line of civilization. After a day or two spent in making his final preparations and getting supplies, he came to see me; observing my lackadaisical condition, he offered me a job to go with him. I jumped at it. My friends were rather troubled with misgivings on my behalf.

"That boy go up into that wild rough country?" said a dear old lady who was mothering me in her lovely home. "Nonsense! What he wants is a good long rest."

"Not he," said my brother in great contempt. "He's had too much loafing already. What he wants is twenty miles paddling upstream in the bow of a canoe for dear life and a few miles over the portage with a tump line over his head and a good-sized pack on his back. The trouble with him is, you are all coddling him to death."

"Nonsense!" exclaimed my motherly friend indignantly. "He's all worn out. That hard work would kill him. And in that wild country without doctors or anything."

"Doctors? When he gets on the trail he won't have time to think of doctors. He'll be too busy keeping up with me."

"What food will he have? He should have nourishing food. Who will cook for him?"

"Good Lord! He'll cook for himself and for the camp."

"It would just kill him! He wants the best of food."

"And he'll get it. Why, my dear lady, he'll live like a lord."

"What will he have to eat?"

"Sowbelly, blackstrap if he's lucky, and flapjacks, fried in pork gravy, washed down with tea that will float a flatiron."

The dear lady held up her hands in horror.

"He will die on your hands! All very well for you a great big— big—"

"Brute of a bully," supplemented my brother. "No fear! We won't let him die. We'll be far too busy. Don't fear for his feeding. At the end of the first week he'll be ready to eat cut nails. No! Don't you worry about him. If he stays in this house with half a dozen women coddling him for a few months he won't be worth a darn for anything but singing you a lot of silly love songs. If he comes with me I'll bring back a man to you when I'm through with him."

"Aw, shut up, you big blowhard," I said in a cold fury. "I've wet the shirt of many a man as good as you, and I'll wet your shirt too before I come back, you hear that?"

"All right, my boy. You keep your stroke with me in the canoe and keep step behind me on the portage and I'll ask no more."

After that nothing short of an infectious disease or a broken leg would have kept me from going.

Before the week was out, on a shiny morning we were standing on the shore of Lake Nipissing, our canoe loaded to the gunwales with our outfit tent and grub sitting like a living thing on the clear blue water and a small group of my brother's pals to see us off.

"All ready?" said Robertson. "Get in."

I had never been in a canoe. Boats, rafts, floating logs I knew the ways of. But a canoe is like nothing else that floats.

Gingerly I reached a foot toward my place in the bow.

"Hey! What the deuce do you think you're doing? Do you want to dump the whole blasted outfit into the drink?"

I knew he was putting it on a bit, but he was nonetheless unpleasant.

Hastily I drew back my foot and stood waiting, with my ears hot.

"Now listen to me and take note too. First, never stand up in a canoe. Remember that. Never stand upright in a canoe. Now do what I tell you, and don't do anything else. Face the bow."

I obeyed.

"Stoop down low.

"Take hold of the gunwale with your right hand.

"Slip your left foot into place.

"Reach your left hand quietly and grab the left gunwale.

"Transfer your weight gradually from your right foot to your left.

"Keep down low.

"Now easily and quietly bring your right foot in and kneel down, at once."

To his evident surprise I managed easily to get into position. The boys uttered a few words of approval in undertones.

"Gets in like a blasted cow," said Robertson.

"Fuss-rate, by gar!" exclaimed Frenchie La Roque. "He's mak one dam good canoeman, eh?"

"He will before I'm done with him," replied Rob with a grunt, stepping into the stern so lightly that I didn't know it till I saw him sitting in his place.

"Well, boys, so long! See you when we do," said Robertson.

"Good-bye, boys!" I said cheerfully, glancing round at the group who were all wishing us good luck.

My eye fell on Robertson's gun propped up against a tree.

"Well! we're away!" cried Robertson. "Let her go! Paddle!"

"Don't you want your gun?" I asked quietly.

"My gun? Great Jehoshaphat! Didn't I put that in?"

There was a shout of laughter from the boys, followed by many cheerful suggestions and warnings.

"You tak care dat beeg brudder of you," said Frenchie to me. "He's forget his paddle sometam, hey?"

"I'll look after him," I promised cheerfully.

"Sure t'ing!" said Frenchie with a delighted chuckle. "You mak heem wan bon voyageur. Hey?"

We were away. I could feel the lift of the powerful sweep of the stern paddle behind me which seemed somehow to give me a feeling of assurance that whatever came our way we would get through. And so I entered one of the great experiences of my life.

We were off for a two months' trip through the country north and west of Lake Nipissing and choosing our own waterways. At times we followed old Hudson's Bay Company blazes grown over with the years, which I could not detect but which to Robertson were like a chart, at times adventuring our own way, like French Indian half-breeds. The Indians and the half-breeds are marvelous trackers, the latter we found not so absolutely sure in the forest. They somehow lack the Indian's intuitive sense of the woods and of its many mysteries, but they have more venture on water. The Indian is inhibited by a thousand things that the half-breed either has never known or has forgotten or has come to ignore. The Indian moves through the forest in absolute silence. He will not converse. Even when he knows what you are saying, he will reply with a low "huh!" as if deprecating speech, his eyes meanwhile darting everywhere with piercing glances. Never for a single instant except at the campfire, and not always there, is he off guard. In the woods he is in his own friendly country, but always, always, he is conscious of sleeping danger. He moves among hostile forces. He is no coward. He will go anywhere, but always he goes aware and alert. The half-breed is a jolly fellow, ready under stimulus at any time to take a chance. An eloquent talker can stir him to great effort, to great daring. He will respond to the appeal of danger, and he is capable of unswerving personal loyalty. If he loves you he will risk life and all he has for you, but he is terribly subject to moods and tenses. He can tire out an Indian, he can outfight an Indian; but for the long, long trail, for endurance to the last gasp, if I have really given him cause to love me, I'll take the pure-blood Indian of the north country every time.

For quite twenty minutes Robertson paddled along in silence. I guessed he was thinking of that rifle. An utterly unpardonable lapse of memory for a woodsman. And in the presence of old comrades of the trail. I did not realize till after long experience of the north country how that slip cut to the bone his woodsman's pride.

Suddenly his silence was broken.

"It was my darn monkeying, getting you into the blasted canoe that did it," he said wrathfully.

"Well, I had to learn somehow," I said. "If you hadn't told me I would probably have upset the canoe."

"Yes, and dumped the whole blasted outfit into the drink."

"It was a good thing you told me." Then I added something about learning the canoe in a few days, an unfortunate remark.

"Few days?" he exclaimed. "If you live a hundred years you'll never learn everything about a canoe. She's as full of whims and quirks as any other female thing."

And many a time I have had cause to prove the truth of his words, at least so far as a canoe's quirks are concerned. For fifty years I have handled a canoe in all kinds of wind and water, but any day she will show me by some quirk that there are mysteries in her yet unexplored. That is one of the tricks she has for making you love her.

But she nearly killed me that first day. To begin with I was in wretched physical condition. The steady thrust of the paddle set agoing a "hotbox" under my shoulder blade. Also, I was in football knickers, tight at the knees, and kneeling checked the circulation, causing almost unbearable pain. My feet, thrust back under the thwart on which I was sitting, rested upon my bent-back toes. The agony was almost insupportable. But remembering my threat of the "wet shirt" I vowed by all the powers I knew that I would make no complaint if I had to fall out of the canoe. Fortunately my skip became dissatisfied with the balance of the canoe. He was finicky about balance. She was not riding just as he would like. We landed to readjust the dunnage. Never have I been so profoundly thankful to the fates as I was when I heard him say:

"She's too low in the bow. She's steering like a cow."

During the readjustment he observed:

"Plenty room for your toes?"

"Well, they are a bit crowded. Could I sit with my feet in front of me?"

"Sit with your feet in front? Good Lord! Say! If you were Paul La Marche you might. But not yet awhile. If a squall struck us with you sitting like a blasted turtle on a rock you'd send us over sure as you're born. You'll get over your toes in a day or two. If not, you'll have to do what the rabbit did when the bear caught him."

"What was that?" I asked cheerfully, unwilling to let him guess anything about my toes.

"He just got used to it. Feeling tired?"

"Not a bit!" I declared, making an attempt at a handspring not very successfully.

"Well, guess I'll have a smoke," he said pulling out his pipe.

I turned my back on him lest he see the joy in my eyes. I was again thinking of the "wet shirt" as I laid myself flat on the rocks.

I could not sleep. The hotbox under my shoulder would not let me, but I lay in blissful rest. Slowly he filled and lit his pipe while I thanked God for Sir Walter Raleigh and his introduction to civilization of the red man's fireweed.

In the afternoon we found ourselves paddling up the west arm of the Nipissing and two or three times pausing to allow my brother to examine some rock ledges, where there was no more chance of finding gold than in the gray stone in the walls of the old varsity. And well he knew it. He knew all about my toes too. Every canoeman remembers how his toes felt during his first day's paddling. In the early evening we drew up at a pine-covered point.

"Looks like good campground," said my brother. "We'll make a camp here. Out you get."

I sat steady, pretending to be lost in admiration of the scenery but in reality shrinking from the agony of waking up the lower part of my anatomy.

"All out!" snapped my brother. "Throw out your paddle."

"All in," I said to myself as I set my teeth and slowly extricated my lower limbs from the jaws of the infernal machine that held them fast.

"Hold her steady!" came the order as he stepped lightly from the canoe. "Hold her while I unload, and remember the sequence. First your paddle out, then yourself, then hold her while the stern unloads. Don't let her touch the rock!"

The unloading done: "Now catch her by the bow and lift her clear! Don't let her touch! Carry her up the bank. Let down gently. Don't drop her! You're not unloading cordwood. You're carrying a baby."

The canoe was to him a living and highly sensitive thing to be handled with meticulous care. Nothing so roused him to wrath as the careless handling of the canoe. To let her graze a rock, to allow her to fall, to leave her right side up, to sizzle in the sun, all such treatment he classed in the same category as larceny or child murder. But after all, when one thinks that to a Far North voyageur the destruction of a canoe may register the loss of the lives of the party one does not wonder at his anxiety for his frail craft. She is indeed dear as life.

The first and second days were my most painful in the way of discipline. The third day I began to eat "sowbelly" with relish. By the end of the third week my record for the evening meal is represented by the menu:

> Pot of flour porridge
>   (eaten with blackstrap)
> One white 4½ pound bass per man
>   (cooked in clay as caught with sowbelly on side)
> One partridge per man
>   (cooked in clay, feathers and all, inside and out)
> Tea ad lib—flapjacks ad lib—blackstrap ad lib.

Notes upon above menu as follows:

a. The batter for the flour porridge had been prepared after the noonday meal before either bass or partridge had been secured.

b. The habitat of the white bass was an ice-cold, ice-clear lake in which you could see the bass swimming under the canoe twenty feet down.

c. The partridge Robertson potted with his automatic in the spruce grove immediately back of our tent. The partridge knew no fear and felt no hurt.

d. Both bass and partridge were cooked just as God made them without mutilation external or internal. Each was rolled in its shroud of clay and buried in a bed of coals and sand for twenty minutes or so. There is no other method of cooking either bass or bird so as to preserve their perfect flavor. Furthermore, this method saves trouble. No scaling, no plucking, no removing of viscera. When the clay jacket is knocked off fish and bird appear clean, perfectly cooked, and with their native juices unspoiled by pot or pan. Anyone partaking of fish or game thus prepared will be really content with no other for the remainder of his natural life.

Another three weeks and we made our way over the height of land by a series of small lakes and streams following the general course of the trails of the Honorable Company of Adventurers of England Trading into Hudson's Bay and the North-West Company. At last we struck the headwaters of a sizable river and began our return journey via the waters of Lake Huron, Georgian Bay up the French River, and so back again to Lake Nipissing. But how completely changed everything was! Now every day was a joy. We were going downstream on a big flow of water, evidently an old timber waterway, for the jams were cleared out and only the heavy rapids or waterfalls forced us to portage. The flies, of course, were annoying, especially when going with the wind, but a coating of pork grease, laced with some appallingly potent flavoring of Robertson's concocting, saved us from all but the deer fly, that gray, flat-bellied emissary of the pit. But we could smash him, for he hated to let go after he had got thoroughly preoccupied with his cocktail.

It is one of the supreme joys of life to be thoroughly fit. Joy is really well-being. At the end of my fifth week I made that great discovery. It was worth all the agony of knees, ankles and toes, all the hotbox of the shoulder blade, all the staggering backbreak of the portage, all the long weariness of the unending swing of the paddle, worth all just to be fit. Ready to meet with a spring everything and anything the hour may bring you. To wake and be willing to spring from your spruce bed ready for your morning dive, ready for sowbelly and blackstrap and flapjack with a fish, if you are lucky, ten minutes from the hook to the pan, ready for the swift, smooth technique of camp-breaking and canoe-packing and heaven help you if you mess up that technique, or worse still if you have no ordered technique—I once had to paddle back five miles for a forgotten and essential pan. I say life is one gay song for the man fit for his day. And a man gets fit by observing the inexorable laws of life, work, food and rest in proper proportion and environment. Here I am at the end of the fifth week fit and bubbling with life. I can carry my load across the portage at the Indian trot. I can pack my canoe, too, over the portage, if the carry isn't too long, for I am no giant. I can paddle a day of twelve hours and come in fresh enough to cook supper or make our beds or get wood for our night fire. And, best of all, I have learned something about a canoe. No man lives long enough to learn everything about a canoe. But I can paddle her, bow or stern, with head wind, side wind, tail wind in anything but white water. I can upset her, "shake" her empty and climb in over bow, stern or belly. I can paddle her standing on her gunwale, not very fast, but fast enough. And therefore I am happy, all day long from dawn to dark, ready for anything and the bigger the better, and this is not bragging. It is simply feeling fit, being right with yourself and your world. It is being as God meant you to be.

Let me moralize a little at this point. Skip a page if you hate it.

The conditions of fitness, or "joie de veef" as Pierre La Roque puts it, I have said are work, food, rest in proper proportions, with adjustment to environment. And I think even the modern psychologist would agree, though he would not say it in those words. What's the use of being a psychologist, a modern psychologist, and use terms a mere wood-runner can understand? But these elementary words must be understood. For instance, almost all my agony of knees might have been avoided by a little adjustment .

"What's the matter with your knees?" asked Robertson at the end of the second day, observing me stamping and rubbing. "Let's have a look."

He gave a brief glance at my tight knickers. "Well, I'll be darned!" He pulled out his knife. "What do you think you're doing? Playing rugby?" Neatly he slit the elastic knee bands.

"Any other pain?"

"My ankles."

"Get your toes down as far as possible into the bottom of the canoe. Loosen your laces. That will ease some of the pain. The rest you'll have to stand for a day or two. Now what else?"

I told him about my hotbox.

"Why the devil didn't you tell me? Hero stuff, eh? Hero stuff's all right, but don't be a darn fool. Paddling is easy work if you paddle right, but the very devil if you don't. I noticed that darn fool swing of yours, but forgot to tell you about it. Remember this. Keep your hands below your chin. I'm not talking about the racing stroke, though a lot of smart alecks think it's a great style to swing their blasted arms, is if they were trying to catch butterflies. But in the all-day bow stroke, keep your hands low. Loose grip, hands low, and get the power from your body, not your arms. Do that and you'll have no hotbox tomorrow. Only fools carry hotboxes."

"Who told you?" I asked.

"Nobody, by Jupiter!" My brother had a rich variety of oaths, but never have I heard him use the Holy Name. "I learned it myself with a driving brute who was trying his best to break me. I kept lifting my arms till I absolutely couldn't lift them again. I was planning how to upset the canoe, for I couldn't quit, not if I died for it. While I was planning my arms dropped, but I kept on going through the motion of paddling. Then all of a sudden, by Jove, I found my-self paddling with hands low down and then I found my body going into the stroke. I had the trick in five or ten minutes. He noticed it too.

"'Hey there! Get into it,' he yelled.

"'Go to hell!' I said and put my body into it. I had a little advantage of the wind too, so I thought I could hold him. Of course the stern has a big advantage. But in spite of that I thought I could hold him. I did, too, in spite of his teeth. After that I had no more hotbox. He had known the trick, too, but he wanted to break me. Was I mad? Well! When we got to the landing he got out and said, 'Loafing, eh? Bushed, eh?' 'You're a liar,' I said and walked up to him and hit him one. That was all there was to it. But I had no more trouble with my hotbox, nor with him either. I should have told you about it though."

It was a fine bit of wisdom. I never forgot it. You don't forget what you learn through suffering. Some suffering we cannot dodge, but most of life's agonies would be saved simply by better adjustment to our environment. Enough of psychology.

We are still a long way from home, but every mile of the way is now a living glory. The unspoiled woods, the shy things that lived in them, the water that is our pathway and our medium of transport, and the canoe alive under us.

One morning at breakfast on the riverbank with the sun appearing over the rocky ridge across the river, and the eloquent silence of the woods all round us, Robertson caught my arm in a quick, hard grip. I turned to him without a word. He had taught me the law of silence in the woods. I learned to say little and, like the Indians, that little in low tones. My eye followed his finger. There fifteen feet from us was a bear, sauntering slowly along. Suddenly he caught our scent. Up went his head with a loud "whoof!" expressing, as I thought, indignant surprise. For a single instant he faced us, then with a perfectly effortless movement he whirled on his hind legs, ambled down the bank and without a sound he was in the river and away with the water foaming in front of him, up the other bank, over the rocky ledges with a speed incredible in so huge and apparently so clumsy a creature. He scaled the hillside and disappeared.

"He'll have a great story to tell," said Robertson.

"So will I," I said. "What amazing speed he has!"

"For a short distance he's a racer. He gave me the hardest hundred yards' race I ever had in my life."

"What then?"

"I fell down between two big logs, and when he found me I was ready for him. I had an army pistol at his ear. He never touched me."

Another ten days found us paddling in the maze of islands through which Lake Nipissing pours itself by the romantically lovely French River into Georgian Bay.

We were heavily loaded with samples of ore taken from two score ledges, some of them most promising in gold as we had proved under the blowpipe and crucible. We were pushing hard, for it was Friday, and Robertson was anxious to get his samples off by the night express from Sturgeon Falls, only twenty miles away. But there was an unpleasant head wind kicking up rough water and with our load we couldn't risk too much. It was most annoying, and behind me I could hear Robertson cursing his luck. From the shelter of one little island we would slip across to that of another, always taking a little more water. And so all forenoon we poked along, Robertson getting more and more wrathful against wind and weather. At length we came to the last island facing the open water of the Northwest arm which lay between us and mainland at the mouth of the Sturgeon, up which we could paddle safely to the railway station of Sturgeon Falls. There it lay, a low dark line on the horizon, only nine miles away, but this wind with its cross sweep of thirty miles from the open lake with a million hissing voices said "No." And with a loaded canoe, that "no" was enough, even for my brother Robertson, with all his imperious will and ways. But he was very cross. He was one of the finest fellows in the world but he had a streak of Satan in him, which at times made him ready to challenge heaven itself.

For some minutes he stood viewing from the island that hissing tumbling white water and scanning the sky, an unpleasant sight.

"Darn you!" he growled, apostrophizing the universe. "We'll have to camp. And a deuce of a place for a camp it is!"

He was right. No underbrush for shelter or bed, no moss, no decent wood for fires, not even trees for our tent guy ropes. The miserable leavings of two hundred years of Huron raiders, Hudson's Bay trappers, North-West Company pirates! And across this miserable nine-mile jump were all the luxurious comforts of Sturgeon Falls! We made camp, guying our tent to piles of rocks and laying our blankets on the unyielding bosom of the Cambrian Cap. Then we cooked our dinner, also of leavings, for our luxuries were exhausted and we were reduced to tea, the tailings of a sack of sugar, sowbelly, flapjacks and half a sack of flour which we had laid in at the last Hudson's Bay post at the mouth of the French River. A dinner of necessities.

"It may clear up toward evening," said Robertson when we had washed our dinner dishes—he was an incorrigible optimist—and sat down to smoke and watch the weather.

The wind dropped, the clouds lifted and appeared to solidify into the arch of the sky, the white water sank into a dark-blue smoothness, heaving slowly. Robertson became cheerful.

"She's going to clear." It has been always a mystery to me why the weather is considered feminine. Even as he spoke a puff of wind struck him on the face and changed his mind for him.

"If it weren't for our confounded load we could easily make it."

But in ten minutes the wind was up again and the blue water was showing white flecks on its glassy surface. We finally made tea and resigned ourselves to camp for the night on this dreary and desolate island. I spent an hour gathering such wood as I could, cutting down stumps and hauling up driftwood and making things snug for the night. Robertson sat smoking gloomily. Suddenly he exclaimed:

"By George! she's clearing! Look at that sky!"

I looked. Certainly there was a patch of blue in the south.

"But look at that sky!" I said, pointing westward. The west was a livery mass shot through with jaundiced bars of yellow, the northeast, the danger point, was a mass of black low-lying clouds.

"Oh, blazes, we can make it!"

"Well," I said, "I think it's foolish to take a serious risk to avoid a little unpleasantness."

I said the wrong thing in the wrong way.

"We'll go," he shouted. "Load up! Jump to it! Never mind packing. Throw things in!"

In a very few minutes our stuff was flung loosely into the canoe and we were afloat, but in those few minutes the whole sky had changed. The blue patch in the south was gone, the west was still lurid and angry, in the northeast the black sky was now billowy with hanging masses of cloud lying almost on the water. Assuredly a dangerous sky. I hated it, but stepped into my place in the canoe. Mine not to reason why. He was my chief. Our job was to get over this nine-mile stretch of water, now an angry purple and heaving with a slow, oily swell, just as speedily as possible. We went to it. I felt the mighty heave of the stern paddle and knew he was as anxious to get over as I. I responded with my best and our stanch but heavily laden little craft was flying up the long purple slope, hanging for an instant on the crest and shooting down the answering slope as if anxious also to get across this bit of water with all possible speed. We had paddled a quarter of an hour when suddenly I felt a faint puff of cold air on my face and immediately was conscious of a heavier heave from the stern paddle. At once I responded with all there was in me. In a minute more a second puff struck us, definite, unmistakable. At once I responded with a quickened stroke.

"All right, my boy, take it easy," said Robertson in a cheery voice. "Just a little breeze!" But his stroke, too, had quickened. Immediately there followed a gust that ruffled the glassy surface of the lake.

"Well! Let her go!" he cried gaily. "We'll show her."

I was fitter than I had ever been and I knew I could paddle at racing speed for half an hour without the slightest distress. So at racing speed we went, all out to beat the gale, which we could see coming down upon us far away to the northeast and carrying with it a long, low wall of white water. In five minutes it struck us, and struck us with a rude, angry slap. At once we were in the midst of a smother of white water rushing at us and reaching for us like a pack of furious wolves. I put another pound into my stroke.

"Hold on, my boy!" came my brother's voice, quiet and cool, as if about to light his pipe. "Now listen, and do exactly as I tell you. No use racing now. We are in for it, and we must fight every foot and very carefully. No matter what comes, paddle your steady stroke. Don't break your rhythm or you'll throw me out. Understand?"

At once a quiet calm filled me and I said:

"All right, Robertson, I'll do my best!"

"You just bet you will! I know you!"

Fifty-four years lie between that moment and this, and even as

I write my heart chokes up in me as it did then with pride. To us younger ones this eldest brother, wild, reckless as he was, stood for all that was splendid, gallant and heroic in manhood. He was a born leader. Men followed him without question into no matter what desperate adventure on river or lake, in peace or in war, as he had proved in the wilds of Mexico.

And now the storm was mounting every minute. The big waves were coming in threes and between the groups a long, sidling lane extended nearly a hundred feet, and then another group of three great masses of water, each with an immense white mane.

"Take it easy, boy; lift her quietly over each wave as it closes, then when the long lane opens before you push for dear life. Understand?"

"I understand."

I tried the next three, edging the canoe easily over each crest and then with desperate quick strokes making her fly for a hundred feet or so. I began to enjoy it. It really was a great game.

"Good boy! Great stuff! We'll make it yet!"

"Yet!" That word gave me my first chill. He wasn't so dead sure after all. But here were the next three to negotiate.

"Charley boy, I can't lift this canoe," came Robertson's voice. "We'll have to dump our stuff."

"How much?" I asked with a definite chill at the pit of my stomach.

"Everything except tent and blankets."

"Samples?"

"Samples, flour, everything not absolutely essential. Now listen carefully." He was speaking quietly and kindly, all bluster gone. "I'll hold the head steady, you reach around, watch your balance, pick things up and ease them quietly over. Be careful, but be quick, boy."

I have carried a vivid picture in my mind of the red lettering of the Hudson's Bay Company on the white fat belly of that flour bag. The dumping was effected safely, and once more we were into this hand-to-hand fight for life.

"Much better!" said Robertson in a cheery voice. But in a few minutes his voice came again with a note of anxiety in it. "She won't lift, boy. I'm going to try to bail her out, the water is round my knees.

You just hold her head steady, don't try to get forward, just hold."

For the next five minutes I had a terrific fight on my hands. The wind from the northeast was now a furious gale. The drift from the comb on every wave swept clear over me for I had to hold her right head on, and this for a bowman alone is something of a job. Meanwhile Robertson was bailing for dear life and making cheerful remarks. At length I heard the bailing tin thrown down and could feel again the lift of the stern paddle.

"By Jove! she's fit again! The old girl is riding! Riding like a duck!"

I could feel her under my knees beginning to dance in her old style. She was again a living thing, not a dead log.

But now a new terror fell on us. We were making for a long low island, dark with dense underbrush and at one end a single pine tree standing like a watchtower. As the storm gathered force the air became thick with a driving, misty rain, which with the gathering night was gradually blotting out the island from our sight. It was now only a dull blur on the water.

"Say, boy, can you see that island?"

"Not so very well. But I can see the tree."

"Boy! Forget everything else, but don't, on your life, lose sight of that tree. I'll watch the rollers. Paddle your stroke, but don't lose that tree."

I lost all anxiety as to rollers, spray, pitching canoe, but like a man holding to a life line my eye held that tree. The island faded to a smudge, hardly differentiated from the clouds on the horizon, but the tree still stuck up its crest from the foam. And to that crest my eye clung desperately.

"Must bail again, boy. Hold her as best you can, but don't lose that tree. We'll beat this blasted bitch of a gale yet."

Somehow the epithet cheered me immensely. He was becoming contemptuous of the gale. Even at the height of its fury he felt that he was beating it. With a canoe under his knees that was given a fair chance, he had come to feel he could outride this storm. His courage was of that fine temper that rose with danger, and asked only fair terms in a fight.

Once more we went on dealing with each wave as it came rushing at us with death in its foaming jaws, mounting it, dodging it, or pushing it aside and riding over its hissing crest. At length we began to see the dark mass of the island again.

"Not far now, boy! Let the tree go! But watch these waves they are cutting across our bow more."

We could now see the mass of underbrush on the island. Suddenly we became aware of a little oasis of calm in the midst of the raging waters.

"Must be a submerged island," said Robertson. "Let's bail out again."

After bailing out and readjusting our load we sat there in the growing dark. We had only a hundred yards or so to go, but that hundred yards was like a black funnel down which the wind was howling like a million wolves, thick with driving spray and impenetrable to the sight.

Robertson studied the situation for a few minutes, grunting imprecations. He seemed to feel that this female canine of a storm was taking a low-down advantage of us. We had beaten her in fair hand-to-hand fight, and now to suddenly try to block our way with this sort of flank movement Robertson regarded as only another revelation of her essentially feminine characteristics.

"Huh!" he grunted. "You would, eh? Well, we'll just fool you, old lady!" He picked up his paddle.

"Now then!" he announced. "We're not going to try to push through that mess of wind and flying spray. It would just smother us and fill us up! Not much! We're no such blasted fools. We'll keep her head fair into the wind and paddling a nice quiet stroke I'll just ease her over and we'll drift down till we find a cove and, by gad! fool her."

He meant we would fool this "blasted bitch of a gale." Everything went according to plan, and in a few minutes we were quietly floating behind a jutting rock in a little cove where the water lapped gently on smooth white sand.

"Well, we're here, thank the good Lord!" said Robertson quietly. I turned and looked at him. His face was bloodless, his eyes large white pools with black centers, his hands were shaking as with palsy, his breath coming in great heaving gusts. "There was once I thought we were for it, when I felt the water up to my knees and I couldn't lift her over the crest. One big wave would have been enough."

"Where did you get the can?"

"God knows. I put my hand down and there it was. God arranged that, I guess," he said simply.

He was a strange mixture. Quick-tempered, imperious, merciless, but with a woman's tender heart and deep down a child's trust that God was his friend.

"Well, get out! We'll make camp."

I tried to rise. I found I had no legs.

"Can't do it," I groaned.

"Stay there, boy!" he said. "There's a fisherman's hut on this island, if I remember right. I'll go and find it."

I leaned forward on the gunwale. I wasn't exhausted but my legs were gone. I recalled the various crises of the last hour, any one of which could easily have been the last. At each crisis each of us did exactly the right thing. We could as easily have done the other. Why was that? And that can? We never *planned* to have an old can in the canoe. How came it there? "God arranged that, I guess" was Robertson's simple explanation. Was he right? My mother would say so too, and in exactly the same simple way. Were they right? I was shocked to discover that I could not truly answer. I would have to face that out with myself later.

Soon I could hear above the gale and soon Robertson came crashing through the brush, and with him a stranger.

"Great luck, boy! Hut, fire and grub! Come along, old chap! By Jove! you deserve it."

Something in his voice released emotions that had been dead in me. I could not speak a single word. I began to struggle out of the canoe. With my hands on the gunwales I strained to my knees and there I hung in agony. Then one foot after the other I got out and stood bent over with my hands on my knees, breathless with the pain. Robertson and the other man lifted me to my feet and got to rubbing my legs.

"I'm all right," I said and staggered up the beach utterly disgusted with myself. I had thought I was fit for anything. "I have only been a couple of hours or so in that fight and here I am no good at all," I muttered.

"No good? You're all right, my boy, as right as God makes 'em!"

said Robertson in a queer, croaky voice. I stumbled up the trail, reached the hut, drank a cup of hot tea, tumbled into a bunk and woke next day at noon. Then I walked down to look at the lake. There she lay, quiet, shiny, a lovely thing. I shook my fist at her.

"Confound your sleek face!" I said. "You would have drowned us last night!"

"Not she!" said Robertson. "She did her darnedest for us. It was that cursed gale that did it. She sure was one bitch of a gale." He was still obsessed with the sense of a certain venomous femininity in the gale. A hundred yards from our shore lay a low but sizable island of rock and sand.

"I never noticed that island there last night," I said.

"There was no island there last night," said our fisherman friend. "It was washed right out. Never seen that happen before, and I bin here ten years."

"Some gale, eh?" said Robertson.

"Never seen such a gale on this lake," said the fisherman. "Two men in a fishing smack was drowned, and a schooner upset in the mouth of the river. When I seen you at my door last night I couldn't think where'd you come from. When you said you come across the lake I thought you was crazy, or a liar. Across that lake in a canoe! My holy cats! I can't believe it yet!"

In the afternoon we paddled up the river to the little village of Sturgeon Falls. Wherever we went a small group of staring inhabitants gathered about us to ask whether we had really come across the lake last night. Had we the capacity we could have drunk the town dry at the town's expense, and with the town's help. As it was I proved a bitter disappointment to our friends. Robertson did his best in honoring their hospitality. But I was rather happy that an early evening train carried us off with a completely new outfit, the best the town could supply and at no cost to us.

"Put up yer roll, you bloody ole whale!" said a trapper with a magnificent walrus mustache who had been aiding in the celebrations. "Whale? Thash what he is. Bloody ole whale! Anybody says he ain't, is a bloody ole kankeroo!"

That day Robertson's blustering, semihumorous, bullying manner toward me completely vanished. He took me as comrade and chum on terms of equality. That day, too, I attained the ultimate pinnacle of my self-esteem, for standing in the hallway of the Sturgeon Falls hotel I heard my brother's voice in solemn asseveration declare:

"No! He don't look it! But I want to tell you he's the best bow paddle I ever had in my canoe. You see he's light, only a hundred and thirty-five pounds, and that's to his good. And tough as iron bark! And guts! By golly! Last night he never lost his stroke, dumped that stuff, never turned a hair! Guts! and fight—" here Robertson became confidentially impressive—"why, he knocked out the Varsity bully over two hundred pounds, till they had to put ice on his head for nearly an hour!" At this climax I moved out into the open air. I had no ambition to meet the town's champion pugilist. It is fair to say that while my brother carried the bibulatory gratulations of his friends with considerable ease, yet I had a fear that in the overflowing hospitality of our friends and admirers there might lie even for him a danger of submersion as complete as that we had escaped.

That night before we went to bed Robertson became reminiscent and gave me an account of two other storms through which he had had to fight his way. "But neither of them as bad as this one, by Jimminy! And when that gale hit us in that open water, I said to myself, 'You know blamed well you shouldn't have tried it, but you lost your temper.' And then I remembered—this was the third time! By Jove, that gave me a queer feeling. Third time, you know!" His voice sank into awed silence. All these old trappers become superstitious.

"What then?" I asked. He hesitated a few moments. Then finally and in a half-shamed way he made answer:

"Well, I'll just tell you. I said to the Good man Up Above. 'Look here! I knows it's third time for me, but it's only first time for him.' And so it was."

CHAPTER VIII

On the Wanapitei

THE WANAPITEI RIVER flows out from the lake of the same name and crosses the Canadian Pacific Railway line about sixty miles from the lake. Our purpose was to make the lake and from it reach the headwaters of another water system farther west.

Fine and fit I was and, as I thought, ready to deal with any kind of water.

We put our canoe into a large pool at the bottom of a rapid and proceeded to edge our way up to the foot of the rapid, whence we should make our portage, saving a carry of several hundred yards, always an important consideration.

"Now take this carefully," instructed my chief. "See that point jutting out? Well, immediately round that point we strike swift water. Take it quietly, then hold her steady till we catch the eddy which will carry us right up to the foot of the rapid."

It seemed quite simple, and it was to those who knew its secret.

We paddled quietly to the point, then pushed the nose of our canoe into the swift water; immediately there seemed a call for a fight. Desperately I dug into the swift water, paddling for dear life.

"Easy!" sang out the chief, but I had missed the eddy and we drifted downstream, then gradually edged across the river once more to the bank far below our starting point.

"Now you'll learn how to take swift water," said my chief with a chuckle. Again he carefully explained the technique of making an eddy help you against swift water:

"Put her nose into the current quietly, hold her with an easy stroke till I swing her stern about, then when the current strikes her put your back into it and she'll walk right upstream. Don't work hard till the stream begins to work with you, wait for my word and then pull like blazes."

It was all a mystery to me, but I determined this time to wait for orders.

Once more we approached the point still in quiet water, pushed her nose out into the current.

"Steady! Hold her!" Gradually the stern swung about. "Now!" yelled the chief. A few quick hard strokes. She held her nose upstream till the current caught her sidewise, then gradually she began to crawl slowly upstream and in two or three minutes we were beyond the point, caught by the upstream swing of the eddy and were soon being carried easily up to the very foot of the fall where we made our landing safely for the portage.

"Nice work!" said my chief. "Got it just right."

I stood looking back on our course in utter amazement. It seemed a miracle.

"How did that happen?" I asked.

"Quite simple. Immediately you pass the point, there is a backflow of the current close inshore. Catch that and the eddy pulls you right upstream. At the foot of almost every rapid there is an eddy on one side or other of the river. Get her nose into that and up she walks."

"She's a wonder!" I remarked, gazing at our canoe with new awe and respect.

"She's like nothing else that floats. She's a wonder but you've got to know her ways. You can't bully her."

I gathered that it was only one more mystery associated with things of the feminine gender. The main thing to remember, apparently, is that they will not stand bullying. A most useful addition to my psychological education.

Three days of strenuous toil fifty miles upstream—and a fierce stream, too, with twenty or thirty lift-outs and portages as it seemed to me—brought us to a large and perfectly enchanting lake, Lake Wanapitei. Next morning at dawn to avoid rough water we crossed the lake, a half day's paddle, and found a little stream flowing into the lake from the opposite side.

"This looks like the trail," said my chief, studying the map which he had from a Hudson's Bay Company agent. Up the little stream we pushed our way through tangles of bulrushes, willows and log jams and found ourselves at the edge of a huge swamp, hemmed in on three sides by a rampart of rocks.

"This is what I wanted to see," explained my chief. "We will make camp, snatch a bite of lunch and explore these ledges."

We spent the afternoon working our way round the rocky ledges, collecting what seemed promising samples. As the sun was beginning to make its descent toward the treetops of the swamp below us, my brother suggested:

"You work your way back along this ledge. I shall go around to the other side, then cross the swamp and meet you at camp." His plan was to follow the arc of rock round to the farther horn of the arc and then, following the string of the bow through the swamp, meet me at our starting point.

Slowly I worked my way back till I approached our meeting point where I sat down on a luxuriant bed of brush to wait his coming. After a wait of an hour or so I began to listen for any sound of his hammer, but could catch none. I could see no sign of him on the ledge about half a mile away across the swamp below me. I raised my voice in a loud call, but there was no reply. Once more I sent forth a long, loud coo-e-e. Far away across the swamp I caught his answering call. A little later I called and again got his reply. He was evidently crossing the swamp toward me. I moved toward our meeting point, called and got his reply just below me in the swamp.

"I'll go down and get the fire going," I called and proceeded to our camp by the stream. I put on the kettle and climbed the hill to meet him. But there was no sign of him. Again and again I called, but no response.

"Hurry up, Rob, the kettle is boiling," I said. But he paid no heed. What could he be doing? There were no rocks down in that swamp. Was he trying to fool me? That was not the kind of thing he would do on a trip like this.

"Hurry up, Rob! Don't be an ass," I said impatiently. "I'm going down to fry the bacon. Hurry up!"

Annoyed at his silly silence I went back to the fire, cut the bacon, got the fish ready for frying. Still no sign or sound of him. Once more

I climbed up the bank and called down into the swamp, "What's keeping you? Hurry up! Everything is ready!"

Immediately at my back, about a dozen yards away it seemed, among the underbrush, there was a wild cry like a scream. Then I was properly angry.

"Look here!" I said. "If you think that's smart I don't. Don't make a fool of yourself. I'm going to have my supper."

So saying I went down to my fire and began to fry the fish and bacon, expecting him every moment to appear. I called, still no answer. Had he forgotten a hammer or something and gone back for it? Could anything have happened? I became anxious. Then I raised my voice in a long, loud halloo, when far across the swamp I heard his voice in reply. Again I called and again came his answer. At length he emerged.

"Well," he said pleasantly, "supper ready?"

I was perfectly furious.

"What sort of confounded idiot are you anyway?" I said. "Do you think that sort of thing is funny? How often have you told me never to fool in the woods?"

"What's the matter with you?" He gazed at me astonished.

"How often have you told me that no one but a darned fool would play that kind of trick? What did you go back for? Anyway, you might have explained to me."

"I don't know what you're talking about, Charley," he said, scanning my face curiously.

"Do you mean to say you weren't here fifteen minutes ago?"

Then I told my tale.

"By Jove, boy, it was a cat, a lynx. And how near did he come?"

"He yelled at me from that clump of bushes right there!"

"Good Lord! You are lucky boy. He might have dropped on you from a limb overhead. It was your fire likely scared him off. They are inquisitive devils."

"But it was your very voice, I would swear to that. Not once or twice, but a dozen times. He answered me just below there at our feet. And then after I came back from putting on the bacon, he screamed at me from that clump. It was exactly your voice." Then I was enraged at the beast. I got my revolver and beat round about and through the bushes but could find no sign of my clever ventrilo-quist.

That night beside the fire Robertson told me of similar experi-ences he had heard of from one of his trapper friends.

"But I always thought they were pulling my leg a bit. The brute can imitate any cry or call, they say."

"Well, he certainly fooled me," I declared, "even to that last wild scream. That, of course, was like no human voice. Still I thought it was you trying to startle me. But all the way across that swamp as he came nearer and nearer I never for a single moment doubted it was your voice answering me."

I slept with my gun under my pillow, hoping my friend might be inclined to pursue his investigations. But evidently he had satisfied his curiosity.

We penetrated the wilds for another week; failing to make con-nection with the waters of the western watershed, we were forced to retrace our way over Lake Wanapitei. We determined to make the run down the river, about fifty miles, with its two dozen lift-outs and portages, in a single day. It was all swift water, tricky and not without danger, but the chief had been down before and he had a mind that registered a course like a map.

At dawn we were away. Pausing twice only to boil our kettle, our grub being all finished, we found ourselves in the evening at the head of the last long sault. The question now was a run or a carry. The carry was long and up over a rocky climb. We should have to make two trips. It was not a pleasant prospect. We were faint from lack of food and tired out with our hard day.

"Let's take a look at her," suggested Robertson. We climbed up to the top of the rocky bank and looked down upon the rushing water, with its long, dark, smooth sweeps and its sharp pitches of white water. Long and carefully he studied the course.

"She looks rather wicked," he mused. "That center chute is a bad one. But if we hugged the left bank we could avoid that chute. That is really the only bad pitch—and she's a devil. Of course I believe we could hug this left bank all right."

"Suppose we couldn't—suppose we were drawn into that center chute, could we make it?" I asked.

"We could, but it would be a close thing. You see that long smooth sweep there just before the drop. If we hit that it would be Kingdom Come for us. But if we did strike that center chute fair a good heavy lift to the right would clear the boulder all right. It can be done. What do you say?"

"Whatever you say," I replied, hoping he would try it.

His eyes were beginning to shine. He glanced at me with a curious searching look. I grinned back at him.

"By Jove, we'll do it!" he said with an answering grin. Again he scanned the course foot by foot, studying the water and explaining it to me.

"If we keep close to the left bank the thing is straight going. But there is a heavy cross current there toward that center chute. Now listen. If we do get caught and are drawn in, a quick heavy lift to the right just before we reach that chute will send us clear. Be ready. If I yell, then lift like blazes and don't lose time. Sometimes a split second of time means eternity."

As I walked back to our landing I was conscious of that curious thrill through my nervous system that I used to get just before the kickoff in a big match with McGill, but with a deeper and more portentous interrogation in it. We made our load snug and taut.

"All right, boy, get in!" His voice had a kind of gay lilt. I got in, kneeling low and spreading out my knees to grip the sides of the canoe. A touch of the stern paddle and we slipped smoothly into the current. At once I became conscious of a quick, strong grip on the canoe, as if someone had said, "Come on here! I've got you! You are mine now!" For twenty-five yards we kept gathering up speed, not by seconds, but by fractions of seconds. We are at the crest. Jove! This looks like a toboggan slide! And feels like it too! We are flying as if in air, a curl of white water smites us in the face! She begins to leap, to plunge, she skips from one wave crest to another, pounding only the tops of these hummocks of water that feel like rocks under us. Suddenly I see that we have missed the current. We are in the center—the big plunge is rushing at us. "Li-i-ft her!" The yell smites like a blow on my senses—what I did I don't know—a wash of water chokes us—blinds us—our craft pitches madly forward, exactly like a bucking bronco—we are under—we are out into the air—gone—no! I am sitting in water over my knees—but—yes—we are through and skimming over crumpled, broken, boiling wave crests—but we are through!

"By Jove, boy, you did it!" gasps Robertson, exultant. "You're a whale."

A loud cheer from the bank greets us. It comes from a little group of men standing at the landing.

"Heh! What the hell? Oh, it's you! Might 'a' known it was some damn fool water hen!"

"Hello, Mike! Glad to see you, old boy," shouts my brother, bringing his canoe up to the little wharf.

"Say, you darned old fish hawk! You gave me the wolly-woogles, all right!" We shook hands all round, then Mike said solemnly:

"Look-a-here now, boss, you'd ought ta knowed better'n that. When I saw you up there at the top of that pitch I says, 'Well, there's another damn fool goin' to hell!' That's what I says, ask Bill here!"

"Yes, that's what he says, all right," replies Bill, slowly squirting a stream of tobacco juice into the river. "Two fellers, lumberjacks, drowned in that water this spring, comin' down in a Hudson Bay pointer too."

"Well, Bill, you see," said Robertson with a little grin on his face, "this isn't any Hudson's Bay pointer, and, by golly! we are not any lumberjacks. See that boy?" he added, shaking a finger at me. "He's—he's—well, look at him! Not much to look at—but you see before you the best bowman in this north country! Bar none!" Which I knew to be wildly absurd, but no less overpowering for that. Furthermore, it expressed his feeling at the time.

My throat was hot and choked. I couldn't utter even a croak. I made a jab at his stomach with my paddle and hastily bent to unload our stuff. Gold medals? You could have them all. But that word, from perhaps the finest canoeman in that land of canoemen, knocked me out. I couldn't see what I was doing, but it took me some minutes to unload my stuff. Good old Rob! Miner, woodsman, canoeman, rifleman, none better in all the Northland. A leader of men who would follow him anywhere, no matter against what odds, and proud to do it. This was not my last trip with him, but never with him or with any other did Death splash water in my eyes as during those split seconds on the Wanapitei.

PART TWO
Northwesterly

CHAPTER IX

Edinburgh

THE ROAD HOME—HISTORICAL SIGHTSEEING—
GREAT MEN AND GOOD FRIENDS: DRUMMOND,
WHYTE, DODS, DAVIDSON

AFTER finishing our university and professional courses the Quintet in 1887 were able to execute a purpose cherished for some years, which was to complete our training with a year's study in Edinburgh. That my brother and I were able to finance this rather ambitious plan I regard as something of an achievement. Ever since entering university in 1879 we had not only paid our way, but we had saved up enough for our Old Country trip, Gib having six hundred dollars to the good and I seven hundred. Obviously we were no spendthrifts, but at the same time we paid our way as we went, meeting all necessary charges, fees, contributions and collections attaching to student life. But that there was no wasting of substance in riotous living can be easily believed.

As I pause to take a look at us I can't help the feeling that in spite of our experiences from the backwoods of Glengarry, through the harvest fields of Zorra, in high school and university and as public schoolteachers and college masters, in spite of all our hard struggle with life, and in spite of our years *we were still very young*. We had no knowledge of life of our country or the world outside. Life was still a wonder.

From Glengarry to Edinburgh, truly a rugged enough road, with light and shade, rough and smooth. To the question, what makes a man what he is? the answer is origins and environment, his race and his road. As we stepped out of the Caledonian Station I knew where we were. We were back among our origins—more Scottish than Canadian.

"That must be the Castle?" I said to my cousin, a handsome youngster, dressed in his kilt, who had met our train.

"That's the Castle," he said with that in his voice that stayed our steps. To the Edinburgh man there is only one Castle. In silence we stood gazing at the rugged rock crowned with its towers. A queer surge of feeling rushed up in me. The Castle! The Bruce, the Douglas, the lovely unhappy young queen and John Knox, the Bonnie Prince!

"Listen!" I breathed, gripping his arm.

Down from the Castle came the throbbing of drums and over the drums the heart-penetrating lilting of the pipes.

"Aw! that's the Seaforths," said my cousin casually. "They are out for a walk. You will see them often enough. They are stationed here."

"We will see them now!" I said fiercely, holding his arm.

"Our train to Juniper Green goes out in fifteen minutes," said my cousin, who as I afterwards discovered never considered himself in time for a train unless he had at least a quarter of an hour to spare. A most trying person.

"They are coming down the hill there!" I protested.

"Come along! We shall surely miss our train," said my cousin in a fever of anxiety.

"Listen!" I insisted. "And look!" Sure enough round the turn of Lothian Road they were coming, and I had my first sight of Highlanders marching. Leading them was the pipe band, stepping with a pride that no other living humans can equal. On they came, streamers fluttering, kilts swinging, white spats flashing, drums rolling their matchless rhythmic beat, and behind them the gay and gallant tartans of the Seaforths.

Down they came upon us, the people on the sidewalks halting to gaze at them as they passed. Edinburgh folk never weary of their Highlanders. There are only a few great moments in life. This is one of them.

The Highlanders! Pipes and drums! Kilts and tartans! History was parading past us, Killiecrankie and Culloden, Lucknow and the Plains of Abraham, Khartoum and Magersfontein, and where you will. Where the flag flies their drums beat and their tartans swing.

My throat was hot and choking, the tears were dimming my eyes.

"The train will—"

"Oh, to blazes with your train!" I roared at him, and he subsided gasping.

We Canadians were very young in this very old world. Even
when I was born Canada consisted of two groups of colonies. The
Maritime group along the Atlantic coast and Lower and Upper Canada for the most part a struggling line of settlements hugging the
St. Lawrence and Ottawa rivers with a vast but only partially developed hinterland. Even at the time of Confederation, twenty years ago,
Canada was just struggling into self-consciousness as a Dominion, as
a constituent part of the Empire. We were still very young. Our lives
had been lived in an environment of newness and youth. This world
in which we now found ourselves was an old world, hoary with ancient history and gray traditions. We had to develop a new sense of
age values.

This process was to begin soon.

Within a week of our landing my uncle Charles, the Free Church
minister at Douglas, with a fine sense of what was due to his Canadian
kinsfolk and their friends, met us in Edinburgh and took us into his
care. He was a grand Highland gentleman, stiff with heather and
broom, reeking with national pride, dripping with Scottish history.

"First you must give a day to Edinburgh," he announced with a
grave and solemn air. "A hasty glance it will be, but you can see it
all winter long between your classes."

We glanced at each other. This was no sightseeing jaunt. It was
to be a solemn pilgrimage. The new West End, a thing of yesterday,
a mere hundred years or so, he summarily dismissed with a word.

"A fine street!" he remarked with a casual wave of the hand,
toward Princes Street, than which with its glorious environment there
is no finer street in Europe. "But we have little enough time." It was
still early morning. "Let us go up to the High Street," he added in a
tone of reverent awe.

We toiled up the Mound by the North Bridge and came to the
High Street.

Walking out into the middle of the street, heedless of traffic,
he took his stand and smiting with his cane the rounded cobblestones of the causeway he declaimed: "This, sirs, is the High Street
of Edinburgh, known as 'The Royal Mile,' reaching from the Castle

there to the Holyrood Palace." He stood looking solemnly at us awaiting our reaction.

We looked up at the gray mass of the Castle and down toward
Holyrood. We saw a long tunnel of cobblestones, rough and none
too clean, flanked on either side with gray grimy walls, rising to ten
stories in height, pierced with rows of small windows, the street cut
crosswise with "closes" or "wynds," narrow, filthy passages whose walls
you could almost touch with your outstretched hands, the whole
thing, streets, walls, windows, closes, wynds and cobblestones violently clamant for a cleaning.

"Rather dirty, isn't it?" muttered my medically sanitary brother.

"Dirty! Dirty!" gasped the old Highlander, "Dirty? Ye barbar-
ian! Do you not realize that you stand in the Royal Mile, that these
'dirty' walls are vocal with great and glorious doings. See that hoary
pile of gray granite, sir? Twelve hundred years of Scottish history are
looking down upon you!"

My irate uncle paused for breath, gazing at us in mingled disgust
and pity.

"Well, shall we go up to the Castle? Or will it be too dirty for
you?" he said stiffly, moving off toward the ancient fortress.

"Sure, we want to see the Castle!" exclaimed my brother. "I want
to see where Prince Charlie climbed up the rocks."

"Prince Charlie? God pity you for an ignoramus! Prince Charlie
marched up this street with pipes playing, banners flying, followed
by his Highlanders!"

"Well, it was somebody," insisted Gilbert.

"Somebody? Aye, it was somebody!" said my uncle with sad
resignation. "Did you ever hear of a person called Robert the Bruce?
Come along, you savages, we will just have to enlighten your darkened minds."

As we reached the Castle gate and moved into the esplanade
Dick Tibb, who was something of a historian, remarked:

"This must be Canada—Nova Scotia, isn't it, sir?"

"Canada? Nova Scotia? Man, are ye wandering in your mind?"

"Well, I understand that in front of the Castle there is a bit of
ground given a long time ago to Nova Scotia."

"Wait now! Man, I believe you are right! I had forgotten! You are right! This must be the spot. Ye have some intelligence," said Uncle Charles, respect in his voice. "But we will look that up."

Edinburgh Castle! Romance and History, War and Love, Treachery and Loyalty—England, Scotland, France, yes, and Canada meet you here!

We "did" the Castle, Edwin'sburgh with the ancient relics and sacred spots, the Crown Room, St. Margaret's Chapel, Mons Meg and the rest of it, Uncle Charles spouting history. Then he led us to one of the most glorious views in all the world. To the south the Pentlands, east the Lammermuirs with the Berrick Law and the Bass Rock in the far distance, north the Forth with the Fife shore beyond, and then our guide turned our eyes northwest and stood in silent and rapt reverence.

A soft blue haze lay upon the New Town. Our eyes wandered beyond the city limits to where a softly undulating plain, dotted here and there with farm steadings and villages, church spires and towers of ancient castles spread itself before our eyes, and came to rest at last at the far horizon at a dim waving line of soft blue mountains.

Glancing at our guide's face we forbore speech for some moments. We knew that something beyond the common lay before us. At length my brother said quietly.

"Uncle Charles—those mountains—they can't be—"

"Sir!" said the old gentleman, a quiver of emotion in his voice, "there they are! The Highlands of Scotland."

Something leaped up within me and took me by the throat. The Highlands! Cradle of my race! Land of song and story! The Home of my father and mother! My eyes could see but dimly, but not for the distance. Not one of us spoke.

"Well! Well!" said Uncle Charles at length with a touch of impatience. Still none of us spoke. The old gentleman glanced at our faces ready to blaze forth at us. What he saw checked his speech.

"Say! Let's go," said Gilbert with grave seriousness. "That's enough for today."

The old gentleman drew a long breath.

"Well, God be praised," he muttered, "ye're not quite the barbarians I took ye for."

After dinner we did Holyrood. Our guide hurried us past the

ghastly array of royal portraits to show us where the wretched Rizzio met his doom.

"And served him right," was my uncle's remark.

"It was Mary's fault though," said my brother stoutly.

"Aw, well, maybe. The less said about Mary, poor thing, the better, but yon feckless creature got his deserts whatever."

"But Mary was—"

"Let her be, laddie! Between them all, that popinjay of a husband, the lords, and that heartless virago of England, she had little chance."

We did St. Giles, the Cowgate, but on our way back through the Canongate he halted us in the Parliament Square, near St. Giles Cathedral, just beside a huge equestrian statue to Charles II.

"Uncover, gentlemen, please," said my uncle, removing his hat. We removed our hats looking up at the statue.

"Never heed yon harlotmonger," he said. "Look at your feet."

Let into the pavement was a small brass tablet on which was stamped "J.K. 1572." It was the great moment of the day. The old minister pointed to the ancient St. Giles Cathedral and intoned.

"There's where he preached and shook Scotland's throne and here's where he lies."

"I heard about that," said Tibb. "His only monument in Scotland, isn't it?"

"No monument to John Knox anywhere in Scotland? What a shame!" I exclaimed.

"The hand of God is in it," said my uncle reverently. "No! God made his monument. Scotland is his monument and the Scottish Church."

He cast a glance of contempt at Charles II.

"The auld wife was right when she said," he said with a grim smile, " 'It's fast eneuch here the noo, but gin he had it wi' him whaur he is, it wad rin fast eneuch.' It's made of lead, you see."

Our first day in Edinburgh was a great day. But much of the full effect of the pilgrimage was lost by our almost complete lack of time-values: St. Giles is a very old building, twelfth century; John Knox preached there in 1570; Holyrood Palace, 1670; the Abbey, 1128—five hundred years' difference, but all the same to us. What are five hundred years in this land?

Dr. John McNeil's descriptive phrase of this queen city of North Britain has somehow stuck, "Westendy, Eastwindy Edinburgh." After an eight months' experience of that city I found it to be neither. It has its east winds from the Firth of Forth, bitter and cold enough, but it has also its fair share of good weather. Somehow the memory in me of Edinburgh weather is not so much of east winds. It is rather of shiny mornings with a misty radiance over the Castle Rock, and in the evenings seen from Calton Hill a plain, stretching to far blue mountains dim through a soft opalescent haze, pricked through with spires and turrets tipped with gold from the setting sun. A man can see only with his own eyes or perhaps with his own heart. Frankly, I may as well confess that Edinburgh gripped me by the heart, for Edinburgh means to me, not its physical content only, but its folk as well. Westendy means stiff with the pride of blood and intellect. But this stiffness is only a mimetic armor of defense against the pride of wealth and the size of richer and bigger neighbor towns, Glasgow, for instance. Edinburgh is not a great and wealthy and populous center of commercial and industrial importance, nor does it seek to be. But it is Edinburgh, opulent in romantic history, in the culture of mind and imagination, as well as in that rare and indescribable loveliness that God and man have somehow built into her very stones. Edinburgh folk, if once they give you the keys of their hearts, utterly cast aside anything of the Westendiness which they show to some. And certainly to us five stranger Canadian students they handed the keys.

Henry Drummond

For the first time in my life I laid eyes upon a man who had written a book that the world was reading.

I met Henry Drummond first in the room in Professor Alexander Simpson's home where his famous uncle, Professor James Simpson, made his first experiment in the use of chloroform as an anesthetic.

To meet Henry Drummond marked an epoch in a man's history.

Henry Drummond was richly endowed with almost every quality that makes a man loved. His body tall, slender, well knit, exhibited in its every movement co-ordinated strength and grace. His very walk with its supple and easy spring caught your eye. His face, in which there was a touch of ruggedness, was aglow with a kind of inner fire that shone most through his large blue eyes. Luminous is the word for his eyes, for they truly radiated light, the light of a cultured mind and of a pure heart. I remember a word spoken by that great old Puritan preacher, Dr. Alexander Whyte of Free St. George's, Edinburgh, when I was walking with him down that glorious pass of Killiecrankie. We were talking of Henry Drummond when suddenly he stopped in his tracks and said with a twinkle in his eye:

"The trouble with Hen-a-ry is he doesna ken anything aboot sin."

A purer-hearted being I never knew. In any company while almost invariably the most brilliant member he never absorbed attention, rather he seemed to elicit all that was best in others. A rare gift. He fascinated women, treating them like comrades, but he was essentially a man's man, winning and holding men's confidence and loyal affection.

The world will remember Henry Drummond by two of his books: *Natural Law in the Spiritual World,* the best known book of its day, and his exquisite booklet, *The Greatest Thing in the World.* His friends will remember him for the beauty, the exquisite beauty of his spirit, and the sanity and saintliness of Christian manhood. It was my high privilege to know him well. I spent some time with him in his home with his beautiful mother. At all times, in all circumstances, even under criticism that was stupid, cruel and unfair, he was never anything but the perfect Christian gentleman. No man I ever knew so completely deserved the title "Christian gentleman." Fine, rare, brilliant, gay, fearless, modest, considerate, these adjectives he fully merited. A modernist in theology, he yet held strongly the great and essential doctrines of the Christian faith.

One night before the fire we were discussing various Calvinistic doctrines, among others the tremendous doctrine of the atonement in its substitutionary aspect.

"We can't go back to that, Gordon," he said.

"No," I agreed. "But there is a profound and mighty something there. You ought to go into that."

"Yes," he said, "there is some deep thing there." Then with a little smile he added, "You do it, Gordon. You do it."

Drummond always acknowledged a great debt to Dwight L. Moody.

"The greatest human I ever met," he said once. It was Moody who led Drummond into his great work for students in Britain and in America. He had marvelous influence over students. An incident illustrating this which I witnessed I will carry with me to my death.

There was a large student gathering, the final meeting of the session, in the Assembly Hall in Edinburgh. Sir William Muir was in the chair. Drummond was speaking on a theme that always released his best, "The Sufficiency and the Supremacy of Christ." All kinds and classes of students were present, saints and sinners, workers and slackers, and all eager and fascinated.

With absolutely rigid attention they listened to him. He spoke with unaffected simplicity, his message clothed in thought forms of limpid beauty and penetrated with an intense and throbbing sympathy. He was not speaking down to them, there was nothing of criticism, no attempt to "convict them of sin." He was a big brother telling his younger brothers what a wonderful person Christ was, how sufficient, how utterly dependable. "He won't let you down no matter what you do." He might have been talking of a Big Brother of his own, as indeed he was. He then took his farewell of them, thanked them for their fine backing of him; then, as if it were almost an afterthought, he said:

"There may be a fellow here whom I haven't been able to help this afternoon. I'd like to help him. If any of you would like to speak to me personally I shall be for a few minutes in the room at the rear." He stood there looking down at us with a little friendly smile on his face, then waved his hand, "Good-bye, you chaps! The best of luck," and was gone. In many a man's eyes the tears were standing.

As Sir William Muir was saying a few closing words I noticed someone slip out through the rear door. A final hymn was being sung when the young man entered from the rear, spoke a word to the chairman and remained standing.

"This young man has something to say to us," said the chairman.

"Most of you fellows know me. My name is Fraser," said the young man. "All my course I have been what's called a 'waster.' I am leaving college tomorrow. I have had a talk with Mr. Drummond.

I have determined from now to follow Christ. I thought it wouldn't be fair to leave without telling you. Pray for me, you fellows that know how."

He turned to go. Sir William put his hand on his arm, held him and said, "Let us pray."

Like a wheatfield before a wind all heads went down, while the chairman said a few words of the simplest kind of prayer for us all, "and especially for this young man who in this hour has committed his life to Thee."

That was one of the great moments in my life. It is vivid with me as I write.

I saw Henry Drummond last in the Rocky Mountains in company with Lord Aberdeen, when I was a missionary there. We rode and swam and walked and talked, talked, talked—at least he talked. I made him talk. I was facing great problems, some of which he helped to straighten out. He had an amazing power to draw the heart out of you. What a hero! He died like one. What a saint! He lived like one.

Dr. Alexander Whyte

Mystic, Puritan, scholar, preacher, writer of books, pawky Scot, all these he was and other things as well.

Our first Sunday in Edinburgh we went to church at Free St. George's. At the door some minutes before eleven we were marshaled into a waiting line, till pewholders were seated. The service is of extreme simplicity. The choir, who sit with the congregation in seats reserved for them, serve only in the leading of the praise service. It is a reverent and expectant congregation. Their expectation is fulfilled. The preacher, short in stature, well set, moves with deliberate, firm step into the pulpit after the beadle has reverently set "The Books" upon the pulpit and then opened the pulpit door. The preacher's face is preternaturally solemn, with deep-set blue eyes that one feels see nothing of his physical environment, but are fixed upon things unseen. His voice is clear, resonant, slightly nasal after the Highland type, and without effort reaches the back seat in the gallery.

This is great preaching, doctrinal without being argumentative. He does not argue, he expounds the truth, he *declares* the will of God, with perfect clarity and authority. No matter what his subject, he will find a place for the *damnation* of sin, but also for *appeal* to the sinner. Great preaching for people with brains and consciences. Those with neither may find another kirk. Vividly dramatic at times, he makes you see things that are invisible. In a truly terrific passage he was picturing "the hunting hounds of sin" on the trail of the sinner.

"Hearken!" he cried, lifting his eyes from his manuscript and gazing into the corner behind me, "Do you not hear? See! You long, lank, lean-bellied hound making up on ye." For the life of me I could not forbear a quick glance over my shoulder. Great preaching! With a swift change of tone and manner he pictured the sinner's escape into the "warm, strong, loving arms of the Heavenly Father."

I found myself one glorious day going for a walk with Dr. Whyte down Tummelside in the Highlands. I was a guest at Bonskeid, the splendid castle of the Barbours, that nobly generous family, famous throughout Scotland for their gracious hospitality to people and causes that stand in need of friendly aid. Dr. Whyte's wife was a daughter of the Bonskeid family, of whom more will be said.

He would walk miles without tiring; at times, silent, almost dour, wrapped in his own thoughts, then suddenly "minding his manners" he would begin to talk. And wonderful talk it would be, a veritable pouring out of his rich treasures of brain and heart and experience. This day after long silence and strenuous walking he suddenly halted and stood pointing out the magnificent view down the Glen Tummel.

"Something like the Delectable Mountains," he said, recalling his favorite Bunyan. Then swiftly he turned on me and like a prophet gave his message. "You are to be a minister, see that you feed your people. Never mind your theological, your scientific, your higher critical problems. Keep them for your study."

"But will they let you?" I asked. "Are not the people demanding discussion of these problems these days?"

"I remember what John Owen said to his people." He was an expert in the great Puritan divines. " 'Why should I take time to expatiate upon that wind called Euroclydon, when your hearts are full of malice, envy and all evil things?' "

"But, Dr. Whyte," I urged, much disturbed at that time in my life with higher criticism, "suppose a man comes to me after my sermon and insistently demands, 'But what about that wind called Euroclydon?' What shall I say to him?"

He stood a moment or two gazing at me, then putting out his hand he grasped mine, shook it warmly and said with that sunny smile for which he was famous:

"I would say, I would say, 'How are they all at home?'"

Was ever a more perfect answer?

Grave though he was in manner, and Puritan though he was in theology and in practice, yet he dearly loved a laugh, even at his own expense.

Once among a meeting of students a clever mimic, A. B. Macaulay, later Professor Macaulay, was doing a sermon in Dr. Whyte's best style. Both matter and man were being reproduced with perfect art amid the delighted cheers of the audience. By some ill fate that night Dr. Whyte himself unexpectedly opened the door and, unseen by the young preacher, stood listening in apparent enjoyment forbidding all interruption. When the sermon was over he walked calmly into the room, and shaking hands cordially with the horrified young student, said:

"Mr. Macaulay, y're indeed an artist. More than that, y're an excellent preacher. I doubt I couldna do as well myself."

Dr. Whyte was the students' favorite in Edinburgh. Both for his preaching and for his courses of lectures through the week they would throng his church.

Marcus Dods

Before I met him as a professor I knew Marcus Dods as a great scholar from his book on Genesis, a book that helped many a student put reality into that great and inspiring revelation of God and His world. But now I came to know him as a great teacher and preacher, and also as a true friend.

The story of Marcus Dods' beginnings as a preacher is a great encouragement to young and timid candidates for calls. For some years after graduation—seven, I think—young Dods went the rounds of the vacant pulpits, enduring with increasing anxiety the humiliating experience of vainly preaching for a call. His friends, who knew his worth did all they could with letters of commendation, personal introductions and all the rest. No congregation would have him. One of his greatest backers was Dr. Whyte, but even Dr. Whyte's influence was of no avail.

"Whatever is the matter with you?" asked Dr. Whyte one day.

"They tell me you just stand like a post and read your sermon, without a move in you. Can you not move your hand a bit?"

Dods sadly acknowledged his inability.

"Now then, Dods, you are going down to preach in Glasgow. A fine congregation. Will you promise me that for once you will put out your hand? Just lift it up and put it out. Promise me, or I will have nothing more to do with you."

After great persuasion Dods made the promise.

On his return he came to his friend again.

"Well, how did you get on?"

"Oh, just the same," replied Dods, sorely despondent.

"Man! Did you put out your hand as you promised me?"

"I did," said Dods.

"Well! What then?"

"I couldn't get it back," replied Dods gloomily.

The day came, however, when Dods got his call and became one of Scotland's greatest preachers, and later one of Edinburgh's most scholarly and best loved professors.

Rabbi Davidson

Professor A. B. Davidson was the greatest Hebraist of his day in the English-speaking world. He was the father of many heretics in Old Testament criticism, the two most distinguished of which were Robertson Smith, the great scholar and Hebraist, who was expelled for "heresy" from his professor's chair and from his church, and George Adam Smith, also a great Old Testament scholar, the man who "split Isaiah in two" but who did more than any other man of his time to make the Old Testament a living word of God. No classroom was so filled with eager students as Davidson's. His lectures, delivered to successive generations of students, often drew back many of his old students to hear again his scholarly exposition.

Whenever, for instance, it became known that Davidson was to deliver "Saul" the room was crowded with students old and new. It is quite impossible to reproduce the scene. The eager crowd of youngsters complacent and superior, especially toward the "old boys" who had come in, and "old boys" staid, shy, conscious of their whiskers and bald heads among those gay lads with mops of hair on their heads but none on their faces.

Before they are aware the professor has slipped in and with a flush on his face meekly taken his place. His opening prayer is simple as a child's, phrased in beautiful English—of which he is a master—and instinct with the spirit of one who lives in touch with God.

His iron-gray hair is brushed off his forehead, his voice is younger than his long, keen, dark face. His eyes are little pools of fire and they startle you when you catch a flash, which is not often. In a voice high, thin, and delightfully Aberdonian—that is, if you like the Aberdonian, which I do when he uses it—he begins his lecture.

No need to ask for order. The attention is breathless, almost reverential, which from Edinburgh theologues may be regarded as a phenomenon.

He is not on "Saul" today, but on the first chapter of Genesis, the Mosaic authorship of which he dismisses with a single phrase, not scornful. The old "Rabbi" is often incisive in his criticism, but never scornful.

"The author of this writing is no scientist. It is well to remember that inspiration offers no short cut in scientific research . . . The author is a poet with a poet's gift of vision and vivid expression . . . He has a vision of God, the Author of Life and of all things, engaged in His work of making a universe . . . The author though a poet is a realist. He says exactly what he means. He pictures God working as a man might work at his day's labor. When he says 'day' he means 'day' not an aeon, when he says 'watter' [the Aberdonian accent here comes out beautifully on the word] he means 'watter' not 'mud.' He is writing simply and truthfully, gentlemen, of the things which as a poet he sees."

Thus in five minutes my difficulties as to Mosaic authorship are blown away. What a simple and blessed relief to troubled souls who have been torn between loyalty to an impossible theory of plenary inspiration and loyalty to simple and obvious truth. My last Old Testament professor in Toronto had spent hours laboring the "long day" theory, a matter of millions of years.

With what vast relief I remembered how impatiently my mind had rejected the theory, and with what grateful satisfaction I accepted the teaching that when the writer said "day" he meant "day" and when he said "watter" he meant "watter" not "mud."

After half an hour of introductory lecture the professor asks Mr. Macpherson to read. Macpherson, his face red as his hair, which is saying something, is much flustered, evidently stricken with a consciousness of the inadequacy of his Hebraic furnishing. However, he gallantly makes the plunge and is soon obviously floundering in deep water. On both sides his friends have come to his aid with more or less helpful suggestions. At length the high voice of the professor breaks in upon his desperate situation.

"Sit down, Mr. Macpherson," he says. "Mr. Macpherson," he adds kindly, "makes no pretension to a profound knowledge of the Hebrew language, but I make the painful discovery that those who are striving to assist him have even less knowledge of the subject than he has himself."

In Professor Davidson's class it was understood that after lecture any student wishing to ask a question might seek the professor in his private room. A certain student who enjoyed many doubts made a habit of discoursing his doubts to great length with the professor. On one occasion he went so far as to ask for an interview with him some evening at his home. The request was granted. Arrived at the professor's house, the young man proceeded to elaborate his doubts, which ranged widely over such matters as the origin, inspiration, authenticity of Scripture, branching off into various questions of philosophy, science and kindred subjects.

The professor listened long in stolid patience, his only answer being "yes . . . oh, yes—yes . . . yes . . . oh, yes—yes," until the student had exhausted the full tale of his doubts. At length after a period of complete silence, he remarked: "Well, sir, I think I must be getting home." Still the professor replied "yes . . . ah, yes—yes" and in silence accompanied him to the garden gate.

"Well," said the student, gazing up at the starlit sky, "it is a fine night, professor."

The professor's face was suddenly illumined with his rare smile.

"Man, ye have no doubt of that, have ye?" he ejaculated with an air of relief.

When on rare occasions the old Rabbi preached in Edinburgh it was always in one of the smaller suburban churches which would be crowded to the doors. His delivery was seriously hampered by his shyness. I have a clear vision of him standing with a wee black notebook in his hand, to which he constantly referred, darting swift and shy glances now and then at his congregation. His discourse was like a clear-flowing stream, exquisitely beautiful, illumined with flashes of rare spiritual insight. To listen to him was an experience of unbroken delight. In the presence of this shy, modest preacher I forgot that I was listening to one of the great scholars of the age.

There is no finer testimony to the deep reverence and affection of Davidson's students than the fact that, though Robertson Smith was expelled for the heresy learned from this shy professor and George Adam Smith, now principal emeritus of Aberdeen University, was remorselessly pursued by the heresy headhunters, their teacher, who had set them in the path of their heresy, was left quite undisturbed in his chair and in his church.

CHAPTER X

Conquest by Song and Story

LIKE TOPSY, the Toronto University Student Quintet never was "borned," it "growed." We were for three years first members of the University Glee Club, one of the most famous singing organizations of its time in Canada. Then we were for three years members of the Knox College Glee Club, which we considered was easily superior to that of the university. Furthermore, the Quintet could furnish a program of music quite remarkable in variety and extent in the way of solos, duets, trios, quartets and quintets. And best of all we had a comique, in the person of Bob Haddow, such as I have never seen surpassed on any stage, and I do not except even George Robey himself. Our repertoire was wide and varied. In addition to the ordinary German, French, English and Scottish music we specialized in college songs, Negro plantation airs and spirituals, and French Canadian river songs, chanteys, choruses. We had worked persistently, patiently at improving ourselves. Every Saturday morning during most of our college course we gave some two or three hours to hard practice.

In Edinburgh University there was nothing, absolutely nothing in the way of male-voice singing. The only thing I ever heard sung by the students was "Old Hundred" without words to the syllable "ah-h-h-." Anything more deadly doleful could hardly be conceived. I don't believe there was a Student Songbook in all Scotland, not because they were not musical, but just because it never happened.

With one single exception, the Quintet had no social introductions in Edinburgh. Our first bass, Mac Hamilton, was the exception. This exception proved fruitful. It chanced that the young lady in question,

91

an active worker in a Cowgate mission carried on by Free St. George's Church was in desperate need of help in a projected entertainment for the denizens of the Cowgate and made known her plight to our first bass. He offered first aid in the shape of the Quintet. The proffered aid appeared to be exactly the quality that appealed to the Cowgate dwellers. The concert proved a "howling" success and by request was repeated with louder howlings and even greater success. The heather was on fire so far as the Cowgate was concerned. But what of the West End? The West End was definitely not the Cowgate. The Cowgate was low in taste, irreligious in character, and wide open to all comers. The West End was none of these, distinctly none of these.

The hour of testing arrived. The Quintet was invited to a students' party at the home of the Rev. Dr. Alexander Whyte. These parties were supposed to exert an uplifting influence upon the students, more especially theological students from the Highlands and from the regions about Glasgow. The Quintet was invited to perform.

At once rose the question, "To perform what?"

The Quintet were a unit in support of a program of German, English and Scottish music with a touch of appropriate Canadian airs, such as "The Canadian Boat Song." The young ladies who had been present at the Cowgate presentations were united in demanding something spicier in flavor. They were all for "The Bull Dog on the Bank," "Polly Wolly," and "Say, Darkies, Have You Seen de Massa?" Above all they demanded a contribution by our jester.

"Who'll be there?" asked Bob Haddow. "The elders and officials of St. George's, I suppose."

"Well—yes—they will be there, but others as well."

"Yes! All the West End swells stiff with culture and propriety? Not me! We will sing anything decent, but that I should do slapstick stuff and make a fool of myself! Not much." Haddow was adamant. He was a theologue himself, an honors man in metaphysics, within one of being a medalist. Was he going to make an idiot of himself? Not if he knew it.

"You might do *The Country School,* Bob. That is more or less educational," suggested Dick Tibb, the second tenor, with a highly developed sense of propriety but an infernal instinct for getting people into holes.

Haddow withered him with a stare.

The program opened with the rollicking French-Canadian chorus

"Alouette," which was approved with well-bred and restrained applause. Then after several German and English numbers Mrs. Whyte in her charming manner approached Haddow and with one of her fascinating smiles remarked:

"There seems to be a general wish, Mr. Haddow, that you should give something in the way of a reading lesson."

"Reading lesson?" inquired Haddow, blank surprise on his face. "I'm afraid I am not qualified to give a reading lesson."

"Mrs. Whyte probably means *The Country School*," suggested Tibb. At that moment Haddow could have cheerfully slain him. Stimulated requests arose on all sides, and after much protesting Haddow proceeded to order up his class of six pupils on the occasion of the Annual Country School Examination, who forthwith began to read in succession verses from Gray's "Elegy." I kept my eyes anxiously upon the solemn and somewhat severe face of the minister of Free St. George's who apparently was waiting for a demonstration of methods of elocution as taught in Canada. His face was a study. As each pupil made his or her attempt the grave face registered first surprise then perplexity. Soon a little smile began to twitch at the corners of his stern mouth, and finally before the third pupil, a giggling miss, had broken down in a perfect gale of giggles, the solemn face broke. He was completely swept off his balance and before the reading was finished was holding his sides and helplessly wiping away tears from his eyes. Thereupon the Quintet cut loose with student choruses, negro plantation songs and the like, while our *comique* went the length of "Solomon Levi" in character.

That evening's experience taught me some things about human nature. For instance, no amount of intellectual culture can resist the attack of pure humor. Nowhere in Britain is there a larger percentage of intellectual culture in the human being than in the city of Edinburgh, and nowhere is its defensive armor so effective against the invasions of financial power, mere caste pride or political influence. But these defenses are completely disintegrated against the impact of pure, clean humor. Humor makes a direct entry to the heart. There is one essential condition, and that condition our *comique* possessed. His type of humor was absolutely free from vulgarity. Haddow was not a "funny man," nor was he that most tiresome of all tiresome people, what the Scottish phrase so perfectly describes as a "jokey man." He was a gentleman and with a fine mind he carried a kindly heart. His humor never offended and never wounded, and never once did I see him fail. No superiority complex could resist the impact of his appeal.

At Free St. George's manse the Quintet had registered another triumph and its fame ran through the city as a fire through a western prairie. Engagements began to mount for college, church, mission functions as well as for private social evenings. Frequently we would find ourselves with three and four evening engagements in a week, and often with two for the same evening. For the four theologues who were simply "attending lectures" without the prospect of exams, the dissipation of time and energy awakened, I fear, rather slight concern. For my brother, however, who was working for his M.R.C.S., L.R.C.P. it involved a terrific grind. But he had great physical endurance and was a keen worker and he won out. Thenceforth, whenever we heard Edinburgh folk described as being stiff and exclusive we craved leave to dissent.

One amusing, but at the time for me a devastating, experience still comes to me in "dreams of the night upon my bed." In an evil hour as we were sitting about the table after dinner in our lodgings Haddow happened to quote a saying of a Canadian friend of his from the country about "two little orphans, a little boy and a little girl whose father and mother was both dead, and who had no parents livin'."

"What?" I said, "no mother?"

"No! No mother!" replied Haddow gravely. "No father either."

"Father dead, eh?"

"Yes, both dead, father and mother," said Haddow earnestly. "No parents at all, only the brother and the sister."

"Oh, of course, the little girl had a brother," I suggested cheerfully.

"Yes, but she had no mother," Haddow explained carefully, "nor father, in fact she had no parents at all, both parents were dead—they were quite orphans. Of course, she had her brother, but he had no father or mother, he was an orphan too, his parents were both dead."

For quite half an hour Haddow gravely emphasized, iterated and reiterated, explained, described, deplored, the lamentable condition of these orphans with grave and deeply interested face, the remaining members of the Quintet being utterly helpless with laughter. The moving little tale seized my imagination and set up quite a ferment therein. One day the Quintet had invited some twenty of their friends to a fish dinner at Musselburgh, a not unusual function in that circle. As we were chatting at table after dinner I asked my friend Miss Charlotte Ada Rainy, a jolly and brilliantly clever girl, and a good sport, who was sitting next me:

"Did you ever hear the story of *The Two Orphans?*"

"No! Do tell me!"

"Well," I said, "it is not much of a tale and it really is a little sad but—"

"Oh, do tell me!" pleaded my friend.

I began the yarn intending a simple recital of the tragedy such as I had heard from my friend Haddow. But almost immediately the impulse seized me to enlarge and expand by means of mere iteration, which I proceeded to do. My immediate neighbors, then gradually others, finally the whole table became fascinated. Back and forth, over and over again in a voice of deadly and impressive earnestness and of deep emotion, restrained with intense effort, I wove the idiotic yarn, introducing such additional and heart-rending facts as that they lived in a little house—they didn't need a big house since they had only themselves, their father and mother being both dead, etc., etc. The little house was down by the river—just beside the river—on the bank of the river.

"Which bank?" asked Miss Rainy solicitously through her tears.

"Which bank? Oh, yes, the bank the house was on—just one bank, of course, etc., etc. Till one day one orphan, the little girl, fell into the river."

"Oh!" gasped Miss Rainy, "into the river."

"Yes, right into the river and—"

"Which river?"

"The river on the bank of which the little house stood, etc., etc.," till the whole table, extraordinary as it may seem, Quintet included, rocked with laughter.

"And what then?" inquired Miss Rainy, wiping her eyes.

"Oh, nothing—you see there was nothing left but the little house—and the river—and the river flowed on—and on—and on—" At each "on" there was a fresh shout of laughter.

"On what?" asked Miss Rainy, faint with laughing.

"Oh—on nothing—just on and on—" again the laughter seized them—"and on—"

"Oh, for heaven's sake, stop!" cried my friend, falling back exhausted in her chair.

Humor is one of the most inexplicable of all human emotions. So many mysterious elements lie behind it. The psychology of the company, their physical, mental and emotional environment, and something deeper than all these lie about the springs of laughter.

I often begged Haddow to adopt and elaborate the silly tale and make it one of his numbers.

"It wouldn't come for me," he declared. "It would be an utter failure and I would look like a fool."

A few evenings later in the home of Dr. Marcus Dods, with Henry Drummond as the only guest besides myself, we were sitting in friendly chat after dinner when some imp within me moved me to ask Drummond, who was sitting next me on a sofa, "Have you ever heard the story of *The Two Orphans?*" intending to get his psychological explanation of the phenomenon I had witnessed at the fish dinner.

"No," said Drummond, and then cried out, "Gordon has a story! Come on, Gordon, let's have it."

In vain I protested that there was no story, just a bit of fool nonsense I had had from my friend Haddow. But Drummond would have it, and greatly fearing, I went at it.

The effect was amazing. In five minutes the whole company were utterly paralyzed. Dods was half lying, quite helpless, on the sofa, his wife in her chair, equally helpless, with her handkerchief pressed to her eyes. Drummond walked about the room, rocking back and forth, and at each new development of the fool yarn uttering faint moans of agonized distress and begging, "Oh, Gordon! stop! stop! For heaven's sake, stop!" till finally he was compelled to leave the room.

When the idiotic tale was finished I went out and found him leaning on his stomach over the banister rail groaning.

"Gordon, you nearly killed me! I've got a most frightful pain!" he said. "I shall find some way of repaying you, if I live."

And he did. The following day was Sunday. On his way home from church he called at the home of Dr. Alexander Simpson to visit Mrs. Simpson, a chronic invalid with valetudinarian tendencies. To her he recounted his experience with *The Two Orphans,* urging her to get me to do the tale for her someday.

The very next day a most untoward fate brought me to an afternoon gathering of ladies in the Simpsons' drawing room in the interest of foreign missions, I think. On more than one occasion I had seen a social gathering of students in Mrs. Simpson's drawing room suddenly and without warning transformed into a prayer meeting at which any theological student might be called upon to lead in prayer. Even to theologues this might sometimes prove a rather trying experience, all the more so that in the full tide of his devotion the student might be arrested by Mrs. Simpson's clear voice: "And, Mr. Smith, would you please remember our Malabar Mission, where dear Mr. Brown is having a difficult time with the girls' school." Whereupon Mr. Smith, who might know nothing whatever of the peculiar and trying circumstances of Mr. Brown and his girls' school, would have to pull himself together and adjust his devotions to the case in point.

With no foreknowledge of Drummond's machinations I opened the door of the Simpsons' drawing room and found it packed with ladies beyond the bloom of their first youth. Immediately upon my entry Mrs. Simpson's high clear voice arrested me.

"Oh, *dear* Mr. Gordon! So *glad* to see you! And you must do *The Two Orphans.*" I almost collapsed on the spot. Then I moved swiftly to the sofa upon which my hostess was lying, and leaning over to greet her, muttered almost savagely.

"Not *The Orphans,* Mrs. Simpson. It would never do here."

"Oh, Mr. Gordon," again her voice rang clear through the room, "you must do *The Two Orphans.* Mr. Drummond told me yesterday all about it. And he said I must get you to do *The Two Orphans.*"

With desperate but vain insistence I declared the thing impossible. It was an utterly fool thing, with nothing in it. And in a meeting like this it would not possibly do. But in her penetrating voice she persisted in her demand.

I offered to sing for her, to make a speech, to do anything for her, but not—certainly not—*The Orphans.* But *The Orphans* she would have and nothing else. Mr. Drummond had made her promise that she would have me do it. Some of my friends gathered round and began to add their persuasions, till at last in utter desperation I yielded. Thereupon I stood up and in the cold gray light of an Edinburgh winter afternoon, and to that Edinburgh gathering of middle-aged spinsters, married and unmarried, in a perfect fury and funk I began that fool story.

Anything like humor was miles distant from my soul. With solemn face I began to unwind the tale. With gravely expectant faces, growing more puzzled every instant, the company listened. As I proceeded their faces grew more and more perplexed. My friends in the company seemed to become anxiously concerned for me. I fancy many of them must have been expecting an interesting and cheerfully inspiring missionary story. Those who might have been inclined to smile at my idiotic performance politely repressed the inclination. My forehead was beaded with perspiration. Down my back and legs I was conscious of cheerful little rivulets running. Determined not to be beaten, I persisted, winding and unwinding my tale—back and forth—again and over again. Still not a smile—only blank and utter bewilderment, mingled in the case of my friends with pity. Finally I surrendered; walking straight across the room to a friend on whose face I had caught a grin, I greeted her wrathfully with:

"Why in blazes didn't you laugh?"

"Oh, did you mean us to laugh? Do you know, I once thought so. But I wasn't sure, so I didn't."

There was valuable material in the experience for a study in the psychology of humor. But I was not in the mood, so I hurriedly made my adieux. A few days later I met Drummond. He was highly amused at my account of what had happened, but he was also rather more sorry than amused.

"You must do it again," he said firmly.

"Not if I am sober and in my right senses," I declared.

He took the thing quite seriously.

"Gordon, you will promise me that before you leave Edinburgh you will do that thing again. It is priceless." He would not let me go till I had promised to reconsider.

I did, and had a glorious revenge. It was in the home of my friend Herbert Gray, now the Rev. Dr. Herbert Gray of London. I left my audience in various stages of hysteria. But the conditions were suitable. It was two in the morning, we were all in a jolly mood and a number of my fish-dinner friends were present. Humor is a funny thing—sometimes. *The Two Orphans,* however, was quite reinstated in the opinion of my Edinburgh friends.

Nearly thirty-five years later I appeared in Edinburgh as a delegate to the various General Assemblies from the New United Church in

Canada. The moderator of the Free Church Assembly introduced me in some such words as these:

"More than thirty years ago when I was a student in Edinburgh a singing band of Canadian students appeared among us and turned our city upside down. Dr. Gordon was the first tenor in that band. I have a vivid recollection of them. I should love to hear them again. But as the Quintet are not here I should be delighted if Dr. Gordon would just tell us the story of *The Two Orphans*." Shouts of "Hear! Hear!" came from various members of that reverend body. Remembering Mrs. Simpson's drawing room on that gray winter afternoon, I need hardly say that I confined myself strictly to my greetings.

After the close of our college year we made brief visits to friends in different parts of Scotland. First to my father's home in the Highlands at Blair Atholl, where the lovely glens of the Tilt and the Garry and the Tummel effect a junction. Never have I suffered so acutely from poverty of speech as on that occasion. The great Bens, their slopes shaggy with purple heather, splashed with yellow gorse and here and there clothed with dark masses of pine while their peaks pierced the blue haze of the heavens above, left me tingling with emotion but with no words to express it. The homes we visited, great and humble, were alike rich in simple and gracious hospitality that satisfied but never embarrassed us.

My grandfather's wee stone cottage stood at the very edge of a tinkling burn whose song was the last thing in our ears as we sank into sleep and the first to welcome our waking moments. From this little cottage had gone forth seven sons and six daughters. Of the sons, Gilbert, the eldest, was the celebrated piper of the Duke of Atholl, two became ministers of the gospel, three won distinction in the medical profession, the seventh died a young man. The pride of Scotland in the native worth of its sons and daughters is amply justified in the service they have rendered to humanity the wide world round.

A short stay at Bonskeid in the Tummel valley gave us a glimpse of a type of a cultured and Christian manner of living that has never faded from my mind. Robert Barbour, who died while still in the full tide of his life service, had been a leading spirit in a group of seven Edinburgh students who did rare service in the university during the visit of Dwight L. Moody to Scotland. Bonskeid was indeed a veritable

House Beautiful, an Interpreter's Home offering rest and refreshment to many a pilgrim in need of both. Those days at Bonskeid form one of the bright spots in my life that time cannot fade.

Our visit to Douglas, the home of Uncle Charles within the bounds of whose parish stands Castle Dangerous, the ancient home of the Douglases reeking with the wild and bloody doings of that noble family. We saw the bloody well, once choked to the top with the bodies of Douglas retainers slain by their enemies, and the church of St. Bride's, memorable for a thoroughgoing slaughter of foes of The Douglas, all in the olden days.

That ancient kirk was worth a visit; there stood the very foundation stones of a thousand-year-old church. As I gazed at that ancient relic I suddenly realized how marvelously had developed in me my sense of time-values since my first day in Edinburgh some nine months ago. I could now appreciate to the full the difference in time between, say, the Covenanter's stone in the Greyfriar's Churchyard in Edinburgh and this hoary relic of St. Bride's.

But to do justice to Scotland's historic memorials, to the splendid glory of its Highlands, its bens and glens, to its murmuring streams and its headlong mountain torrents, its sunny Lowlands, its shining lochs and swift rushing rivers, is beyond the art of man.

Through the wide world the Scot has wandered far, but be he Highland or Lowland he aye carries in him a heart that beats quick at the skirl of the pipes, that grows tender at a song of the gowans or the heather, that thrills at the story of high deeds of Scotsmen, be it at Bannockburn or at Culloden, and that aches with a dull pain at the memory of the wee but and ben that sheltered his tousy head when he was a bairn.

Aye, and in his sons and daughters—yes, to the third and fourth generation—that same heart beats quick with pride, grows tender and aches with the same dull pain, as they wander here and there in that magic lovely land of their forefathers.

CHAPTER XI

From Leith to London

BICYCLING ON THE CONTINENT—RHONE JOURNEY—
GERMAN MILITARISM — AN UNCONQUERED PEOPLE
— SWISS MEMORIES — PARIS—ENGLAND — COASTING
AND KINDNESS

FEELING the need of recreation and relaxation after Edinburgh and
its arduous scholastic and other activities, we decided upon a Continental tour. For our mode of transportation we selected bicycles,
partly under stress of financial stringency and also for the adventure
of it. No one, so far as we could learn, had ever done the Alps on
a wheel. So on a cloudy April morning we pedaled down to Leith
and embarked on a little steamer for Antwerp. We knew no language
but our own, for guide we had only Baedeker and some rather vague
bicycle road maps. But we were keen for experiences of lands unknown. We had no fear of our fellow men, so why not?

Our wheels were the first safety bicycles ever made, and with
hard tires. How hard they could be we never guessed till we struck
some of Napoleon's pavé roads; they were eminently suitable for
cannon and cavalry, but after our first day we longed with a new ardor
for Waterloo.

Antwerp! Then along the shaded canal roads of Holland by
Ville Vordt to Brussels, Waterloo where we blew out our chests a
bit, by Aix to Mainz, then up the Rhine by steamer, singing German songs on deck in the evening, to Cologne, Bonn—sleeping as
often as possible in the villages, seeing the people at their work. One
day as we were wheeling from Cologne to Bonn along a beautifully graded road lined with trees in their fresh spring loveliness we
paused for a bit of a rest and to enjoy the evening air and the exquisite
beauty of the rolling countryside. As we lay on the grass we heard
from a neighboring field a birdlike whistle and looking over the
hedge we saw a man hoeing potatoes and whistling an exquisite air.

"I'm going to see a man who can whistle like that," I said, and over the hedge we went. He was a young man with long dark face and dark hair, very unlike the ordinary German. None of us could remember the word for whistle. We tried "singen." Yes, he understood "singen" and away he went, singing a lovely German song. He wrote the words for us while I, by means of Donald Alec McRae's sol-fa method took down the music from his lips. On our return to London a musical friend of Mac Hamilton's found the song in an old book and copied it for us. We have it still and no lovelier song is there in our repertoire. Here it is:

> Still lies the lake! The birds are sleeping,
> Awhispering low their rest reveals.
> The gloaming falls and night draws nearer,
> A lovely dream o'er nature steals.
>
> Still lies the lake! The branches rustle,
> The breath of heaven is passing there,
> The flowers by the lake's broad margin,
> Bend low and breathe their evening prayer.
>
> Still lies the lake! The stars in heaven,
> With holy calm and peace are blest.
> O troubled heart, give o'er thy fretting,
> Thou too, thou too, shalt find a rest.

At Bonn, an old university town, we continued on a Rhine steamer and for another whole day drank in the glory of vine-clad hills and the patches of dark forest, and thrilled to the splendor of ancient castle and rockbound fortress. Then off again on our way down through the Black Forest, taking in ancient Heidelberg and many another romantic town, each with its own story of the great days of old.

At Strassburg with its mighty fortifications and big garrison, holding this outpost of the German Empire in an alien and hostile land, we paused a day. In this country with all its loveliness, its perfect orderliness, its rich vineyards and farm lands, we become conscious of a darker reality behind this pleasant front. We get it from the fortifications, from the marching troops we meet everywhere. We get it from the absence of men from the fields where women and girls are at work, hoeing, plowing with teams of oxen, or a cow and a horse, or, as we saw more than once to our horror, of an old woman and a cow hitched together to a plow.

It is gradually driven into our consciousness that this is a war-cursed country, a conquered land under military rule and military discipline. All this daily toil of Germany is not for the feeding, cloth-ing, housing of its people, but for the feeding, making, drilling, or-ganizing of a vast military power with which she means one day to dominate the world. To us this whole military business which they seem to take with such desperate seriousness appears silly. Soldiers with us are chiefly useful to give a splash of color to our Queen's Birthday or Dominion Day parades. In this country they constitute a terrible and solemn institution.

After we had become aware of this we took every opportunity to observe soldiers at their drill. The desperate earnestness of the officers seemed to make them brutal in their treatment of the men under their command. Once on a village green we stood watching an officer trying to perfect a company of recruits in a certain evolution. Over and over again the officer, cursing them furiously, put them through the maneuver. One soldier, slower than the rest, apparently aroused his wrath. He called him from the ranks, poured a stream of abuse over him, then tried him again. Once more the soldier failed. With a fierce imprecation the officer drew his sword and with the flat of it struck him heavily over the shoulder. The soldier took the blow like a block of wood. That was the first time we had an exhibition of the brutality of the German officer toward a soldier wholly at his mercy, but not the last. Often we were shocked and in-furiated at the outrageous and absurd insolence of the German of-ficers, not only toward their men on parade but toward the ordinary citizens, on the street, in beer gardens. The people of Strassburg carried themselves with a sullen indifference in the presence of these officers; indeed, so far as it was possible, ignored them, yet there was no doubt as to their state of mind. They were a conquered people, but un-subdued and waiting. Always we thanked God we were from a land where this silly militarism was unknown. Alas, we were to learn later by a terrible experience that it was not simply silly.

In Strassburg we visited the old Cathedral, with its wonderful clock which registers not only the passing hours but the movements of various heavenly bodies. At the noon hour every day the clock presents a quaint and marvelous drama. A figure of the Christ takes His stand and before Him the twelve apostles parade in succession, each bowing reverently as he passes. As Peter approaches a cock appears on a pinnacle at the right, flaps its wings and crows. Judas appears, and high up at a little door the devil is seen watching him eagerly. When the traitor reaches the Christ he turns his back upon his Master, who makes no response, and passes on to be greeted by the devil at the exit. A gruesome spectacle. A little human touch awakens our amusement during the parade. As the cock appears and crows a child's voice rises shrill from the company:

"Maman! Maman! Voici le tot! Voici le tot!"

"Never heard French baby talk before!" said Haddow, greatly delighted.

We entered Switzerland at Basel and began to climb and continued to climb for some days. It seemed as if we did nothing but climb for, though no doubt after each mountain range surmounted we had a corresponding descent to the intervening valley, the impression of each flying descent was so transitory that it was speedily erased by the long and painful grind of the following climb. Our trip through Switzerland remains in our memories as one long succession of laborious climbs from one mountain to another, with momentary, but glorious flights between. At times, however, there are little touches of human interest that make us kin to the delightfully friendly people of these valleys.

For instance, as we prepared for one of our downward flights a voice startled us from the door of a wayside pension:

"Hello America!"

We looked and saw a handsome, dark-faced, young fellow with a red feather in his Alpine hat.

"Hello!" we said, "but not America, Canada!"

"Ah, Canada? So-o—? This is—is—new to me."

"How long were you in America?" we asked.

"Three years."

"How did you like America?"

"Fine! Splendid."

"Why did you come back?"

"Ah-h-h!" he said and gazed upon the panorama before him. Then with a sweep of his hand toward the magnificent ranges about us, he said, "There were no mountains in America."

Money he had made in plenty in America, but the mountains drew him home. And with our eyes upon this glorious sweep of mountain and valley we understood. He took us into his pension, regaled us with bread, wine, Swiss butter and cheese and reluctantly bade us farewell.

"Good-bye," he said, "give my love to America. Someday I may go back. But"—again his eyes swept the scene before him—"I could not stay."

We understood then as never before the glorious story of William Tell and the Swiss fight for freedom.

We lingered at Lucerne, climbing the Rigi, and again at Interlaken, feasting our hearts and eyes in the evening twilight and at sunrise upon the distant splendor of the Jungfrau, that loveliest of all Switzerland's lovely snow-clad peaks.

At Interlaken another human touch left on our hearts an ineffaceable memory. One early morning we were roused from our slumber by loud shouting and ringing of bells. Springing to our balconies we looked down upon an interesting scene. The sidewalks were thronged with people in gala dress and down the street came a herd of cows, well-groomed and decked with garlands of flowers, each cow with a melodious bell. Before them two or three men gaily decked with ribbons, silver buckles and silver chains came dancing, shouting and singing, leading the herd. As they made their way along the street they were frequently halted and regaled with cakes, fruit and goblets of wine by enthusiastic admirers. This procession, we were told, was the annual bovine welcome to spring by the herdsmen of the district. Before leading their cows to their pastures for the summer they considered it necessary to take them out for practice walks preparatory to their mountain climbing. The most beautiful and most productive cow bore the finest bell. Those bells are often preserved in a family from generation to generation and are greatly cherished by the owners of the prize cows.

Our tour led us out at length over the Col de Pillon at the eastern end of Lake Geneva, most famous of all Switzerland's lakes. In Geneva, being good Presbyterians, we paused to do homage to the

memory of two men. We visited the modest little church where John
Knox once preached and we stood in his pulpit. We also visited the
ancient and noble Cathedral of Saint-Pierre and gazed up with due
reverence at the lofty pulpit from which John Calvin was wont to
inspire and indoctrinate the good people of Geneva over whom he
ruled with iron hand. It would have been quite impossible to persuade me that day that forty-five years later I should stand in that
same pulpit and preach the annual sermon to the League of Nations
there assembled.

Time and money are ruthless tyrants whose commands all men
must obey. We took a night train through France and woke in Paris.
We seldom confess that we "did" Paris in two days! The Louvre, doing homage to the "Venus," the Madeleine, Notre Dame, Napoleon's
Tomb, the Bois, the Champs-Elysées with the two draped figures of
Strassburg and Metz that kept burning in the heart of France the
fires of revenge for a later day. Then we pedaled off for Normandy
with its fertile fields of grain and poppies, its great orchards, which
reminded us of the orchards of Zorra. Taking ship at Dieppe, we
bade farewell to the continent of Europe with its history, its geography
and its humanity, a wonder world, but carrying in memory and in
imagination and in heart a vast and varied treasure that fifty years
of time have not been able either to filch from us or to destroy.

And so we stand again on English ground, none too happy or
comfortable after our Channel crossing. Newhaven greets us with a
glorious sunny welcome, but our unhappy experience with the English Channel dampens our patriotic ardor and we long to sleep the
clock around. But now the financial pressure has become acute. We
discover that the two meals which will carry us to Croydon where
we can replenish our funds will leave us with exactly 13s. 2d. between
us. We must push on. We pedal in a kind of mechanical nightmare,
dead even to all the sweet beauty of the English countryside.

An hour or so out of Newhaven we met with our first serious
accident of the whole journey. After a long hard climb we came to
the top of a winding hill down which we let ourselves go.

"Don't coast, you little idiot!" shouted Mac to Haddow, over
whom he always exercised a kind of fatherly supervision. "You don't
know what's round that bend. Keep your feet on the pedals."

His warning came too late. Already Haddow, who was perhaps the least expert of the company with his wheel, had set his feet upon the rests and was coasting downhill quite merrily. Suddenly at the turn we saw coming up the hill a man driving before him half a dozen cattle. Immediately the four of us with our feet on the pedals had our wheels under control and made our way easily around the herd. Poor Haddow, however, coasting gaily along with his wheel out of control and rushing furiously down upon the beasts, began frantically to ring his bell and to shout for a clear way.

The startled beasts only bunched and crowded the road. Haddow's wheel crashed into a stone, he was flung into the hedge and lay there entangled in the branches. We rushed to his aid, but before we could reach him he had struggled to his feet and was brushing the debris from his clothes.

"All right, Bob?" said Mac in an anxious voice, putting his arm about him.

"All right, Mac," replied Bob quite cheerfully, but in rather a shaking voice.

"You little fool," exclaimed Mac wrathfully. "Don't you know any better than to coast round a bend like that? You might have killed yourself! And served you right too!"

Bob stared at him in amazement.

"Why, Mac, what's wrong with you?" he asked. The big chap was white and shaking.

"You might have knocked your brains out, Bob," said Tibb.

"Knocked his brains out? He couldn't do that," said Mac, regarding him with disgust, "he hasn't got any."

"I am all right, Mac. That hedge saved me, I guess, but my wheel looks rather a wreck."

It was a wreck and London forty miles away.

A committee of the whole on ways and means was called. Mac, our treasurer, reported 13s. 2d. in the treasury.

"And he's got to go by train," said Mac in disgust, "and his blasted bike, too." He consulted his guidebook. "That means for both seven and tuppence. He'll have to eat too, I suppose."

"No, I won't need any lunch," said Bob penitently. Mac glared at him.

"A cup of tea will do," said Bob, eager to atone.

"Give him two shillings, Mac," said Tibb. "You never know what will happen."

"That's true. You never know what he'll do next," agreed Mac sullenly. "That will be nine and tuppence."

"There'll be tips, too, Mac," said Tibb. "Give him ten shillings."

Poor Haddow could only glance at him gratefully. No one else in the Quintet was so particular about tips.

We accompanied him with his bicycle to a small-town station and got him aboard.

It was long after the lunch hour when we rode into the beautiful little village of Brambletye and pulled up at the door of the village inn. Having been unable to eat breakfast, owing to the effect of our Channel voyage, we were ravenous. We had three shillings and tuppence. Our treasurer interviewed the barmaid as to lunch. Lunch was over, but she would see. She returned to announce she could give us a steak or chop with bread and butter and tea.

"And how much will that be?" enquires our Business Manager.

"That will be six shillings for the four."

Mac emptied his purse into his hand showing three shillings and tuppence.

"We are on our way back from the Continent. We have met with an accident. This is all the money we have. When we have eaten what that will buy, tell us and we'll quit."

"I will see the head," she replied, smiled at us and ran away.

In a few minutes she returned and announced:

"It will be a steak."

It seemed to us the best lunch we had had for many a day. When we had finished Mac went with his three shillings to the innkeeper, but he waved him and his money away.

"Keep your money, you may need it," he said. Then after a few moments he came to Mac:

"Can't I lend you some money? You never can tell what may happen."

We thanked him and took our journey with grateful farewells.

"After all," said Tibb, "we are a long way from Canada, but we're at home all right."

CHAPTER XII

The Great Superintendent

JAMES ROBERTSON—SETTLING OF THE CANADIAN WEST—MISSIONARY PREACHING—BACK HOME— SECOND RIEL REBELLION—DEATH OF MOTHER— —PRESBYTERIANS ON THE FRONTIER—BANFF

AMONG the makers of Canada perhaps no one has done more to determine the character and quality of its early civilization than the Rev. Dr. James Robertson, for twenty years superintendent of missions in the Presbyterian Church in the West. A man's influence upon his country is determined by the elements that go to make his personality, the characteristics of the period in which he lived and the quality of the influence which he exerted upon his generation.

In Dr. Robertson's personality were to be found the qualities of a statesman, vision, organizing ability, power to inspire to heroic deeds, selfless devotion to his country, a courage that never faltered and a persistence that never swerved from the line of duty.

His period of service synchronized with that of the exploration and settlement of Western Canada, and of the unification of the Dominion of Canada, by means of the construction of the Canadian Pacific Railway.

The work to which he, together with other pioneer religious leaders, devoted his great physical, intellectual and spiritual powers was laying broad and deep the educational, social and religious foundations of the nation's life.

It was at a Sunday evening service in the historic St. Andrew's Church in Toronto that I first heard him speak. I was then a graduate of Toronto University and a theological student in my first year, and with all the self-assured, critical faculties belonging to my stage of development keenly alert. The superintendent was in the fourth year of his office, but he had not yet made for himself the sure place in the confidence of his church which he afterwards attained.

He was introduced by the minister of the congregation, the cultured and popular Dr. D. J. Macdonell. The contrast between the two men was strikingly to the disadvantage of the superintendent, whose rugged face, angular form, hard voice and almost uncouth pulpit manner intensified the critical attitude of mind with which I waited for his message.

In three sentences he had me disarmed, seized with a grip that never let go till his last word was spoken. He began with a lesson in the geography of the new Canada that lay west of the Great Lakes and stretched for nearly two thousand miles to the Pacific Ocean. He showed us the sweeping vastness of the prairies, the rolling beauty of the foothill country and massive grandeur of the Selkirks and the Rockies, a few years ago the paradise of the buffalo hunter and the Hudson's Bay trapper. He pictured on that map the great Saskatchewan and the Bow, the Mackenzie, the Fraser and, in the Far North, the Peace, the Athabasca, the Yukon. Then he proceeded to tell of the tide of humanity, spreading over the new land, which from 1881 had been gathering in force and volume year by year. The church must care for these people. She was beginning to care for them. In the first year of his superintendency 50 new stations were opened, the next year 51, this year 70. "These tides of immigration will not wait for us," he said. "If we lose these people now we shall have a wild and godless West. Already we have two belts of land taken up and settled, one 300 miles by 50, another 250 by 25. These new settlers are your people—your sons and daughters.

"The Presbyterian Church has a large stake in this new country. Over forty per cent of the immigrants into Manitoba are of Presbyterian blood and in the western territories over thirty-two per cent. The church is responding nobly," he declared, a ring of pride in his voice. "For the Church and Manse Building Fund within two years $63,726 has been contributed, of which over one-half has been raised in the West."

The voice was harsh with a Scottish burr, but it compelled attention. The urgency of a rushing multitude was in his plea. He wanted men and he wanted money, and he wanted both this year— now. The large congregation was held rigid for nearly an hour.

"There's a man," said Gilbert. "What a rugby center forward he would make!"

During that college year 1885 I signed up for a mission field in Manitoba. But before the close of the term the war drum was beating and Canada was facing the second Riel Rebellion, which threatened to develop into an Indian war. Early in the spring various volunteer battalions were ordered to the front and were on their way west via the uncompleted Canadian Pacific Railway along the north shore of Lake Superior. Though not a member of any volunteer organization, my brother Robertson organized a corp of mounted scouts and offered their services to the government. I begged a place in his company and he promised it to me, but the volunteer forces appeared to be sufficient and all others were held in reserve.

Early April found me in my mission field in Southern Manitoba riding the plains, rounding up the scattered settlers into congregations and Sunday schools, organizing Bible classes, baseball teams and singing classes. It was a glorious summer and I went back to college hot for the new western country and for my rugged-faced superintendent.

After graduation and after our Quintet year in Edinburgh and our trip over the Alps, I spent a year at home taking work for my father whose health had broken down. It was a quiet home. My five brothers had married and settled down or were finishing their college courses, my sister was settled in Toronto. Gilbert, too, was settled in Toronto and busy with a growing practice. My work was not very satisfying, but I found a wonderful compensation in helping my mother with her parochial duties and in her work in connection with the newly organized Woman's Foreign Missionary Society, in which she took an important part and to which she gave much of her mind and heart. These few months at home were among the happiest in my life, and in some ways to me the most useful.

In the early spring of 1890 my mother went to Toronto to attend the annual meeting of the W.F.M.S., making her home with Gilbert, where a baby was being awaited with great interest. In the last days of April a telegram summoned us to her bedside. On May Day her six boys carried her to her grave and spread the earth over her dear dust. The manner of her going seemed so much a part of her beautiful, brave and bright life that the loss did not at first seem so appalling. She left us with words bright with hope and courage. Her thought was for us who were being left behind.

"Stick close to one another and be good to your father," were her last words. Tender words and wise.

It was only after I had gone back to our old home to close it up forever that the full weight of my loss smote me with an appalling desolation. Nearly fifty years have elapsed and even yet the memory of those first months without my mother brings back the ache to my heart. The other members of our family had already found other love ties that bound them to life's interests, but for ten years no such experience came to me. That chamber of my heart I kept fast shut. I could never mention my mother's name. That was a fatal mistake, and one that tended greatly to impoverish my life. Fortunately I had kept in close touch with the superintendent of our western missions. At my brother Gilbert's suggestion he came to me one day and told me of a vacant field for whose rather special needs he could find no suitable missionary.

The main station of the field was Banff in the new National Park, which the Dominion government in collaboration with the Canadian Pacific Railway was trying to make into a world center of tourist travel. But the superintendent was a wise man. Banff, it is true, was the center of the field, but with it were associated two mining villages, two or three railway stations and some lumber camps.

"A large field and a needy field," the superintendent explained. "It is in the new Presbytery of Calgary, the largest presbytery in the world. Your nearest neighbor will be in Calgary on the east, some eighty miles away, but on the west your next neighbor will be at Donald, a hundred miles distant."

"I hate to have you go so far away," said Gilbert as we talked it over. "Two thousand miles and more. It will be awfully lonely for you."

"Lonely?" I said. "More lonely than this country?"

To this he made no reply.

I accepted the superintendent's invitation and went to Banff, and have thanked God for it ever since. I had the good fortune to work with one of the greatest, in some senses the very greatest, man I have known.

In June, 1890, I was ordained at Calgary. The ordination service was exceedingly primitive. Rules of order were sometimes forgotten and at other times ignored. After my ordination I sat listening to the "fathers and brethren," mostly brethren, who were really anxious to get at the reports from the various fields.

These reports dealt mainly with the experiences and observations of the missionaries in regard to the country and people: the new people coming in, and how the old-timers helped them to get themselves adjusted to the new life; the old-timers and their manner of living, were they coming to church? How about the young men and the "Permit System" and the big jamborees? Light and shade, success and failure, comedy and tragedy.

One missionary, a new man, was evidently down and almost out. His people were indifferent to religion, except the few women and they were often too sick, lonely and discouraged to be interested in anything. Another missionary reported in the same strain and then another. Then followed a red headed, queer-looking missionary originally from the North of Scotland, slow of speech, with a touch of pawky humor. His mistakes, his misunderstandings, his failures, all of which he apparently regarded as one huge joke, soon had the brethren in roars of laughter. Then followed discussion.

The old-timers among the missionaries, all but two under thirty, refused to accept failure as possible. Their various experiences had carried them along over failures, as over crests of waves, to success. The discouraged and near-quitters listened with growing excitement. They began to see the joke in failure. They began to laugh at themselves and their experiences. Their laughter was an indication that they had got their second wind. Long before presbytery had risen they were prepared to go back to their fields with a new light in their eyes, new courage in their hearts, and filled with a new scorn for their failures. It was all an amazing experience to me. The presbytery closed with a full-dress preaching service in Dr. Herdman's church, the preacher in gown, choir in gowns, the church filled with earnest and enthusiastic worshipers and the preacher Dr. Herdman himself, a scholarly Modernist, glowing with an intense spiritual flame. The service was extraordinary for its exalted optimism and its note of triumph. It gave me just the tonic I needed. It came to me suddenly that I was meeting with the brethren of the largest presbytery in the world, whose bounds in the instrument of its creation were set forth in the following terms: "The eastern limit shall be the one hundred and ninth degree of longitude, the southern limit the forty-ninth parallel of latitude, the western limit a line passing north and south through the western crossing of the Columbia River by the Canadian Pacific Railway, the northern limit the Arctic Sea." Over this vast area, comprising thirteen fields, these nine ordained men had supervision, together with an equal number of student missionaries during the summer months.

As I listened I had a sudden realization of the magnitude and splendor of this work. Dr. Herdman's penetrating voice was analyzing the type of Christian needed in this age and especially in this new land. "He must be a man to whom God is more real than His universe." This was great preaching, fresh, spiritual, inspiring, apostolic in its sweeping outlook.

About two o'clock, some hours before daybreak, the Presbytery of Calgary adjourned to allow the brethren from the West to get ready for their train. With great hilarity and the most jovial fellowship we snatched a lunch provided by the ladies of Knox Church, after which in a dazed state of mind, but feeling small amid this bunch of roughriders I made my way to Banff, where I was to spend four glorious years.

I felt myself like a man caught in a moving avalanche swept along I knew not whither, but sure of arriving at some terminal I knew not what. Nor did I care much. There was no uncertainty in the minds of these men. They were laying deep and broad foundations, let other men worry about superstructures. Each had his own particular field to cultivate, but ever their eyes were on the horizons, foothill or mountain peak, for what was coming to them. For something was surely coming to them, something big.

A year later I found myself one of them sharing their fortunes and their outlook. How great was the change in me I realized when at a meeting of presbytery at Medicine Hat I came into touch with a new missionary, an old friend of mine, Tom Rogers, fresh from his college in Toronto and under appointment to Nelson, a new wild West mining town in the South Kootenay. On his journey west he had fallen in with an American missionary superintendent from the western states, who was loud in his lamentation over the needy and neglected fields in his own land. "He told me," said Rogers, "there were thousands of square miles without a single missionary. He offered me full charge of a town of twelve hundred people. Now in Nelson, I understand, there are about two hundred people, my particular congregation there numbering twenty-two members, and there is an Anglican missionary in the same district. Across the line I would be the only man in the place. I have only one life. I want to invest it where there is a chance for the biggest returns."

I watched our superintendent, who happened to be with us at our presbytery meeting, handle the young man.

"Mr. Rogers, you are a Canadian—"

"There are no national lines in the Kingdom of God," broke in Rogers.

"True, but you are a Canadian. Educated by the Presbyterian Church in Canada. This country needs missionaries to deal with the incoming people. Nelson needs a man if it is to be saved from utter godlessness."

"But there is—"

"Wait please! Never heed the Anglican. He will have all he can do. The Presbyterian Church is responsible for Presbyterian people first. Wait now! I make you a proposition. Go you to Nelson. Do your work as you should. If in one year from today you wish to be relieved I shall pay your way to your western American town and with no recriminations or criticism."

Reluctantly Rogers accepted the challenge. In six months he came to presbytery breathing fire and fury.

"The situation in that southern Kootenay country is a disgrace to the Christian church, and especially to the Presyterian Church in Canada," he announced in a flaming speech that ran to the quite unusual length, in that presbytery, of half an hour and was filled with statistics as to the situation in the various mining towns of the district of which Nelson was the center. "I must have at least two men immediately and if we are to meet the needs of this growing country at least four more men next year."

The old-timers in the presbytery listened with grinning faces but with glowing eyes. It was an old experience for these men, but the story was as new as their need for daily bread. Rogers got the definite promise of one man immediately and the others at the earliest possible moment.

"I won't accept that," shouted Rogers. "I'll go down to Toronto myself and get the men, if I have to pull them out by the hair of their heads."

"Where?" asked the superintendent.

"Knox College! My own college!" replied Rogers.

"Go!" said the superintendent. "I visited the eastern colleges. I asked for fifty new men for next spring. I got the promise of twenty-two. But perhaps you can get more."

Rogers immediately wilted.

"I beg your pardon, sir. I didn't mean that," he said in a husky voice. "But it's a shame. If you can't get them, who can?"

"You see, sir, some of them can't see as far as Nelson," said the superintendent with a twinkle in his eye.

"Again I apologize, sir. I remember well what a fool I was last spring," said Rogers. "But I've seen the country since."

The superintendent reared up his lanky form. He was deeply moved by the flaming enthusiasm of the young man, but he spoke quietly:

"It is our simple duty to care for our people and this can be done only if all Canadians do their full duty by all Canada." It was one of the superintendent's great dicta which have become the heritage of all Canadians.

"Great, old boy," said Rogers to me afterwards. "Guess I made an ass of myself."

"Yes," I said, "the kind of ass we need in this country, but more in Eastern Canada."

CHAPTER XIII

Sky Pilot in the Foothills

VISITORS TO BANFF—EVENING IN A VALLEY—
I MEET MY MOTHER AGAIN—AS LITTLE CHILDREN
—RELIGIOUS ROUNDUP—PERMIT SYSTEM—THE
COMMUNION SERVICE

EVERY settled and ordained minister in the presbytery was supposed to exercise a kind of supervision over the missionaries in his neighborhood, and do a certain amount of exploratory work. Hence in addition to my work in Banff, in Anthracite, a mining town, and Canmore, a railway divisional point and coal mining center, I had oversight of lumber camps in the neighborhood and the railway points as far west as Field, a distance of fifty-five miles. During the tourist season from June to September the work in Banff was engrossing. It was my duty not only to hold a service every morning for the people of Banff and in both Anthracite and Canmore, some twenty miles away, but to call upon visitors as far as possible, a duty which made large demands upon one's time but had its compensations. For one thing, it brought me into touch with most interesting people and enabled me to form new and valued friendships. Many friends from the Old Country were visitors to our National Park. What was my delight one Sunday morning to see Dr. Hugh Barbour and his charming wife worshiping with us in our little church. At another time Henry Drummond walked into our service and to my great joy spent a few days exploring and enjoying the wonders of the park. More frequent visitors were Lord and Lady Aberdeen, at times accompanied by their daughter, Lady Marjorie Gordon. No visitors to the park took a deeper interest in the missionary's work than did Lord and Lady Aberdeen. Indeed, they came to regard themselves as regular members of the Banff congregation from the fact that on their periodic visits to their beautiful Coldstream ranch in the Okanagan valley they would always contrive to spend at least one week end at Banff. On one occasion Lord Aberdeen had occasion to run up from Banff to Field to spend the week end there. I was billed for afternoon service that day in Field, but owing to a washout on the line I was unable to keep my appointment. It was thoroughly characteristic of Lord Aberdeen to send me a wire announcing that he would take my appointment for me, which he did to the delight of the congregation.

Visiting preachers, though I hated to break in upon their holidays, were always ready to take a service which would allow me to give supply to some outlying mission. A visiting minister from England was good enough to take my work for two successive Sundays. This gave me the opportunity to make, at the request of the superintendent, a tour through the foothill country, some two hundred fifty miles south as far as the boundary. It was a wonderful experience; first, because I made the trip on Romeo, a stunning bronco colt belonging to Guy, the young son of Dr. Lafferty of Calgary, one of Dr. Herdman's elders and a dear friend of mine for many years. The colt was one of the most beautifully formed broncos I ever saw. His one fault was an incurable aversion to any but first place on the trail. A horse coming up behind him, or on the trail in front of him, would drive him frantic. I rather judge that for this characteristic of his the responsibility must rest upon young Guy, who like his bronco hated second place.

This trip lives with me still. I set out on a gorgeous September morning and began to climb the run of hills that enclosed the straggling town of Calgary. This trail led southward to the American border, through the country of the great ranches, a country of vast empty spaces rapidly filling in with new settlers from everywhere in the world.

The march of fifty-seven years has not obliterated from my memory certain happenings of that trip.

One day near the end of the first week as the sun was making for the western horizon I came to the edge of a lovely little valley. It was like a cup with a rim of gold and blue round it, and at the very bottom of the cup a neat and cozy farmstead set among the willows beside a little lake.

"Someone lives there that is worth knowing," I said to myself and loped down the hill till I reached the gate of a little garden where some late prairie flowers were in full bloom, goldenrod, asters and others whose names I did not know; but such goldenrod and asters as I had never seen. They had evidently been carefully nursed. The sound of my horse's feet brought to the door a little lady with dark hair, dark eyes warm with a smile like the dawning of a spring morning. I saluted her and introduced myself. She greeted me as if I had been a long-lost brother.

"I am Mrs. Hugh Gibson," she said. "My husband is away from home, but wait—" She ran into the house and brought with her an old gentleman with long white hair and patriarchal beard, tall, spare and carrying an air of distinction but walking with difficulty, using a cane.

"My father-in-law will show you where to put up your horse. What a beauty he is!" she said, rubbing my Romeo's nose.

The old gentleman greeted me with a nod and a curt "good day," but though I chatted with him as I made my horse comfortable for the night, he spoke in reply not more than half a dozen words. As a matter of fact, I was uncertain whether he was taking in my chatty remarks. He maintained the same attitude of dignified silence as he brought me into the house.

Mrs. Gibson greeted me warmly as I entered the large living room behind which was the kitchen, in and out of which she tripped. "Tripped" is the only word that properly describes the movements of this trim, neat, bright-faced little woman.

"You will find basin and towel in the shed at the back of the house. Come with me, I will show you."

As we passed out through the kitchen she said to me, in a low thrilling voice, "I met your mother once."

"My mother? When? Where?" I asked in surprise.

"It was at a Woman's Foreign Missionary meeting in Woodstock. She had driven down twenty miles from Harrington with a young brother of yours. The meeting was in the home of a dear friend of mine, Mrs. Ball."

"Mrs. Ball!" I exclaimed. "A dear friend of my mother's and a dear friend of mine too."

"Well, I must tell you." She was speaking hurriedly and under deep emotion. "We went upstairs to lay off our things and had about fifteen minutes together. Those fifteen minutes changed my life. I was in great distress—oh, great distress and darkness! I can't go into that. But she was so kind, so understanding, so bright. She had such a grip on the worth-while things. Well, as I say, I owe all that is finest and best in my life to those fifteen minutes and to the hour at the meeting downstairs which followed. So this house is yours, and all that it holds. There's my little girl now with the cows." She ran around the house to meet her daughter and left me to my ablutions and my thoughts. "My mother! Fifteen minutes! Yes, that would be enough."

Her little girl, of about eleven I should say, was like so many of these western youngsters quite grown up. Shy, silent, except when I talked about her pony, which apparently was a quite wonderful cattle pony, but with an air of quiet self-reliance. She had never been to school but she knew more schoolbook stuff than many an eastern girl of fifteen.

Mr. Gibson arrived home just as we were sitting down to supper. His welcome home was the guarantee of his character as husband and father. After the supper things were cleared away we spent some time in talk and then the father took down his fiddle from the wall, began to tune up and without apology away he went into the kind of fiddling Billy Sutherland of the old Oatmeal Mill used to do.

"Do you play any instrument?" the mother asked me.

I confessed to thumping a piano, tooting a flute and strumming a guitar.

"Can you play this?" asked Mary, holding up her mouth organ.

I admitted some amateurish skill.

She ran to a shelf and produced a second mouth organ, wiped it carefully with her apron and handed it to me.

"Let's all go," I said and away we went at the old reels, and had half an hour of rare fun.

"Can you sing, Mary?" I asked.

"Yes," she said, " 'Old Black Joe,' and Grandpa can too."

"Come on," I said and began to play "Old Black Joe." The fiddle joined in, the mother took a part, the silent old man contributed a bass, soon I abandoned my harmonica and put in a tenor. For another hour we went through a varied repertoire of Negro, Scottish, English songs, till finally the mother placed a Bible on the table and said:

"May we have worship? We always have worship in the evening."

I passed the Bible to the father, saying, "Every man is high priest in his own house."

"Not me," he said with a little laugh, "the lady looks after this."

Ah! Those fifteen minutes with my mother. I could easily fill in the picture.

I suggested that we sing a hymn.

"What do you like best, Mary?"

"'Unto the Hills,'" she answered promptly. "They're just out there," she added pointing toward the west. Following the lead of the violin our worship began with the Marquis of Lorne's noble version of the 121st Psalm, ending with the words:

> From every evil shall He keep thy soul
> From every sin.
> Jehovah shall preserve thy going out
> Thy coming in.
> Above thee watching, He whom we adore
> Shall keep thee henceforth, yea, for evermore.

"Have you any church service here on Sunday?" I asked when we had finished prayers.

"No," said Mrs. Gibson. "The people are widely scattered and until a few weeks ago we had no place for meeting. But now we have a new school quite near us, just finished a week ago."

Next morning soon after daybreak I was ready for the road. As I was saying good-bye, the old gentleman said quite abruptly:

"Come back this way and we shall get a meeting for you."

His family were apparently quite startled.

"Are you coming back this way?" he asked. "Could you come back this way? You should come back this way. We will get you a congregation." Still they gazed at him in wonder. "We need you here. We will get you a congregation," he insisted.

I made a quick calculation and a sudden resolve.

"I'll be back here two weeks from today, if you promise me a meeting."

"Very well. We will get you a meeting. Won't we, Mary?"

"Yes, grandpa, we will," said the little girl eagerly.

"I'll come," I said, shaking hands with the old gentleman and then with the others.

Mary was standing beside me with her pony saddled.

"I'm going to show you a short cut," she said and off we went up the trail, Romeo frantic to take the lead and the pony equally determined to challenge his right.

After a mile of hard fighting we got our horses down to a trot.

"Your grandfather is keen about the meeting, Mary," I said.

"I never saw him that way before. He never speaks to strangers. He is very funny today."

As we trotted along Mary told me her life story, as far back as she could remember from the day they drove their team into the valley some seven years ago. From her point of view she had had a very happy life. She had no friends, no school, no church. She often went off for a day and a night up into the Pass with her parents. Her father had discovered a coal mine from which they would bring down a load of coal every now and then. The grandfather had never been outside the valley and had made no friends at all, but he was her great friend. He listened to her lessons, and made her read books.

"What books?"

"Oh, Shakespeare and *The Pilgrim's Progress* and *The Golden Treasury*," was the astonishing answer.

After a ride of an hour we came to a deep valley in the shadow of two crags, the first outposts of the Rockies.

"Down there Mrs. Mallock lives. She has two dear little girls."

"Come down and introduce me, Mary."

"No, I'm afraid of her. I saw her once. She looked awful. Don't go!"

"She won't hurt me, Mary. Good-bye. See you again soon."

"Yes, in two weeks," said Mary, and waving her hand she galloped back over her homeward trail, while I trotted down to the shack in the valley before me. Fifteen minutes! And a lovely, well-bred little girl like this in a lonely valley among the foothills!

It was a wretched dwelling for any human being. Built of logs with a pent roof, covered with sod, two windows with missing panes, stuffed with rags. In front was an enclosed plot that had evidently been intended for a garden but was filled with weeds and rubbish.

Two hungry dogs came rushing to meet me, followed by a man dressed in rough hunting shirt, leggings and cowboy hat. From the door peeked two ragged little girls, through whose tousy locks sharp little eyes peered curiously at me.

"Good day!" said the man. "Nice day! Here, shut up! Down there! Damn you!" he shouted to the dogs.

I introduced myself.

"Oh, preacher, eh? Well, we've been pretty free of them since we came here. But like the wild oats and potato bugs, they're bound to come."

"And railroads and schools and doctors and other things," I suggested.

"You're up early, where did you sleep?"

"At Mr. Hugh Gibson's."

"Nice folks. Not much snap about him."

"They have a beautiful home there."

His face grew suddenly dark.

"Money means paint I guess," he growled.

"Must be hard to make money on these ranches," I said.

"Didn't use to be before those darn railroads came."

"Jim!" a fretful voice called from within.

"All right, Edith." He went into the house, leaving me on my horse outside, a gross breach of foothill manners.

Through the open door peeked the bright eyes at me.

"Hello!" I said, "come out and see my horse."

Like a flash the eyes disappeared. I waited. Again the eyes peeked round the jamb of the door.

"I can see you!" I said. "Have you a pony?"

A little face appeared and a sharp little voice answered, "I got a hen!"

Another little face appeared. "I got a hen too!"

"Where are they?" I asked. "In the stable?"

"Naw!" replied a scornful voice.

"Under the bed!" came another voice. "It's got a nest and some eggs too."

"What? Eggs? How many? Two?"

A burst of giggles made answer, followed once more by a scornful voice. "A whole lot of eggs. She's settin'."

"She's goin' to have chickens." One little girl came wholly into view.

"Chickens? Splendid! How many? Two?"

A second little girl came into view and shouted. "Oh, a lot! A hundred!"

"I have a hen too," I said. "Do you want to see it? Come on, I'll show it to you."

Shyly they drew near while I brought from my bag an illustrated children's book, and slipping from my saddle I dropped the reins over Romeo's head, which as with every well-trained bronco anchored him to his place.

"Look!" I said.

Shyly they peered at the picture of a gorgeously colored cock, crowing lustily. In silent and amazed rapture they gazed at the splendid creature.

"It ain't a hen! It's a rooster," scornfully said the bigger girl.

"It's a rooster!" echoed the smaller one.

"So it is! But there's a hen, too." I turned the page.

"Oo-oo-oo-h look at the little chickies!"

I moved over to a log and sat down with one on each side of me and displayed before their fascinated gaze a glorious succession of barnyard fowls, hens, roosters, ducks, geese. They had completely forgotten their shyness. The smaller girl, Eva by name, was on my knee, the larger one, Ethel, leaned against my shoulder, their eyes popping at a picture of a magnificent turkey cock with tail displayed in all its gorgeous splendor.

A glance over my shoulder revealed the father in the doorway and the mother just behind him apparently astonished at the temerity of their children.

I heard a word or two in a woman's voice.

"Oh, all right. Ask him."

"Hello!" said the man. "What are you doing to the preacher?"

"Oh, look mammy!" The wee one caught the book, sprang from my knee and rushed toward her mother. "See, the man has a hen, and a rooster and ducks and everything."

It was a most satisfactory introduction. Mrs. Mallock came out and invited me in, apologizing not at all for the woeful condition of her house, which I took for a good sign. Her husband was taking Romeo to the stable, but I told him I must hurry on.

"Oh, do stay for dinner," said his wife. "We live very simply but—"

I was firm in my refusal, at which I observed relief, and while the children were busy with the book she gave me in a few sentences enough of her story to explain a good deal.

"Seven years ago I came over those hills," she said, a bitter note in her voice. "I have never been over them since."

"No neighbors?"

"We have few neighbors. My fault I suppose. I don't make friends easily."

"We all need friends and especially in this country."

"Circumstances are sometimes too much for us." Immediately she changed the subject.

I studied her face. She had been beautiful one could easily guess. Sickness, loneliness and deprivation are hard on beauty in this country. But something deeper, more cruel I guessed, had stamped those deep lines on her face. When her husband came in I was startled at the quick flash of contempt, almost of hate, in her eyes. I understood now the lines on her face. I was deeply shocked and felt terribly sorry for her.

"You'll stay for dinner," he said in a pleasant voice. "I'll just put up your horse."

A plan came into my head.

"Thank you, I can't stay. I have a long trip ahead of me. I am riding down to the border and then away round by Pincher Creek. Here's my map."

He looked at my map.

"That's a long ride, all right."

"I have two weeks to do it in."

"Well, if your bronco can stand it, and he looks all right, I guess you can do it, if you have good luck."

"I can do it. But I want to send a message to Mr. Gibson. Does your little girl ride?"

I wrote a note and enclosed it in an envelope.

"They all ride in this country," he said.

"Could she take this note to Mrs. Gibson for me?"

"I don't—we don't know the Gibsons," said his wife.

"Nonsense," said her husband angrily. "Give me your note. I'll see they get it."

"Thank you. I'm coming back in two weeks. Now I must go," I turned to the little girl. "Now, Ethel, I want you to keep this book and your mother will show you the words that tell about the pictures. What's that?"

"A hen," said Ethel promptly.

"A hen!" corroborated Eva.

"Now see that word. 'H-e-n' that's the name of the picture. When I come back I want you to show me the name of every picture in the book, 'hen,' 'duck,' 'goose,' 'chicken,' will you? Never mind the letters, just the words."

"I'll try."

"I will too," said Eva.

"I bet you will. Good-bye."

"Don't go," said Eva. "Tell him not to go, mammy." Her lip began to quiver.

"I'm coming back in two weeks. You find out every hen and duck, will you?" She promised and with mutual regrets we parted.

What a life for this woman! And what a future for these little girls!

And so went my ride. In that roundup of some hundred and fifty miles through this southwest country, I found eleven families and seventeen bachelors living in their lonely shacks, a few in comparative comfort and decency, some in beastliness. Small wonder. The Permit System flourished in this so-called prohibition country and too often did its diabolical work.

The details of that roundup would make an interesting book. For two weeks of glorious weather Romeo and I threaded the valleys of that foothill country, along the bases of the Rockies, often sleeping in the shelter of a big rock or in a clump of spruce with Romeo nosing about me. I envied our men their job in fine summer weather but I shuddered to think of their lot in the rains and in winter. My respect for our missionaries rose immensely during this trip.

At one point I ran into a "Permit Night." A young Englishman, well bred and well educated, had cashed on his "remittance" from home. After "liquidating" his permit he had summoned the boys for twenty miles round for one glorious blowout. But that story, a sad story, must wait. Something like it can be found in *The Sky Pilot,* every word of which, though fiction, is terribly true. But I must tell of my return, which fell on the day before the close of my two weeks' ride.

I arrived at the Mallock house and was welcomed by the whole family like a lifelong friend. We had supper, after which I held a regular "examination" of the progress made in the little book. The result was quite marvelous. Even little Eva, five years old, could point out every "hen," "duck," and "chicken" in the pages of the book, and a good many other words as well. I gave them each another book with pictures of dogs, cats, squirrels, bears, which they promised to learn.

"You are coming to our meeting tomorrow, aren't you?" I asked as I was leaving them.

There was silence for a few moments.

"Well, Gibson brought us your message, but I hardly think we can make it," said the father.

"I am awfully disappointed," I said. "I wanted to see everyone belonging to this neighborhood at the meeting. Everyone I have asked is coming. And the Gibsons promised to get all the people up north."

"Well, I guess we can't just make it," said Mallock. "We'd like to all right but—hang it all—you see we—"

"We will be there," said his wife with a sudden fierceness. "They are no friends of mine. But the meeting is in a school, isn't it?"

"In the new school," I said. "Fine! Good-bye! I'll look for you all."

That service in some of its features lives in my memory. It was a rare September day. From near and far the people had gathered in lumber wagons drawn by oxen and by horses, in democrats and in buckboards, many riding broncos. Arrangements had been made for a Communion Service, though without any special examination of communicants. To this there was a single exception, the little girl of eleven, Mary Gibson. And in her case there really had been no examination, unless one would count some self-examination on the part of the missionary. After a short conversation with her the words had come to me.

"Except ye be converted, and become as little children, ye shall not enter the kingdom of heaven."

According to my form of service I asked her to stand and make her confession, and receive her admission into the Christian church. This she did with utter simplicity and serenity. On her face was such a look of simple gladness as almost broke down my self-control. Immediately after I had received her by giving her, as we say, "the right hand of fellowship," the whole congregation, as well as myself, received a shock.

From his place in the congregation her grandfather came slowly to the front and stood beside his granddaughter.

"Mr. Gordon, I wish to do today what my mother wished me to do more than fifty years ago. I should like to profess my faith in Jesus Christ as my Saviour and Lord."

I was so overcome that I could not find my voice for a moment or two. I took his hand in both of mine and held it fast, then managed to say: "In the name of Jesus Christ, my Lord, I receive you to the membership of His church." As I saw many of the congregation before me in tears, I went on to say: "This is a very informal and very wonderful meeting. And I am going to say that if any others present desire to accept Jesus Christ as their Saviour and Lord, in His Name, I bid them welcome."

Immediately there was a swift movement in one of the back benches and with her handkerchief pressed to her eyes Mrs. Mallock came forward and in a low broken voice asked:

"May I come?"

"Gladly in His Name I bid you welcome." I paused a few moments, hoping her husband would come. But he was sitting in his seat, his face in his hands, apparently unable to stir.

The whole scene was so strange that I hardly knew what to do. I have been thankful ever since that I broke through all the restraints of form and ceremonial and said:

"This is a most unusual service to me, but I am quite sure I am speaking for my Lord and Master when I say, if any of you would like to show your love to your Saviour and your desire to serve Him by joining with us in this memorial service, I will gladly make you welcome."

How many came I do not now remember, but it seemed to me that almost all those present joined in the Holy Communion.

"It was quite irregular, I know," I said to my superintendent as I described the scene to him some months later.

"Irregular?" he exclaimed. "And who are you to stand between sinners and their Saviour?"

In that new land we had to do many unusual things.

After the service I was forced to hurry away, but I was glad to see Mrs. Mallock and her husband and her two little girls in tow of my friend Mrs. Gibson, going into her clean and cozy home.

"Fifteen minutes!" I said to myself, remembering that dear woman's words, as my eyes followed them. "Not much time, but enough."

CHAPTER XIV

A New Adventure

AFTER a year and a half at Banff a call came from a Winnipeg church carrying with it strong personal backing from influential friends. I referred it to my superintendent.

"Stay where you are most needed" was his answer. So I remained at Banff. I was quite delighted with his decision, for I had grown to love the country and the people among whom my work lay. Especially was I intrigued by the magnificent sweep of the work carried on within the bounds of the Presbytery of Calgary, and I had come to love the splendidly heroic men carrying it on, every man a comrade in a great enterprise and every man a friend. It was worth while living to be engaged in such work and with such men. There was no soft stuff in them, no sentimental sloppiness in their religion. Sane, strong, they fought their fight with a gay courage that laughed at danger and hard luck.

In my own field changes came. The mine at Anthracite was closed down. At Canmore a church was built and a vigorous congregation of miners and railway men set agoing. The lumber camps ceased to operate. But mills and mines were being opened in many places in the mountains. Life was strenuous and aggressive and work was expanding every month. It was good to be alive and to have the privilege of taking a hand in this extraordinary development in this truly wonderful country.

But after two years more at Banff another call came from Winnipeg, this time not from a going congregation, but from a new mission in the western outskirts of that rapidly expanding city. The moving spirit in the organizing of the mission was my old minister in Toronto during my university course and my good friend, Dr. J. M. King, then principal of Manitoba College. His letter forced me to seriously consider the call, but the pull of the mountains and the foothills and of the men who were my comrades there, I believe, would have kept me in the West had it not been for a word from my old chief. "Better come," he said, "there is work for you to do here." I went but as I watched the white peaks sink below the rolling curves of the foothills country I felt as if all the color was fading out of my life. How little we know what the future holds for us!

But before settling down to working in Winnipeg I asked and obtained a year's breathing space to brush up my reading which for four years had been completely neglected. So I went to Edinburgh and once more came under the spell of my old professors, Rainy, Dods, Davidson, and renewed my fellowship with such great souls as Dr. Whyte, Henry Drummond, George Adam Smith and with such charming families as the Barbours, the Browns, the Nairns, the Greys, the Simpsons.

I was, however, fresh from my experiences as a missionary in the new Canadian West, to which hundreds and thousands of Scotland's young men were making their way. Everywhere I found the most eager interest in that vast new land. It happened that one evening I went to a drawing room meeting to hear Henry Drummond tell of his trip over the Rockies, and a thrilling tale he made of it. After he had finished his address a number of questions were being asked about the mission work carried on in Western Canada. No sooner had the questions begun than Drummond, who had seen me come into the meeting, said, "Gordon, come up here."

I demurred, but he came to me, took me by the arm and walked me up to the front and introduced me in some such words:

"Most of you remember that wild bunch of Canadians, the Student Quintet, who turned this city upside down some few years ago. Here is one of them. I met him last in the Rockies where he was doing mission work. Ask him any question you like."

They kept me on the grill for nearly an hour. I finished with the statement that we were in desperate need of both men and money.

"Thirty-eight thousand new settlers came into that country last year, forty per cent of them from Scotland. The Presbyterian Church must look after her children."

That night Professor Hugh Barbour, at whose home I was spending a few days, said to me, "Gordon, you must capitalize that story of yours. Carry that story to our students and to our people and you will get both men and money."

We talked the matter over with some of our friends, with the result that a small committee was formed to set the thing agoing. It consisted of Henry Drummond, Hugh Barbour, George Brown, his brother-in-law, the son of the late Honorable George Brown, one of Canada's greatest statesmen. I wrote my superintendent, who as usual acted with vigor. From the moderator of our General Assembly, the Rev. Dr. Cochrane, the Convenor of Home Missions in our church, came a formal document appointing me as a deputy from the Presbyterian Church in Canada, with authority to present to Presbyterians in Scotland the cause of missions in Western Canada. Very soon I was overwhelmed with requests for addresses to small groups. My committee then took up the matter vigorously. The final result was that a Union committee, representing the three great Presbyterian churches in Scotland, was appointed to organize and direct my work. A Union committee of these three churches had never before been known in Scotland.

As a fresh step, with the co-operation of Hugh Barbour and George Brown, a relative of the Nelsons Publishing House I prepared a brief pamphlet illustrated with scenes from life in Western Canada and filled with stories from our western mission fields, stories humorous, tragic, and all true. The pamphlet became immensely popular. It ran into several editions, numbering finally many thousands of copies. And why not? They were reading about their own sons and daughters in that far-off lonely land.

My first plan was to tell my story, after which an offering would be given which might run to five pounds and at times to ten. I soon realized that in the brief time I could give to this work the amount of money raised in this way would not go far to avert the serious financial crisis in our work in Western Canada. An inspiration came to me. The average annual grant to a mission field in Western Canada was $250. I decided to accept no collection, but instead I offered to assign a mission field as their own to any congregation contributing fifty pounds per annum for three, later increased to five, years; the field would report annually to the supporting congregation. The plan touched the imagination of the people. And it worked. At first it was a little difficult to get a hearing on this new understanding. Scottish people have a reputation for being "canny" with their money. So they are, none more so. But show them a good investment and none are quicker to respond.

The largest and most important congregation in Edinburgh of the Established Church was St. George's of which the Rev. Dr. Scott was minister. If I could get Dr. Scott and his people interested my entry to the Established Church would be assured. I had never met Dr. Scott. I determined to call upon him. I called, he was engaged. I asked if I might wait till he was disengaged. I was invited to enter. He was a dignified and slightly pompous old gentleman. I could see that he was annoyed at my persistence.

I thanked him for his courtesy. I told him my mission.

"Young man, do you know," he said, "that every second Sabbath during this coming winter I shall have in my pulpit a beggar for some cause, from every mission in the world, home and foreign missions, London missions, European missions, missions from every country under heaven?"

"This is a mission to your own people, Dr. Scott," I said, "who are in desperate need in the wild West of Canada. Did you ever see a map of the new Canadian West?" Before he could reply I laid the map before him on his table.

A map is an eloquent thing. "It is a big country. From where the boat lands here in Montreal to Winnipeg is as far as from Edinburgh to Constantinople and then you are as far again from Vancouver."

His eyes began to study the map.

"And from Calgary, my own presbytery, the biggest in the world, bigger than the whole of Scotland—north and south, the distance is over six hundred miles. I have ridden the whole of it on a bronco, so I know." I talked hurriedly, intensely as though fighting for my life. I gave him not a moment's pause. I told him of Mrs. Gibson's wee house and of the service I had held in the little school. I told him of the young men from the Old Country and the Permit System. I hurried him up the line through the mountains to the new mining towns, Rossland, Nelson, Kaslo. I pictured the deadly dangers of these camps.

Suddenly he smiled at me.

"Young man, you've won. You will speak to my people on Sunday morning, but on the condition that you ask for no collection."

"I never ask collections," I said. "It is too big a thing for collections."

"What then?"

I explained my plan.

"Ye're no blate, young man! But come next Sabbath."

"Thank you, sir!" I said. "Good-bye, sir. I'll tell my superintendent of your kindness."

I left him. I had been talking exactly thirty-five minutes. I was wet to the skin and walked out exhausted.

On Sunday morning he introduced me to his congregation and I made my plea asking only for their prayers and their sympathy for their sons and daughters in that faraway part of the Empire.

Then Dr. Scott rose. He told his people of my visit to him and of his reception. He told them he had made me promise to ask no money.

"The young man has kept his word, but I am going to ask any of you interested in this story, this marvelous story, to remain after the benediction."

It seemed to me half the congregation remained. I explained my plan. I made no plea. I told them yarns. But I came away with a promise of support for two missions for five years. I was limp but amazed and grateful. These canny, careful Scots! Show them a worth-while investment and there are none like them in the world.

At Free St. George's and with Dr. Alexander Whyte I had a different experience. He was a warm friend of mine, but no less canny for all that. His congregation was the stamping ground for every religious tramp and every needy cause in the world. He could not give me a full service. People came from all lands to hear the minister of Free St. George's preach. He must keep faith with them. He would give me ten minutes. My heart sank within me. Ten minutes for Western Canada and its needy people! But my committee, Hugh Barbour and George Brown, were on their job. They saw that a copy of my pamphlet was sent to every important member in the congregation during the week preceding my appearance.

Ten minutes! What I said I don't know, I only know I lost no time in preliminaries, but I was quite disgusted with myself.

Dr. Whyte followed me. Holding up a copy of my pamphlet in his hand, he cried out to his people, "Have you seen this wee book? Get it! Read it! Man, it's literature! If I know my people I can assure my young friend something will be done by Free St. George's."

That was all. I walked home with him to lunch, sick with disappointment at my miserable failure and said so.

"Oh, never heed it," he said with his cheery smile. "I'll say to you what an old minister said to me when I was a young man feeling as you do now. 'Hoots!' he said to me. 'Dinna fash yersel'! There's nae buddie thinkin' aboot it but yersel'.' That has helped me over many a dark hour, and it may help you."

It did then, and many a time since.

Free St. George's gave me five missions for five years and for longer after the five years were done, in all over six thousand dollars. But there was in all Britain no man like the old Puritan divine, Dr. Alexander Whyte, and no congregation like Free St. George's.

To Glasgow I went where Dr. Black, the grand old minister of Wellington Church, gave me welcome and Dr. Orrock Johnstone of Kelvinside, Dr. Marshall Lang, father of the Archbishop of Canterbury, minister of The Barony and others stood by me, to Paisley where Hugh Black, that beautiful saintly soul, afterwards assistant to Dr. Whyte, now a distinguished traveling professor in homiletics to a number of colleges in the United States, gave me a glowing introduction to his people; also to other centers in the west. I went to St. Andrew's, Dundee and Aberdeen in the east, where George Adam Smith and Lord and Lady Aberdeen backed me splendidly. Up to the north as far as Inverness I carried my fiery torch and everywhere was kindled a fire that burned for many years, as you shall hear.

The success attending my mission in Scotland stirred up my committee to greater efforts. They communicated with the Presbyterian Church in Ireland and also in England. I was invited to both churches. I had time for only a few engagements in these two churches, but the response in every instance amazed and humbled me. I say "humbled me" advisedly. I don't think I acquired a swelled head. I knew quite well that the response from Great Britain was due not to the advocate of the cause, but to the cause itself. It was a cause of magnificent possibilities, not for Canada only but for the Empire and through the Empire for the whole world. For a "wild West," the stamping ground of the "gunman" and the "Vigilance Committee," in Western Canada as in the western half of the United States would have changed the history not of Canada only, but of the Empire and to a certain extent of the whole world.

I do not think this is extravagant talk. The mission work of the Christian churches in the western half of the Dominion together with the marvelous work done in that vast new land by the Northwest Mounted Police—and I add this with the fullest confidence and writing from intimate and personal knowledge of that splendid body of men—created not in the West alone, but throughout the whole Dominion, a mighty force for reverence of law, for orderly government and for national righteousness, whose world influence it would be difficult to overvalue.

In 1895 the General Assembly of the Presbyterian Church in Canada was meeting in St. John, New Brunswick. The moderator is the old war horse from the West, Dr. James Robertson. The reports from the West were quite discouraging. The year before some thirty-eight thousand new settlers had come to the West, hence the duty of the Presbyterian Church to assume its share of responsibility for these newcomers. But funds were low. It would be impossible to maintain the fields already established and to open out the necessary new fields unless more funds were available. It was at this juncture that the Assembly's special deputy to Scotland put in his appearance fresh from the boat.

His appearance is not unexpected, nor is the General Assembly wholly ignorant of the spirit shown by the home churches in Scotland, Ireland and England. But he is not prepared for the gusty welcome accorded him by this revered court. His chief, the superintendent, who is in the chair of the supreme office in his church, that of moderator, gives him warm welcome with that swift downward grip of his. This gives the deputy confidence. Also his friend, Dr. D. J. Macdonnell, has him by the arm and is piloting him through the standing, cheering crowd of "fathers and brethren." Fortunately the rather obvious explanation of all this to-do occurs to him. He is a "hunter home from the hill," and he carries home a quite astonishing bag. Money? Yes, but infinitely more than money, the love, admiration, confidence, gratitude of thousands and tens of thousands of fathers, mothers and kin in the homeland across the seas, to the daughter church that is undertaking their spiritual care in the far, dangerous land of Western Canada. It is this thought that gives the returning deputy his first word as he stands facing that august body. And his nerve too.

"Moderator, well do I know they are not cheering me," I said, sweeping my hand toward the General Assembly, "they are cheering Scotland!" Once more the cheering breaks forth. "And they are cheering you, Moderator, whose great service has made this day possible." Again the Assembly rises to its feet and breaks into louder cheering than ever. It is a lucky inspiration and a fortunate word.

The tale I have to tell is really quite a wonderful tale for I am able to lay upon the table that day the promise of between fifty and sixty thousand dollars from British Presbyterians, in trust for their children in this far-off land. The moderator is deeply moved. He is worn and thin, but his blue eyes are bright as ever and his great voice rings out in its deep burr, and with its old-time passion as he summons his church to renewed consecration and sacrifice.

Seven years more are left him. Seven strenuous years for the country he has served so well from the Great Lakes to the new gold diggings of the Klondike, his last adventure. When those seven years are done we shall look down upon his rugged face quiet in the solemn beauty of death and carry him to the West which he loved and lay him there with that gallant band of old-timers in Old Kildonan, to await his Lord's awaking.

CHAPTER XV

St. Stephen's

AUGUST, 1894, found me settled as a missionary in the western outskirts of Winnipeg, a hustling city fresh from its big boom of '81-'83
with its soaring hopes and prices, its inflated ambitions and real
estate, its vast and daring investments.

Winnipeg was a city of contrasts. A magnificent site for a great
city at the confluence of two historic rivers, the Red and the Assini-
boine, but apart from the shops and stores on Portage Avenue and
Main Street a city of shacks and mud roads. It was the distributing
center for the business of the whole West, but the self-confidence of
its old-time merchants had been so badly shattered by the experience
of the Big Boom that anything like daring enterprise was throttled.
However, at the time of my coming the city was on the eve of a new
development. The western boundary was practically Colony Street,
now a thoroughly downtown section, and my little new mission was
out on the brown prairie where the streets were black trails radiating
in every direction over the prairie, fine for driving in dry weather,
but the rain made them long black lines of impassable bog. By "impassable" I mean that foot passengers were forced to stick to the
wooden sidewalks if they could and all horse traffic was a matter of
speculations. You might, with luck, get through. I have frequently
seen a light unloaded delivery wagon bogged to the axles so that the
horse after being unhitched could with difficulty get himself out of
the viscous mud. But most of the inhabitants were youngsters who
had come west after the city had begun to recover from the boom,
and were full of "pep and git."

My little mission was composed of young people for the most

part with a few old hands to hold us down, the wisest and best of whom was Dr. J. M. King, the principal of Manitoba College, a saint and a scholar, but with a shrewd head for affairs.

The story of St. Stephen's Church is quite a remarkable one. It was my good fortune to be its first minister. The growth of the church was extraordinary. One secret was youth. The city was young, the people young, the minister young. At my first communion in 1894 the roll showed fourteen members. The quintennial record for the first twenty years is an index of its spirit. Here are the figures of its membership: 14, 222, 400, 728, 1,000. Seven times during those twenty years was the church capacity enlarged, at a cost of over $150,-000.

The missionary spirit of its people is indicated in its missionary adventures. In 1903, when its annual revenue was less than $3,000, the congregation with a membership of 333 undertook the building of a beautiful stone church at a cost of over $50,000. In the year following it assumed the support of a foreign missionary in India, and within the next three years established two home mission churches in the western suburbs of the city.

Through these years the social service work of the church in Canada was growing rapidly. In Winnipeg there was an awakening sense of responsibility for the increasing stream of immigrants from Eastern Canada and from Europe as well. To meet this responsibility and to cope with the demands for social service work, St. Stephen's undertook a new building enterprise by erecting at the cost of over $50,000 above the value of the land a Church House on a lot adjoining the church. The Church House soon justified its existence not only by providing accommodation for the senior Sabbath school and various other organizations and also for the many social and club activities, but also by providing temporary living quarters for young men newly arrived in the city.

Its earliest women's organization was a Woman's Foreign Missionary Society, which was followed almost immediately by a home mission organization, carrying the name of the home mission superintendent: The James Robertson Auxiliary.

In addition to the usual Sunday school and Bible classes, two organizations more than any others gave form and color to the life of the congregation. So unique were they that I consider them worthy of more than a passing reference. The first of these was the Brotherhood, an organization of mature men whose primary function was that of discovering and welcoming to the congregation men newly arrived in the city.

A stranger entering the Sunday afternoon meeting of the Brotherhood would find from one hundred to two hundred men assembled. The program is carried through with snap and precision. The chair is held by a layman, not by the minister. He has his own place near by and acts as referee at times when discussion grows hot. First, there are opening exercises, prayer and vigorous singing by the whole company, quartets, solos, etc., being regarded somewhat in the nature of frills and nonessentials. The group in charge of the study period are in control. Every man has his own Bible. The subject is the Life and Teachings of Jesus, with the Mark record as a basis. The discussion is wide open, nothing, no theory, no heresy, is barred. Heretics especially are given the utmost liberty of expression. No one is shocked, or if he is he tries not to show it. The leaders in charge are thoroughly prepared. There is no guesswork, no taking things for granted. The Record is the only authority. What does the Book say? When that is decided, then for that day at least the matter is settled. Many a man in Western Canada dates his intelligent interest in religious truth from the stimulus received in St. Stephen's Brotherhood. Sometimes the lesson for the day is a question bearing upon social, economic or other matters, but there is no spoon-feeding by merely eloquent talkers, uplifters, religious fakirs, emotional rhapsodists.

After the lesson there is a report of cases of sickness, unemployment, absence, marriages, births, deaths. Then strangers are introduced and the members all shake hands with strangers after the close.

The collection is not forgotten.

The final hymn is sung and the meeting "skales," but there is no hurrying away.

The meeting takes an hour and a half or even longer if the argument becomes unduly fierce. But it is a friendly, even jolly hour, a marvelous opportunity for human kindliness and Christian fellowship to operate. The Brotherhood represents the deep religious and social life of the manhood of the church, without which the church would not be St. Stephen's. There are also weekday activities, bowling, baseball and, in winter, curling.

St. Stephen's Club is different. Its members are young people of both sexes, the age limit seventeen to thirty, but "we don't look at their teeth." They meet every Sunday evening in the basement, a cheery room with an open fireplace and a kitchen adjoining. The minister himself runs the meeting. He knows what he wants to get out of it. The program, except in its outline, is generally impromptu. Bores, cranks, exhorters are barred, hot-air artists or humidifiers are courteously but effectively turned off. First a straight twenty minutes of singing, the best we can prepare, choruses, solos, duos, quartets all are welcomed with a word or two from the minister, who handles this half hour. The singing, though bright, is never simply for fun. There is purpose in it and sincerity.

Then comes an interlude and a ritual.

"Stand up! Right turn! Shake hands! Left turn! Shake hands! Now you are all friends! Get acquainted—while we have a cup of tea."

Now comes the characteristic feature of the Club, the introduction of strangers to the minister and to one another. Dan Fraser comes up with a friend, a stranger. "This is Tom Stewart. He comes from Halifax, Nova Scotia. He is not a member of the church yet." Dan backs out and I do my best with Tom Stewart. I find out about his home, his family, his church, his business.

"You're not a member of any church?"

"No!"

"Anything against the church?"

"No, oh, no! Used to go to church every Sunday."

"Never really faced up to it, eh?"

"I guess so."

This is a crucial moment for us both. Everything depends on the boy's look, tone, attitude. Often before the interview is closed the boy has an appointment with me some night next week. If he comes and faces up to the matter of religion and relation to his Lord that boy will be very probably one of the new members at the next Communion. Often it is not so simple. Then I hand him back to Dan Fraser with an injunction, "Look after him, Dan." And in most cases Dan will. There are fifteen or twenty young people who regard it as their job to do the decent thing to the stranger, which is to help him to a right relation to his Lord. For this they receive special training. This

Club is the main gateway for young strangers to enter the church; more, it is the powerhouse of the young congregation for the highest and best things in life. Forty or fifty per cent of the new members each year come to me through the Brotherhood and the Club. Before these organizations began to function ninety per cent would come by mere routine or by the personal touch of the minister, at best a rather haphazard method.

At the end of the hour and a half a jolly, kindly meeting is closed with brief devotions. Too many prayers sometimes kill a good prayer meeting. Some things I learned in that Club. For instance, it is the church, not the minister, through whom the Lord of the church establishes living contacts with the world. It is because this is forgotten that the church has so conspicuously failed to establish among men the Kingdom of God.

St. Stephen's Club is a dominating force in the social, educational, athletic as well as in the religious life of the youth of the congregation. Without St. Stephen's Club, St. Stephen's would be something quite other than it is.

Pre-eminent among the forces tending toward the stimulation of religious life in the congregation was the Woman's Foreign Missionary Society and for the very sufficient reason that the Society by reason of its regular, close and continuous study of the needs of the non-Christian world with all its unhappy and degrading social and moral conditions keeps alive that flame of love and compassion for the needy, the unhappy, the outcast, which is characteristic of the Christian religion.

But in every department of work the energizing power came definitely from the deep spiritual contacts with the eternal verities of our religion.

The demands upon the time and powers of the minister by every department left little for any other kind of work. But there was one field of activity that the minister could not possibly ignore. He kept in touch with the superintendent of missions in the vast and rapidly expanding missions in Western Canada. Year by year the streams of immigration were growing in volume. Hence it came that my first vacation from my congregation I spent in 1896 with the superintendent in an extended tour of our western missions.

Our route took us first through the small new mining centers in the South Kootenay, thence through the Crow's Nest Pass, toward the older settlements in the foothill country.

It is a hard year for the people in that section. For four successive seasons the wheat crops have been destroyed by early frost.

The superintendent's purpose is mainly to hearten and encourage the missionaries and their tiny congregations, to investigate their needs, to advise, stimulate their church boards and officials in the support of their work.

An instance of this last comes to my mind. It was in a little village whose ambitions had outrun its prudence, a not-uncommon situation in this rapidly developing new country. A church had been built, a little manse was in process of construction. Then partial crop failures had checked their activities and discouragement and apathy seemed to have settled down upon the congregation. The superintendent's method of procedure was to hold a public preaching service, after which he discussed the general situation with the congregation and finally had a heart-to-heart talk with the Board of Management. Following this order we found ourselves about 9:30 face to face with the board, the secretary of which presented a most depressing statement as to the finances of the congregation.

"Is your minister's salary paid up?" was the superintendent's first question.

"No! We are behind there," acknowledged the secretary.

"How much? Last year's paid up?"

"Yes, yes," said the minister hurriedly. "I mean just about."

"Of course, we have had bad years, doctor," said the secretary.

"I understand your marsh hay crops were rather above the average," said the superintendent, "and your cattle brought a fairly good price." His intimate knowledge of everything never ceased to amaze me.

"Yes, oh, yes, fair," said the secretary.

"Fair?" The superintendent quoted the prices for hay and for cattle, and actually gave the amounts of hay and the number of cattle disposed of in the district.

The committee sat astounded.

"Have you paid your interest on the loan from the Church and Manse Building Fund?" This is a real touchstone of spiritual life with the superintendent.

"No, we have not," rather truculently replied the secretary. "We thought that under the circumstances that might just stand."

This was too much for the superintendent.

"Sir, the Presbyterian Church is composed of people who make an effort to meet their obligations. The fund is supported by contributions from rich men, but also from ditchdiggers and washerwomen. The fund is a sacred trust from them, and is intended to be expended in the service of those who, but for it, would be deprived of gospel ordinances."

For fifteen minutes he told them stories of how the fund had been raised, with the result that the secretary then and there guaranteed that the interest would be paid and the missionary's back salary would be raised, "before the snow flies, doctor."

Next day we drove through the ranch country where here and there fields of ripening wheat were standing like tiny yellow squares of gold on the vast expanse of tawny rolling prairie.

The superintendent was silent as we drove past these yellow squares. "Too bright! Too bright!" he muttered from time to time, glancing up at the cloudless sky. Throughout that night he rose from his bed beside me and went out to gaze up at the hard moonlit sky. "I'm afraid of it," he would report. "I am very much afraid of it."

Next day we were off on our journey with the bright sun shining down upon us. At the first wheatfield he stopped my horse, ran to the wheat, plucked a few heads and rubbed them out and shook his head again sadly. Again and again throughout the day he repeated his examination. As evening drew near, our anxieties were fully justified, frost had fallen. These beautiful fields, while they might furnish wheat fit for fodder, were useless for the market. To him this blight was a heavier blow than if it had fallen upon his own wheatfields.

That night he was due to address a meeting of farmers and ranchers. A silent and sad-faced group of men met us in the little school building, every man of which had lost the fruit of a year's toil. He had intended making an appeal to these men that this year they should make an effort to reach self-support. Now a new program was necessary. "Gordon, you will take the meeting," he said as we entered the little school. "I have no heart for it."

I read the great words of the Shepherd Psalm.

"The Lord is my Shepherd;
I shall not want"

and made such comment as I could, but in the presence of these grave men it was hard work.

When I had done, the superintendent stepped down from the little platform and stood among them. Never have I seen or heard anything finer in the way of handling a meeting. They might have been members of his own family, as indeed they were. He began with a word of greeting to old friends. He knew them all by name. Then he told them of a new wheat that had been produced which would ripen in ninety days.

"That wheat of yours has been in the ground fully a hundred days," he declared as if he had a grudge against it. "Don't blame God and don't blame the country. Blame the wheat. We will get you better wheat, please God. You have had five years of disappointment. Hold on. Feed your wheat to your beasts. Boil it into porridge for your bairns. It won't be as good as oatmeal"—a grin ran round the glum faces—"but it makes good porridge, I have tried it. Trust in God. Hard times make brave men. It was true of your fathers. It will be true of you." He paused a few moments, letting his eyes rest kindly upon them.

"And remember, you have a great church behind you. Your church won't forget you. We will pay your minister's salary. And behind your church is your Father in Heaven. Remember, the Shepherd brings his flock through the worst storm. I have seen him in old Scotland. So have some of you." By this time their heads were up, their eyes were beginning to shine.

Then as if they were a group of children he prayed with them.

I am not ashamed to say that by this time the tears were running down my face.

"Great, old boy!" I was saying. "God made you for this job! You've done the trick again!"

To see those rugged, hard-faced men crowd about him, shaking his hand, gripping his arms, patting his shoulders, almost putting their arms about him was worth driving a thousand miles. If the "Big

Boys" down East with the money could only see him now, there would be no need to beg them for money for the Home Mission Fund.

It was right on the back of this vacation jaunt that I was sent to Toronto as representative of our Western Home Mission Committee, to meet the General Assembly's Committee in Toronto.

The atmosphere surrounding the committee was heavy with gloom. The magnificent contribution from the homeland had already been absorbed in expansion work. Again the funds were low. The word from the committee was "Halt! Rightabout-turn!"

In vain the old chief told his best tales, pictured in his most glowing colors the splendid heroism of the missionaries of the West and their people. The committee were solid for a halt, if not for retreat. After the meeting I went to see my old college friend, Rev. J. A. Macdonald, the editor of our church paper, the *Westminster Magazine,* later editor of the Toronto *Globe* and by all odds the greatest editor in Canada and one of the greatest in all America.

In Jim Macdonald's sanctum I let myself go. My language, I will confess, would have required editing before publication. I gave him a picture of my recent trip with the superintendent.

"Sit down, Gordon," said Jim. "Be calm!"

It was the wrong word. And for the next fifteen minutes Jim sat listening to my language with evident enjoyment.

"Well, what are you going to do about it?" he asked.

"What are *you* going to do about it?" I shouted at him. "What's that sanctimonious *Westminster* of yours going to do? Westminster! Heavens above, what a name!"

"The name's all right," said Jim.

"Yes, it's a great historic mausoleum for ancient creeds, beautiful rituals, saintly preachers and d-d-"

"No, no, don't say d-d-d-amn."

"You say it then for me."

"You know I can't say d-a-d-amn," which was unhappily true. Jim's stutter always halted him at that word. A serious impediment at times.

"But say, Charles, my boy—I've got it! I've got it! You write me something when you go back to Winnipeg!"

For three years he had been one of my assistant editors on our *Knox College Monthly.*

"Me write? What good would that do? Isn't the superintendent writing all the time?"

"No—no—write me a little personal thing. A story out of your own experience—put it in the form of a yarn! Yes, sir!"

Jim's hands began to go through his shock of red hair. He sprang to his feet and paced the room.

"Charles! I have got it! A story! You remember that thing you did about your first summer in Southern Manitoba. That's it! Promise me! Do it! You'll get your money."

I promised to think about it.

"Think about it? I know you too well. No! Before you leave this room you will give me your word of honor that you will write me a short sketch. I'll put it in my Christmas number."

I promised and left him in a bitter mood. When I reached Winnipeg I was so overwhelmed with back work that any attempt to write my sketch was impossible. Soon I began to get letters from the editor of the *Westminster*—then telegrams—I cursed him in my heart. But one Wednesday night after coming home from my prayer meeting I sat down, took pencil and notebook and at three o'clock Thursday morning I had in my hand: *Christmas Eve in a Lumber Camp.*

With scarcely a word of retouching I sent it to Jim Macdonald.

In a few days a wire came: "Ms. too long for single article. Rewrite. Make it into three."

I was too late for the Christmas number. I went at the thing with more care and deliberation, and in ten days I had a story in three chapters. That story was the beginning of *Black Rock.*

CHAPTER XVI

The Coming of Ralph Connor

BIRTH OF A NAME—INTREPID PUBLISHERS—
RELIGION IN THE NOVEL—THE FLOWERS OF THE
CANYON—SOURCE MATERIAL

BLACK ROCK is an example of that rather rare thing in writing, a successful novel with a purpose. *Black Rock* is really a phenomenon in a way, indeed in several ways. I am too far on in life now, I hope, and moreover I have seen too much of the real things in life to lay myself open to the charge of egotism if I speak frankly about Ralph Connor and his books. When I sent those first three articles to Jim Macdonald I had no more thought of a book in my mind than I have now of flying to the North Pole. Slightly less in fact, for I should dearly like to encircle the pole in an airplane.

My sole purpose was to awaken my church in Eastern Canada to the splendor of the mighty religious adventure being attempted by the missionary pioneers in the Canada beyond the Great Lakes by writing a brief sketch of the things which as clerk of the biggest presbytery in the world I had come to know by personal experience.

When Jim Macdonald received my sketch he found no name attached as author and under the urge of the "printer's devil" he wired me in a frenzy, "What name shall I sign?" Now the choosing of a nom de plume is no easy matter. Desperately I scanned every horizon in my mind for a name, but all in vain. Nothing would come to me. In this crisis my eyes, roving over my desk, lit upon the heading on the note paper I was using as secretary of the British Canadian Northwest Mission, which was abbreviated into the form "Brit.Can.Nor.West Mission." The two contractions in juxtaposition caught my eye. I ran my pencil round them and had Can.Nor. So I wired Macdonald, "Sign article Cannor." The telegraph operator had never heard of such a being as "Cannor," but the Irish cognomen

"Connor" was perfectly familiar to him. Hence the wire reached the editor "Sign article Connor." But this left my editor friend still in a quandary. Everyone would know it was a pseudonym. I can see him with his great hands tearing his shock of red hair as he vainly tried to fit all the Irish names he knew to Connor—"Mike," "Pat," "Terence"! At length straight out of the blue came "Ralph" and thus was born into the world of letters "Ralph Connor"—not an uneuphonious name. I have from the first quite liked it.

The name for the sketch with three chapters was found, but as yet there was no book and no thought of *Black Rock*. After reading the three chapters Macdonald wrote asking for three more. With my characters clearly conscious in my mind and with abundance of material lying at hand this was no difficult task. I sent to my editor three more chapters and followed with a third three. Thereupon Macdonald wrote me saying, "We will make a book." Having decided upon "a book," the next consideration was to find a publisher. With his nine chapters Macdonald went to New York. But America at the moment had slight interest in making books—she was busy making war with Spain. Besides, *Black Rock* would never go in America. It was "too religious," "too temperance." But Jim Macdonald thought he knew better. He determined that he would publish the book in Canada and publish it himself.

This was a daring venture. Few novels had ever been published in Canada, but he decided to risk the thing. But how large an edition? Macdonald was advised by leading Canadian booksellers to risk an edition of 800 copies. But the extraordinary interest which had been aroused in Canada by the nine chapters already published made Macdonald reckless. He determined "to go the whole hog," as he wrote me and publish an edition of 1,000 copies. Before the day of publication the element of risk had vanished. The first edition, I am glad to think, was published in Canada and reached the hitherto unapproached figure of 5,000 copies.

By this time, too, an American publisher had been discovered. In the publishing house of the Fleming H. Revell Company of Chicago there was an enterprising young clerk who was developing a nose for books, George H. Doran by name, a Canadian by birth and a bookman by the gift of God. He had followed the chapters in the *Westminster Magazine* and came to Macdonald with an offer for

Black Rock which, though it was too late now to copyright in the United States, he was eager to publish. Macdonald accepted his offer and thus I came first into touch with George H. Doran who became eventually one of the three greatest publishers in America and one of the best and closest friends I have made during my life. Though he is no longer a publisher I am glad to say he is still one of my intimate friends. Before a year had passed, Jim Macdonald and George Doran's faith in me had been more than justified. *Black Rock* had gone some hundreds of thousands while with *The Sky Pilot,* which followed during the succeeding year, and *The Man from Glengarry,* two years later, the total issue was estimated by my publishers as over five million copies.

I have often tried to analyze the reaction upon my mind of this unique experience. But I have always failed. The comments and criticisms in the magazines and newspapers in both Britain and America were amazingly enthusiastic. I have attempted to explain this reception by a variety of reasons: *Black Rock* and *Sky Pilot* gave an authentic picture of life in the great and wonderful new country in Western Canada, rich in color and alive with movement, the stamping ground of the buffalo and his hunters, the land of the trapper, the Mounted Police and that virile race of men and women, the first pioneers who turned the wild wilderness into civilization. Then, the pictures were from personal experience. I knew the country. I had ridden the ranges. I had pushed through the mountain passes. I had swum my bronco across its rivers. I had met the men—Hi Kendal and Bronco Bill and the rest were friends of mine.

Another cause of the phenomenal editions of these Ralph Connor books, and a very influential cause, was the fact that though in fiction form they possess a definitely religious motif. Religion is here set forth in its true light as a synonym of all that is virile, straight, honorable and withal tender and gentle in true men and women. And it was this religious motif that startled that vast host of religious folk who up to this time had regarded novel-reading as a doubtful indulgence for Christian people. I have received hundreds of letters expressing gratitude for a novel that presented a quality of religious life that "red-blooded" men could read and enjoy.

Of all men, the most surprised at this reception of his books was Ralph Connor himself. He had not the slightest ambition to be a

writer. He made little effort after polished literary style. Things just
came to him and he put them down. Let me give a quite remarkable
instance of that fact. While I was writing *Sky Pilot* it happened that
one Sunday morning I was addressing a congregation of children and
young people on the general topic, "The good that pain can do for
us," a difficult enough problem to deal with. As I was standing before
that gathering of youngsters there flashed upon my mind a picture
of a canyon I knew well in the foothill country and then and there
without preparation I told them the story of "how the canyon got
its flowers":

"At first there were no canyons, but only the broad, open prairie.
One day the Master of the Prairie, walking out over his great lawns,
where were only grasses, asked the Prairie, 'Where are your flowers?'
and the Prairie said, 'Master, I have no seeds.' Then he spoke to the
birds, and they carried seeds of every kind of flower and strewed them
far and wide, and soon the Prairie bloomed with crocuses and roses
and buffalo beans and the yellow crowfoot and the wild sunflowers
and the red lilies all the summer long. Then the Master came and
was well pleased; but he missed the flowers he loved best of all, and
he said to the Prairie: 'Where are the clematis and the columbine, the
sweet violets and windflowers, and all the ferns and flowering shrubs?'
And again he spoke to the birds, and again they carried all the seeds
and strewed them far and wide. But, again, when the Master came,
he could not find the flowers he loved best of all, and he said: 'Where
are those, my sweetest flowers?' and the Prairie cried sorrowfully:
'Oh, Master, I cannot keep the flowers, for the winds sweep fiercely,
and the sun beats upon my breast, and they wither up and fly away.'
Then the Master spoke to the Lightning, and with one swift blow
the Lightning cleft the Prairie to the heart. And the Prairie rocked
and groaned in agony, and for many a day moaned bitterly over its
black, jagged, gaping wound. But the Little Swan poured its waters
through the cleft, and carried down deep black mold, and once more
the birds carried seeds and strewed them in the canyon. And after
a long time the rough rocks were decked out with soft mosses and
trailing vines, and all the nooks were hung were clematis and columbine, and great elms lifted their huge tops high up into the sunlight,
and down about their feet clustered the low cedars and balsams, and
everywhere the violets and windflower and maidenhair grew and

bloomed, till the canyon became the Master's place for rest and peace and joy."

I am not ashamed of that canyon picture. One Sunday night after I had preached to a great congregation in Pittsburgh on the theme, "The Problem of Pain" the minister of the church, after the genial American custom, invited any who desired to come forward and shake hands with the preacher. A thousand people and more passed before me shaking my hand. I remember only one, a girl, piti-fully deformed, who paused before me and holding my hand in both of hers lifted a face pale, and bearing the marks of pain, but radiant and said in a low voice, "Oh, thank you for Gwen!" Then with a quick rush of tears in her eyes, "the flowers are beginning to grow in my canyon too." Of the many hundreds I have received I cherish the canyon letters most. They bring me the love and gratitude of those whose canyons of pain have been brightened with the flowers that bloom only in the canyon.

The Glengarry books, too, received an extraordinary welcome. George Doran has often said to me that it was *The Man from Glen-garry* that won for him his place among American bookmen. His first American edition ran to ninety-eight thousand copies, later edi-tions to many hundreds of thousands. One thing is true of the books. They grew out of Glengarry soil, out of Glengarry humanity. Let me tell you a story which I had from a young Glengarry lad whom I met in Winnipeg some years after the publication of the books.

"Those old Glengarry boys," he said, "believe them as they do the Bible. One old patriarch who in all his life had never read a novel until *The Man from Glengarry* and *Glengarry School Days* said to me, 'I know every man of them fellas except wan and him I cannot place.'

"'But, Mr. McKenzie, you don't think that Ralph Connor is writ-ing about actual people,' I said.

"'And what else would he be doing?'

"'Well, Ralph Connor is a novelist. He just makes up those things, you know.'

"'Makes up them things, is it?' The old gentleman became in-dignant. 'And do you mean to tell me that a meenister of the gospel would be writing lies?' My old friend had not grasped the distinc-tion between a novelist and a liar."

No one ever paid me a finer compliment than Mr. McKenzie.

The material of *The Man from Glengarry,* its color, action, its historic background, its human quality, all account to a certain degree for its extraordinary vogue. But not altogether. The best of the book I drew from the same source as that from which I drew my life. That Highland preacher with his mystic fire, his indomitable courage, his passionate loyalty to Scotland and all that belonged to it, its glens and lochs and purple heather hills, its weird ghost stories, its pibrochs and its Calvinistic theology, had much to do with the making of *The Man from Glengarry.* But the soul of the book, whatever of intellectual quality it has, its response to the appeal of beauty whether of the woods and wild flowers or of the things of the spirit, and all that is best in it Ralph Connor had from the Lady of the Manse. From her, too, he inherited a photographic quality of mind. Let me illustrate.

At the age of ten I left Glengarry with my family. Fifty years later I was driving with a school friend, Johnnie Robertson, north from the eighteenth concession.

"Johnnie, I know this road," I said. "It takes a turn to the left through a swamp about half a mile from here."

"Well," said Johnnie, "the turn is there sure enough but the swamp is gone."

"Yes, and half a mile farther you come to the Brick Church and across the road to the east is Malcolm Fisher's house and beside it old Widdie Matheson's and to the north the little wooden Congregational Church."

"They're there still."

"And going east from the crossroads on the right were the Munroes and beyond them the Sinclairs and across from them Donald Alec used to live and next to him was Dickson's brick yard and beyond him the McNaughtons and the Fergusons."

"Every one right! Man, it's amazing!" exclaimed Johnnie.

And so I went on giving him a perfect photographic reproduction of the whole countryside. That quality, too, helped make vivid the Glengarry books.

Indeed so many persons, places and things entered into the making of those books that Ralph Connor's part seems almost incidental. However, he got hold of the string and "as he pulled the story grew."

CHAPTER XVII

A Very Great American

GEORGE H. DORAN's business brought him into touch with many great
men, for he had a genius for detecting greatness. Most publishers have
had to suffer the humiliating experiences of seeing manuscripts rejected
by them become the world's best sellers, but with Doran this was an
exceptional occurrence. He had to an unusual degree a genius for
making and keeping friends, which is a natural fruit of loyalty. Doran
would go to any amount of pains to help his friends, and such was his
power of organizing results that he seldom failed in his goodwill efforts.
He was a truly amazing man at getting things done. For instance, one
morning when walking down Fifth Avenue with him in company with
W. E. Robertson, apropos of this quality I made the remark to Robertson: "If I asked Doran to get me an elephant, he would say, 'Certainly,
C. W., when do you want him?' and he would produce it on time,
wouldn't you, George?"

"Most certainly, C. W. Want him this morning?"

An extraordinary thing happened. We walked on down Fifth Avenue a few blocks when sure enough what did we see walking up that
great New York thoroughfare but a huge elephant coming to meet us.

"There's your elephant, C. W.," said Doran quietly. "He's slightly
before schedule, but what are you going to do with him?"

Doran was generous in his use of friendships. He was most eager
to have his friends come to know one another. That very morning he
was taking me down to his office to meet Samuel L. Clemens—Mark
Twain—with whom I spent a delightful hour.

"Come in, Robertson, and meet Mark Twain," he said.

"Oh, no, Mark Twain doesn't know me from a hole in the ground.
This is Gordon's show."

"Nonsense, come in, all my friends are my friends' friends," answered Doran with characteristic cordiality. He came in and we had a delightful hour together.

Mark Twain was a clever, droll talker, not one of those professional funny men, but human, sincere and altogether delightful. A little man he was with a great shock of white hair, a huge mustache and strangely youthful face for a man nearing his three score years and ten, and a pair of eyes of extraordinary brilliance.

It was my good fortune to meet many great Americans through Doran's introduction, but by far the greatest of them in many ways was Theodore Roosevelt, who was his warm friend. That meeting is worth recording.

Shortly after the beginning of Roosevelt's second term as president, we were invited through Doran's good offices to meet him at the White House. The President's secretary, who knew Doran well, showed us into the Blue Room.

"You will have to wait some little time, I fear," he said, as he showed us in. "The President has quite a number of appointments this morning. But you may find it interesting to sit here and observe."

"Fine!" said Doran. "We'll have a chance to see the President in action, which will be something worth watching."

And it was.

We sat at one end of the great room with the secretary beside us annotating the proceedings.

First there was shown into the room a deputation of forty or fifty American matrons, gorgeously attired and decked out with garlands of expansive smiles.

"Daughters of the American Revolution," said the secretary, "from the New England states."

A United States senator was making the presentation. But he did not get far, for the president of the Daughters, after being welcomed by Mr. Roosevelt, waved the senator aside and took full charge of the introductions herself, and in a ringing, not to say penetrating, voice presented each matron with descriptive notes as to origin, office, services rendered to the organization, etc., etc.

It looked to me as if we were in for a ceremonial of at least an hour's duration and I whispered my fears to Doran.

"You watch the President get into action," said he. "This is going to be good."

The secretary smiled with confident complacence. I watched and waited.

The President began with great dignity, but with the utmost urbanity, shaking each member warmly by the hand. Soon, however, his warmth and heartiness speeded up the action. The lady in charge of the ceremonial found her descriptive notes cut short by the President's "Dee-lighted to see you," and his quick grip of the hand and as quick reaching for the next candidate, all the time carrying on a running fire of ejaculations, comments, questions, but all the time keeping the procession on the move. Each lady received some special mark of interest and attention. The presenting official was forced to cut short her notes in the gale of hearty, jolly but all the while dignified words of welcome which poured from the President's lips. She found herself reduced to uttering a name with a single comment when the President's welcoming "Dee-lighted to see you" or some other word of recognition or remembrance would crowd the next candidate upon her attention. The scene reminded me a little of a threshing operation on the prairie where the feeder standing in front of his humming cylinder grabs a sheaf from the attendant, shakes it loose and shoves it in with one hand while reaching for the next sheaf with the other.

The Daughters of the Revolution lingered in the Blue Room chatting with the senator and the President.

"I must go now," said the secretary. He moved to the President's side and spoke a few words.

"Ah!" exclaimed Mr. Roosevelt regretfully. "Here is my boss with my marching orders."

In ten minutes more the Daughters had vanished, having taken about thirty minutes of the President's time. Thereupon the President approached us, greeted Doran with great cordiality and then turned to me with both hands outstretched.

"Ah! I know you well, Mr. Connor. I know your country, lived across the line from you for two years. I know your books. I could pass an examination in *Black Rock* and *The Sky Pilot*."

He really was an amazing man. He gave me the feeling that he was genuinely glad to meet me, that he loved my books, and that he knew something about my work in the new wild West country. He became serious and gravely earnest as he spoke of "that big raw West country with its vast possibilities and its perils."

"It's a great country, but it is wild, the 'wild West' all right with its lawlessness and—"

"Lawlessness? Why, Mr. President, the law runs in the western country that I know just as it does in Toronto. I never saw a man offer resistance to one of our Mounties. And what's more I never saw a Mountie pull a gun to enforce the law."

He was intensely interested.

"Never pull a gun in making an arrest? You amaze me! And you have seen men arrested?"

"Yes," I said, "and gunmen, too, from across the line. They do come across, you know, Mr. President."

"Oh, don't apologize. I know them. Splendid chaps, but—wild, wild! But go on. I have a few minutes yet. Your Mounties hold down that country amazingly."

"Hold down? Not exactly. Why, those laddies are rather like dry nurses to the whole community. They are everybody's friend. They look after the sick, they rescue men from blizzards, they pack in supplies to people in need."

"And what about the whisky runners? I understand your Mounties can't be bought," said the President.

"Well, let me give you an instance. There was one of them, Sergeant Bagley, used to sing in my choir and play duets at concerts with me—fiddle and flute, you know. A splendid chap. One day in Calgary a fellow offered him six hundred dollars if he would keep to the west side of the town for an hour, when Number One from the east pulled in. Bagley took the money. When Number One pulled in half a dozen kegs were dropped off and claimed by the bootlegger. Bagley stepped out from behind the car, tapped him on the shoulder, 'Get aboard, McDougall,' he said quietly.

" 'What the devil do you mean?' said the bootlegger. 'Didn't I give you your money?'

" 'Yes, Corporal Finch has it. You ought to go to jail. But you're not a really bad chap. You've just gone rotten for a while. Corporal Finch will see you over the line. My advice is get back to Inverness and start again.'

"The man was absolutely flabbergasted. Without a word he got on board, where he was taken care of by Corporal Finch. Bagley told me six months later that McDougall spoke hardly a word one way or another till he was on the train at Vancouver heading south. Then he said, 'Finch, I've been a damned fool. Tell Sergeant Bagley I'm going to Inverness. But I'll look him up when I come back, you bet.' That's the kind of thing our Mounties consider their business."

Teddy's rugged face was fairly shining.

"Wait here!" he said with warm interest in his voice. "Don't go, Doran. This will take only a few minutes."

This time it was a group of girls in their teens, hair down their backs, really lovely, charming young things, delightfully shy, but eager to show their loyalty and their love for their great President.

The change in the President was amazing. He was like a big brother among a lot of adoring young sisters. He chatted to them, laughed with them, took them by the arm, patted their shoulders, he made jokes and altogether he had the dear sonsie lassies utterly daft about him, all the while moving with them toward the exit door at the other side of the room. The whole reception took about fifteen minutes, but in those fifteen minutes he had bound to his electioneering chariot wheel several million impassioned voters. And the point is that he enjoyed the thing immensely and obviously loved them dearly. And why not? They were all entirely lovable, and they were his people.

Hardly had the bevy of young things disappeared across the lawn before a deputation of quite another quality appeared over the horizon. This consisted of a senator from Montana and with him a big and rather pompous individual. The secretary said a few words to the President, whose face changed instantly. He moved forward to meet the senator with outstretched hand.

"Ha! Senator!" he exclaimed. "Dee-lighted to see you!"

The senator presented his friend.

Cordially, but as if "on guard," the President greeted him, placing him on a chair facing the window and seating himself directly before him.

The senator began explaining his errand in a hurried, rather apologetic manner. I felt that he did not like his job any too well.

Teddy was like one of Dumas's fencers facing two antagonists. He was alert, cheery, but his face was like a bit of rugged granite.

When the senator had finished, the President faced him.

"No!" His voice was like the explosion of a gun. "Impossible!" The big man was evidently pulling himself together for an attack.

"Look here, my dear fellow." Teddy's smile broke through his set face like a gleam of sunlight through a blizzard as he turned toward the senator. For a few minutes he talked with forceful ejaculations and gesticulations. Then turning to the senator's big friend he leaned forward, placed his hand on his knee and began to talk. As he went on he grew more and more intense. Everything about him talked, his eyes, his hair, his hands. The big man had not the ghost of a chance for his scheme. He ventured a protest, but he only tapped a new reservoir of persuasive and compelling speech from the President. The senator ventured a mild suggestion.

"No. No!" The President's explosion was likely to blow him off his chair. "You are wrong, senator! It would never do! You see—" The voice became low, persuasive, friendly. It was soon quite apparent that the deputation was doomed to failure. Whatever it was they were after, I felt it was utterly impossible, that they ought to have been ashamed to ask it. And that is exactly what did happen. The senator became apologetic. He turned on his friend and I am quite sure he said:

"You see! I told you it was impossible."

The big man was glum. The President rose, the deputation rose. The President's hand was through the big man's arm, piloting him toward the door. He was talking in low, confidential tones and with a pleasant smile on his face.

The deputation departed, empty-handed, but apparently quite apologetic for having given trouble and not too bitterly disappointed with the outcome of their visit.

The President's time was exhausted. With many regrets he came to us. "You must bring Connor again to see me, Doran," he said in a tone of profound regret. "We must arrange something, eh? I want to hear about that fellow Bagley."

We went away feeling important and greatly pleased with our visit.

"Doran, he is a wonder!" I said. "Fancy his remembering Bagley's name."

"Remember? If he met you in Timbucto ten years from now he would shout out your name and ask for Bagley."

"No wonder he is president," I said.

"Make no mistake," said Doran. "He is president because no man in America has served his country as he has. He is absolutely honest. You can't buy him and you can't frighten him. He cleaned up New York in 1886, reconstructed the Civil Service Commission in 1899. Some job! Reorganized the navy in 1897."

"And now he is on the way to clean up the United States," I said. "I don't envy him his job."

"Watch his smoke," said Doran. "He'll do it."

Roosevelt made a magnificent start at that job. But that is another story.

CHAPTER XVIII

The Fight for a Clean Country

LAW ON THE FRONTIER—THE CHURCH IN POLITICS—BLOOD AND THUNDER—SPIKED GUNS

IN THE great resounding nineties the tides of life were flowing strong and free. Every spring the railroads continued to pour out at every station floods of immigrants, who with their weird bundles and boxes disappeared over the prairie's rim to form new settlements as best they could. These settlers became the care of two great nation-building institutions: the church and the famous Royal Northwest Mounted Police. These two forces worked together in mutual understanding and with a common purpose to aid these new settlers, strange to the new country, unprepared to deal with new conditions and hardships and perils, to establish themselves in safety and in comparative comfort. In the western territories they joined in a common effort to protect settlers from the cattle and bronco rustlers and whisky runners from "across the line."

In the Province of Manitoba law and order were in charge of the provincial police operating directly under the government. The social life of Manitoba in the early nineties was unhappily largely under the domination of a very powerful liquor ring, which in turn exercised a powerful influence over the government liquor policy. Drinking habits had gained a dangerously strong hold over the people in the urban communities and in many cases throughout the rural districts. The churches and temperance organizations vainly tried to limit the operations of the liquor dealers, seeking to secure the legislative enactments known as the "Local Veto" and "Banish the Bar" laws.

The church was so closely associated with the life of the new settlers, so eagerly devoted to their material as well as their spiritual wellbeing, that it soon found itself in direct opposition to the government in its liquor policy and to its laissez-faire attitude toward commercialized vice. Unfortunately, the reform forces were lacking in cohesive unity, while the government forces, political, social, commercial, were a disciplined and compact unit. The Reform forces were divided by demoninational differences, by different theories in regard to method and extent of temperance reform. For some time the Anglican Church leaders held aloof from other Protestant churches and the various temperance societies in their fight against the liquor interests which supported the government party. Gradually, however, the bitter experience of successive defeats forced the party of Reform into a solid and disciplined fighting force. The first definite and effective move toward solidarity was taken in 1907 by the General Assembly of the Presbyterian Church, when its Committee on Temperance, Social and Moral Reform, impatient with the lack of cohesive and definite action in the church memorialized the General Assembly asking for a consolidation of the various committees. The result was the creation of a Board of Social and Moral Reform, through whose agency there was set up an interdenominational body, representative of all the Protestant churches in Canada and those of organized labor as well. This body was known as the Moral and Social Reform Council of Canada. This was recognized as a decided step forward. The Moral and Social Reform Council, or the Social Service Council, as it came to be called, united into one solid phalanx the Protestant churches, the labor organizations, the various temperance bodies, the farmers' institutes and associations and other bodies whose aim was the building of a cleaner and better country. Of this organization the minister of St. Stephen's Church was asked to become president. It meant time and work, and what with his congregation and his writing and all that that involved he had little enough time and strength to spare for a fight with the liquor forces entrenched behind the impregnable defenses of the Conservative party. He had no illusions about the nature of the fight. It would be bitter, dirty and ruthless.

His church put him into it by electing him convenor of the Assembly's Committee on Social and Moral Reform, which led to his being chosen president of the Social Service Council for the Province of Manitoba. He consulted his session. All its members were sturdy temperance and antivice men. They promised to back him if he went in for the fight. It was a question largely of time and strength.

The Brotherhood really decided the matter. The question of temperance and commercialized vice came up for discussion at a Sunday afternoon meeting. There was a considerable opinion that the church should keep out of party politics. A sturdy and steady Scot, an elder and shrewd businessman, had been studying the question for weeks. He settled the question of the church's relation to policies by reading from the last Report of the General Assembly's Committee on Social and Moral Reform, which set the General Assembly of the Presbyterian Church squarely behind the Manitoba program of Local Veto, Banish the Bar, Government Control of Liquor, and the utter extermination of Commercialized Vice.

"It seems simple enough," said the Scottish elder quietly: "the question as to the attitude of church officials and church members toward politics evidently is settled. The General Assembly is definitely opposed to any party that opposes local veto, refuses to banish the bar, and to wipe out professional prostitution. Our choice is either to oppose the Conservative party in Manitoba or to oppose the General Assembly. No loyal Presbyterian can do the latter."

I accepted the presidency of the Social Service Council and entered the bitterest fight of my life; it lasted for another ten years, costing time, money, strength, friendships, and brought upon me the most ruthless slander, vilification and scurrilous abuse that any public man in Canada was ever called upon to endure. At two successive provincial elections the Reform forces were beaten hopelessly. As the third contest approached, the Reform forces were immensely strengthened by the loyal affiliation of the Roman Catholic Church leaders with the Social Service Council. This was an immense gain.

The chief difficulty came finally to be the wavering and uncertain attitude of the leaders of the Liberal party on the questions of temperance and moral reform. While violently condemning the policy of the government in power and promising in general terms an advanced and enlightened temperance policy, and while individual Liberal leaders were members of the Social Service Council and were supporters of its platform, the party officials refused definitely to put into the campaign platform the three planks of the Social Service Council: Local Veto; Banish the Bar; Government Control of Liquor. To take this extreme attitude was bad tactics. The thing to do was, first, "turn out the rascals" and then trust the Liberal party to put into operation an advanced and enlightened social and moral reform policy.

In the most desperate stage of this conflict an incident occurred which brought the minister of St. Stephen's a certain amount of notoriety and inconvenience.

In the summer of 1914 a by-election for the provincial legislature supervened in the town of Portage la Prairie. The government forces were in desperate straits and in their distress summoned to their aid the newly appointed and brilliant Solicitor General for the Dominion, the Honorable Arthur Meighen, an able campaigner and exceedingly popular in his home town of Portage la Prairie. I was at this time holidaying and resting after a strenuous year's activity in literary, political and religious work at my island home in the Lake of the Woods. I received a wire followed by a letter summoning me to the front line of battle. Mr. Meighen hurried up from Ottawa, called at the Conservative headquarters in Winnipeg, got into touch with the editorial staff of the Winnipeg *Telegram,* a peculiarly venomous and unscrupulous news sheet, the mouthpiece of the government, whose editor had made it his special metier to empty the inkpots of his office over my person.

Filled up with material supposed to be of a peculiarly devastating character, Mr. Meighen proceeded to Portage la Prairie, opened his campaign with a most violent attack on my unfortunate person as president of the Social Service Council of Manitoba. In addition to a bitter condemnation of my general wrong-mindedness in this campaign, he made three specific charges against me personally.

Mr. Meighen was at once challenged by an official of the Social Service Council present at the meeting, and was dared to make the charges in the presence of the gentleman he was vilifying.

Mr. Meighen promptly accepted the challenge. A date was fixed for the meeting in Portage la Prairie.

All this was reported to me in my island retreat by the secretary of the Social Service Council, Mr. W. W. Buchanan, who insisted on my appearing at the time and place appointed.

Much disgusted, I wrote to the secretary denying the charges as ridiculous and declining to ruin my holiday by rushing through the July heat to meet such preposterous statements. Letters and wires came in swift succession, beseeching, demanding my presence. Therefore, on a blistering July day I found myself on the platform of a packed hall in the little town of Portage la Prairie with the able and indefatigable Mr. Buchanan in the chair, awaiting the appearance of my accuser, the Honorable Arthur Meighen, Solicitor General of the Conservative government in Ottawa. A few minutes after the hour the gentleman entered the hall, a small black brief case in his hand, and walked toward the platform.

Immediately a solid block of the audience occupying the center of the hall rose and broke into wild cheering, which continued till Mr. Meighen had taken his seat. So far as the audience was concerned, there was no doubt as to who was who.

The chairman made a statement explaining the purpose of the meeting and invited Mr. Meighen to repeat in my presence the charges he had made in my absence or to withdraw them with appropriate apologies.

Loud and ribald laughter rose from the center block at the suggestion of withdrawal.

Mr. Meighen began with an expression of regret that it had been his misfortune to be the one to make these damaging charges, but in the interests of truth and of decency in public life he had been forced to do what he felt was his duty. He deeply regretted the necessity, all the more because he was a graduate of the same high school and of the same university as Dr. Gordon, whom he had always held in high regard. He would welcome any statement from Dr. Gordon that might possibly clear up this painful matter.

Immediately I rose and said:

"I understand that Mr. Meighen in this hall made certain definite charges which impugn my character as a minister of the Presbyterian Church, and my honor as president of the Social Service Council. I am ready to hear Mr. Meighen acknowledge these statements as false and slanderous and make public apology for his disgraceful conduct in making them."

The uproar from the center block was immediate and terrific.

The chairman succeeded in restoring order and called upon Mr. Meighen.

He deeply regretted the necessity that forced him to do what he was now forced to do, but he had a duty in this matter which he must perform.

First Charge. Collusion with Liberal leaders in this campaign and planning with them to overturn the Roblin government. Dr. Gordon was well known as a Liberal in politics, using his office and his position as president of the Social Service Council to defeat the Conservative government. The evidence from the public press was enough to make good this charge, but he had personal testimony from gentlemen whose names he would submit to the chairman as to the truth of his charge of partisanship and collusion with leaders of the Liberal party. To the chairman he handed a list of names.

Cheers, wild and excited, from the center.

Dr. Gordon's friends were ominously silent.

Second Charge. He presented a more serious charge, challenging Dr. Gordon's honor as a gentleman, his integrity as a minister of the Presbyterian Church and his sincerity as president of the Social Service Council of Manitoba. The charge was that when acting as chairman of the committee arranging the program of the last annual meeting of the General Assembly of the Presbyterian Church, Dr. Gordon had used his influence as chairman of the committee and his great personal influence to prevent the Rev. Dr. John Pringle, a greatly respected and loved missionary of the Presbyterian Church, recently returned from the Klondike, from making a speech on the floor of the Assembly, because Dr. Pringle in letters to the press had openly condemned the liquor policy of the Liberal government, in that Far North country, and had declared his intention of bringing this matter to the Assembly's attention. Dr. Gordon, actuated by his partisan prejudices, had prevented the missionary from securing a hearing from the General Assembly.

The *Third Charge* was an equally serious charge, indeed in one sense an even more serious charge. He charged that, though Dr. Gordon on the public platform had denounced the liquor traffic as sinful and debasing to public and private life, though he was president of the Social Service Council of Manitoba, whose mission it was to utterly destroy the liquor traffic in Manitoba, yet this same gentleman had invested money in a hotel in this province, from which investment he was now drawing a dividend. In proof of this, Mr. Meighen held up a check and handed it to the chairman, who scanned the check with noncommittal face. Then the speaker passed the check to me, saying:

"Your signature, doctor?"

I bowed, acknowledging my signature.

Dead, solemn silence.

"This is all very painful to me," continued Mr. Meighen, "but knowing these facts, I felt I must do my duty and reveal them to the people of this province who have been led to believe that Dr. Gordon is a sincere temperance worker and an honored minister of the Presbyterian Church."

The center block rose in wild cheering, hurling at Dr. Gordon insults and gibes, and began to move en bloc from the hall.

At once I stepped to the front of the platform and called to them.

"Sit down, you cowards! if you have any sense of British fair play. Give me ten minutes and I'll prove your man a fool or a liar, or both. Sit down. Show a little sense of decency."

Immediately the uproar ceased, the center block hesitated, wavered, then sat down still laughing and jeering. Mr. Meighen took his seat at the back of platform in silence. I also took my seat. When silence had fallen, the chairman said:

"I have no knowledge of what Dr. Gordon is going to say, but I know the man, and I want to assure you, gentlemen, that when he has finished what he has to say your representative will be ashamed."

I stepped to the front of the platform, stood looking at the center block for a few minutes.

"First, let me say that I am sincerely sorry for Mr. Meighen. I have watched his career with great interest, a career of great promise, but if this is a sample of his character and method I predict for him a brief career."

They listened in utter silence.

"Now, as to the first charge. I confess that I had many conferences with the Liberal leaders, who in this province naturally were anxious to secure the support of the Social Service Council in the coming provincial elections, and whose support I was anxious to secure for the program of the Social Service Council in the coming elections."

"Oh! Of course, you were!"

"The conference, I regret to say, was a failure. I tried to get the Liberal leaders to accept the platform of the Social Service Council. They refused. I had to inform them that in that case the Social Service Council could not support the Liberal party at the coming election, that not a single Liberal voter who was a member of the Social Service Council would vote for the Liberal party, because we had his signed pledge to that effect, in which case the Conservative government would very likely be returned to power."

At this point a voice inquired, "You believe the present Conservative government is corrupt?"

"Thoroughly so."

"Yet you are planning now to put them back in power. Nice patriot you are."

It took just a moment for this to soak in, then the whole center block again rose in wild cheering, certain that they had me one way or the other.

I held up my hand.

"I would regard it as a calamity to have the Conservative party returned to power but—"

Yells— "But you're putting them back."

"But it would be an infinitely greater calamity to elect a Liberal government and have it sell us to the liquor interests in this province, as the present Conservative government is selling this country."

Dead silence for a moment. Then for the first time during that hour our friends on the side aisles and our friends on the platform rocked the building with cheering, which expressed a long pent-up emotion.

"How does that suit you? If the country is to be sold out again to the liquor interests, I'd rather you'd do it than that the Liberal party should."

Again our friends tore the air to ribbons, the center block sitting in glum and puzzled silence.

"Now for the second charge: my partisan action in preventing my very good friend Dr. Pringle from addressing our General Assembly lest he might expose the iniquities of the Liberal government in their liquor policy in the Klondike. You'd like to hear about that, wouldn't you?"

"Oh, go on!" cried the center block.

"Ten minutes will do for me on this, and then you and your champion will be wishing to heaven he had kept quiet.

"Oh, go on!" "Shut up!"

"Listen! It is true, I was convenor of the General Assembly's program committee. It is true that the suggestion was made that our missionary from the Klondike, Dr. Pringle, should speak. It is true that this was opposed on the ground that it would be highly improper and unwise to discuss political issues on the floor of the Assembly."

Cries of "Oh, oh! Terrible thing!" "Never do!" with derisive laughter from the center.

"But you will be sorry to learn I insisted that public morality demanded that the matter should be discussed upon the floor of the General Assembly. Still the committee opposed me. They wouldn't agree to make a bear garden of the General Assembly."

"Oh, no! Too holy, eh?"

"Do you know what happened then? You will be sorry to learn. It is really quite sad! Mr. Meighen will be sorry to learn."

"Oh, go on!"

"Well, what happened was this. A member of the committee rose and said, 'If you decline to ask this missionary to address the Assembly, I myself from the floor of the Assembly will demand that Dr. Pringle be heard, and you know I shall carry the Assembly in spite of you.' Then they consented. Dr. Pringle did address the Assembly. Now, who was that member that forced the committee to allow Dr. Pringle to address the Assembly? You will be sorry to learn. Mr. Meighen will be grieved to learn. Do you know who it was?"

Breathless silence.

I leaned out over that center block tapping my breast and said gently with a smile: "It was this man."

There was a moment's silence and then some of the friends of the defense went on riot.

When silence was finally restored, I once more took up my story.

"Now as to that check. I'm sorry for you," I said, leaning out toward that silent and humiliated center block. "I'm beginning to be sorry for the Solicitor General of the Dominion. I used to admire him greatly. I once predicted a great future for him. Today I'm not so sure. Too bad he has such a bunch of liars and slanderers for his friends and too bad he was fool enough to listen to them."

Not a word from the center block, not a murmur, dead silence.

"Now about that check—do you really want to hear about it?"

"Yes," yelled the side aisles. "Give 'em their medicine! Go on! Do 'em good!"

"Well, that is my check." I said in a sad and deprecating voice, "I am sorry to say I did make a mistake that time. I'm sorry, but we all make mistakes. I had some money. I was offered some shares in a hotel at a low price. I took them."

The center block brightened up greatly.

"Aha! Nice minister! Fine temperance man!"

"The hotel needed the money."

Ironic cheers from the center.

"It was a hotel in Neepawa."

A chilly silence fell.

"Let me tell you about it. It was a temperance hotel, built to meet the needs of the town of Neepawa, when a local veto vote closed the drink shop and your liquor party refused to play the game, but did their best to keep the traveling public away from the town and kill its business. The temperance people built a temperance hotel. I put my money into it. The hotel failed, I regret to say, you killed it. The check which Mr. Meighen showed you was not a check of dividends. It was salvage from the temperance hotel wrecked by the liquor interests, who were not sports enough to accept the vote of their fellow citizens and play the game. I am sincerely sorry for Mr. Meighen. His own people must have lied to him. Sold him up, exposing him to the contempt of all honorable men. That's the kind of thing the liquor interests will do. What do you think of your party? That's the way it sells out its friends!"

There was no cheering—a deadly silence held all parties.

Mr. Meighen was so completely overwhelmed with surprise and humiliation that without a word to me or to any man on the platform he left the building by a side door. The liquor candidate was swamped in the election that followed.

"It was that blankety-blank speech of Meighen's did it," said the organizer of the Conservative party for Portage la Prairie to me some weeks afterwards in Winnipeg.

But within four weeks a sound was heard which stilled all other sounds. It was the tap of a drum. The next time I saw Mr. Meighen was at a great meeting of the Canadian Club in Winnipeg assembled to hear the Solicitor General of the Dominion set forth what the government considered to be Canada's duty in the World War. It was a noble speech. I went home and wrote a letter of appreciation to Mr. Meighen. He replied warmly and gratefully. We have been the best of friends ever since.

CHAPTER XIX

Return to the Highlands

IN 1913 the General Assembly did me the honor of naming me as a delegate to the Pan-Presbyterian Council in Aberdeen. With its usual generosity my congregation extended my summer vacation some weeks
and in consequence my wife and I found ourselves the guests of Dr.
George Adam Smith, Hebraic scholar, brilliant author of the *Historical
Geography of the Holy Land,* and principal of the ancient and honorable University of Aberdeen.

The appointment involved a special speech before the delegates to
that world-wide organization for the preservation of the marvelous body
of Christian dogma promulgated by John Calvin of Geneva.

With my speech out of the way, we felt more or less free to enjoy
or suffer speeches from other delegates, to renew our acquaintances with
the "diamond-studded," granite city of Aberdeen and its Deeside en-
virons, and more especially to luxuriate in the hospitality and delightfully human atmosphere of one of the most "homelike homes" in all
bonnie Scotland.

George Adam, as his friends affectionately name him, is a great
scholar, a famous preacher, an educator of note. But the guests who sat
about his dinner table will, I venture to say, remember him chiefly as a
prince of storytellers. He was a master of the dialects of both Highland
and Lowland Scots.

One such gathering is vividly present to my memory. Some half
dozen Pan delegates, an old retired dominie of the famous Aberdeen
Academy for Boys, George Adam, his fine lady who was his able abet-
tor in anything he set out to do, my wife and myself constituted the
dinner party.

171

We had hardly finished the soup when George Adam "cracked yin." After due allowance of time for the laugh to subside, the auld dominie matched him and the game was on. Two American professors, no mean adepts in the taletelling art, made contributions, I modestly brought forth my most effective Royal Georges. But before the roast was finished, all lesser lights were dimmed and these two, the principal and the dominie, were alternately flashing their headlights upon us till we were reduced to a mere speechless and breathless audience, waiting for the next.

Mr. H. V. Morton in his fascinating book *In Search of Scotland* has a cleverly diverting chapter on the Joke Exchange in Aberdeen. Had Mr. Morton been present at dinner that night he would have done the best chapter in his book under some such caption as "The Doctor Dings the Dominie," or vice versa. We had reached the nuts and raisins when our hostess, with a sensitive conscience, managed to catch the eye of my lady, endowed with a conscience even more tenderly sensitive. But before the signal for departure could be given, George Adam exclaimed "Did you ever hear of the Highland elder who—" and everybody sat down again. The dominie, like a hound on the scent, could hardly give time for a decent interval till he had matched his host with another so pungent that not a lady's eye could be caught by the hostess. It was nine o'clock when one of the American delegates ventured an inquiry as to the Pan program for the evening. It was discovered that the really worth-while speech of the evening, by a distinguished Continental professor of comparative religions, had been set for 8:30.

"Too bad!" exclaimed George Adam penitently.

"Well," drawled one of the American delegates, "I haven't had such a whale of a time since my graduation dinner, and if there's any more stuff on tap like what we've had I'm all for it."

"Oh, that reminds me—just this one, my dear—did you ever hear of the American going out to his first shoot with the Highland gillie?"

"Say! He's away again! Let her bust, Principal," said the American. And George Adam "let her bust" with the auld dominie in hot pursuit.

The Pan-Presbyterian Council closed its various sederunts with due formalities. The principal of the University of Aberdeen made a most valuable and learned contribution to the obsequies of which the delegates would doubtless make full report to the various bodies which they represented. But I have little doubt that what will live most vividly with these same delegates who were present at the dinner in the home of the president of the university will not be his address before the Pan.

My wife and I spent a happy week with Lord and Lady Aberdeen at their beautiful home near Aboyne. To me they were old and dear friends of Banff days and at the Coldstream ranch in the Okanagan valley of British Columbia. Our closest fellowship, however, we had enjoyed during their residence in Canada when for two successive terms Lord Aberdeen was Governor General. In those days he had made it his custom to attend my little frame church in Winnipeg on the occasions of his official visit to that city.

The House of Cromar is not a great castle. It is a simple, homelike mansion but in its setting of hills, forest and lake possesses a restful charm. We were the only guests and from the moment we entered the door were made to feel that we were members of the family. Indeed, Lady Aberdeen insisted that we were, being of the Clan Gordon. We had the rare opportunity of coming into close touch with an aspect of Scottish life that few Canadians have had the privilege of knowing. We saw the Highland chief among the people of his own clan. I confess to being something of a radical. Furthermore, the traditions of the Glengarry folk, dispossessed from their native glens, among whom my childhood days were spent were not such as to waken any feeling of loyalty or affection in my heart for the aristocracy of Scotland. But our days spent in the home of the Aberdeens at Tarland opened to me a new world of social relationships. It had been a hard year in that part of Scotland. Crops had been a failure and the prices for cattle and sheep were low. From the factor of the estate I heard tales of the laird's attitude toward his tenants that gave me some new opinions in regard to class relationships in the old land. Laird and tenant are of the same blood. Every clansman is cousin to the chief.

The spirit of this home is democracy of a very simple and also very beautiful type, a type that some Canadians apparently could not understanding during the Aberdeen regime. But whether at Coldstream or at Ottawa or at Dublin the spirit was always the same, a frank recognition of the worth of humanity and a simple and courageous attempt to serve humanity. Best of all, they found in their life a flowing spring of joy in giving joy to others.

After dinner we would talk and sing and tell stories—at least Lord Aberdeen told stories. He ran a neck-and-neck race with George Adam as a teller of Scottish tales and he told them with a racy touch of pawkiness that even George Adam might envy. Jolly evenings they were, free, full of kindly fellowship that is the very heart of happy living. No spot in all the world holds for us kindlier and happier memories than the House of Cromar.

A curiously interesting aftermath came to us immediately after we had concluded our stay with the Aberdeens. We were going on a visit to a friend up Glen Lyon way. It was from Glen Lyon, by the way, that the murderous Campbells stole out one black night to perpetrate, what is regarded not only by Scots but by all decent people of any land as the vilest act of treachery recorded in any history, the massacre of the Macdonalds of Glencoe. We drove past Glen Lyon House where the final details of the bloody deed had been perfected, till we came to a grassy road which ran past a wee stone cottage, a mere "but and ben," beside a little singing burn. We were searching for an ancient mill, the Eonan Moulin, the last remnant of what had been a great monastery with its gardens and clustering huts about it. At the door of the cottage stood a tidy and comely-faced woman of whom we inquired the path to the ancient mill. "You will be wanting the Eonan Moulin?" she said in her soft Highland voice.

"Yes, we want to see the old mill."

"The mill is interesting, but the walls of the old monastery can be traced, and the millrace. You will go through the gate yonder and follow the path."

We thanked her and followed the path. It was a most interesting ruin, and we explored it thoroughly. But just as we were taking our departure my eye fell upon a half circle of stone hidden under moss.

"What's this?" I cried in a fearful ecstasy. "It can't be! But it is! It's the old millstone!" We dug away the turf and there it lay, the ancient millstone with which hundreds of years ago the monks had ground the meal for their porridge, and doubtless for the porridge of the whole clachan as well. It was a glorious find.

We returned by the path and through the gate to the road, and saw waiting at her door our Highland lady now in her decent Sabbath blacks, with white collar and cuffs, her hair waved from the forehead, and altogether looking the fine lady she was.

"You found the mill?" she asked, coming toward us.

"We did indeed; more than that, we found the old millstone."

"Ah, I am glad you found that. It was my husband dug it out some two or three years ago. He wrote to the papers about it but nothing was done. It is a peety."

"It's a shame!" I said with indignation. "And when I get to Edinburgh I shall certainly see that something is done."

"Och aye! They will listen to Ralph Connor, I doubt," she said, a smile parting her lips.

"And how do you know Ralph Connor, pray?" I asked.

"Oh, my husband brought back a paper with him from Aberdeen," she said and hurrying into the house she brought out an Aberdeen paper carrying a picture of Ralph Connor.

"He heard your speech at the council."

"Your husband? At the council?"

"Oh, aye!" she replied, modestly covering her face with confusion. "He is an elder, Donald McLeod is his name, and he was chosen as a representative from this glen to the council. And he heard you."

At this a daughter appeared, a lovely dark-eyed girl, quite smartly dressed.

"Oh, yes," continued the mother, "but he likes Ralph Connor better than he does the Rev. Dr. Charles Gordon. Bring the books, Jessie."

"Oh, mother!" exclaimed the girl and ran into the house. She came back with copies of *Black Rock, The Sky Pilot* and *The Man from Glengarry* and handed them to her mother.

"There! You can see, they have been up and down the glen. And Jessie was wondering if Ralph Connor would be so good as to put his name in the books."

"Now, mother, you know quite well it was yourself that suggested it," said Jessie. "Not that we would not all be pleased. Will you come in?"

We went into the wee house; it was neat as a pin, with an open fireplace and on the "sweigh" a kettle singing. Here and there were hanging bunches of heather and broom, in the corner a bookcase holding the English poets from Shakespeare to Keats, and on the table in another corner a family Bible, a *Concordance* and *The Pilgrim's Progress*.

I wrote my name in Ralph Connor's books, keenly conscious of the honor done me, and I said so. While I was poking about examining the contents of the bookcase I caught fragments of a conversation between Mrs. McLeod and my wife, who has the rare gift of getting into the hearts of people. They were exchanging confidences about their families, Jessie meantime setting out the tea things.

Such a tea. Scones with butter and honey and black currant preserves and tea! Why is it that you nowhere else get tea such as they give you in the cozy homes of the Scottish people?

"You are not of the Clan Campbell," I said.

"No, we are not Campbells," said Mrs. McLeod quietly.

"We came past Glen Lyon House where the massacre was planned," I ventured.

Suddenly it was as if a curtain had been drawn down over a window.

"Of course, that was a long time ago," I added.

"Yes, it was a long time ago. There are things in Scotland's history we like to forget," said Mrs. McLeod, and something in her tone seemed to forbid further reference to that ghastly crime. "And indeed the Campbells have done for Scotland and for the Empire much to redeem their name," she added.

"Sir Colin," I said quickly, "at Lucknow."

"Yes, at Lucknow, and wherever the tartan has waved on Britain's battlefields," she added with a proud lift of her head.

I accepted the rebuke. With these folk the massacre of two hundred years ago and more was still an old wound that hurts under a rough touch. They were not Campbells, but they were now in the homeland of the Campbells, and a Campbell was their chief. I took my rebuke and turned back to the ancient Eonan Moulin in the lore of which our hostess was an authority.

"Is there anything published about that ancient monastery?" I asked.

"Not much except in some of the *Annals* in the Edinburgh Public Library."

"And in some of the songs of local bards," said Jessie with a little laugh.

"Now then, Jessie!" said the mother. "She is making fun of me. Well, bring it then."

And Jessie from "ben the hoose" brought out a leaflet bearing a poem of some dozen verses.

"It is something her father did in his idle moments," said the mother with a smile of mingled pride and apology.

I glanced at the lines.

"Read them to us," I said, knowing well that from her lips the lines would carry something I could not get from them.

She handed them to Jessie, who strenuously demurred.

"Read them yourself, mother. You know them by heart and can do them better than I can."

"Do please, I should love to hear them."

With a little flush on her cheeks, but without any further fuss or apology, the mother recited the lines, her soft Highland tone and accent lending them a beauty and wistful charm far beyond anything I could have drawn from them.

We said good-bye to these people as if to old and dear friends. What a country! And what a people! In what other land in all the wide world, among the humble cotter folk, could be found a home where gentle manners, cultivated minds and self-respecting dignity could redeem poverty from all the sordid meanness, the narrow outlook, the unhappy misery that are its usual accompaniments? Here in this two-roomed turf-covered cot lives a workingman, who is chosen to represent his church in a council whose members represent the highest scholarship and the finest Christian culture to be found in the world, and with him two women whose quiet self-respecting dignity, whose mental and spiritual attainments would fit them to mingle on terms of equality with the highest in the land. Scotland! The old bard of Ayr had it right:

> From scenes like these old Scotia's grandeur springs,
>   That makes her loved at home, revered abroad;
> Princes and lords are but the breath of kings:
>   "An honest man's the noblest work of God."

Robert Burns, poet of the people, champion of the rights, the dignity, the worth of the common man! And John Knox, to whom among other things the Scottish people owe the Scottish home, the Scottish school and the Scottish kirk. Other peoples have their worth. Let those who know them tell their story.

CHAPTER XX

Embattled Ladies

BRITISH FIGHT FOR WOMAN SUFFRAGE — SYLVIA
PANKHURST — CAT AND MOUSE LEGISLATION — A
QUAKER HOUSEHOLD — HYDE PARK — SIDNEY AND
BEATRICE WEBB

No PLACE in all the world is of such absorbing interest to a Britisher as London. If you remain long enough in that center of the world you will meet, if you have the luck of introductions, some of the most interesting people in the world and witness some of the most interesting scenes in the world.

After our visit to Scotland we went to London and spent some days "doing" that mighty city. One particular Sunday remains vivid in my memory. In the forenoon I was due to preach in Whitefield's old Tabernacle. A little incident occurred that I always take pleasure in relating, as it affords an example of one of the rare occasions on which I rather "put one over" on my wife. The church was packed to the doors. We were taken to the vestry where we met the minister, who gave us cordial welcome.

"Will you kindly see that Mrs. Gordon has a good seat, where she can see and hear well?" I said to one of the church officials. He hesitated just an instant, then brightened up and said, "Oh, most certainly. Come with me, Mrs. Gordon."

After we had agreed upon the order of service I was escorted by the minister to my place in the pulpit and I began to look for my wife. Every seat was taken. Chairs were crowded about the Communion rail. I could see her nowhere.

"I wonder where they have placed Mrs. Gordon," I said. "I can't see her anywhere."

The minister immediately began an anxious search of the front seats.

"I can't see her," he said, standing up to scan the crowded seats about us.

"I'm here, Charley!" said a meek voice near me. I turned sharply and there she was behind me on the pulpit seat, with a delighted and mischievous grin on her face.

"Hello! How in the mischief did you get up here?" I asked.

"The wretched creature told me to follow him and before I knew he had me up here," she said in great indignation. "But if you preach too long I'll pull your coattails."

I fear my devotional mood was slightly disturbed.

That afternoon I witnessed a thrilling and amazing scene illustrative of the British manner of enforcing police regulations for the maintenance of public order. My friend and Canadian publisher, W. E. Robertson, successor to J. A. Macdonald as editor of the *Westminster*, called at our hotel and told me that Miss Sylvia Pankhurst was to address a public meeting in Trafalgar Square in the interest of woman suffrage. Sylvia Pankhurst, the daughter of the heroic little pioneer of woman suffrage in Britain, Mrs. Emmeline Pankhurst, was at the moment under arrest for some violent and lawless exhibition of her devotion to the cause which she represented as the honorary secretary of the Woman's Social and Political Union in Britain. She had just come through one of her nineteen hunger strikes, and for some days had been living in freedom but under police supervision, recovering health and strength, preparatory to another prison term. Today was her last day of freedom, and she had decided to signalize her return to prison by a last appeal to the British public for what she believed to be the rights of British women. It promised to be a meeting worth seeing, so we took our way to Trafalgar Square.

It was still about three-quarters of an hour before the time of the meeting, so we moved about admiring the lions couchants at the corners of the base of the immense column carrying the figure of England's greatest admiral gazing out to sea. Five of London's busiest streets converge upon the square, which is flanked on all sides by noble structures, great shops, churches, banks, hotels, offices, their roofs, doors and windows affording excellent points of vantage for viewing the square and any doings therein.

When we arrived the square was partially filled with well-dressed people strolling quietly about or chatting in groups, and here and there a helmeted policeman calmly enjoying the quiet of the Sabbath afternoon. But every minute and from every mouth of the five streets people are arriving, men and women, but mostly men, and are seizing points of vantage from which to view whatever may happen. A couple of policemen walk toward the plinth of the great column and begin quietly to move from the immediate area surrounding the plinth the groups of people gathered there. Rapidly the doorways and windows commanding the square, the roofs of the buildings and every jutting ornament that can hold man or boy fill with sightseers until half an hour before the time advertised for the meeting the four sides of the square are black with human beings, humming like a great hive of bees aswarm. There is absolute order. To us that is the outstanding and amazing feature of the scene. There is no jamming, no rushing, or crushing, no loud talking and apparently no extra cordon of police. A few officers stand listless and indifferent at the various points of intersection. And everyone is perfectly good-humored and ready to oblige his neighbor, if it does not involve any loss of vantage ground. The big crushing, crowding bully so frequently in evidence in Canadian or American crowds is not here. As the hour approaches a stillness falls upon the crowd. Even conversation ceases. Soon I understand. They are listening. Far down a street leading up from the East End there is the faint shrilling of a cornet, and the throbbing of a drum. A soft sigh, exactly like the first movement of a rising wind through a Glengarry cedar swamp, passes over the crowd, then a strained stillness, through which soon pierces the notes of a marching band. Listening intently, I begin to catch the terrific notes of that fiercest of all war songs:

> Aux armes, citoyens!
> Formez vos bataillons!
> Marchons, marchons . . . !

Ruthless, starving men, panting for freedom and mad with blood lust, had shrieked their way from Marseilles to Paris with this song issuing through bared teeth, in the wild days of the First Commune. Whether the cornets are of a special make or are blown with particularly savage blast, there is something peculiarly fierce in the shrilling notes of this band and the step is shorter, quicker than that of an ordinary marching column. A man explains that quick short step as being adapted to the march of women. Whatever the reason the impression made upon me is that of passionate eagerness to arrive. It is an amazing column. In the lead appears a Junoesque figure of a woman all in white, a shining silver helmet on her head, and flanked by groups of girls also in white. Next to these a solid block of young men in black marching with the quick, trained step of disciplined soldiers, the fighting bodyguard of Sylvia who is marching bareheaded in their midst. Next a silver band, not so much playing as shrieking forth the strident notes, and in the chorus employing a device I have never heard before. In rendering that terrific call "Aux armes, citoyens!" the tenor cornets blare forth the fifth note in the scale, the sol, and persist in sounding that most arousing of all the notes straight through to the end. The effect produced by this barbaric disregard of the ordinary rules of harmonization is something appallingly fierce and savage. One could almost hear the sullen roll of the wheels of the tumbrils over the rough stones of the streets of Paris. Following the band comes a weird and motley crowd, the denizens of London's East End. Their appearance clutches at my throat. I find myself breathing fast, choking breaths and with hot tears in my eyes. Whoever staged this parade had a highly developed dramatic instinct. And most amazing feature of this amazing parade, on each side of the marching column there is a line of marching policemen, guarding, protecting this lawbreaker and her sympathizers from all possible violence.

I grip Robertson's arm. "Where else under God's shining stars could you behold such a scene as this, Robertson? Policemen protecting a lawbreaker on her way to preach lawbreaking to a crowd only too ready to break the law."

"She's a funny old lady is Grandma Britain. She protects lawbreakers till they lose interest in their job. But somehow she gets there."

Here is Sylvia marching to music through London streets with a long procession of belligerent followers all rebels against government and ready to break windows, but now all carefully guarded by the officers of the law. Now she is lifted upon the plinth of Nelson's column, amid the mad cheers of her own followers, and welcomed by polite but quite hearty handclapping of respectable London citizens. Pale, worn, weary-faced, she stands looking at that crowd of comfortable folk, tens of thousands of them, all of whom are quite hostile to the idea of having their own windows broken, but most of them secretly rather sympathetic with the general idea of window-breaking as a sporting proposition. The musical crashing of breaking glass and the positively thrilling sensation attached to the hurling of a stone with a splendid crash through a good-sized pane of glass is a survival of adolescent days, dear to most middle-aged steady-going householders. That is, if the window is a neighbor's.

For some moments she stands there before the adoring eyes of those whose wrongs have driven her to prison and to hunger strikes, indeed to the very gates of death. Her speechmaking is a feeble effort. She is too spent for eloquence, she is telling that crowd of freedom-loving Britons whose digestive organs are dealing satisfactorily with their Sunday dinners, she is telling them how she held up the majestic march of British law by a slow process of voluntarily dying for what she believes to be the rights of British women. To this hour I see the worn face and the burning eyes in their hollow sockets, and hear the thrilling note of scorn of "the big thirteen-stone men who rather pulled me about." With startling swiftness the climax comes. From her breast she draws a roll of paper, and waving it high, she shrills:

"Men and women, the time for words is past! The time for deeds is come! I hold in my hand a petition signed by sixty thousand women and girls. The Prime Minister has refused to receive it, but today we shall carry it to his house at Number Ten Downing Street and place it in his hands. Come on! Follow me!"

Two young men spring to take her outstretched hands and lift her down. About her a solid phalanx forms into a wedge and before we know has pierced its way through the crowd making for No. 10 Downing Street. That instant a shrill whistle blows. As if they had materialized out of thin air lines of stalwart officers of the law are moving with apparently easy strides, but with amazing swiftness, into position. Within five minutes a cordon of police is stretched about that square, closing up every one of the five streets but leaving open the entrance to Downing Street into which the flying wedge, led by Sylvia, is allowed to pass. Following close upon this wedge, Robertson and I find ourselves, after a swift rush, suddenly halted and unable to advance or retreat.

A convenient street bus affords us an observation post. We climb to the upper deck and see at once what has happened. Behind us the entrance to Downing Street has been closed by a line of tall police. Beyond No. 10 the way has been blocked by another bluecoated line.

There is no rushing about, no flying clubs, no rough handling, but quietly here and there men and women are being picked up, put into cabs and driven off. Quietly but swiftly the street is cleared of the crowd of sightseers. Citizens are politely being sent wherever their business calls them. They obviously have no business here. The petition has been carried to the door of No. 10. A tall policeman listens gravely to the demand for the Prime Minister, then informs the excited deputation that the Prime Minister does not receive visitors on Sunday afternoon. Expostulations arise. A police officer moves forward.

"I'll take that paper," he says.

"We must deliver this into the Prime Minister's hands," shouts an excited woman.

"Madam, I shall see that this paper is delivered to the Prime Minister," says the officer with calm politeness.

"But we must—"

The officer makes a slight motion with his hand. Cabs pull up to the curb. Fighting fiercely, the petitioning women are lifted into the cabs and driven off.

A young man attempts a rescue. A heavy hand falls upon his coat collar. A swift downward jerk and the young man's heels fly from under him and he is flung out among the crowd.

"Be off!" orders the officer, for the first time drawing his club. At once the crowd give back, moving slowly and pouring forth vile but futile abuse upon the approaching tide of blue helmets, which keeps moving steadily upon them with the relentless advance of the incoming tide. Here and there through the thinning crowd men and women are being arrested, thrust into cabs and driven away.

We drop down from our observation post and begin to move toward the square, when we come upon an amusingly pathetic scene. A great two-hundred-pound bluecoat is escorting a well-dressed middle-aged lady to a waiting cab. Her bonnet had fallen from her head, revealing disheveled gray hair. With all her puny strength she is fighting her vain fight for freedom and for women's rights. Calmly, without violence, but with steady step the officer moves on with his victim. On the other side a little redheaded man, about five feet tall, middleaged, with red face and fiery eyes, is trotting along beside the policeman, looking up into his face and pouring forth an unbroken stream of scornful abuse.

"Hey! You're an' 'ero, ain't yeh? Knockin' a laidy abaht, eh? Wot's she been doin' to yeh? 'Urtin' yer feelin's, eh? W'y don't yeh 'it 'er? You're an' 'ero you are! W'y don't yeh pull 'er 'air?"

He would have been priceless on a London stage, but somehow the whole thing shamed me. But the big man feels no shame or at least shows none. Occasionally his glance wanders to the frothing little man at his side as if he were a yapping poodle, but there is no anger in his eye, hardly any interest. The lady is deposited in a cab and driven off and the policeman turns away to the next item of duty. The little man follows, still barking at him.

With a swift movement the big man turns on his heel.

"What are ye da'en here, ye puddock?" he said sharply. "Be aff wi' ye!"

Immediately the little one scuttled off and disappeared into the crowd.

I caught the North Country accent.

"You're having a busy day," I said, edging up to him.

He glanced at my ministerial garb.

"Ooo aye!" he said.

"Not very pleasant job, eh? I mean arresting women?"

"Ooo, it's no what ye might call exheeliaratin' wi' the weemin, puir buddies. I dinna like it when they're gray-heided. It gars me think o' ma auld mither, ye ken."

"You are from Aberdeen," I ventured.

"Aye. How did ye ken that?"

"I've just come from there. And a lovely old city it is."

"Man! Did ye see the feeshin' fleet comin' hame?" he said with a wistful cadence in his voice.

"I did indeed. I wonder you could leave that country."

"Aweel! It's a bonnie country, but close, awfu' close. There's naethin' in it."

"But this job?" I said, sweeping my hand over the crowd as we walked along.

"Aweel! It's unpleasant whiles. But the paiy's no bad."

He saluted as we left him and made our way back to the square. There we found lines of policemen quietly moving the crowd without insistence or hurry, but moving them. As we reached the monument a well-dressed man on the plinth was attempting to harangue the crowd. A policeman moved slowly toward him.

"The meeting is over, sir," he said.

"I protest against the action of the police in—"

"Come down!" ordered the officer.

"I protest—"

The officer caught him by the leg, gave him a quick jerk and landed him on his back.

"I protest," began the gentleman angrily.

"Move on, please!" ordered the policeman.

The man continued to protest but he moved on. And London moved on, and Sylvia moved on to finish her prison term with its periodic hunger strikes and releases under the operation of the nefarious Cat and Mouse legislation, which legislation it took the German guns to blast forever from our British system of law.

My visit to London brought me an entirely new experience in matters of the spirit. We had the good fortune to be invited to spend a few days at the home of Mr. J. Allen Baker, member of Parliament for the Willesden district of London, a large manufacturer and a man wholly trusted by all who knew him. Mr. Baker was born in Canada and had visited us in Winnipeg, but he had spent most of his life in London.

I have never known a more simplehearted, sincere and altogether Christian-minded man. He belongs to one of the famous English Quaker families that have done so much to ennoble the manufacturing and commercial life of England. This was not my first experience of Quaker folk. It had been my good fortune to come into personal touch with one other Quaker family in my life, the family of which my dear friend Mrs. Robert Barbour of Bonskeid, Scotland, was a member. Hence I was quite eagerly looking forward to another delightful experience. I was not disappointed. There was the same atmosphere of fine and beautiful simplicity in the manner and style of living, the same high intellectual culture and fragrance of spirit that made their home a veritable Interpreter's House for the wayfarer. The atmosphere of the home was definitely religious, but the religion of the home was not a thing of special forms or practices, it was a thing of air and light, a thing of spirit. You felt it, breathed it, were rested and refreshed by it. There were the father and mother, two daughters and a son, Philip, later known as Noel Baker, away at Cambridge, a world-famed athlete, a European champion middle-distance runner, who came to his own in later years in the world of national and international affairs. I came to know him better during and after the war.

We spent the week end and went to church with them on Sunday, an experience I have never forgotten. I knew, of course, in a general way the Quaker mode of worship, but this was my first experience of it. The utter quiet I could not understand. There was no audible praying, no voices raised in worshipful praise, no sermon. I sat waiting for something to begin, with a more or less indefinite impression that precious moments were being wasted. I was so placed that I could see the quiet faces about me, more particularly those of our hostess and her daughter. At first I saw nothing but impassive quietude, but as the silent minutes passed I became sensitive to a living something. I studied those two faces. The mother's face, strongly serene and withdrawn from her physical environment. She was seeing the invisible, and in her face there was response from the things unseen. She was refilling her soul from those wells of living water that spring up to everlasting life. Her daughter's face startled me. It, too, was serene, but not quiet. It was not the serenity of an unruffled pool in a shady forest. It was the serenity of a deep-flowing river, unruffled by vagrant winds, moving with steady current to the sea. This was not mere contemplation, much less the quietude of mere musing. There was concentration of thought, vibrant feeling, tense and controlled. It was not the face of one conscious of struggle, of conflict. The struggle was past, and now there was a vivid realizing of the consequences of decision. She had pledged her soul, now she was envisaging and estimating results. But her soul knew no fear, nor even anxiety.

I turned my eyes away from these faces with a definite impression of immovable strength. Resolves made in this hour and in this spiritual environment could not be shaken. This quiet hour held the secret of the calm invincibility of the Quaker conscience. And I realized for the first time that this serenity of soul was not mere passivity. Passivity? Anything but that, as this Baker family taught me within the next month.

The last quarter of an hour I gave to an intensive stocktaking of my own spiritual furnishing. I came away from that meetinghouse with a disturbed mind and an unquiet soul. I was contrasting with this reverent silence of spirit the "bright" bustling vocalizations of communion with the unseen so frequently characteristic of our ordinary public worship. Our praise services, lanquid or hearty according to the mood or temperament of the directing minister; our often appallingly heartless reading of the divine message of prophets, poets, saints and sages from what we call the Bible; our prayers in which the minister too often seeks to instruct Almighty God in the formularies of an outmoded theology; our noisy, cajoling, bullying, "announcements of the congregational activities of the week"; our sermons, at times smart and catchy on up-to-the-minute themes, at times ponderous with half-baked ologies that have lost reality, at times denunciatory of present-day vices. "Alas, alas!" I said to my soul, "I will take heed to my ways, I will keep my mouth with a bridle, that I sin not with my tongue."

One other thing that hour of quiet in the meetinghouse explained to me—the extraordinary fact that these gentle Baker ladies were convinced and devoted suffragettes. I am not sure that they ever broke windows, but I am quite certain that if they could be convinced that a brick or two hurled through a Bond Street jewelry store window would advantage the sacred cause of women's rights, they would delicately, but effectively, hurl those bricks, and gladly go to prison for the lawless act, and hunger strike too if necessary.

Before the end of our visit we learned that a vast Hyde Park demonstration of the suffragettes and their sympathizers from all parts of England and Wales had been arranged for the following week.

"I think I should like to march with you," I was rash enough to declare one morning at the breakfast table.

"Oh, would you?" said Grace Baker.

"Of course I would, but a mere man would not be eligible."

"Oh, we can easily arrange that."

"And, Helen, you will march too, of course," I suggested.

"Not I!" exclaimed my wife, the shyest of shy mortals.

"But you can stand at the Marble Arch and see us all pass," said Grace. "Our uniform is blue with a white sash."

"Yes, I think I should like that," said my wife.

"All right then," I said. "Helen and I will take our stand at the Marble Arch and cheer wildly as you go by."

"But you are going to march," insisted Grace, determined to make a recruit of me, who had no more intention of walking in a suffragette parade than of climbing the Nelson Monument.

"Oh, all right, I shall join you at the Marble Arch," I concluded with a smile, but with not the slightest intention of parading.

But I reckoned without Grace, who was resolute that I should appear in the parade. "I am not going to let you back out," she declared. "We will arrange to have someone to look after Mrs. Gordon."

I agreed, but I was nonetheless resolved that no suffragette parade should claim me as a sympathetic marcher.

From about noon on the appointed day the various detachments of uniformed and beflagged suffragettes began to converge upon the Marble Arch and sure enough my wife and I took up a first-class station just inside the arch, keeping a keen lookout for the detachment in blue with white sashes.

For a full hour we watched and admired the marching column. We were amazed at the large numbers of quite young girls in the parade.

"What a splendid-looking lot they are," I said to my wife. "I rather expected a lot of old maids in poke bonnets."

"Nonsense!" said my wife. "They are mostly young, and they are perfectly lovely, I think."

"So do I. And awfully jolly-looking. When Grace comes along we will just step in with her."

"Don't you dare," she said, clutching my arm. "I won't march. And you daren't leave me here all alone. Oh, there they are! The blue and white! And there's Grace!"

At that instant the parade halted just before us.

Grace caught sight of us and waved.

"Let's go and speak to her just a moment," I said and ran over to her, my wife following timidly and unwillingly.

"You're coming!" cried Grace, in an ecstasy. "Oh, splendid! We have only a little way to go to our platform now. There are our platforms."

"No, no!" said my wife hastily. "We're not! *We are not!*"

At this moment the band struck up. The parade stepped out, my wife dashed back to the side. I followed in step with Grace calling out: "Come on, Helen! Hurry up! It's only a little way."

It was rather a low trick on my part. She hated to come. She was terrified at being left alone in the heart of London. A few seconds of distracted uncertainty and she dashed to our side and stepped out gallantly in the grand suffragette parade, darting indignant glances at me the while.

It happened that our contingent gathered about the platform from which Sidney Webb and his brilliant wife were to speak. I found Mr. Webb rather dull, but his wife, with her bright wit, her clever sarcastic humor, kept the crowd interested, alert and vastly amused. I was enjoying myself immensely when a gentleman touched me on the arm.

"Ralph Connor, I believe?" he said.

"Well, some people call me that," I said.

"Mr. Sidney Webb would like to speak to you. Kindly follow me, sir."

"But what's up?" I asked.

"We will wait for you here," said Grace. "I know the Webbs very well. They are charming people. You had better hurry."

Off I went with the man rather pleased at the courtesy of being invited to a seat on the platform. As I glanced back at my wife I saw the two girls in gales of laughter, but could only wonder what funny remark of Mrs. Webb's I had missed.

Mr. Webb greeted me warmly. He had long known me, had read *The Sky Pilot* and *The Man from Glengarry* with real pleasure. He was delighted to have me sit beside him on the platform. "And we should also appreciate greatly that Ralph Connor should say a few words in favor of our cause. I understand you attended Sylvia Pankhurst's meeting. Brave girl she is! A gallant soul. So good of you to support her with your presence. Mrs. Webb will finish in a few minutes. I shall then introduce you. Just a few words. We should consider it a very real help."

I felt that it would be mean to refuse. It would be a coward's trick to back out. I saw Grace Baker and my wife grinning at me and I well knew that it was Grace who had put the Webbs up to this trick.

Well! I determined I would become there and then a suffragist of the most violent type, and I did.

Mr. Webb introduced Ralph Connor, whose name was known

throughout the English-speaking world and loved wherever it was known. "He is also, I am glad to say, an enthusiastic supporter of our cause. Ralph Connor will now address us."

The reception I got almost knocked me out. But it warmed my blood and I went at it with my whole soul and body.

"I took as my theme "Canadian Women in Public Affairs in Canada." I told of their work in social service, of their remarkable work in the church, and so on and so on. I told them yarns of my mother in the old Glengarry days, of the heroic women of the foothill country. I had plenty of stuff and I served it up hot, and right from my heart. When it was all over we took a cab home; both girls were tired, and so was I.

"Nice trick you played on me, Grace," I said. "Oh, I know. Mrs. Webb told me all about it."

"It just served you right," said my wife, "for the trick you played on me."

"But I'm afraid, Helen, he still is ahead of us a few blocks, as you Canadians say. He made the speech of the day."

"Oh, he wasn't so bad," grudgingly acknowledged my wife, who has never been known to unduly praise her husband. She thinks it not good for him.

"It was God's mercy I got through," I said. "It was old Glengarry that saved me." And it was.

CHAPTER XXI

Asquith

TEA ON THE TERRACE—BRITAIN'S PRIME MINIS-
TER—WILL THERE BE WAR?—SIR WILFRID LAURIER
AND CANADA'S FOREIGN POLICY—DOMINION
AUTONOMY

BEFORE we left the Bakers' lovely home Mr. Baker arranged for an afternoon tea on the Terrace of the House of Commons, and also for a meeting with Mr. Asquith at No. 10 Downing Street. Both engagements proved of extraordinary interest.

At the tea on the Terrace we were introduced to a number of people, among them Mr. A. Richardson, a most interesting Liberal member of Parliament and a warm friend and admirer of Mr. Baker. There was also a Chinese general representing his government in London in support of a bill just passed by Parliament for the suppression of the British importation of opium from India into China, and Mr. Ramsay MacDonald, recognized leader of the Labor party in the House of Commons, belonging to the Fabian school, and a pronounced pacifist. As yet, however, he was greatly despised by the militant Tories, and held in high regard by only a few outside his own party.

Tea on the Terrace is a thoroughly British institution. The Terrace is a spacious sort of parade ground just outside the Parliament Building and immediately overlooking the slow-moving, muddy Thames. Members of Parliament have a pleasant practice of inviting friends to take afternoon tea in a most charmingly informal manner, something in the way of a picnic. Little tables are set here and there and uniformed attendants move about with the supposed dignity of archbishops and come for orders as if taking part in a state ceremonial or a religious service. The members are in a free and jolly mood, quite like little boys out of school. Their lady guests sport their best afternoon frocks and their most fascinating manners. Everything is informal, almost irregular, but at the same time there is not a scintilla of anything that savors of bad form. No loud voices, no backslapping familiarity between the men, for all their good-fellowship. All shoptalk is avoided. There is no reference to what is going on in the House. If a question is asked as to legislative matters the answer is given in the tone and manner of one absolutely bored. Mr. Baker, however, in introducing the Chinese general made an exception in my favor, and in low tones told me about the Opium Bill which had been passed within the hour.

"The point at issue was, what was to be done with a shipload of opium from India at present in the harbor at Shanghai, now that the sale of opium had been forbidden in China. The bill has arranged that this opium shall be disposed of *pari passu* with opium which is still grown in certain parts of China and sold by the government, which seems fair enough. The general is quite delighted with the success of his mission."

What an Empire! London, Shanghai, Winnipeg, all meeting on the Terrace!

Mr. Ramsay MacDonald sat most of the time drinking tea in dreamy silence, answering a question and then relapsing again into silence. As leader of the Labor party he had his own trials. A pronounced pacifist, he was forced to suffer much unfair and bitter criticism on the part of the vast majority of his fellow members of Parliament. He knew little of Canada and was but slightly interested in Canadian affairs. He had read some of Ralph Connor's books and said nice things about them. But he seemed to me like a man whose heart had been numbed with a heavy blow. Mr. Baker told me later that he had lost his wife, a brilliant and lovely woman, a true comrade and helpmate to her husband.

As we were walking along the Terrace front on our way out, we stopped to watch the Thames rolling by with its varied traffic.

"Muddy stream, eh?" said Mr. Baker.

"Yes, but it is the Thames," said my wife quietly.

"Let me tell you a story," said Mr. Baker. "Mr. John Burns was on one occasion showing the House of Commons to an American, who when he stood where we are now looking at the river, remarked: 'Muddy little crick, eh?'

" 'Sir,' replied Mr. Burns, 'do you know what you are looking at? You are looking at "liquid history," the noblest mankind has known.'

"I must have you meet John Burns," continued Mr. Baker. "He is one of England's greatest men." And when some three years later I met John Burns I remembered Joseph Allen Baker's estimate of him and felt that the words were true.

Two days later Mr. Baker took us to No. 10 Downing Street to pay our respects to the Right Honorable Herbert Asquith, premier of Great Britain. Mr. Asquith was a busy man, and I felt that we could expect to have only a few minutes of his time. We arrived on the stroke of ten, the hour appointed; instead of spending ten minutes with this man so charged with many and heavy responsibilities, when we left his room the hands of his clock pointed to 11:15. I can remember no other hour and a quarter of such rapid, intense and stimulating mental effort to keep pace with the ever-changing stream of thought.

After a few general questions regarding Canadian politics, I changed the subject abruptly and said:

"Mr. Asquith, may I ask your judgment as to the imminence of war with Germany? If I am asking something I should not, please do not answer, but I should greatly like to carry back with me to Canada the Prime Minister's opinion on this important matter."

"The question is perfectly correct," he said. He thought for a moment and then added slowly, "The answer, however, is not so easy." He paused again. Mr. Baker, Mrs. Gordon and I stood tensely waiting his reply.

Then with studied deliberation he said:

"If you had asked that question six months ago I could not answer as I do today, but the mission of Mr. Haldane, and the visits of those most useful deputations representative of the Christian churches of both countries, which we owe more to my friend Mr. Allen Baker than to anyone else, enable me to answer that I do believe the imminent danger of war between Germany and this country has passed away."

"You authorize me to say that in Canada?" I asked.

"I believe you can safely say so."

"Well, thank God for that," I said. "We have been very anxious in Canada, you know."

"What?" he said sharply. "Very anxious in Canada? Canadians are really, I mean seriously, concerned over the possibility of a European war?"

"I am rather surprised that you ask such a question, Mr. Asquith," I said. "Have you forgotten South Africa?" I fear my voice carried a touch of indignation.

"Please don't misunderstand me, Dr. Gordon. Nothing in my lifetime has so deeply moved the hearts of our people as Canada's magnificent contribution in the recent war. Never can that be forgotten. But may I speak to you frankly, man to man, and without reservation?"

"Mr. Asquith, let me assure you that Dr. Gordon's work in Canada and his place in the confidence of his people is a guarantee of his prudence. Besides, I know him."

"Thank you, Baker. Now I shall speak frankly. You are a Liberal in politics?"

"I take no part in party politics, except when they impinge upon social and moral questions."

"I am thinking of Sir Wilfrid Laurier's speeches when the proposition was first made to send a contingent to South Africa. Sir Wilfrid Laurier is a French Canadian and a Roman Catholic—wait, please—I know he is no narrow bigot—but he needs the votes of French Canada and—"

"Mr. Asquith, will you let me interject a word here? I may save time. Do you remember Sir Wilfrid's attitude on the Remedial Bill and his campaign throughout Canada on that question, which stirred French Canada tremendously?"

"Of course, not clearly—but—"

"Then let me recall one fact. In that conflict which extended from 1890 to 1896 Sir Wilfrid had the massed weight of the Roman Catholic hierarchy against him. Every archbishop, every bishop, every priest in French Quebec—indeed throughout all Canada—was fanatically against him. He won out, but he won by the votes of the French-Canadian people. Protestant and Orange Ontario gave him 44 seats against 48, but French Roman Catholic Quebec gave him 48 seats against 17. He is French and Roman Catholic, but he carried Canada for constitutional freedom against the fanatical opposition of the whole hierarchy of his church."

"Very interesting indeed. Intensely interesting," said the premier. "What happened finally?"

"The hostility of his church was so fiercely resented that a group of prominent lay members took the matter to Rome. The Vatican spoke and the bishops were silent."

"Extraordinarily interesting! Now about South Africa. I want your version on that. This is really a matter of the greatest importance to me."

"In the matter of the South African contingent," I replied, "I believe Sir Wilfrid's attitude was quite constitutional and quite sound. It is true that when the proposition of a Canadian contingent was first mooted Sir Wilfrid did point out the constitutional difficulties— but have you read his speech in Parliament, in defense of his government's action in reply to Bourassa's challenge?"

"Most certainly I did and was thrilled by it, but there seemed to be at the first a slight hesitation."

"Pardon me again, Mr. Asquith, if I ask you if you read his farewell to the troops as they sailed for South Africa?"

"I must have read that, but I'm afraid I do not recall it now."

"Then, Mr. Asquith, I venture to say you have not read it. For if you had you could never forget it. It is in my opinion one of the noblest speeches ever delivered on Canadian soil. Forgive me if I speak warmly."

"Dr. Gordon, I am glad you have revived my memory of these speeches and especially in view of the discussion at present being carried on in the Canadian Parliament."

"The naval policy, I suppose you mean?"

"Yes. Again I seem to be a little uncertain of Sir Wilfrid's attitude."

"Mr. Asquith, I am glad you have raised that point. I think I can confidently say that I believe I know Sir Wilfrid's mind on the whole question perhaps as well as any man in Canada. May I tell you why?"

"Do. I should be most grateful."

"I am afraid I am taking up too much of the time of the Prime Minister of Britain," I said.

"Let me assure you, Dr. Gordon, that there is nothing the Prime Minister is more keenly interested in at this moment," said Mr. Asquith earnestly.

"Well, you may have noticed a remark of Sir Wilfrid's in our Parliament, that it was not to be regarded as an axiomatic truth in Canada's relation to the Empire that when Britain is at war Canada is also automatically at war."

"I caught that. I certainly caught that," the Premier replied quickly.

"I confess I was shocked when I read that and immediately wrote Sir Wilfrid regretting his statement and suggesting that his real mind might be more clearly set forth if it were put in some such statement as this, that while it was true that when Britain was at war Canada was also at war, it still remained for the Parliament of Canada to determine what action, if any, Canada should take and when. In other words, though technically Canada is at war when Britain declares war, still the Canadian Parliament alone gives the word to march."

"Excellent! What was Sir Wilfrid's reply?" asked the Prime Minister eagerly.

"He wired me a cordial acceptance of my suggestion and invited me to dine with him a week later when he was to visit Winnipeg.

"I did dine with him and for an hour and a half he expounded his views on the subject. There is no doubt about two things, so far as Sir Wilfrid is concerned. First, as to his utter loyalty to the Empire and, second, his conviction as to Canada's complete right to self-government."

"Fine. Very fine! I am really most grateful to you for what you have told me."

"May I venture a step further, Mr. Prime Minister?"

"Do, please."

"Perhaps I should not say this, but I don't think your secretary helped things much by his telegram to one of our Cabinet ministers a few months ago."

"Telegram? My secretary?"

"I am thinking of Mr. Churchill's wire indicating the line of action by our Parliament which would be most acceptable to your government."

The Prime Minister gazed at me in shocked silence, then said slowly:

"I want to assure you I knew nothing of that."

"I am stating a fact. The thing ran through our Parliament like a fire through prairie grass. It was only Sir Wilfrid's prompt and authoritative action that prevented what might have been a most unpleasant crisis."

"You have done me a very real service today, Dr. Gordon," said the Prime Minister, as he was bidding us good-bye.

"I am going to be bold enough to offer the Prime Minister a bit of advice. I know I may be presuming, but I am going to take a chance and venture this opinion: It would not be a good thing for the Empire if the British government should accept any naval contribution as from Canada if it represented the will and pleasure of only half the Canadian people."

He was silent for a few moments. He walked over to the window and stood gazing out into the Green Park. Then he came back and said, slowly and with quiet emphasis:

"Dr. Gordon, you may rest assured that my government will accept nothing from Canada that does not represent the will and opinion of the great majority of her people."

I came away limp as a rag. The story of this interview, of which I give the exact words as I remember them, may read quietly enough, but to me every moment was one of keen mental strain and at times of tense emotion. Mr. Baker was equally excited.

"I am amazed at the Prime Minister," he said. "I know him well. He is usually very reserved, very close-minded in his interviews. Never once have I heard him speak so freely as today. Of course, he could be freer with you from Canada than with his own people here, but all the same he astonished me."

PART THREE
The Camerons in Flanders

CHAPTER XXII

World Conflagration

PRAIRIE FIRE — THE SPARK — WAR COMES TO BIR-
KENCRAIG — UNITED CANADA — THE FIRST CONTIN-
GENT — COLONEL SAM HUGHES — THE CAMERONS
SAIL

ONE AUTUMN evening I was visiting a bachelor friend in Western
Canada, a member of my flock. We were returning from a day's fall
plowing to his little shack set down upon the broad prairie. As he
was about to unhitch his team from his plow and turn them in to
the stable we observed far on the southern horizon a smudge of smoke.

"Some Yankee farmer burning rubbish across the line there,"
said my friend.

For some moments we stood looking at that dark line of smoke.

"How far is the border from here?" I asked.

"About twenty-five miles. A prairie fire is no joke," he mused.
"I ought to have a firebreak round my stacks and buildings here.
I must do it tomorrow."

"Why not today?" I said. "You have your team and plow."

"Oh, I'll do it after supper. Well, I don't know. I guess I might
as well do it now, I've got the team hitched up anyhow."

I walked with him as he plowed a succession of furrows round
his little farm steading. After we had done two or three rounds I
glanced toward the American border.

"Say, that fire is nearer than it was," I said.

He stopped his team and together we looked toward the south.
"And it is coming like a race horse."

He quickened the pace of his horses and soon had them going
at a smart walk, the plow was giving him some difficulty, so I took the
lines. At every turn we paused to look south. We could see a red glow
at times flaming up through the black rolling volumes of smoke, and
the smoke was raging toward the clouds above.

"Say," he exclaimed, "get them horses going!"

Before we had completed our firebreak a raging wall of smoking fire, blotting out the horizon, was coming at us like a line of charging cavalry. Our horses were tearing round the steading at a swift trot, a fierce wind had been blowing toward the fire. My friend had all he could do to keep the plow in the ground. Before the break was finished the wind suddenly turned and was now coming with the fire on what was almost a gale. Soon we began to feel the heat of the approaching flames and we were surrounded with rolling clouds of smoke.

"Let's get the horses in," he shouted.

We unhitched and raced them into the stable. Then seizing some bags we soaked them in water and began to beat out the flames which were already started on the inner side of the break. We had an hour's desperate fight to save the little shack and the steading. In a few minutes after the first tuft of burning grass had struck across our break the fire was past us and raging across the prairie. We learned afterwards that it ran for sixty miles, destroying everything not properly protected with firebreaks.

We later learned that the fire was started by an American settler, new to the country, burning up some rubbish about his stable. He was able to save his own home, but he wrought destruction for his neighbors.

So it was with the World Conflagration.

It is not an idle question to discuss the responsibility of the Great War, but it is a difficult question to answer.

On the morning of June 29, 1914, a headline in the Winnipeg *Free Press* announced the murder of Archduke Francis Ferdinand in Austria by a half-crazed Serbian pressman at Serajevo in Bosnia. I glanced at the headline. I had never heard of Serajevo. Assassinations seemed to be one of the chief outdoor sports of the semicivilized peoples of those Central European countries. We were packing up for our annual trek to our island home. Next day headlines of varied interest were in the paper and we forgot Serajevo.

Four weeks later we were camping on our island, Birkencraig, in the Lake of the Woods, near the little town of Kenora. It was glorious weather. With our canoes and boats, with our swimming and tennis, with our campfires and singsongs our life was full of rest and happy

peace. It was a good world. On Thursday, July 30th, our boat returning with supplies from the little town brought back a newspaper with
red headlines splashed on its front page. Austria had declared war on
Serbia and her armies were bombarding Belgrade. Germany had
called together its Council of War. Bethmann-Hollweg, German chan-
cellor, had intimated to Britain the extreme importance of local-
izing the conflict between Austria and Serbia, in other words, suggesting that Austria should have a free hand with little Serbia.
Sazonov, Russian ambassador in London, had called on Sir Edward
Grey to warn him that the only chance of averting a European
war lay in the united effort of Britain, France and Russia. Paul Cam-
bon, French ambassador in England, anxiously inquired from Sir
Edward Grey as to Britain's attitude, and received an indefinite answer. Lichnowski, German ambassador in London, was told by Sir
Edward Grey that Germany must not count on Britain's standing
aside in case of a European war. This was a full month after the
Serajevo murder, which we had all forgotten.

On Sunday morning, August 2nd, we motorboated in to church.
A little group of men were standing on the wharf listening to one
of their number reading from a morning paper, in which red headlines announced that Germany had declared war on Russia. Germany, Russia, Austria, Serbia were at war, but thank God! our
Empire was out of it and would doubtless keep out.

On August 4th, after several days of furious diplomatic activity
between the ambassadors and chancellors of Germany and Austria,
Russia, France and Britain, the British ambassador at Berlin informed
Sir Edward Grey that he had received his passports. Half an hour
later Britain declared war on Germany and the old world had passed
away.

I remember taking the newspaper from my son King and going
off into the woods to look at the thing and to consider what it had to
do with me. With me and with my wife and my children. I was thinking of them, I am afraid, more than of the great world outside. It so
happened that I was chaplain of a Winnipeg kilted regiment, the 79th
Cameron Highlanders. I was proud of my battalion, the smartest
and most gorgeously arrayed in all Western Canada. I had loved the
splendid, historic, romantic glory of the kilted Highlanders, but this

day a new, a terrible and ugly thing looked at me from the red headlines. But I was no fighting man, I was a chaplain. Besides, I was within six years of being sixty years of age. For the first time in my life, in spite of the great wars that had shaken the world during my time, I looked the thing in the face. I called King and together we slipped away to town without a word to anyone. Groups of camping men were on the wharf. One man arrested my attention, a big shrewd businessman and a friend of mine. He was hurrying to catch the train that would leave for Winnipeg in a few minutes.

"What do you think of the situation, Mr. Ashdown?" I asked

"The world is changed. Everything is changed and we must meet that change."

His answer startled me. There was no shrewder man in Western Canada, "Everything is changed." The weeks immediately following showed how true the words were, but it took four years to make their full truth clear to the world.

Within a week my colonel had wired Ottawa announcing that every man of the 79th Cameron Highlanders had offered service overseas and asked for orders for his battalion.

There was no question this time as to whether a contingent should be sent or not. Without parley or hesitation Canada, from Halifax to Dawson, was alert and aware that world-shaking events were impending. Canada was instantly on the war line and with the full strength of her men and her resources. From the Governor General, His Royal Highness the Duke of Connaught, to the humblest workingman there was one spirit, one purpose, one resolve. The Canadian government at once approached the Governor General and obtained his permission to appeal to the Home government that he be permitted to remain in office in Canada. The British government immediately consented and the Duke of Connaught remained Governor General throughout the war.

On the 30th of July, Colonel Sam Hughes, the redoubtable and forceful Minister of Militia, hurried from his home in Lindsay, Ontario, to the capital. Members of the government came rushing from their holidaying in different parts of the country. Sir Wilfrid Laurier at once issued a call for cessation of all party strife. "In view of the critical nature of the situation," he wrote, "I have canceled all my meetings, there must be a truce to all party strife." The Premier, Sir

Robert Borden, gratefully acknowledged this announcement of the Leader of the Opposition, and together they assumed the direction of all Canadian war activity. Everything that savored of race, class or party distinction was immediately obliterated. Even before the declaration of war by the Home government, during those first hectic days of August, enthusiastic groups of both French and English paraded the streets of Montreal and Quebec together, flying French and British flags, singing French and British songs—"La Marseillaise" and "Rule, Britannia." Telegrams and letters from all parts of the Dominion, from the far Yukon under the Arctic Circle to Halifax down by the Atlantic, came pouring in to the government demanding a chance to stand on the Empire's battle line.

On the 18th of August, the earliest date allowed by the constitution, the Dominion Parliament met. It took exactly one minute to pass a vote of $50,000,000 for Dominion defense and to pledge to the limit the Dominion's resources and manhood to the defense of the Empire. Sir Wilfrid Laurier stated the attitude of the Opposition in this country: "Speaking for those who sit around me, if in what has been done or what remains to be done there may be anything which in our judgment should not be done, or ought to be differently done, we raise no objections, we take no exception, we offer no criticism and shall offer no criticism so long as there is danger at the front." In a House rigid in the intensity of its emotion, he closed with these impressive words: "It is our hope that from this painful war the British Empire will emerge with a new bond of union, the pride of all its citizens and a living light to all other nations."

Sir Robert Borden made reply, concluding: "In the awful dawn of the greatest war the world has ever known, in the hour when peril confronts us such as this Empire has not faced for a hundred years, every vain and unnecessary word seems a discord. As to our duty all are agreed, we stand shoulder to shoulder with Britain and the other British dominions in this quarrel. Not for love of battle, not for love of conquest, not for greed of possessions, but for the cause of honor, to maintain solemn pledges, to uphold principles of liberty, to withstand forces that would convert the world into an armed camp, yea, in the very name of the peace that we sought at any cost save that of dishonor."

The daily papers brought to our island home by my son King,

not yet fourteen years old, were read aloud at the tea table: a few friends and our six children, one boy and five girls, down to a baby sitting in a high chair.

"Will you go to war?" asked my eldest girl, Mary, her big hazel eyes fixed upon my face.

"Sure, he will go," said King with scornful impatience.

But at that time I had not the slightest expectation that it would ever seem my duty to go. True, I was chaplain of the 79th Cameron Highlanders, organized by one of my elders and my friend, Colonel R. M. Thomson, but at that time I did not even know whether chaplains went on active service. Within a few days Colonel Thomson was able to report to the Minister of Militia that his battalion was up to full strength, with hundreds of eager Scottish Canadians clamoring for a place on the battalion roster.

It does not enter into my plan to describe the organization and dispatch of the First Canadian Contingent. It is enough simply to say that on the 22nd of September, exactly thirty-five days after meeting of Parliament, the first contingent of 33,000 soldiers were afloat in thirty British vessels of whom ten were battleships, on their way to the war, with the second contingent of 22,000 already enlisted, and literally hundreds of thousands eager to go.

As the reports from the front line came back to us it soon became evident that Canada's contribution, which was first set at 25,000, would have to be materially increased. By the middle of September our island home was broken up and we were all back in Winnipeg.

I found myself overwhelmed with engagements, speaking in different parts of the West. My speech delivered before the Canadian Club in Winnipeg was reported in the *Canadian Annual Review,* as follows:

> The news as to the 2nd Contingent was well received everywhere and Ralph Connor (the Rev. Dr. C. W. Gordon) of Winnipeg issued one of the most stirring appeals for prompt and large enlistment. In it he declared that "our government has done well, has given a splendid exhibition of efficient despatch in mobilizing, equipping and transporting to England's shores between 30,000 and 40,000 men in the short space of two months. But it is not, I repeat, a matter of Contingents,

one, two, or three. Rather must Canada, with calm, deliberate, clear-eyed purpose, make resolve that she is committed to this world conflict to her last man and her last dollar, not for the Empire's sake alone, but for her own sake and for the sake of her national ideals, for the sake of human rights. If it is clearly understood that every fit Canadian man is pledged to this war, then first let the government take immediate steps for the enrolment, not of 20,000 but of 100,000 or 200,000 or even 300,000 Canadians available and offering for active service. Then from these enrolled men let Contingents be selected for immediate training and sent on to the Front as they can be equipped and fitted, and as they may be needed." He concluded with verses which were afterwards published, as the only Canadian contribution, in *Princess Mary's Gift Book*, for the aid of Belgian Relief Funds:

O Canada! A drum beats through the night and day,
Unresting, eager, strident, summoning
To arms. Whose drum thus throbs persistent?
Whose? Old England's, Canada, Old England's drum.

O Canada! A sword gleams leaping swift to strike
At foes that press and leap to kill brave men
On guard. Whose sword thus gleams fierce death?
Whose? 'Tis Britain's Canada, Great Britain's sword.

O Canada! What answer make to calling voice and throbbing
  drum,
To sword-gleam and to pleading prayer of God
For right? What answer makes my soul?
"Mother! To thee! God! To Thy help! Quick! My Sword!"

When I had finished my speech the Canadian Club appointed a committee to consult with me and to perfect a plan for giving effect to these suggestions. The proposal was put into shape and I was asked to go to Ottawa and lay it before Sir Robert Borden and the Minister of Militia.

On my arrival at Ottawa I went first to see Colonel Sam Hughes.

I had known Colonel Hughes in my university days. He was a famous lacrosse and football player. Strong as a bull, fearless as a lion, and on the field ferocious as a tiger. He was never at his best, he used to say, until he felt the warm blood running down his face. I shall never forget his appearance in a famous match between our Toronto University rugby team and the Argonauts of Toronto, in which he was easily the most effective halfback. Over and over again in that hectic contest it was my brother Gib's luck to meet Sam Hughes in head-on collisions. My brother was his superior in technique and his equal in physical strength. Hence in every clash between the two Sam came off second best. But after that famous match he retained for my brother a great admiration and affection.

I went first to lay the plan before Colonel Hughes. I found him in a large room filled with desks and chattering typewriters, two or three of which apparently he was able to keep simultaneously on the go.

"Hello, Ralph Connor," he shouted as I entered the room. "What do you want here?"

"I have just come down to help you win the war, sir," I replied.

"Don't you worry, we are going to do that, all right."

"Rather serious looking," I ventured. The accounts of the Mons retreat were just beginning to trickle through to Canada.

"Ah!" he said. "Mons, you mean? Great bit of work! If only the French had backed our men up we could have ended the war right there," exclaimed the redoubtable Sam. "But wait for the second half, my boy! The British never fight until after they get a good spanking. Now you watch 'em."

He then proceeded to demonstrate where the Expeditionary Force had been guilty of grave errors in strategy, and raged with furious fire at the French generals who had failed to back us up. He was an extraordinary mixture of shrewdness, bluster and common sense.

"Well," he repeated, after he had finished his demonstration as to how the whole German First Army might have been destroyed, "What do you want?"

I explained with due modesty, feeling something like a worm in the presence of a steam engine.

"Humph! Two hundred thousand men, eh? I can get two hundred thousand men just like that." He turned his hand on his desk, "just like that!"

"That's fine, colonel," I said.

"Yes," he continued. "No trouble to get men." And he went off into the enumeration of the various organizations, male and female, who were panting to pour recruits upon him.

"Splendid, colonel!" I exclaimed enthusiastically. "The only point I am making is this, that it might be a good idea to get them enrolled, while they are coming to you, so that when you need them you won't have to go for them."

"Can get them any day," he said.

"Besides, colonel," I said, "when we are discussing terms of peace with Germany"—we all had a feeling at that time that within a few months Germany would be suing for peace—"it would be much more impressive if our representatives could say, 'we have in Canada two hundred thousand men enrolled waiting to come,' than if we said, 'in Canada we can get two hundred thousand men.'"

"Peace!" he shouted, smashing his fist down on the table. "I'll never make peace until that German military machine is smashed." Thereupon he began to elaborate the terms he would impose upon the beaten enemy.

I listened with reverent respect. He was simply amazing. In the midst of his talk with me clerks and messengers kept coming to his desk. With furious energy he scribbled replies, shot out orders, answered questions. More than anything else he was like a threshing machine I had once seen on the prairie, with three men feeding it so as to keep it humming. All the time, however, his brains were working.

"Say," he said at last. "Put that thing of yours down in writing, with your reasons and let me have it. Good day!"

I left his presence like one escaping into shelter out of a hurricane. I went to my hotel, and still under the spell of his concentrated energy set down the bare bones of our scheme and sent it to him by special messenger.

Thereafter I proceeded to call upon Sir Robert Borden. As I was waiting in the anteroom, who should come in but the Solicitor General, Mr. Arthur Meighen, who had just returned from the West where he had been delivering a series of speeches, setting forth to the people the gravity of the war situation, which Canadians had not yet begun properly to esteem. He greeted me warmly. I confess I felt somewhat embarrassed, remembering our last famous meeting in Portage la Prairie.

"What are you doing here?" he asked.

"I am waiting to see Sir Robert Borden," I replied.

"Ah! Can I help you? I should be glad to introduce you."

I am ashamed to say that I received his offer somewhat coolly and assured him that Sir Robert would see me in a few minutes.

"Well, if there is anything I can do," he said, "I will gladly do it."

Whereupon, ashamed of my attitude, I explained my errand and handed him a copy of the draft of the scheme drawn up by the Winnipeg Canadian Club.

He read it with eager care. Read it a second time and part of it a third time. Then he shook my hand, saying: "Doctor, that is a fine statement. It is just what I have been trying to say to the people of Western Canada for the last three months, only you have put it much better. Now," he continued, "I will go with you to the Prime Minister and if he does not back it up I will carry it myself to the War Council."

His friendly manner, his eager enthusiasm made me quite ashamed of myself. Thereupon I proceeded to explain to him the spirit and attitude of the Canadian Club which was responsible for my presence in Ottawa. In ten minutes we had established a basis of friendship that has strengthened ever since. Throughout the war no man served his country more effectively than Arthur Meighen. He went with me to the Premier, went over the points of the proposed scheme, warmly endorsing it. There was no need for me to say a word. The Prime Minister immediately became interested and after a brief discussion promised to bring the matter before the War Council.

That same evening when I was in the rotunda of my hotel waiting to go into dinner, who should arrive but the Minister of Militia himself. He bore down upon me and said: "I have been looking over that thing of yours. It's all right, but do you think that *we could get* these two hundred thousand men enrolled?"

"Why, colonel," I said, "with all those organizations of yours and with the Canadian Clubs to help you I think we could."

"I will do it," he said. "I will take it to the Prime Minister and if he does not take it up, I will take it myself to the War Council. Come and see me tomorrow at ten."

At ten the next morning he received me cordially and in a few brief sentences set forth a plan to give effect to the scheme.

"Now," he asked, with a little grin, "what do you want?"

"What do I want?" I replied. "Nothing."

"Oh, come on now, everybody wants something," he said. "I remember your brother Gilbert. He is a great man, one of the best I ever met on the rugby field. He was a devil to tackle, but he was a man. Now what do you want?" The colonel was passionately loyal to his friends. If a man was his friend he must therefore be quite all right.

Suddenly I remembered that I did want something, and badly. Already scores of men from our 79th Cameron Highlanders, too eager for war to wait for the dispatch of the battalion as a unit, had enlisted in other battalions. Some had sailed to join Highland battalions of the Imperial Army.

"Well, colonel, there is something," I said. "Not for myself but for my battalion."

"Oh, yes," he exclaimed. "The Seventy-ninth Cameron Highlanders. Your colonel has been plaguing the life out of me to send them as a unit to the front. I know them. I know them, a lot of damned Scotties—the colonel himself is Irish—but they are a fine body of men. I know your colonel, a good soldier, a good disciplinarian, but we are getting away from the plan of sending battalions as units."

I eagerly pointed out the importance of capitalizing the clan feeling of the Highlanders. I expatiated upon their extraordinary cohesion, their loyalty, their pride of race. I became enthusiastic. He listened with glowing eyes.

"Connor," he said, "you've said something. There won't be any trouble in the discipline of that battalion. By jingo! They shall go. Don't say anything about it just yet. But they'll go! They are the right kind, they won't give any trouble. I will write your colonel. He is a soldier, but don't say a word to a soul. Now what do you want for yourself? Your brother was a friend of mine."

"Well, colonel," I said, "Colonel Thomson and the boys would like me to go as their chaplain."

"You would go?" he snapped at me.

"Well, I have not finally decided, but I almost feel it would be my duty to go, if the battalion went. You see, some three hundred of them are members of my congregation, also two of my elders, three of my managers and over fifty of my Young Men's Bible Class are in the battalion."

"My God, doctor!" he exclaimed. "What a battalion!" He called a clerk, scribbled a note and sent him off. "Doctor," he said earnestly, "that is the kind of stuff we want in our army, good solid Presbyterian churchmen. I am a Methodist myself, and for fighting men whom you can depend on we want clean-living religious men. I am sick of these drinking, woman-chasing soldiers. We haven't got many of them, thank God, but a dozen of them lowers the morals of a whole battalion. No, sir, give me good clean fighting men in our army and we will knock hell out of those squareheads."

In a few minutes the clerk returned and handed him a paper. He glanced over it, signed it without a word and handed it to me. It was my commission.

"Thank you, colonel," I said.

"Say, doctor, what about your wife? Have you a family? Look at this." He reached for a file and showed me a stack of letters. "These letters are from wives and mothers asking me to send their husbands and sons back to them. Their husbands I sent back, not their sons. How many children have you?"

"I have a son fourteen years of age and five little girls."

"Five girls! My God!" he exclaimed in a low voice. "What does your wife say?"

"If I think it my duty to go, colonel, she will not let me stay."

He sprang to his feet, grasped my hand with a grip that almost cracked my bones. He caught me by the arm with his other hand and held me fast.

"Say, boy!" he said. "If your wife wants you to stay, don't say a word about that paper and I won't."

"I will do what she says, colonel," I replied.

"Damn it all, man, I believe you will go."

So I left him with a new conception of our Minister of Militia. Bluff, blustering, bullying, a dynamo of energy, reckless in his speech, but a true Canadian, honest, devoted to his duty, fearing no man, an organizer of action.

The Minister of Militia was true to his promise. The 79th Cameron Highlanders of Canada remained in being as a base recruiting unit in Winnipeg, but the whole battalion, 1,100 strong, under the caption of the 43rd Cameron Highlanders, sailed for the front as a unit early the following year. And no finer battalion ever stepped on French soil than the 43rd Cameron Highlanders of Canada, at least so we modestly thought. Three hundred and fifty were members or adherents of St. Stephen's Church, two of my elders were officers, one the colonel. I could not bear the thought of sending them off to the front without their own minister. What of my wife and her family of little ones? I took the matter to her. Some things cannot be put down on paper, and that conversation is one of those things. My wife is the kind of woman that speaks with difficulty of the great things, but like Mary she "ponders them in her heart." Her last word, quietly spoken, I put down here:

"I always knew you would go. And—and—" there was a little catch in her voice—"those boys need you—more. Their mothers will be glad that you are to be with—them."

Nothing more was said. As for my kiddies, their pride in my going was rather disconcerting. Children have an uncanny insight into the very heart of things. They had read in the papers or had heard that those terrible Germans were killing women and children in Belgium and France. Naturally, they must be killed themselves. All those boys were going from St. Stephen's. Our own boys. Of course, Daddy would go. Every night of their lives during the war those children would pray for our soldiers. Their prayers were sometimes rather startling. My third, a fiercely loyal little flaxen-haired soul of eight, shocked her mother one night in her prayers.

"O God," she prayed with fervent passion, "bless the poor wounded soldiers and make them better quick so they can go and kill the Germans."

"Where did she get that bloodthirsty desire?" I asked later.

"Certainly not from me," declared her mother. "It was entirely of herself."

The departure of the 43rd Cameron Highlanders brought 50,000 people to line the streets of Winnipeg to watch their swinging kilts and hear the wild, weird shrilling of their pipes, and bid them God-speed. I could not know on that day that another day would come when I should see them march up to the dreadful Regina Trench on the Somme, some 580 strong, and see them march back a poor remnant of 68 dazed soldiers, but grim and unconquered, leaving their comrades in colored swaths before the uncut German wire.

CHAPTER XXIII

Lighter Interlude

AN EXPERIENCE which particularly interested me in those dark war days, and even more so in these days of peace, was the occasion on which I accompanied a Russian delegation on a visit, arranged by the British Admiralty, to the Grand Fleet, safely ensconced at Scapa Flow.

To me, as a Canadian, a more than ordinary interest is contributed by the fact that our delegation was under the charge of John Buchan, then busily engaged upon his great *History of the War,* now the esteemed and honored Governor General of our Dominion. The Russian delegates comprised a general, an admiral, a cousin of the great Tolstoi, and two others.

We traveled together via Inverness and reached our destination late in the evening. After dinner Mr. Buchan gathered us about the wheezy old hotel cabinet organ and led us in the singing of some Scottish songs to the great delight of our Russian guests.

The following day we visited certain battleships of the Grand Fleet, among them the *Queen Mary,* on which we had lunch. I sat next to Admiral Hood. I began talking of the war and the prospects of the Grand Fleet's being engaged with the enemy in a great naval encounter. Admiral Hood, with the face of a medieval saint and the gentle voice of a scholar, led the conversation to the discussion of Browning's poetry with which, fortunately, I was fairly familiar. Although he was a great admirer of Browning he did not hesitate to offer some acute criticisms both as to the involved and labored poetic style and in regard to the poet's philosophy. He quoted some beautiful bits from "Paracelsus" and from some of the shorter pieces, which he held in high esteem. "My Last Duchess" he regarded as high art.

His spirit, gentle as a woman's, his cultured mind, his lofty

215

Christian idealism, seemed strangely foreign to his profession as a fighting admiral in His Majesty's Grand Fleet. But at Jutland he showed his courage, taking his own ship into action between two of the enemy battleships, sinking or disabling both, if I remember rightly, but going down himself in the encounter.

I made my way to the midshipmen's quarters. I thought I had never met a finer looking, better spoken, and more gentlemanly lot of young fellows. They were keen on their job but avoided speaking about it. Everything else we talked about. They were eager to talk of Canada, its sports, its fishing and shooting, its wild West, in regard to all of which I could give them some personal experiences. Just as I was about to leave one youngster asked me eagerly:

"Do you think they'll come out, sir?"

I knew what he meant. Would the German Grand Fleet, upon which German hopes had been so elaborately built up, adventure a great sea fight with ours?

"If they are as wise as I think they are they will not."

"I hope they come out, sir," said one boy eagerly.

Some weeks after our arrival I was appointed chief chaplain of the Canadian forces in England. This made it necessary for me to report from time to time to the chaplain general, Colonel Stacey, whose headquarters were in London. On one occasion as I was entering our orderly room to get leave of absence to proceed to London, I met the pipe major of our band, who appeared to be quite downcast.

"What is the matter with the pipe major?" I inquired.

"Oh," said the colonel, rather brusquely, "the pipers are going on leave, and I have given them an alternative between taking a teetotal pledge or leaving their pipes behind them."

"Rather a tough proposition," I ventured. "A piper without his pipes is like a Highlander without his kilt."

"Quite right," replied the O.C. "But these are valuable pipes. These pipes were made specially for our battalion, and presented by our honorary colonel, Alexander Macdonald, as you know. They are the best that can be made, I'd hate to have them lost or injured."

"But after all, colonel," spoke up Major Grassie, the second-in-command, "drunk or sober a piper takes care of his pipes, just like a woman with her baby."

"When do they go?" I inquired.

"In two days," replied the colonel. "They go to London and take in the Lord Mayor's Show, and thence to Glasgow and the North Country."

"Going to see the Lord Mayor's Show?" I inquired. "What a pity they cannot march in the parade with the Canadians. They'd make a sensation. Do you know whether or not our Canadian contingent has a pipe band?

"I think not," replied the second-in-command.

"Well, it does seem a pity," I said, "that when this band is in the City it could not give the Canadian contingent the benefit of their assistance. They would certainly make a sensation and reflect glory on the Canadian contingent, not to speak of our battalion. Don't you think something might be done, colonel? Couldn't you pull some wires? What about General Carson?"

General Carson was the administrative chief of the Canadian forces in Britain, and had his headquarters in London.

"Also there is Sir Max Aitken," said Major Grassie, who was greatly interested in the pipe band. "He is a great friend of yours and of this battalion, and he admires our pipe band enormously. Something might be worked."

"If we had a couple of months," replied the O.C., "we might get something done, but in two days the thing is quite impossible."

"Well, colonel, I am summoned to London today. Give me a free hand and I will see what I can do."

"I will give you nothing of the kind," replied the colonel. "When you go to London you can do what you like. I assume no responsibility."

"Well, it really would be a great thing if our boys, since they are in London anyway, could take their place in the Canadian Contingent."

"That, of course," replied the colonel rather shortly, "is just nonsense. That parade is arranged months ahead. It is absurdly impossible that any change can be made at this date."

"But you don't mind my trying?" I persisted.

"I give you no authority whatever. Do as you like, but if you get into trouble don't expect me to pull you out."

Four days later I was sitting in the mess with the rest of the officers. After "the King" was drunk the colonel inquired: "Oh, by the way, padre, did you see the parade?"

"A bit of it," I replied.

"A bit of it?" echoed the colonel.

"Well, you don't see much of a parade when you are in it."

"Oh," he said scornfully, "of course you were in it. And by the way, did our band see it, do you know?"

"Yes, they saw a bit of it too."

"What do you mean?"

"Well, as I say, you can't see much of a parade when you are marching in it."

"Oh," said the second-in-command, "of course you and the band were leading the parade, I have no doubt."

"Not all the way, only the last half," I answered quietly.

"What do you mean, the last half?" By this time the whole table was listening intently.

"Well, you see," I replied casually, "we didn't get our order to move up to the head of the column till the show was half over."

There was a shout of derisive laughter.

"The Lord Mayor sent for you, naturally," said one of the officers.

"No, not the Lord Mayor, it was the colonel in command of the Canadian contingent. You see, they were leading the parade and they couldn't find us at first."

"Look here, padre, you know damned well you never saw the show," said the second-in-command.

"Oh, but I did," I replied. "So did our pipe band, and what is more important the citizens of London had an excellent opportunity of seeing and hearing our band play."

Again there were shouts of derisive laughter.

"Come on now, padre, you can't pull my leg like that. Don't tell me you were in the Lord Mayor's Show," said the second-in-command.

"Didn't you hear me tell you," I said quietly, "that I was in the show?"

"And the band too?" demanded the colonel.

"And the band, sir," I replied.

"For heaven's sake, what happened?" asked the second-in-command.

"Come on, padre! . . . Tell us . . . And tell the truth," came from the officers.

"Well," I said, "if you care to hear, it takes a little time."

"Go on," they all shouted.

"It is rather an interesting story. There were times, however, when I must say the interest became rather intense, but if you care to hear I shall be glad to tell you."

"Aw! go on. . . . Pipe up," they clamored.

"Do you wish me to report, sir?" I said to the colonel gravely.

"Go on, padre, we will listen to you," he said with a little grin.

"Well, sir, you will remember that you gave me permission to put the pipe band into the show—"

"Permission to put the pipe band into the show!" exclaimed the colonel. "Not on your life."

"Well, I mean you did not forbid me to do so."

"I simply told you the pipe band were to be on leave, that they were to be in London during the Lord Mayor's Show. What they or you did in London was no business of mine," he said, "so long as you all kept sober."

"I can assure you we all kept sober," I replied. "At times we were very sober indeed."

The officers were becoming impatient. The second-in-command said to the colonel: "I suggest, sir, that you order the padre to give us the full and detailed statement of what occurred during his recent visit to the City. It is part of his duty."

"Go on, padre. Don't waste time," said the colonel.

And away I went.

"Well, sir, after I reported to my chief, Colonel Stacey, I went to call upon General Carson, whose headquarters, you know, are at the Hotel Cecil. In conversation I brought up the matter of the Lord Mayor's Show and expressed my deep regret that our pipe band had not been invited to play for the Canadian contingent, which had been chosen to head the whole procession. 'You know our band,' I said; 'just think what a touch of perfection it would give.'

" 'Too bad,' he said. 'If we had known of it three months ago I believe it could easily have been arranged.'

" 'I suppose nothing could be done now, general,' I said.

" 'Why, my dear sir,' replied the general, 'the show is tomorrow.

The line of parade and the place of each unit in it was settled months ago. As I say, if I had known, even a few weeks ago, we might have done something.'

" 'Do you know who is the chief officer commanding?' I asked.

" 'I understand it is Sir John White, but I know nothing about him.'

" 'You have no influence with him, then?'

" 'Not the slightest.'

" 'Are there no wires you can pull at all in regard to this parade, general?' I asked.

" 'Not a wire, and if I could I shouldn't try at this late date.'

" 'I know one of the aldermen of the London County Council,' I said, 'Mr. Hodder-Williams. He is my publisher here.'

" 'Call him up,' said the general, with a grin. 'He no doubt will be able to arrange the whole thing.'

"I took him at his word, called up Mr. Hodder-Williams, who is a great friend of mine, and put my case before him.

" 'You are an alderman,' I said, 'and surely you can do a little thing like this. Get a pipe band added to the present Canadian contingent; that would require little influence.'

"He fairly shouted at me.

" 'I would have you remember,' he said, 'that you are now in London, that the London County Council is a body of grave and distinguished gentlemen. These arrangements are in the hands of an influential committee and have been perfected for three months. The place of every man, every company, every guild, every military unit is now fixed and published. Nothing under heaven could make a change.'

"I did my best with him, but he simply jeered at me. The thing was impossible. I made an appointment, however, to call upon him later in the afternoon.

"The general was greatly amused at my failure.

"Then I thought of your old friend," I said, turning to Major Osler, "Sir Max Aitken. He is a great admirer of the band, indeed of the whole battalion. I called him on the telephone, but he couldn't be seen. Several times throughout the afternoon I renewed my attempts to get him but failed.

"I spent an hour with Mr. Hodder-Williams, but he absolutely ridiculed the whole proposition. 'Why,' he said to me, 'the King himself could hardly make a change in that procession now, and certainly nobody less than the King.'

"Late at night I went back to see General Carson and report to him my complete failure.

" 'What did Sir Max say?' he inquired.

" 'I have not been able to get him. I wonder if I could try him now.' It was ten o'clock.

" 'Try him,' said the general, much amused. 'Don't tell him you are speaking from my office.'

"I called Sir Max Aitken. I got his secretary. No! Sir Max could not be seen. As a matter of fact, he had been ill in bed all day. I expressed my profound grief, told her to say who was speaking and sent a message of sympathy.

" 'Wait a moment, sir,' she replied.

"In a few minutes I heard Sir Max's voice. He made some pleasant inquiries about the battalion and the officers, and then I said:

" 'I have been trying to get you all the afternoon, Sir Max.'

"He was very sorry and asked me what I wanted. I told him my story.

" 'I say, padre,' he said, 'have you been taking anything today with the general?'

" 'No, I am perfectly sober.'

" 'Then you are crazy,' he said. 'You are not in the wild West of Canada just now, remember, you are in the City of London. If I had even a week to work on it I might do something, but on twenty-four hours' notice, why, the thing is nonsense.' He became almost excited. I set that down to his illness.

"Gently I tried to show him how easily the matter might be arranged. The Canadian contingent was there and would be in place, all he had to do was to suggest to the O.C. to take on a few more men. 'And you know, Sir Max,' I said, 'what a contribution the band would make to the whole Canadian contingent.'

"He just laughed at me and told me to go to bed.

"So I apologized, expressed the hope that he would soon be better, gave him the greetings of our whole battalion, and ended up with the suggestion that I would still cherish a hope that he would be able to get somebody to do something, and that I would be at the hotel that night and next morning.

"He practically told me to go to blazes and I left him to his repose. Of course, I gave the whole thing up, but really I felt very disappointed. It seemed to me such a simple thing."

The whole mess broke into a roar of laughter.

"Well," I went on, "I had arranged with the pipe major that I should meet him at Charing Cross Station next morning. So bright and early at half past seven I met the band. I had arranged with the general that the band should serenade him before breakfast next morning and he was delighted. So we paraded up to the Hotel Cecil, marched into the courtyard. I sent word up to the general, and he came out onto the balcony. The pipes treated him to their best. Afterwards the general took them down, gave them some refreshment, though I warned him that our colonel was very particular about his pipe band. Then he treated them to breakfast and the interview was over. By this time the line of the march was being crowded with sightseers. I was terribly disappointed. Here was one of the finest bands in England and there was the procession and the two could not be brought together.

"As we set out from the courtyard into the street and I saw that solid mass of citizens lining each side of the line of march, I made a sudden resolve. There wouldn't be any harm in our marching down that empty street and if we saw a space we might slip into it. I explained the proposition to the band. They were game for anything."

"Was the band playing?" asked a member of the mess.

"Certainly not," I replied. "We were much too modest for that." This remark was received with derisive laughter.

"On we went until we came to a turn in the street. A policeman stopped me, but before he could say a word I asked him: 'Can you tell me where the head of the procession will be at this moment?' "

" 'Yes, sir,' he said, 'somewhere down about the Guildhall.'

"By this time it was a little after nine. The parade would be setting forth in about three-quarters of an hour.

" 'Well,' I said, 'I would be glad if you would direct me.' I explained that we were Canadians and would like to join the Canadian contingent. At once he cleared a passage through the crowd, called another policeman and sent him with us to show us the shortest cuts by which we could reach the head of the procession.

"Away we went again, the police officer making the crowd stand back for us. We crossed several streets and finally found ourselves back on the line of march. I suggested to the officer that we would be all right now.

"'Certainly, sir,' he said, saluting. 'Jist keep till the way!' Again he made the crowd stand back, ushered us into the open street and away we went. Soon we came upon a mounted officer. 'This,' I said to myself, 'will be our finish.' An idea came to me. I halted the band, went straight up and said to him: 'Where do you think I could find Sir John White? I believe he is in command of the procession.'

"'I could not tell you that, sir. He will be somewhere near the top.'

"I thanked him. We were stopped at intervals by officers stationed on the line of march. I always made the same request as to the where-abouts of the Canadians and Sir John White. However, nobody stopped us and finally we arrived at the Guildhall. Here all the side streets were packed with dense crowds of sightseers and with various con-tingents of troops, guilds and so on, waiting to swing into the proces-sion. I halted our band near the Guildhall and went up to an officer in command of one of the waiting contingents and asked him where the Canadians were located.

"'Up at the head,' he said, 'about half a mile from here. Are you Canadians?'

"'Yes,' I said.

"'Well,' he said, 'I am afraid you cannot get through now, sir.'

"'Too bad,' I said.

"'Why not swing in behind us here?'

"I thought a moment and decided that it might be as well not to get too close to the Canadians and that it might be better to swing in behind this officer who happened to be commanding a detachment of the West Surreys.

"'All right,' I said. 'We'll swing in after you.'

"As we were waiting a crowd gathered round our kilts and began chaffing them.

"'Play up, Jock! Gie us a skirl!'

"I looked at the officer. He nodded. I spoke to the pipe major and they were off. In an instant we were surrounded by a group of Scotties —London, you know, is full of Scotties—cheering and cracking jokes and finally when the pipes struck into a Scotch reel we had three or four sets of men and women dancing, snapping their fingers, whooping wildly. Of course, you will remember that at this time the Lord Mayor and the great officials and high dignitaries were at divine service in the Cathedral. It occurred to me that it was a lucky thing the Cathedral was some distance off, for our contribution would hardly fit in with the service being conducted there.

"After a while I began to notice that the contingents were falling in line, getting ready for the march.

"'Who follows you here?' I asked the officer of the West Surreys.

"'The Manchesters there,' he said, pointing to a company of soldiers in a side street.

"I looked across at them, some twenty yards away.

"'I think I will let the Canadians go,' I said to the West Surrey officer.

"'Quite all right,' he replied. 'Step in smartly after us and pay no attention to anybody. We will soon be moving now.'

"I stopped the dancing and told the pipe major that we should give up our attempt to reach the Canadians. As a matter of fact, there was nothing I desired less than to meet the officer in charge of the Canadian contingent. I explained our plan to the pipe major and said: 'Pay no attention to anybody. We will swing in after the West Surreys here. Keep right up close.'

"Soon the procession was on the march. As the West Surreys stepped off I followed immediately after them. A young lieutenant from the Manchesters came rushing up.

"'Excuse me, sir,' he said. 'I believe the Manchesters march in succession to the West Surreys.'

"'Oh,' I said, 'it really doesn't matter much, there has been a change. Just fall in behind us here. It is quite all right.' I paid no more attention to him and off we went. But I was none too sure what was going to happen to us.

"With brief halts now and then, we marched along, our pipes playing up whenever the band marching before us gave us a chance. As the noon hour approached we came to a halt to allow the men to have their lunch and I suddenly remembered that we had no rations with us. However, as I was planning a raid on some shops near by I noticed that we had halted immediately before the Australian House. I called the pipe major and told him to strike up. Again we had a riotous crowd around us. The windows of the Australian House were packed with enthusiastic listeners. Presently an Australian officer came down and invited me up to visit the Australians. I explained to him that I had to look after my men, but under persuasion I thought I could run up for a few minutes.

"In the room there was no less a person than Prime Minister Hughes of Australia and his distinguished friends. They gave me a warm welcome. I explained that I had to look after my men and that we were without rations, as I had been unable to get in touch with the Canadian contingent.

" 'Don't worry,' they assured me, 'we'll look after them.'

"They carried down a lot of stuff to the band. I took care that the drinks were of the right quality, and presently the band began playing again, with an enthusiastic crowd about them, dancing and whooping in great style.

"After lunch the procession set off once more. But we had hardly got started when I saw a mounted officer coming down upon us. He was inquiring for Major Gordon and his pipe band. I confess that a sudden panic seized me. Now I did not know what was going to happen.

"The officer came to me, presented the compliments of the O.C. of the Canadian contingent and an invitation from him to bring the pipe band up to the head of the procession and join the Canadians there. We were quite all right where we were in the procession and enjoying ourselves. I explained to him that perhaps we had better stay where we were, that we were quite all right and so on.

" 'It is the O.C.'s orders, sir,' he said. This was different.

" 'Orders?' I said.

" 'Yes, sir, it's his orders.'

"So off we went, marching along past all the various contingents, ancient guilds, etc., etc., and receiving enthusiastic cheers from the crowds on both sides. I was becoming more and more anxious as to what might be awaiting us. But there was nothing to do but follow the officer. At intervals the whole procession would halt, but we kept marching straight on up toward the head.

"Finally we arrived at the Canadian contingent, which had a cadet pipe band whose playing was rather terrible. I fell in at the rear and told the officer that this would be quite all right for us, that I would report later. I instructed the pipe major to play alternately with the cadet band, and said to him, 'Now give us all you've got.' I never heard the pipes sound as they did then. The high stone walls on either side and the stone pavement on which we were marching gave back our music in a perfectly glorious way. I had never heard band music to such advantage. I began to feel easier in my mind and to think that our troubles were over.

"At the first pause in the march, however, back came the officer with the request from the O.C. of the Canadian contingent that we should proceed to the head and lead the column.

"I was completely flabbergasted, but I said that I hardly liked to supersede the cadet band. Furthermore, I was quite sure that the music of our band would really be more useful at the rear of the column than away out in front, and suggested that the present arrangement would really be much better from a musical point of view.

"The Colonel was good enough to accept my suggestion. So we carried on. The truth is, I did not want to 'crowd my luck' unduly. Just as the parade was about to finish it occurred to me that the band must have dinner before taking their train, and that it might be wiser for us to fall out quietly and allow the procession to finish without us. So I sent my compliments to the O.C. explaining the circumstances and thanking him most cordially for his courtesy, expressing the hope that we had been of some assistance and emphasizing the importance of our catching the train.

"The O.C. was very decent about it, sent back his warm thanks for our fine assistance and expressed his delight at the music furnished by the band of the Forty-third, and wished us all good luck. I have not heard from him since.

"It was all quite interesting and the pipe band really covered itself with glory."

My story was enthusiastically approved, especially by the juniors of the mess, as a great lark. The seniors, on the whole, ostensibly considering it a piece of unparalleled cheek, secretly were delighted, I think, that the thing had been successfully pulled off by their padre. The colonel felt in duty bound to condemn the whole thing as utterly irregular, but contented himself with the remark:

"Well, padre, you put it through, but I make a guess that we have not heard the last of the Lord Mayor's Show."

His guess proved right. Two weeks later he called me into the orderly room, and handing me a blue envelope said with a grin: "Take a look at that, major." I took the chit:

Attention the O.C. 43rd Battalion Canadian Highlanders of Canada

Please inform this department, etc., etc.
1. Did the pipe band of the 43rd Cameron Highlanders of Canada march in the recent Lord Mayor's procession in London on such and such a date?
2. If so, by whose orders did the band appear in the procession?
3. What officer was in command of the pipe band on that occasion?

"Well, sir, I don't suppose there is any rush in this matter," I suggested. "I shall do all I can to secure the information."

"Oh, very well. Don't say I didn't warn you," replied the O.C.

"Of course, sir," I said, "I suppose there is no immediate rush in this matter. I shall be absent on duty for a few days. Meantime, the usual army practice of 'stalling' may perhaps be followed."

He grinned at me. "We shall do what we can. But seriously I'm afraid you haven't heard the last of this. The chief chaplain of the Canadian forces in England is an officer of some importance."

"All right, sir. I'll take it when it comes. But it was a great lark. The laugh is on them really."

"A great lark? Well, the best laugh is the last laugh."

I left the orderly room with unpleasant visions of a court-martial, with dismissal of the chief chaplain from the Canadian forces and return to Canada.

It was the war that saved me. Within ten days the 43rd Cameron Highlanders of Canada were ordered on active service to France. I resigned my command as chief chaplain to the Canadian forces in England, and proceeded to Boulogne as senior chaplain of the 3rd Division in France. The last laugh was mine, after all.

CHAPTER XXIV

A Padre in the Trenches

THE CHAPLAIN's service is a time-honored institution in the British army. The duties of the chaplain were largely confined to the formal parade services, to the care and comfort of the wounded and sick and to other more or less formal social functions.

At the outbreak of the war the chaplain's service was regarded somewhat as a concession to the general religious spirit of the nation. Similarly, the Y. M. C. A. service was considered unnecessary by the authorities. But before the end of the first year of war the chaplain service had won its right to a place within the war zone, and the Y. M. C. A. had proved its usefulness to the army in its ministry to the wounded and sick and to every department of the army service.

As senior chaplain to the 9th Brigade, I accompanied the 3rd Division to Boulogne and up to the Ypres salient, where we were to have our first taste of actual war. The 43rd Cameron Highlanders were stationed at Camp E, a little beyond Poperinghe, from which we could see at night the glare of the Very lights and of the bursting shells some miles away. Occasionally a shell from a long-range gun would drop near our camp.

Near by were various hospital units which I visited from time to time and where I got my first sense of the ruthlessness of war. My first reaction was amazement at the uncomplaining endurance of our wounded. In rows within a former wayside inn they lay awaiting their turn at the hands of the medical officers. The worst cases were rushed down to base hospitals, the others had to wait.

I have seen thousands of wounded men, have ministered to them, have aided the medical officers in their work, but I never once heard a wounded man curse his luck or curse an enemy. They took their wounds as part of their routine; as to the Boche, they did not seem to cherish any violent hate for a fighting enemy. He was doing his job and it wasn't his fault.

After ten days or so in Camp E we were "sent up into the line." Our route lay by the ruined city of Ypres, thence by way of Zillebeke and on to Sanctuary Wood and Maple Copse, in whose shelter were our lines of dugouts among the tree roots.

It was a black night with a drizzle of rain. A good thing, we were assured, because the visibility for the enemy gunners would be bad. A train took us to a huge red brick building on the outskirts of Ypres; it was known as the Asylum and was used as a collecting station for the wounded. Immediately upon debarkation the order for silence had been passed.

"How far off are the enemy?" I asked the colonel.

"A couple of miles or so, I guess."

"Well, they can't hear us very well at that distance."

"No, but this country is thick with spies, who have all sorts of means of communicating with the enemy. I should be surprised if our train hasn't been already reported." This was not very cheering.

We were met by two guides and set off in the black darkness by a narrow side road slippery with mud. Suddenly there was a vivid flare of light high up in the sky, illuminating the whole country.

"A shell," I thought and waited for the explosion, but to my great relief no explosion followed, only a soft "plop."

"Very light!" said the colonel.

We tramped through the mud in dead silence for about a mile. I was beginning to get a little tired of this everlasting slush when suddenly I heard a soft muffled thud, then a vicious whine increasing in volume and in speed every fraction of a second, then over our heads, it seemed, a vast explosion and in the field to our right a great upheaval of earth.

"That's the spot!" remarked one of our men with a chuckle.

"Hit 'em again, Fritzie," said another. But I noticed that the battalion pulled itself together and that its step was considerably quickened. For myself, I lost all sense of weariness. Soon came a second muffled sound—a long savage whine—another appalling explosion as another shell pitched into the field beside us, throwing mud high into the air.

"That'll do now, Fritzie," remonstrated a soldier seriously.

A little later our guides halted and began to consult with each other.

"What's the matter?" asked the colonel sharply.

"Not quite sure if this is our turning point."

"What? You don't know your road? Nice set of guides you are!" The colonel never could bear anything like slackness or mistake.

"Excuse me, sir. I'll go ahead a bit." One of the guides disappeared in the dark. It was an unpleasant feeling. I hated it worse than the shell. We were a few hundred yards from the enemy trenches. If we should take a wrong turn we might easily stumble into one—a most unpleasant surprise for all.

We were taking over from a battalion of the Princess Pats, a smart battalion with considerable social prestige behind it and, though we didn't know it then, a fine fighting record before it. We found guides to place our men and officers into their appropriate quarters. The dugouts seemed to me to be ghastly underground dens, whose earth walls and roofs were only partially covered with timbers. By good luck my batman had been able to get the loan of a primus stove from the outgoing medical officer, a priceless acquisition, as we found out later, for warmth and for producing hot drinks for stretcher bearers, wounded men and for ourselves.

We soon made ourselves ready for bed. Our bunks were of bare boards, upon which we laid our blankets and slept in our clothes. I had just got myself settled down, after comfortably adjusting the angles of my bony structure to the ridges of the slats, when a little scratching noise drew my attention to the wall next my head. Looking through a crack in the wall I saw two gleaming points of light which in a few moments I decided were eyes in the gray head of an enormous rat. I pounded on the slats, the eyes never blinked. They seemed to regard me with the calm insolence of an old-timer for a new settler. We discussed the situation, the M.O. and I, and finally came to agreement as to the priority of the old-timer's residential rights and decided to let it go at that. The M.O. called him Old Joe, but before the end of our time we found it necessary to have a fresh christening, for we discovered Old Joe cuddling a bunch of hairless, grubby-looking creatures, whereupon Old Joe at the M.O.'s suggestion became Jemima and so remained during our sojourn with her. It became one of the minor outdoor sports of our men to take pot shots at the huge rats that infested our quarters, but no one ever thought of molesting Jemima. We felt that under the rule of international law, which we were fighting to maintain, Jemima's rights were supreme.

* * * *

In the front line work the chaplain's job brings him into frequent touch with death. Every hour one lives under its shadow. The first night the dugout which I shared with the medical officer was bitterly cold, a cold that blankets could not keep out. My cold feet made my sleep rather broken. Before daybreak a stretcher bearer came with the news that a man had been shot during the night in the front trench and that he must be buried at once. I hurried into my tunic and overcoat and followed the man to the little cemetery in an open glade in the woods. There the lad lay. I uncovered his face. He was the brother of our sergeant of stretcher bearers, and had a tiny bluish hole in the middle of his forehead. The burial party, which consisted of a file of soldiers, was in charge of Lieutenant Arthur Sullivan. The gray dawn was flushing into morning. It was my first burial. I could hardly fix my mind on my task. I was thinking of his little home in Winnipeg and of the mother in that home. I could see the men about had their eyes fixed curiously upon me. I remembered that I was the officer in charge of this job and must go through with it in proper form. For my life I could not remember how I should begin. As I stood there looking down upon that quiet face, the lieutenant said:

"Shall we lower away, sir? This is rather open. And they say it is a bad spot."

"Lower away," I said and didn't recognize my own voice. All the proper words for a burial service fled from my mind. They covered the boy's face with his gray blanket and lowered him into a shallow grave. The words of the old Psalm came to me:

"The Lord is my shepherd; I shall not want. . . .
Yea, though I walk through the valley of the shadow of death,
   I will fear no evil."

My mind began to work. Other words came to me—and I heard myself saying:

"Let not your heart be troubled: ye believe in God, believe also in me. In my Father's house are many mansions. . . . I go to prepare a place for you. And if I go and prepare a place for you, I will come again and receive you unto myself."

At this point an enemy machine gun opened fire somewhere. A queer patter as of raindrops on the leaves sounded overhead. The men dropped on their faces. I never heeded the patter. I was trying to get through my service for the dead. The sight of the men cowering before me on the ground gave me back my nerve. I found myself talking to them.

"I will fear no evil, for thou art with me. . . . I will come again, and receive you unto myself.

"These are God's words, the words of our Lord Jesus. In the case of our comrade here, they have been fulfilled. He was doing his duty when death came, but the Heavenly Father was with him. Our Lord Christ took him, and so no evil has befallen him. He is with his God and Saviour."

I was relieved to note that my voice was quiet and steady. A few words of prayer—the committal—the benediction, and the service was over.

They filled in the yellow earth upon the gray blanket, placing a board at his head with his name, the battalion, his age, the date of his death, and the platoon marched off in charge of a sergeant. There is no volley firing in the front-line burial. I stood for a time beside that lonely grave. The machine guns were still spitting about us. I forgot all about them. The lieutenant touched my arm.

"I think, sir, we had better move into cover," he said.

That patter on the leaves above me might have been rain. I was saying to myself, "God in heaven, can I stand this thing?"

"Cover?" I said. "Yes, of course. It's a lovely place. These trees are beautiful."

We went to breakfast at the headquarters mess.

The colonel greeted me cheerfully.

"Well, you were on duty early."

"Yes, sir!" The sadness of my burial service was still upon me.

"Fine chap Macdonald. He was peering over the parapet, where he had no business to be, and a sniper got him. They have the line all set and they keep sniping even in the dark on general principles. Our men will have to learn to keep their heads down."

His words grated terribly upon me. They seemed heartless. I ate my breakfast in silence.

"We will take a walk along the front line right after breakfast," continued the colonel in a matter-of-fact tone. "Care to come along?"

"Thank you," I said. "I think I'll get my dugout straightened out."

"Better come along," he said somewhat sharply. "Must see our men are all right."

Suddenly it came to me how right he was. An officer's duty lies with the living. It was the lesson I needed and it did me good. Since then I have buried men in rows, but once my service was over I turned resolutely to my next duty, which was with the living. How right it is. After the volley over the grave the firing party marches off to a merry tune.

* * * *

Courage is an undefinable quality of soul. In the war I had occasion to revise my psychology in many particulars, indeed my whole ideology in regard to human emotions and passions was recast. Courage is an attitude of spirit toward danger that I am quite unable to define. I have seen men who would not quail in the midst of a bombardment become incapacitated as they approached the shell-fire zone.

I think of a young lieutenant who on three distinct occasions, when we reached the zone of fire and as a desultory shell came now and then over our heads, fell to the ground, his face blue, his breath coming in gasps, utterly unable to carry on. He made the most desperate attempts to struggle forward, but each time fell helpless in his tracks. Once in response to his entreaty I put him on my horse and carried him forward a half mile or so, but it was all in vain. He had to be carried out on a stretcher. But if a bombardment caught him in our trenches, he could carry on without fear.

I rarely came in contact with a man whom I might call a coward. After a heavy bombardment in which we had the misfortune to lose an efficient and gallant medical officer another M.O. was sent up to take over. It was his first experience of the trenches. He shared my dugout. After a quiet night we were suddenly roused out of sleep by a brisk little bombardment. At the first shell we both sprang up from our bunks and dressed with all speed, for we knew we would soon have work to do.

I noticed he was shivering as with a deadly chill.

"It's d-d-d-a-m-n-e-d c-c-o-old," he said as he fumbled with his buttons and buckles.

"I'll make tea," I said, got my primus stove going, and made tea with all speed. As we were drinking a wounded man came staggering in with the help of a stretcher bearer.

"Wounded man, sir! Arm messed up a bit," said the stretcher bearer, MacRae by name, easing the man to one of our cots.

I proceeded to help the stretcher bearer get off his coat and cut off his shirt sleeve. It was quite messy, but though he was weak from loss of blood, the wounded man was making light of it.

"Guess it's a blighty for me all right, sir," he said with a grin.

"Right you are. You're a lucky beggar!" I said.

The M.O. was fussing rather helplessly with dressings and bandages when bang! came a shell not very far away. The bandages dropped from his fingers.

"God! that was near!" he exclaimed, shivering like a man with St. Vitus's dance.

"You're cold, doctor," I said, picking up his bandage. "Here, get this chap tied up, he's losing blood."

"Yes, yes! He's bleeding bad," he muttered as he took the bandage and in desperate haste skillfully tied up the wound. We gave the wounded man tea and soon had him ready to start for the first-aid station.

"I'll go along to help this stretcher bearer," I said.

"No, no! You mustn't go!" said the medical officer. "I mean—I may need you. There may be another soon."

The stretcher bearer and the wounded man cast him a queer look, glanced at each other and then at me.

"This man is rather weak," I pointed out. "We may have to carry him."

"No! you mustn't—I can't. I mean I must have help with the wounded!"

"I'll be all right, sir," said the wounded man. "This is quite comfortable now."

"What about it, MacRae?" I asked. "Can you manage?"

"Sure thing. I'll make that beggar walk. What has he got legs for? He'll walk all right. Come on, you lucky devil."

And off they went joshing each other.

I could not make up my mind about the M.O. I hated to think he was afraid. I had seen doctors and stretcher bearers under fire often, but never had I seen anything but the coolest indifference to danger.

"You're not well," I said.

"No," he said, his head in his hands. "I'm desperately ill."

Bang! came another shell rocking our dugout.

With a little cry he leaped from his cot and stood shaking.

"Well, that one won't hurt us anyway," I said. "Come on, take another cup of tea and a biscuit. You're probably hungry."

"Hungry! No! No! I couldn't eat a bite! I'm sick! I'll have to get out of this! I must see the colonel!"

"I shouldn't do that," I suggested.

At this two stretcher bearers brought in a man lying on his face. When I stripped off his helmet we saw that his back was a mess of blood and torn flesh. They laid him down on the table.

I got bandages ready and stood waiting. The sight of the lacerated back seemed to steady the M.O. He went swiftly to work, cleansing the wound.

"Can't do much with this here. We will just tie him up." He laid some lint soaked in disinfectant on the wounds and with clever fingers fastened his bandages. "There, that's all we can do. Take him along."

"Fine, doctor," I said. "Take him along, boys. He'll soon be on his way home, lucky beggar.

"Don't forget," I went on quietly, "your Heavenly Father is near you."

"Yes, sir," he whispered. "I know that."

The little doctor glanced at me with a kind of contempt as they left us.

"I guess the Heavenly Father can't stop those shells," he said.

"Don't be an ass!" I said. I had little patience with him. "The best medical authorities recognize the therapeutic value of a quiet mind. Fear lowers vitality. You know that."

Bang! a shell shook our dugout.

His fear was pitiable. "My God! I can't stand this," he wailed. "I simply can't stand this!"

"Nonsense!" I said. "You'll get used to it. Come on out with me, and see the boys carry on."

There is no tonic for fear like the sight of courage. But he refused to leave the dugout. He lay down on his face in his bunk. He was quite incapable. He would struggle to his feet and under the protestation and stimulation of the stretcher bearers he would help till the next shell came, when once more he became incapacitated.

The O.C. made short work of him. He went down that night with the wounded. His trouble was that his supreme interest in life was himself.

I remember on one of my trips through the northern woods of Ontario I was going along a quiet trail when suddenly I was startled by a vicious rustle just at my feet. There was a mother partridge, her feathers all on end, rustling furiously at me while a dozen little chicks scurried to cover. In half a minute they were in hiding and then this desperate, fearless mother bird fled. She thought first of her little brood. She feared me, but her gallant little heart was filled with a greater passion, mother love. Fear is the triumph of self-love.

A month or so later I came on this M.O. in a dressing station down the line, loud-mouthed, foul-mouthed, retailing a smutty story to the group around.

"Hello, doctor!" I said. "All right again?" He stared at me. "Last time I saw you you were ill. Sanctuary Wood, you remember?"

We had less out of him for the rest of the night. I have seen men scurry for cover under shell fire, as was their duty. I have plumped at speed into a shell hole or friendly trench. A shell is a marvelous accelerator. But that is not cowardice. It is common sense and duty. I have seen shell-shocked men, half a dozen or so, and have been sorry for them. But that little filthy-mouthed M.O. was one of the few cowards I saw in the war. On the other hand, I have seen medical officers and their assistants, stretcher bearers and runners under shell fire, "carrying on" at their duty without pause or falter, noncombatants, but heroes every one.

I have seen medical officers carry on at their work under shell fire for twenty-four hours at a time, till they went staggering through their work, blind with weariness, stopping only to swallow a cup of hot cocoa or coffee, but never quitting till after their work was done or they were relieved. Then they would stumble to their cots and fall dead asleep in their clothes.

It is strange how war reveals traits of character, possibilities of endurance, courage, self-sacrifice, unsuspected in the majority of men. I never could have imagined the qualities of the human spirit that were revealed in the terrific experiences of war.

* * * * *

Communication lines are the nerves of war. The telegraph and telephone, the heliograph and semaphore are absolutely essential. But nothing can take the place of the "runner." There are messages that cannot be entrusted to any other means of communication. As a rule the runners were mere boys. No rank of service furnished finer examples of cool courage, and of resources in the exercise of duty.

One black, rainy night there came into headquarters up in the line a slip of a youth, his pale face lit by large black eyes, his soaked uniform clinging to his thin figure. Smartly he snapped his salute, from his pouch he drew a chit, and handing it to the O.C., stood at attention.

"All right, boy. Give him a cup of tea," said the O.C. who was extraordinarily careful of his runners. "Bad night, eh?"

"Not so bad, sir," said the youngster. "Poor visibility."

"That's lucky, eh? Good lad."

The O.C. read the chit, sent for his adjutant and consulted for a few minutes and wrote his answer. The moment he was ready the little runner was on his feet and at attention.

"Sit down, boy. Finish your tea."

"I'm all right, sir," said the youth eagerly.

"Do what I tell you. Sit down and take another cup of tea. Have you no cake, batman?"

"Yes, sir, there's not much—just a bit, sir," answered the batman, regardful of his chief's needs.

"Give him a good slice!" ordered the colonel. "How far have you come?"

"Camp E, sir."

"Camp E! Good Lord!"

"Took train to the Asylum, sir."

"Even so, that's a long run a night like this. The duckboards must be slippery, eh?"

"Yes, sir."

He finished his tea and was on his feet again waiting.

"Rest for half an hour. Lie down on that bunk there."

"I'm quite all right, sir. The general said to hurry, sir."

"He did, eh? You do what I tell you. Lie down on that bunk for half an hour." He wrote a few words on the outside of the answer and gave it to the boy. "That will keep you right."

The youngster took off his tin hat and belts and overcoat and lay down. In one minute he was gone, his pale face looking almost boyish in his sleep.

"What a hell of a thing war is!" said the O.C. The batman removed the boy's boots, dried his feet and anointed them with an evil-smelling mixture.

"What stuff is that, batman?" enquired the O.C. "It smells a little like hell. Do you recognize it, padre?"

"Can't say I do."

"Yes, sir," said the batman. "There's sulphur in it, sir."

"Yes! Oh, I see! Quite all right," said the O.C. with a grin. "That's in your line, padre, eh?"

"Not so sure about that, sir. Rather hope not."

"Wake him in three-quarters of an hour, batman. Give him something to eat and let him go."

I had another experience of a runner, alas, more terribly tragic.

Once I was called out from the front line in Sanctuary Wood to perform a burial duty at the Château Belge for a young officer of another battalion. My batman, taking his rifle as always, stepped in behind me and we set off in the early forenoon for a six-mile walk. My batman, Edward Ledger, was something of a character. In peace days he had been my stableman and gardener, his wife was maid to my wife. When war broke out Edward was quite indifferent. It was no particular business of his. He was no soldier. But as battalions began to fill up, and as men began to enlist he became uneasy and often would make comments on the movements at the front. The English papers made him thoughtful. When I made up my mind that I should go to war, Edward came to me and asked to be allowed to go also.

"Edward," I said, "I need you to stay here and help Mrs. Gordon to look after things."

He agreed with me for a time and was content. But soon his wife came to me and said: "I wish you would let Edward go. He is quite miserable. There is no living with him."

"Do you want him to go?"

"No, but I know he will be miserable at home."

"Well, it is as you say."

"He wants to go. Better take him with you."

"If he asks me I shall take him," I said.

Next day Edward came to me with his request.

"You've thought this over, Edward. You might get killed, you know."

"So might you, sir," he said.

"You may go."

That same afternoon Edward appeared in khaki.

I told my brother Dr. Henry F. Gordon, who with his eldest son was also enlisting, about Edward's resolve to go to war.

"I can't understand Edward's wanting to go. He is anything but a warrior," I said, "rather a lamblike person."

My brother looked at me curiously.

"You don't know Edward, I guess. I said yesterday to him: 'What are you going to war for, Edward? You'll get killed.'"

"'Oh, I guess not,' he said. 'Don't you know why I'm going? I am going to look after the doctor.'"

It was a revelation to me. Edward was a faithful and loyal servant, but that he had any special regard for me I had never suspected. Events proved the truth of my brother's words. Edward's devotion to me was almost amazing. It became a joke in our mess. He not only had me a shining example for all other batmen, but his care for my comfort and health was unfailing. And in the front line I could not step out of the dugout but Edward would seize his rifle and be at my heels.

Immediately upon our emerging from the shelter of the woods in which our trenches were dug, a shell came over our head and lifted a huge cloud of earth some fifty yards away. Like a hunting dog after a hit bird, Edward was racing over the field toward the shell hole, heedless of my calls. He sprang into the shell hole and began digging frantically with his hands. After some minutes of strenuous effort he returned.

"What the deuce are you doing there? Don't you know these shells often come in salvos of two or three? There's the second now! Get down!" A shell came whining as I spoke and plunked down a little nearer as I lay hugging mother earth.

Again Edward sprang to his feet.

"Keep down, you fool!" I yelled at him. He dropped, evidently quite disappointed.

"I wanted to get that nose-cap for Mrs. Ledger, sir," he said in explanation.

"Don't be an idiot. She'd rather have you than any nose-cap. Now don't you ever do that again till you are sure the shelling is over. Here comes the third! Down, down!" I flattened myself on the bosom of mother earth—but there was no explosion. It was a dud.

Edward was all for investigation. Never once did I see him show any signs of fear.

"Leave that alone, and lie flat on your belly," I ordered. "You never can tell about those duds. They may have delayed fuses."

It was with some exercise of authority that I kept him from digging for nose-caps, and we finally went on our way. We reached the Château Belge, where the burial was to take place. I performed my duty, had lunch with the officers in charge and set off on my return journey.

"Before you reach the next crossroads a quarter of a mile up," the officer warned me, "wait in the old ruined stone building beside the road. The Huns always have a little spell of 'hate' there about this time. They spray the crossroads four ways every day at the same hour and with the same number of shells. They are most methodical. Give them time to get through their little ceremonial."

"All right," I said. "Who am I to intrude upon Kaiser Bills' religious exercises?"

We came to the ruined stone building and waited. Sure enough, the daily service began. Having no desire to share in the Hun performance, we waited.

Along came a runner at a smart walk. I hailed him into our shelter and bade him wait. I got his name and battalion, as I always did. He was anxious to go on. As I was explaining the situation, the "hate" kept steadily on. With marvelous accuracy as to time and direction the shells fell upon the crossroads, leaving great holes on the hard roads.

After the shelling had ceased for some time, the runner was for going on.

"No! Wait a little," I advised. "Give them time to finish. You never can tell. They have an unpleasant trick of dropping an Amen or two at the close of the service."

As I finished speaking two shells in quick succession dropped on the crossroads. After an interval of quiet, again the runner was for off, but I ordered him to wait.

Five, six, seven minutes passed.

"That will be all now, I think, sir," he said. "This is a rush message, sir. I had better go, sir."

"Wait a few minutes longer," I said. "You have a long time to be dead, you know."

"Yes, sir, but my time is marked down."

I held him back for some minutes, but finally giving him a bunch of cigarettes, rather unwillingly I let him go on.

Saluting smartly he stepped off at a brisk pace waving his hand cheerily to Edward. We watched him to the crossroads. As he turned to the left, just at the cross a shell came whining and lit just at the turning upon the hard road.

"It's got him, sir," said Edward, setting off on a run. I followed. The boy lay on his back as if asleep. I lifted his head, my hand came away bloody. A splinter of shell had pierced his brain.

"Go to the château and get a stretcher," I said, and sat down on the grass.

Who could explain this mystery? It was the very last shell. "My time is marked down," he had said.

I buried him at the château beside the officer, saw that his name and necessary data were duly recorded on his headboard, and wrote to his O.C. enclosing a letter for his mother.

"A fearless soldier and keen to do his duty," I wrote. "We may safely leave him with God."

But—alas! in war there are so many unanswered questionings.

CHAPTER XXV

Under Fire

IN LINE OF DUTY—UNEXPLAINABLE ESCAPE—A
SOLDIER'S MOTHER—DEATH OF EDWARD—STILL
BRAVELY SINGING—THE LINE BENDS—BURIAL
BY NIGHT—BOMBARDMENT

IT WAS our third go in the front line and for the first two weeks the enemy treated us to a more or less perfunctory bombardment. We were camped under the cover of two thick bits of forest known as Maple Copse and Sanctuary Wood. The beginning of the third week found us quite fed up with our experience and waiting impatiently for our relief. On the Wednesday the shells began to rain in upon us rather steadily and the men were ordered to take cover.

My dugout, a hole in a slight hillside with a tin roof, flimsy enough, I shared with the M.O., a first-class surgeon, a cool and cheery officer popular with the mess and greatly loved by the men.

We had just finished tying up a wounded man whom we had laid upon a ledge of earth running round the walls of the dugout. In our dugout were the M.O. and his batman, my batman, the sergeant of the stretcher bearers and one of his men, when in came the second-in-command, Major Grassie, for a "wee kailie" as he said.

The bombardment was growing in intensity, the shells dropping about us in unpleasant proximity. Already a number of our trenches had been blown up. Some dozen yards away a company of men were completing the construction of a large deep dugout.

I said: "Boys, there are too many of us in this dugout. It is against regulations. Besides, this tin roof gives no protection."

Edward Ledger looked up at the galvanized iron ceiling and said with a grin:

"It may not be safe, sir, but it looks kind of safe."

No one seemed inclined to move, so I said to Major Grassie:

"Major, let's go and see how these men are getting on with the new dugout."

"All right," said the major, and we stepped out into the trench. When we reached the new dugout we found that the men had knocked off work and had gone to shelter. We were examining the work and calculating its value as a "funk hole" when suddenly we heard the whine of an approaching shell. We flung ourselves face down on the floor of the trench. The burst seemed to be right over us. The shock left us almost insensible. In a few moments we rose and moved to our dugout. There we found a ghastly spectacle. The shell had blown the dugout to bits. Before us lay the mangled bodies of five men: my batman, the M.O., his batman, the sergeant major and another stretcher bearer. The wounded man carried into the dugout was untouched. The M.O. and his batman and the stretcher bearer were dead. My batman and the sergeant major were desperately wounded. We had them carried down to our first-aid station. We did what was possible to ease the sufferings of the wounded.

The sergeant major we set propped up in a sitting position. He was quite conscious and eager to make his report.

"Have you any pain, Aleck?" I asked him.

"No, sir. I have no feeling below my waist at all. Isn't that strange? But, major, I must make my report of the wounded."

"Oh, never mind that, Aleck, I can attend to it."

"No, sir, I must make my report. There was the M.O. and his batman, and your batman, and my stretcher bearer and—I can't just remember—"

"Don't worry, Aleck. I can get all the names and make your report for you."

"No, sir—you see—I must—report. There was—the M.O.—and—" again and again he tried to give the full list but could not.

"Aleck, don't worry, boy," I begged him. "I can get all those names."

"Yes, major, but—I must—report—" with a great effort he seemed to gather up his remaining strength and once more began.

"There was—the M.O.—and his—batman—and your—batman—and my stretcher bearer—and och yes!—of course!—that—wounded fella—yes, that is all—major—it is—my duty—" He settled quietly back against the roll of blankets behind him. "Yes, that is all—I tried —to do my duty—you will—tell—my mother."

I said a prayer with him and repeated the words of the Shepherd Psalm, which he tried to say with me.

> "Yea, though I walk through death's dark vale,
> Yet will I fear none ill;
> For Thou art with me, and Thy rod
> And staff me comfort still."

"Yes—that is good," he whispered. "My—mother—taught—me that—you will—tell her." He snuggled down into the blankets, gave a little sigh and was still.

I must complete the story by telling about his mother. On my return home I went to Aleck's mother and told her of her son's last moments. She was a tall woman with a strong, dark face. She listened, with no loud weeping, but with the tears quietly running down her cheeks.

When I had finished she said quietly:

"Major, I dinna grudge my boy, I wadna hae him back."

That was all. Then it was that I understood her son's brave words: "That is all. It is my duty."

Edward they laid on a stretcher outside the dugout in the shade of some trees. He was semidelirious. Once and again he cried in a loud voice, "God bless the man that fired that shot! God forgive the man that fired that shot!" He had no hate in his heart. Occasionally he broke into a rather rollicking Alexander chorus we used to sing in our club meetings in St. Stephen's Church on Sunday evenings:

> "Count your blessings, name them one by one,
> Count your blessings, see what God hath done.
> Count your blessings, name them one by one,
> And it will surprise you what the Lord hath done."

The incongruity of the hymn rather shocked me. We are told that in delirium the deep things come out. And perhaps in the simple heart of Edward there was a deeper religious strain than I had thought.

I waited beside him as he grew weaker. Whenever I spoke he came back with an apology for giving trouble. The shelling was rather bad, occasionally breaking over our heads. A number of men were about watching these men die. They were all deeply moved. At every shell burst they would dash into their dugouts, but they would come out again to show their sympathy. The M.O. came to me and said: "Major, you can do nothing for this man. You'd better get away. I'll look after him."

"He wants me, doctor," I replied. "I'll just stay with him. Could you give him something to ease his pain? I can't leave him."

"He is really not suffering, you know, but—yes—I'll help him—" He gave him an injection. Soon he grew quiet—and finally fell into a slumber from which he wakened no more.

Edward's death brought me a sense of desolation as I had never known. It was as though a member of my own family had gone from me. I am sure his complete absence of fear in the worst shelling was largely due to his concern for me. A simple, brave and gallant soul was Edward, if ever there was one.

Shortly after this experience the battalion was withdrawn from the front line. Our position was taken over by the Canadian Mounted Rifles, and we set out for Camp E. We had been in the line for fourteen days, had been rather roughly handled, as we thought. As it turned out, however, the enemy were really only getting the range, preparatory to the real bombardment that was to follow. We marched out on a black night of heavy thunder and lightning. The crash and glare of the storm mingling with the crash and glare of the bursting shells, which kept hurtling over our heads as we made our way out of Sanctuary Wood and Maple Copse.

We, the headquarters staff, made our way without casualty. The storm passed and morning found us out of the shell-fire zone in a lovely peaceful countryside, fields in crop, flowers abloom, houses all in ruins, but women at their work in the fields or about their doors. We came to a ruined little farm steading and lay down upon the green grass. How heavenlike after fourteen days of that hell of smoke and blasting fire. Of that quarter of an hour's rest I carry a vivid memory. As we lay there a little bird came and, lighting upon a wire that had been a clothesline, bobbed up and down, and gave us its lovely call, "Coo-coo! Coo-coo! Coo-coo!" How many I did not count. Right out in the open, not more than ten yards away, that shy bird, so prone to deep shade, came and sang to us its heart-moving little song. Not a word was spoken by any of us. Then it flew away. Not a soldier moved, not a word was said for some moments after the bird had gone. Then came a quite earnest and reverent voice, "And damn the Kaiser!"

"Thank God, the coo-coo can still sing," said another, equally earnest and reverent.

As I write I can see that little bird bowing so gallantly and piping so gaily. Still I carry in my heart a dull pain and wonder at the folly and wickedness of men who for any cause soever would make war again in the world.

We reached Camp E in the early morning, worn out and in a kind of dull apathy. We could with difficulty respond to the enthusiastic welcome tendered by the other battalions in camp. Everything in life seemed comparatively trivial to us who had been looking for fourteen days and nights into the glaring eyes of death. The men went to their huts. I made my way to the chaplain's quarters, which in this camp were somewhat removed from those of the battalion and the other officers. First the glorious luxury of a bath. I had forgotten how heavenly was the feeling of hot, clean water and soapsuds. Then I rolled into bed. Bed! To think of the thirty-odd thousand times during my life I had tumbled into clean sheets without a single anthem of praise. Verily, we are of the earth earthy!

I had thought I could sleep the clock around, but somehow the comfort and peace of it were too great to permit of sleep. After six hours of rather broken sleep I woke. It was the silence, I think, that woke me with a start. I listened. Not a shell! But hark! A dull reverberation like distant thunder! I sprang to the window. Not a soul in sight, except about the horse lines. My batman came sauntering up, looking rather lost. I hailed him.

"Well, the boys all asleep, eh?"

"No, sir, they're all gone!"

"Gone? What do you mean?"

"They're all gone, sir. I can't find any of them."

"Go down to the officers' quarters and find out what has happened, and then we'll have dinner."

I proceeded with my bathing and shaving in luxurious deliberation. I was still engaged in my leisurely toilet when my batman returned in anxious haste.

"They're all gone, sir. No one knows exactly where. But up the line somewhere."

"No word left for me?"

"No, sir. I can't find anyone that knows. The battalion has been 'standing to' all afternoon, and they just moved off an hour or so ago."

"Take a run over to the next camp and find out where our battalion has gone, and be quick."

I was quite annoyed that no word should have been sent to me. That wasn't like the colonel. I was in my uniform again and ready when my batman returned.

"They're all gone up the line, sir, somewhere about Zillebeke. There's been a big fight! The Germans have broken through and are coming right down on us."

This was startling, but I had already learned to discount camp rumors at least a hundred fifty per cent.

"Well, we'll get dinner and then we will pack up and get ready to run away," I said.

"Run away, sir?" My batman was apparently quite shocked. He was a Scot.

I found that really grave news had come. The enemy had driven in our line. Under a furious bombardment our men had been forced to evacuate Sanctuary Wood and to retire. How far no one could say. But our battalion and every other that could be requisitioned had been ordered up to strengthen the line. There was no doubt about it, something serious had taken place. The transport was all ready to move at an hour's notice. But not a sign of an order for me could I get anywhere. I was really annoyed. The chaplain's service didn't count for much in this battalion apparently. We hurried through dinner, packed our stuff and set off on our march.

"Which way, sir?" asked the batman anxiously.

"Zillebeke," I answered.

"Yes, sir," said the batman with alacrity. I gathered that he had feared we were really going to run away.

As we went marching up the road we were met by streams of wounded men in ambulances, in transport wagons and walking. The news confirmed the first reports. Our line had been pushed back. The C.M.R.'s had made a great fight but had lost heavily and been forced out of Sanctuary Wood. The Princess Pats on the left had held Hooge, but from Kemmel mountain on our right rear the enemy were pounding us.

"What of the Forty-third?" I asked a wounded C.M.R. officer, slowly and painfully making his way to the base hospital.

"Don't know. Gone up to Zillebeke behind the lake, I rather think."

It was dark when we made Zillebeke. There we found our battalion. Properly indignant, I made my way to headquarters.

"Hello!" said my colonel. "How did you get here?"

"Walked," I said. "I've been searching Belgium for the battalion. Why didn't someone send me word of this move up?"

"Forgot all about you," he said with a grin. "As a matter of fact you know you have no right to be up here at all. It is clear against your standing orders."

He had me there, for the new regulation forbade chaplains going up into the front line at all, unless special arrangements were made with the battalion commanding officer.

"But, sir," I answered, "I think you will agree that I have sufficient authority for being here tonight."

"Well, since you are here, major, we are glad to see you. And, gentlemen," he said, turning to the officers, "may I remind you of a saying of Wellington's before Waterloo when a colonel of a regiment on reconnaissance duty had lost his way: he arrived in time for the battle because he marched toward the sound of the guns. We left our padre safely asleep in camp but he found his way as did Wellington's officer, he marched to the sound of the guns." A ripple of approving murmurs ran round the group. Our O.C. was very chary of approval. I was completely rattled by his absurd words, but the semihumorous tone, and especially the warm welcome given me by my fellow officers, warmed my heart.

"I couldn't do anything else, sir," I protested. "I was all dressed up and nowhere to go."

A shout of laughter greeted my quotation from one of George Robey's latest skits. The colonel went on: "And now, gentlemen, let me once more go over our dispositions. Our front line is not broken, remember, but it is bent a bit. We have found it necessary under a somewhat severe bombardment to surrender, temporarily, Sanctuary Wood. But already the advance guard of the 43rd is in Maple Copse, and it is our purpose to straighten out that line. Sanctuary Wood is Canadian territory, and we are going to get it back. Now if any officer has a question to ask, or if any point is not quite clear let us have it, for we can't afford to make any mistake."

Some questions were asked and answered. There was to be a slight advance in support of our line holding Maple Copse, but for the night there was to be no general attempt to recapture Sanctuary Wood.

"And now, gentlemen, since our padre has seen fit to push in where he wasn't asked to come, we shall make use of him. I think it would do us all good if he made a little prayer."

Again there was a quick, warm ripple of approval, and after a brief service, one by one the officers came and shook hands with me. I was deeply moved by their generous reception.

The colonel then called me aside and said: "I have just got word that Sergeant Major Laird has been killed. His body lies up in Maple Copse. It ought to be buried, of course, but that I think might wait till tomorrow."

I thought a moment.

"We don't know just what may happen tomorrow. I think I had better go up tonight, sir."

"It's a rotten, nasty night, and there is no cover. Our approach trench is blown up and in a beastly mess. Besides, we don't know what may happen up there."

"Have you a runner who knows the route?" I asked.

"Well, yes, but—better wait—we'll see what will happen tomorrow."

"If you get me a runner I shall go up after I have a bite to eat."

"Good Lord, you've had no supper." He called an orderly.

I got my supper and set off with a runner whom I didn't know. He didn't belong to the 43rd, things were a bit mixed.

When we came up to the trench leading up into Maple Copse, I found it practically obliterated, blown out of existence. The night was black enough but Very lights lit our way with unpleasant distinctness. We obeyed the law of the district, which was to cease all motion during illumination. It took about two hours' hard going to reach Maple Copse, which was really an expansion of Sanctuary Wood beyond. The lovely wood was a scene of indescribable desolation. When I had passed through some twenty-four hours earlier it was a beautiful wood consisting of large trees up to two or three feet in diameter, and with thick leafage and abundant underbrush. Now the great trees lay in a tangled and mangled mat on the ground. One could walk on the tree trunks from one side of the copse to the farther side of Sanctuary Wood without touching earth. Not one single tree remained in its original position. Bare trunks were left standing and splintered stubs stripped of limbs and foliage. My runner led me to the dugout of the officer in command, whom I discovered to be Lieutenant Arthur Sullivan.

"Good heavens, padre!" he exclaimed in dismay, as we pushed his blanket aside and stepped into his dugout. "What in blazes are you doing here?"

I explained.

"Well, we buried him just outside there, but he had no service at all. I'm mighty glad you are going to have a service, because it didn't seem right that a fine lad like Bill Laird should be put away without a word."

Lieutenant Sullivan was a Roman Catholic and set great store by the formularies of religion.

"But, major, you shouldn't have come up to this hell hole."

"Shall we proceed now?" I asked.

"Sure thing. Let's go." As he was speaking the blanket was pushed aside again and there stepped into the light a runner, an undersized, white-faced lad, who swaggered in with the air of a sergeant major, saluted, handed a chit to the officer and stood at attention.

"Where in hell do you come from?" asked the lieutenant in wrath. "This is no place for youngsters."

"Brigade headquarters, sir," said the youngster, with a smart salute.

"Sit down there," ordered Lieutenant Sullivan, and read the chit.

"All right. Lie down there," pointing to his cot. "We are going out to bury our sergeant."

"May I come with you, sir?" asked the lad.

"How far have you come?"

"Brigade headquarters, sir, Ypres ramparts."

"You lie down there till we get through," ordered the lieutenant.

"I should like to attend the service, sir," said the white-faced youngster, an indomitable spirit blazing in his blue eyes.

"Let him come," I said, and we went out into the rainy night, my runner, the lieutenant and the little white-faced runner standing close about me. That was the strangest service of my many weird burial services in the war. The black, wet night close about us, the recurring, startling flare of the Very lights revealing with vivid clarity the criss-cross mat of fallen trees that two days ago had been a thick forest of living green, the lonely, closed grave amid this mass of debris, the dead silence about us, the absence of any burial party. I went rather deliberately through the whole service, conscious of an air of unreality, vividly conscious of the cruelty of this war, and of its futile wickedness, but also, thank God, conscious that in spite of the evil, mad folly and wickedness of men there was God, pitiful and patient, merciful and loving, striving to teach us poor stupid mortals that, after all, among men love and goodness and patience are best.

We came back into the little dugout half covered by the fallen timber. Lieutenant Sullivan was silent. I could see as he was getting his pot boiling on the primus stove that he was nervous.

"Here, runner!" he said, "get your boots off and get in at the back of my bed. Quick! Get a move on!"

The boy obeyed and got in under the blankets. We were waiting for the tea to boil, the lieutenant said, "Major, I wish I could believe all you were saying out there, but—well—you know—a God of love and goodness—and all this hell of a mess about us—eh, what?"

"It is a tough proposition and quite beyond me," I acknowledged. "But we haven't got the whole story yet. Eternity is a long time, a century is like a breath, and man is a queer mixture."

"Damn queer! Kaiser Bill, eh?"

"I wasn't thinking of him, he is rather a fool; but think of these men of ours, think of their fine qualities of soul. Courage, loyalty, patience, their kindness to one another, and to their wounded prisoners too. You know, Sullivan, there is something of God in every man of them, but wanting development, eh?"

"Say, major, there's your tea. Get at it and get away," he said suddenly.

"Can't I sleep somewhere on the floor? I've had a long day." I told him my experience.

"No, no! You can't do that! This is no place for you! You'd better get right away, sir."

Suddenly I saw what was the matter with him.

"I see, Sullivan, you are worried about my safety."

"Partly. But frankly you would be rather a nuisance in case they began to push down on us. I don't believe they will. We have got them pretty thoroughly stopped. You see, our boys were all in place under that mess of tree trunks. The very best cover possible, and the Boche would have a devil of a time to move them. But there is always the chance of shelling. You'd better go, padre. I'd love to have you with me. But I want you to go—and go quick."

"What about that runner?"

"Oh, he'll be all right. He's a soldier—a fighting man, as good as any of us. Jove! He is sound asleep, poor little beggar."

"You mean I would embarrass you," I said.

"Well, padre, don't laugh at me, but I feel that you know I'd love to have you stay—but if the scrap began—I'd have to look after you."

"I see, Sullivan. I appreciate your embarrassment. I'll get out."

We got our kits and stood ready to go.

"Listen to this, Sullivan," I said. I took out my little book and began to read:

> "The Lord is thy keeper. . . . The Lord shall preserve thee from all evil. . . . The Lord shall preserve thy going out and thy coming in from this time forth, and even for evermore."

I said a few words of prayer and then said good night.

"Good night, padre, awfully glad you came up. It was really decent of you and the boys won't forget it."

"Good-bye, old chap. This world is an awful mess. But in spite of everything, I believe God is all right and we may trust Him."

"You're damned right, padre. Oh, I beg your pardon. I mean—"

"I know exactly and so does He. Good night."

There was no fighting that night. Our men held the line. That matted welter of trees proved an impassable defense. And for the next ten days—night and day—there was a steady and silent concentration of guns of all kinds in our sector, a lot of them the result of Lloyd George's furious driving energy. When all was ready some of us officers of the 43rd stood one night upon the embankment of Zillebeke Lake waiting the zero hour in tense silence.

Then through the quiet night there came the deep soft thud of a single big gun. Immediately all hell seemed to break. From behind us guns of all sorts and sizes began to speak and for an hour kept up a continuous and appalling roar till the whole enemy horizon was one red glaring conflagration.

At first I was conscious of a feeling of profound satisfaction. They had mauled us savagely and now it was their turn. But after the first half hour our satisfaction became disturbed. Even our second-in-command, a professed "hate" artist, began to feel uneasy.

"Poor devils, they are certainly getting hell," he observed.

"Well, they're devils, ain't they?" said a younger officer. "They're only getting their own."

But I could get little satisfaction from that.

"The trouble is, the fellows responsible for this hell are not the fellows getting it," was my reply.

And that was the terrible pity of it. We all as a people must share our responsibility for our national attitudes. We have the governments we deserve; therefore, peoples must suffer for the sins of the governments they tolerate.

Immediately after the bombardment, the most terrific yet carried out in the war, our men regained our trenches and pushed forward and took possession of the enemy lines, from which they were never again driven back.

CHAPTER XXVI

Front-line Light and Shadow

A THOUSAND DOLLARS FOR A PRISONER—THE
CHAPLAIN'S SERVICE—IRISH GUARDS—PREPARA-
TIONS ON THE SOMME—THE FIRST TANK—REGINA
TRENCH—THE FLOWERS OF THE FOREST

ONE DAY General Byng, our corps commander, was paying our battalion headquarters a call. In the conversation he expressed the great
desire of G.H.Q. for a prisoner for purposes of identification.

"We want to know what enemy troops are in front of us. Our
G.H.Q. would give a thousand dollars just now for a prisoner."

"All right, general," said Major Grassie. "I'll get you one at that
figure."

Within a week one of our strong points in No Man's land was
being held by a file under command of Lieutenant Gordon Young,
the nephew of our O.C., a member of my church and my namesake.
He was a fine young chap, clean-living, plucky, an excellent officer.
Suddenly there was an attack, our men were driven out and the strong
point passed into enemy hands.

Gordon was much chagrined as he reported his misfortune to
Major Grassie.

"What shall I do about it?" he asked. "I hate to let those devils
get our strong point. They came up on us quietly and before we knew
they were bombing us out."

"Too bad, Gordon. The colonel will be disgusted but of course
you couldn't help it."

"Say, I'd like to go out there and blow them to hell," said the
young chap, smarting under his mishap.

"Well, I don't know—"

"Let me go, major. They won't be expecting anything tonight.
Let me go!"

"Could you do it?"

254

"Give me the same men and we will do it. They are very sore over this business." Major Grassie gave him leave.

Filling their pockets with bombs, the party crept out into No Man's Land. Within an hour Gordon appeared with a prisoner.

"Where did you pick up that?" asked Major Grassie.

"Well, we threw some bombs and our fellows dashed right in. I was running round the strong point and came bang up against this chap. I had a bomb in my hand, but I hadn't time to pull the pin so I let him have it. It caught him fair in the forehead—and here he is."

That night the major dispatched his prisoner to General Lipsett with a note:

"Kindly acknowledge delivery of one Hun prisoner. Your check for one thousand dollars as per agreement will be gratefully received."

I never heard that G.H.Q. paid up.

Lieutenant Gordon Young, a modest fellow, took his congratulations with a single remark.

"It was a mighty good thing for me that the pin stuck or we would both have been blown to bits."

Some six months later Gordon had his reward. In the Somme push, shortly before the tragic disaster at Regina Trench, he was leading his platoon in an attack one black night when he received a bullet through the lung and was carried back to our lines, as we thought dying. After a short interval he seemed to recover strength. I went to our O.C. and urged that he be carried at once back to our first-aid station and sent out to our hospital at Contay by ambulance, twenty-five miles back. The colonel was opposed to the idea.

"He'd die on the way," he declared.

"He certainly will die if left here," I urged. "Give me a carrying party and I will see him back to Contay. It is so pitch black, we shan't be seen, and at any rate there is a chance."

The M.O. favored my plan. The chances of life if he remained with us were very slim.

"If he can be pushed right through—"

"Let me go, colonel. I'll get him through," I urged.

That trip through the black drizzling night was for long like a nightmare to me. Through the muddy trail we carried him and reached the main road. As we were going over a rising ground, suddenly an enemy searchlight revealed us as if it had been day.

"Drop!" I ordered. In the mud we lay sheltering our wounded officer with our bodies. Almost immediately a succession of whiz-bangs screamed over us. It seemed to me that they were only inches above us. But no one was hurt. We waited till another gleam had played over us, then went on. We had the good luck to come upon an emergency tram line used to convey supplies. I commandeered a truck and horse and got our wounded man to the first-aid station and thence by ambulance to Contay.

Gordon's fine pluck and his cheery spirit and his clean life carried him through. He is now in Winnipeg, as fine and fit as ever. But for many nights after the ghastly carry I used to wake up with the whistle of whiz-bangs grazing my backbone.

* * * *

The chaplain was no fighting man, but his service called for the same spirit that breathed in and animated the best of his comrades whom he served. In addition to his preaching and worship service, he found his best opportunity to help his men in the dressing stations and hospitals with the wounded. This service brought him at times under fire, for neither emergency dressing posts nor hospitals were free from shell visitation, but his orders forbade his adventuring the firing line. Under a special arrangement with my colonel, however, who was one of my elders at home, these orders were relaxed in my case. The majority of the 43rd Cameron Highlanders were members or adherents of my congregation of St. Stephen's at home. I put it to him that it was largely to minister to these men that I had felt it my duty to follow them to the war. Under protest, he agreed. The only time I was prevented from accompanying my comrades into the firing line was at the Regina Trench on the Somme, of which more later.

My chaplains were a fine lot, as good soldiers as the best. Only once did I see a chaplain exhibit any signs of funk. He was a rather fat and unwieldy person and had never been under fire. After we had arrived at Camp E he went up for a preliminary survey of the approaches to the front line, as far as Ypres. His experience of some shells dropping on the road up and down was too much for him. He became quite incapacitated, and at his earnest request was withdrawn to base hospital work. After the close of the war I was interested to find him a president of a soldiers' organization in Ontario, and extremely active in furthering its interests. His devotion to this duty was equaled only by his eloquence in describing the heroic fortitude of "the boys" at the front line. A rather high average that of all those I came in contact with one chaplain, one M.O., and one officer only were unable to carry on under the stress of crashing and bursting shells. And these I am quite confident would have overcome the nervous shock of active front-line experience if they had been able to stand up under the first few hours of shelling.

Once a man became genuinely and actively interested in his duty and in helping other men, he seemed to become indifferent to personal danger. Furthermore, nothing so pulls a man together as the sight of the heroic patience, the fortitude, the consideration for other sufferers shown by the wounded toward their comrades.

After much hesitation I have decided to include here a letter I wrote to my wife from the front line. After twenty years it brings back to me the very soul and spirit of my comrades in those desperate hours, their patient courage, their almost absurd gratitude for any little service done them. It makes me wonder at their simple faith in their Heavenly Father—some of them wild enough too—and His invariable response. They make me believe in the worth of man and in the availability of God. I confess I read these words again with an ache in my throat, as I recall that all the splendid and noble sacrifices of my comrades in the interest of a better and happier world seem to have been in vain. This is the letter:

ON ACTIVE SERVICE

Chaplain's Service Canadian Corps.

On the Flanders Front.   16-8-1916

My dear Helen:—

We are just finishing our tour and expect to be relieved tonight. We are in excellent health and our boys are fit to go to their limit whenever they are called on. I never cease to wonder at them whether I see them behind the parapet or in the dressing station. They show the same splendid spirit of heroic fortitude, cheerfulness and patience. Many and many a man have I seen carried bleeding, torn, battered into the dressing station, and while they have not always been able to fight back the groans, never once have I heard one single word of complaint

—never one single word of regret for having come to the war—
no single word of impatience. It really breaks one's heart sometimes to see their gratitude for any little help—a drink of water
—a roll of sandbags for a pillow—an easing of arm or leg. The
grateful smile, the sigh of deep content—and they look up at
you with such wistful eyes.

The other night a young chap was brought in with bad
wounds. My heart went out to the lad, but his smile was bright
and brave. The doctor fixed him up. He chatted away with me
quite cheerfully. We took him into the adjoining dugout or cellar
to await the ambulance. I got him some cocoa and made him
comfortable. Oh, he was grateful. In a little while I went back to
him. I saw he must soon go. I spoke to him of his Father in
Heaven. He listened eagerly.

"Shall I pray with you?" I asked.

"Yes, sir, but I am not your religion."

"You are an R.C.?" I said.

"Yes."

"Have you got your crucifix?"

"No, I left it in my kit."

I sent round to find a crucifix among the boys round about,
but strange could not find any. I made up my mind I would carry
one with me after this and I always have. I went out, and cut
two little twigs. The doctor tied them together in the form of a
Cross. I held up the Cross before the boy's eyes, now growing
dim. His eyes brightened, his face really shone in a smile.

"I see it, I see it," he said. "Lift up my head."

I lifted him up.

"I can't pray," he said.

"Never mind, God knows, say after me: 'God, be merciful
to me a sinner. Forgive my sins for Jesus Christ's sake and receive
me now.'"

He said the words after me, his eyes fixed on the Cross. He
moved his lips. I placed the Cross against them, he kissed the
symbol of Infinite Love and Mercy. Again that marvelous smile
lighted up his face. In a few minutes he closed his eyes and was
gone.

Poor boy, poor boy. I felt it was worth my while being here, worth while leaving you all and coming away just to help this poor lad in his extreme hour of need.

Dear Helen, I know you are often lonely and you often feel the burden almost too heavy for you. But things like this will help you to bear up, my darling. I can't do much but what little I can do I am glad to do.

The other day we got word that our artillery officer had been wounded up the line. The M.O. and I went up and found a young fellow, named MacDonald, who turned out to be the son of Miss Ewing, now Mrs. MacDonald, whom we used to know in our university days, and whom your father knew. He was awfully glad to see one who knew something about him and his people. You can't understand the feeling of loneliness that comes over a man when he is sick or wounded in this war. I spoke to him of the Good Shepherd and of His care and love.

"I know," he said quickly. "I have long trusted Him."

Afterwards in the evening he was brought down to the dressing station and fixed up.

"He will do well," I wrote his mother, so that she would not be unduly anxious.

Into the dressing station in the dark cellar adjoining the operating room where the wounded men wait I went and said:

"Now, boys, we are going to have an evening prayer. But first we will say the beautiful words of the Shepherd Psalm."

I began and here and there I could hear voices joining in saying these great and tender words. MacDonald followed me right through to the end. Then a short prayer for those at home, for our comrades in the front line and for ourselves. I know God was near us and seemed very precious to us. Poor brave lads, they give their all. How much do we give?

* * * *

After two or three more experiences in the Ypres salient in the game of give and take, our battalion was so reduced that we were pulled out and sent down the line for recuperation and reinforcement. The whole Canadian contingent had been battered ruthlessly but we came out with our heads up conscious that we had not disgraced our name. And wherever we fell in with any soldiers or officers of a British battalion they didn't say much, but made us feel that the Lion's whelps had not altogether shamed their breed.

I remember as we were marching into Poperinghe, where we were to entrain, one evening on our way out we came upon a detachment of cavalry resting beside the road. Our colonel called the battalion to attention, ordered the pipes to strike up. Like a flash that squadron of British cavalry swung into parade order and gave us everything they had in the way of a salute. It was worth coming all the way from Canada to witness their magnificent evolutions, and to note the superb quivering salutes of their officers. They were the Irish Guards in all their prideful splendor. What they were doing there I could not find out, but they were wonderful to look at.

A few weeks later when our reinforcements from Canada had arrived we were put through a course of intensive training in the new tactics developed in this war, especially in advancing under a creeping barrage and in a new method of trench attack. Thereafter we entrained, and after a couple of days' run we camped near the battered town of Albert in the Somme valley. Here we found a tremendous massing of troops of all sorts, and very especially of artillery.

We soon became conscious of a strange and mysterious thrill of excitement running through the whole army. Something was coming, nobody knew just what. Some officers spoke under their breaths of a new kind of cavalry. Then one day as I was riding with our second-in-command through the ruins of Contalmaison we observed crowds of soldiers running together and yelling madly. We saw an unwieldy, monstrous object waddling along on caterpillar traction wheels. As we watched, it came to an old trench and climbed over it, it reached a stone dike and without hesitation climbed right over, it struck the ruined wall of a house and waddled straight through, it found a battered grove of smallish trees in its way and simply squashed them flat. The monster was a Tank. The first the world had ever seen, the new form of mechanized cavalry which was to transform war methods in many important particulars.

Our battalion arrived at the Somme shortly after the great British and French advance had begun, which finally two years later and after the most terrific trench warfare the world has ever known was to sweep the mighty German army back across the Rhine. This is no story of the Great War nor is it a record of the achievements of the 43rd Cameron Highlanders. I am trying to picture some of the reactions of the war upon my own life.

Our first adventure into the Somme war zone was in the region beyond the Pozières. With one of our officers I went forward to look over the ground taken. I could find no sign of Pozières. I concluded that we had missed our objective, an easy thing to do in this district of obliterated landmarks. My eyes dropped to the ground before me. I received a shock. There at my feet yawned, bare and empty, an open grave lined with marble slabs. I was standing in the ancient cemetery of the town. About me stretched a plain swept bare of churches, public buildings and dwellings, without mark of street or other sign of human habitation, except that about a hundred yards to my right a bit of broken garden wall and two fruit trees bare of limbs were left stark and lone. We had captured Pozières, but Pozières was not. No sign of civilized man could I detect anywhere in the landscape before me except where some black puffs of smoke floated on the sky line. And at my feet after nineteen centuries of Christian civilizations this open grave robbed of its dead. The conviction was forced upon me with appalling certainty that humanity had been moving in the wrong direction. And yet—somehow I could see no other way out of this wilderness of desolation than a further advance toward those floating banners of death on the sky line. On and ever on over farmsteads, villages, towns and cities apparently lay the path to a better world. At least humanity was learning by bitter experience that the road to a better world must lie in some other direction than that which the nations had been pressing for these thousands of years. This way, obliviously, had not been God's way. Yet after some months of experience of war in this Somme area, the settled conviction had seized the minds of our soldiers that surely, if slowly, they were en route to Berlin and that the world would truly be a better place when they had dealt with that capital of the militarized nation. Our artillery was gradually asserting its dominance over that of the enemy and under its devastating barrage the Allied armies were painfully but surely advancing to victory.

The padre's mind and heart were in the meantime beset with

mental and moral entanglements. Every day, every hour of the night and day he was forced to justify his country and himself to his conscience. He found himself forced to accept the vicarious principle by which those guiltless of the crime of war must purge the world of this evil by their sufferings. But who were the wholly guiltless, who could say?

After a preliminary engagement of minor importance in the capture of some small towns, the regiment on the evening of October 7th was ordered to join in a wide forward movement upon the Ancre Heights, north of Courcelette. My escape from that catastrophe can be explained by an extraordinary piece of luck or by the operation of the ordinary army regulations or by the grace of Providence, which indeed may all be the same thing looked at from differing points of view.

On the afternoon of the 5th the 43rd were camped in an orchard in a little village a short distance west of Albert. It was a lovely day. Taking advantage of the quiet environment I had arranged for a Communion Service conducted after the ritual adapted from all Protestant churches. In response to a general invitation given to all who desired to participate in the ordinance, the great majority of the battalion "came forward," the officers, who so desired, acting as elders. Immediately before the "distribution of the elements" a young lieutenant stepped forward and said:

"Sir, I am a Presbyterian but not a member of the church, but I should like to commune. If you allow me I promise you that at the first opportunity I shall make my public profession of faith."

"You understand what this means," I said. "You are expressing your faith in and your allegiance to our Lord Jesus Christ."

"I do."

"Then I do gladly receive you into this Communion of His church."

May I interject here this word: Some months after the close of war I was conducting a service in Regina, Saskatchewan. At the end of the service this young fellow came to me and reminded me of this incident. I was delighted to see him again.

"You know this man?" asked the minister of the church.

"That I do," I replied and told him where it was that the young soldier had made his first Communion.

"Well, he has kept his promise," said his minister. "He is one of the most active young men in my church."

I always recall that Communion Service with the deepest emotion. I can see the lovely little orchard bathed in the brilliant sunlight of that Sabbath morning, whose peace was only accentuated by the sound of the shells dropping some few miles away.

That night we moved to the Brickfields Camp in the suburbs of Albert. Next day orders came for a move into the front line, where we knew our battalion would be heavily engaged.

Early on the following morning, according to our custom, after the battalion was paraded previous to our moving I had a brief service with them. At the close a mounted runner came and handed a chit to our O.C. He read it and handed it to me. It was an order that I should immediately proceed to the hospital tent in Albert for duty.

"What shall I do, colonel?" I said.

"What can you do but obey orders?"

"But," I remonstrated, "you know I have always gone up with the battalion. You can arrange this, can't you?"

"Arrange it? What do you mean? Orders are orders."

"But surely you can do something. Explain that I am on duty with the battalion."

He smiled at me. "I can't very well arrange an act of insubordination."

"Well, let me go up and see General Lipsett. I know him well." I urged him and finally he agreed and I rode off to our divisional commander.

The general was not at headquarters nor could I get in touch with him anywhere. I rode after the battalion and caught up with them as they were having a bit of a rest.

"Too bad, major," said the O.C. with a little grin. "After all, though, you will be of more service likely to some of them in the dressing station."

I said good-bye to him with an ominous foreboding. He was one of the most active of the elders in my church of St. Stephen's, and my friend. I sat my horse and waved to him and to the other officers, my farewell. I watched my comrades march past and took their salutes as rank after rank went by. An awful sense of desolation swept over me, as they swung out of sight. These were my comrades from my home town, most of them my people into whose faces I had often looked Sunday after Sunday in St. Stephen's. Except for a poor remnant I never saw them again.

"What is God doing?" I said to myself and rode back to my dressing station reporting for duty to the M.O. in command.

Next day in the dim light of a rainy morning news of a terrible disaster reached us, we began to receive walking cases. As broad day broke on us the ambulances began to arrive. By noon the tent was full to overflowing and we were forced to lay our wounded on the grass outside in the bitter October rain. My M.O. was distracted. He came to me his tunic off, his arms bared to the elbow and bloody.

"Major," he said, "you know this district. Can you think of any place where we can get shelter for these men? Every hospital in Albert is full. What in God's name can we do?"

I suddenly remembered the large Y.M.C.A. tent where our battalion had slept the previous night.

"I think I can get you a tent," I said and rode off to the Brickfields.

The Y.M.C.A. officer in charge was up to his job.

"Sure thing, if you can get transportation. I'll get this thing rolled up."

I went to some horse lines near by, explained my situation.

"These wounded men are lying there in the rain."

It was a British outfit. The M.O. was absent, the sergeant was trained to observe military discipline, but his heart was in the right spot. Without a single moment's hesitation he began shouting orders and his men leapt to their duty. In less than six minutes he had an army wagon galloping toward the Y.M.C.A. camp and in ten minutes more he had his wagon loaded with tent, cookstove, dishes and all the other equipment necessary for serving hot coffee to wounded men and was away at top speed for Albert. The M.O. was utterly amazed when he saw us. He received me with weird oaths popping out like pistol shots. It wasn't profanity, it was gratitude. His ritual was slightly different from mine, but his spirit was as truly devotional.

All day long the stream of wounded from the front was pouring into the tent and another stream kept pouring out toward Contay, where a regular hospital was operating.

From the 43rd men I could learn little. They had attacked the
enemy line at a point known as Regina Trench. They had been held
up by heavy wire which should have been cut, they had been enfiladed by guns from a strong point which should have been blown
up. Just what had happened they did not know, but they did know
something had gone wrong. They could not go forward, they would
not go back. They could only dig in and wait for relief which came
late in the day. Too late for them—and too late for their comrades
lying in swaths before the uncut wire.

Men don't really mind taking the fortunes of war as they come,
but they grow bitter when they have to suffer for some fool's blun-
dering. Of the colonel I could get no word. They had heard he had
been wounded and had got out of the line. I waited till evening when
the stream of wounded had slackened a bit. Then I went to the
M.O. and begged to be allowed to go up the line. He at once gave
me leave and I rode up to General Lipsett's quarters.

"Any word of our colonel?" I asked.

"Come in, major," he said. "Had anything to eat?"

I had forgotten all about food.

"Any word, general?" I said.

"Nothing definite. But first drink this."

I obeyed.

"Now eat—no! Not a word—Eat!" he ordered.

I obeyed. He was more than kind. I might have been his brother.
I had no need of words from him. His face told me enough.

"He was a fine officer," he said. "No better in the Canadian
force. The terribly sad thing is that he might have been saved. His
battalion headquarters was blown up and twenty men were killed or
mortally wounded. He could walk. They helped him out to the
emergency dressing post and fixed him up. The ambulances were
using a road which was occasionally shelled. The M.O. at the emergency dressing post tried to persuade him to cut across country and
pick up the ambulance farther down. But he was very tired and weak
from loss of blood and his wound was painful. 'Oh, I think I'll take
a chance with the ambulance,' he said. The ambulance drove a hundred
yards. A shell got them all."

"Where is he now?"

"In Albert. The body is being cared for."

I rose to go.

"Sit down," he ordered.

"I must—see—about—things," I said, struggling after self-command.

"Everything necessary is being done, major. The funeral we shall arrange tomorrow."

"I'd like to see the men, general."

"Lie down and sleep," he ordered. "The men are being looked after."

I slept nearly ten hours.

Next morning General Gough came into our general's office. He was quite sympathetic with Lipsett over the heavy losses that had fallen upon a regiment of whom he was especially proud and over the death of an officer who was an old and deeply loved friend. Yet it seemed to me he was rather jaunty about the affair.

"Too bad! Too bad!" he said in a brisk tone of voice, "but fortunes of war, general. I understand they came upon wire. Very important that scouting should be thoroughly done."

Lipsett's answer came back sharp and quick.

"Yes, sir, extremely important. That wire was reported uncut and we were advised that all wire had been cut. That was a mistake."

"Ah! You reported that wire? You were assured that the wire had been cut?"

"Here is the report, sir."

Gough glanced at it.

"Too bad! Too bad, general! Very sorry indeed. Not your fault."

"Furthermore, this strong point here"— General Lipsett's finger rested upon the map—"was reported blown up. It was quite intact. Its guns enfiladed our line held up by uncut wire. We lost five hundred men." His manner was perfectly respectful, his voice was quiet, but it had a knife edge to it.

"Five hundred! Great God, Lipsett!" exclaimed Gough, but he said no more about the fortunes of war. He was terribly shocked. There was no further conversation, and Gough left with a brief word. "That wire and that redoubt—I shall see about them at once."

Lipsett stood gazing down in silence at the map, then said rather bitterly:

"That won't bring back your Highlanders, Gordon, nor your colonel."

Next day through the streets of Albert crowded with soldiers of many regiments our Highlanders in their kilts carried their colonel to his grave to the music of the pipes wailing out that most poignant of all Highland laments, "The Flowers of the Forest." They laid him in a soldier's cemetery just outside Albert. A quiet little corner it was, under a spreading plane tree looking much like a Canadian maple.

Near the grave stood in sad silence the pathetic little remnant of the battalion which had been the pride of their colonel's heart. I saw no man in tears. They had not yet recovered from their terrific experience before that uncut wire. They had always been proud of their colonel, but as soon as they came into the zone of actual fighting their pride had deepened into a warm affection. He was a soldier with a soldier's devotion to duty and a soldier's instinct for the care of his men.

At the close of the service and after a few words by the divisional commander the 43rd officers stood round the open grave in silence for a few moments. Then each dropped a sprig of evergreen on the coffin and turned away. After the final volley of farewell, the little company formed up, the big drum struck a startlingly heavy beat, the pipes shrilled into the silent air the regimental march "Pibroch o' Doniul Dubh," and with heads up, chests out and kilts swaying that gallant remnant swung away through the little foreign town to meet whatever it was their duty to meet and to do whatever it was their duty to do.

The remnant of the 43rd was temporarily withdrawn from front-line service and after some slight reinforcements from our reserve battalion proceeded to the Arras district where for the time they were employed in the duty of holding the line at Neuville-Saint-Vaast, our battalion taking over from a British regiment.

"What strength do you bring?" the British O.C. asked of our colonel.

"How many men have you?" inquired our O.C.

"Eleven hundred men. What have you?"

"Two hundred and fifty-seven," replied our colonel cheerfully.

"Good Lord!" gasped the Britisher. "You can't carry on with that number. Quite absurd!"

"Oh, I don't know," said the O.C. "You see, our chaps are used to all sorts of work from shoeing horses to building railroads and running tractors."

"My word!" exclaimed the British colonel. "I wish you luck, but I certainly should not like your job. Two hundred and fifty-seven men to carry on where the normal force is eleven hundred!"

"Oh, we'll just carry on. We are expecting reinforcements very soon."

"But this is sheer madness. I shall certainly raise the devil at headquarters. Well, the best of luck to you, Canadians! Well, really —you know!"

Our Canadian chests stuck out just a little. We remembered Mons and were not unduly uplifted.

CHAPTER XXVII

On Leave

SHORTLY after the death of my batman, Edward Ledger, my leave fell due and I hurriedly made my preparations. However keen a soldier may be as to his duty, leave is regarded as one unmixed and greatly desired blessing.

I had only a few hours in which to prepare for my journey to London. Most of the time at my disposal I spent collecting letters, packages and messages from my fellow officers and my other comrades. Among the packages, my most treasured was a collection of two German rifles, a bayonet, two revolvers, which I had got together. I was informed by our adjutant that I should not be allowed to carry them out of France, as all were to be turned over to the authorities for service. But I hoped for the best. My farewell dinner at the mess was quite touching. The officers ragged me, toasted me, praised me and abused me to their hearts' content, and sent me off with ringing cheers. They were a great crowd.

After I had got myself snugly settled in a compartment with one of our lieutenants, Hugh MacKenzie, and three British officers, I made myself as comfortable as possible, lit a candle and set it under the skirts of my overcoat for warmth, and was proceeding to get to sleep for I was desperately tired when a sergeant came along shouting for "Major Gordon."

In dread that perhaps something had gone wrong with my leave, I made myself known.

"Major Gordon?" asked the sergeant, saluting.

I acknowledged the fact.

"These papers are for your information, sir, as officer in charge of this leave train. You will be in command of the train en route and will hand over to the receiving officer at Boulogne, sir."

"But," I gasped, "I am a padre. I never commanded anything in my life. I know nothing about it. Get some of these combatant officers for the job."

"Can't do that, sir. It is very simple. There will really be nothing to do, sir. They are all going on leave. They will stick to the train—different from coming up, sir."

He saluted and disappeared.

"But this is absurd nonsense!" I exclaimed. "What's your rank?" I inquired of one of the British officers.

"I am a major, sir."

"Then you take over," I said.

"I'm afraid I can't do that, sir. But after all, it will be quite simple, as the sergeant pointed out, no one will leave this train. They are all too keen for London."

I carried on much disturbed. Had I known what was before me I should indeed have been in a funk.

It was a bitterly cold night, but after many unsuccessful attempts I fell asleep.

I was wakened by a crash. I was hurled from one side to the other of my compartment, now on my head and again on my feet and finally came to rest on the floor, dazed, only half conscious. Outside were loud cries and shrieks, inside were groans, moans, calls for help. I climbed to my feet, found my matches and struck a light. MacKenzie lay groaning at my feet, one of the officers huddled in a corner, the other was standing up clinging to an upturned seat.

"Shell, I fancy, sir," he said quietly.

Our car was lying on its side. Above our heads was the door of the compartment with its window shattered.

"Are you all right, sir?" he asked.

"All right," I replied, "and you?"

"Quite fit, sir."

"What about you, Mack? You're bleeding. Let me see—" I examined his head. "Scalp wound only, Mack, anything else?"

"My shoulder, sir. Can't move—"

The other officer was sitting up, dazed.

I remembered I was O.C. this train.

"Major I must see about this train. Help me out through this window. Tie up this man's head. I'll send help. Sure you're all right?"

"Right, sir," he said. "I'll see to these men."

With his help I struggled through the window. Outside I found a lot of men running about in wild confusion, shouting, calling, cursing.

I climbed up a little bank and called out "Officers! To the front!"

A group of officers came running up.

I seized a major by the lapel.

"Your name?"

"Major Renton, sir."

"Major, take this bunch of officers, get the noncoms at work. Line up the men. Arrange details to see that all the wounded are got from the cars."

"Right, sir!" He saluted smartly and went at the job as coolly as if it were an ordinary parade he was handling.

I grabbed another officer and sent him for the railway officials. Soon they came running with a lantern. From them I learned that we had run into some coal cars which had broken away from a train, that we were not far from a station.

"Can any officer here speak French?"

A young lieutenant responded with a grin. "Yes, sir, not Parisian, but—"

"Go with this official to the station. Find out the nearest hospital, order all the medical help you can get, ambulances—stretchers—and for God's sake—get a move on!"

"Right, sir!" he said with a salute. He grabbed a railway official. "Come along with me," he said, and disappeared on a run into the darkness.

"Major Renton!" I shouted. Immediately my word was caught up and passed down the line. In a few minutes Major Renton came running and saluted.

"Rather a nasty smash, sir. Quite a number wounded. Some killed, I fear."

"Major, I want you to take charge of these men. Get them into

line. See that every car is searched for disabled men. Detail an officer to get all the baggage piled in one place and set a guard over it.
Don't let any civilians near this train."

"Right, sir," he said and was off. I went down the length of
the train. It was a ghastly mess of cars pitched on their sides, on their
ends, everywhere men groaning, some lying still. But there was absolutely no confusion. The officers were carrying on with smart precision in the light of some flares which had been found by the railway
officials. Baggage was piled up with a guard in charge. Already some
civilians had come about, but not a man of them was allowed near
our train.

"Fine work, major!" I said, as we returned to my car.

"My God, sir, look!" Major Renton exclaimed, pointing toward
the front cars piled up near the engine. The baggage car, which was
next the engine, was blazing furiously and from the second car,
which had been ours, a little flame was beginning to rise.

"Major, get a detail and see what can be done about that fire.
Get shovels, anything you can, and choke that fire down. There are
three men in that second car. I'll look after them."

"Right, sir!" He snapped an order to a junior officer. "Never
fear, sir, I shall see to it. Shall I help you with your men?"

"No! You may not!" I said. "There may be men in that first
car."

"Right, sir. Leave it to me. If you want help sing out."

I ran to our car. Climbed up and looked into it. The three officers were still there.

"Get out of this car!" I shouted.

"It's quite comfortable here, sir," said the British officer, who was
coolly smoking a cigarette. "Can we remain here till relieved?"

"Get out!" I ordered. "This car is on fire!"

He grabbed his bag.

"Never mind that," I said. "Get out!"

Without further parley he hoisted himself up through the broken
window of the door. I tossed his bag out after him and he was gone.
The second, with more difficulty and with some assistance, also made
his escape.

"Come on, Mack!"

"Major, I don't believe I can make it. My shoulder is broken I think."

"Come on, Mack, I'll give you a hand."

He stood under the window. I reached down and caught him by the hand and wrist. I could not lift him. He groaned desperately.

"Let me get down there," I said and slipped into the car.

"Get on my back, reach up and get hold of the sash."

He did so. "Now your foot on my shoulder." He got his one foot on my shoulder and the other on my back. I straightened up and his head and his good shoulder were out of the car.

"Now this is going to hurt, but you've got to get through, to let me out. I'm not going to be burnt alive in this car." The fire was burning merrily over the edge. He made a desperate struggle. I hoisted for all I was worth. He was outside. I climbed through, slid down the side of the car, got him on my back and carried him off to where the wounded lay.

Soon ambulances and stretchers from the neighboring hospital were busy carrying off the wounded. I got Mack into an ambulance and away, the walking cases were all on the march. I passed down the lines of the train. Everything was in perfect order. The dead were laid in a row, the wounded had been attended to, but there were none of the other men in sight and none of the officers. I ran round to the other side of the train. I saw a dense crowd of men frantically digging up earth with sticks, boards, bare hands, a shovel or two and flinging the clods and earth upon a fire that was blazing vigorously.

I ran to the head of the train. There a ghastly and unforgettably horrifying spectacle met my eyes.

"What is it, major?" I asked of Renton.

"Some men under that car; some say two, some more. Ghastly, sir! And we can't do a thing."

While a hundred men were shouting, cursing, clawing the earth and flinging it on the crackling fire, cries and groans were coming from underneath the blazing car.

"Can nothing be done? Where is the engine of this coal train?" I shouted at Renton.

"Gone, sir. These cars broke away. The coal trainmen have never missed them—and our engine, as you see, is on its side and the cars piled up on it." For all his cool efficiency the Britisher was white as death, his eyes staring.

"Any medical officer here?"

"Yes, sir." Two came running up.

"No hope there?" I said.

"None, sir."

"Have you any dope?"

"Yes, sir." I had seen them dope men who were hopelessly wounded.

"Can you get at them? Try for God's sake," I begged them.

"Overcoats!" shouted one M.O.

A dozen were thrown at him. He filled his syringe, wrapped a couple of overcoats over his head and arms. "When I kick, pull me out," he said, and actually crawled in under the car, worked like a demon, digging his way into that vortex of fire. A few moments of hell for him and for us. His legs kicked. He was pulled back and lay gasping. "There's another—to the—right," he said rolling in agony.

"Give me your syringe," said the other M.O. He filled it, arranged his coverings and crawled in under the car to the right, delivered his dose and was pulled back gasping. In a moment or two all cries and groans ceased.

"Your name?" I asked one of the M.O.'s.

"Oh, go to hell!" he gasped.

"Major, get these men down to the hospital and get me their names," I said.

"Certainly, sir. Better get away yourself, sir."

"Oh, go to hell!" I heard my voice say through my sobbing. But whether anyone else heard me or whether I actually used the words I don't know. The major solemnly assured me I said nothing.

The hospital corps took all our men down to headquarters, fed them, looked after them, treated them like brothers. There I found them in the afternoon. I promised that they would get full leave after they were fit again.

After twenty years I saw Captain Hugh MacKenzie the other day. He has a prosperous warehousing business in Winnipeg. He still parades with the old 43rd and he still is my very good friend.

Our casualties were:

Killed—Officers 4
    Other ranks 12
    Civilians 2
                                     — 18
Wounded—Officers 18
    Other ranks 59
                                       — 77

Total killed and wounded......................... 95

We had on board 44 officers and 262 men. Major Renton prepared a full report. I added a few words of commendation of the officers and men, with special reference to the service rendered by Major Renton and to the fine courage and endurance of the two young medical officers.

We left the wounded in charge of the hospital corps, we took our dead with us, and reached Boulogne on a special train next morning. There was a transport officer awaiting me. He already had a full report of the horrible affair.

He was a typical British colonel, walrus mustache, eyeglass and everything else. He shook my hand warmly, and grunted out: "Very nasty affair! Damned rotten railway service in this country. Very fine work, major, very fine work indeed!"

"Yes, sir, my officers and men were really splendid—Major Renton—Ah! here he is—Major Renton looked after everything splendidly." The colonel shook hands casually with my major.

"All details in my report, sir," he said, handing the R.T.O. a paper.

"Those two medical officers were—really splendid!" I added and gave him a history of their work.

"It's all in the report, sir," said the major.

"Ha! Yes! Very fine indeed! Damned fine bit of work," said the colonel.

"These men, sir," I said: "some of them have lost their kits, and they have lost some leave too."

"Tut, tut, major, I shall look after them. Everything is in my hands, major. Fine bit of work, sir. Congratulations and that sort of thing. Your boat will sail in an hour."

"My boat? Oh yes, thank you."

He insisted on taking me to the hotel, was deeply disappointed when I declined a drink, came to see me off, and stood waving his stick at me casually when our boat sailed.

London rather shocked me, I must say. Thronging streets, crowded cars, rushing taxis, noisy cafés and hotels and packed theaters greeted me. There was no sign of anxiety or worry. But thank God, there were no sloppy patriotic exhibitions, no parades either. A big meeting in a soldier Y.M.C.A. disgusted me. The chief speaker was Horatio Bottomley of the *John Bull* magazine. He was at that time on the crest of the wave. His oration, in which he lauded "the glorious deeds of our hero boys on the front line," quite sickened me. I took in a Shakespearean play—*Romeo and Juliet*—magnificently produced and a first-rate company. I could hardly stick it out to the end. It seemed so ghastly unreal and trivial. I went to a revue in which George Robey was carrying on. The great George hardly made me smile. The whole business seemed almost sacrilegious when I thought of the scenes from which I had come. I went to the Savoy and to bed for a couple of days. I was feeling quite rotten, no appetite, sleepless, temperature, and all the rest. Visitors came, I would not see them. I called in a doctor. He diagnosed "liver, kidney, stomach, nerves out of order."

"That all?" I asked. He was a returned wounded M.O.

"Oh, there are other things as well. Really, you know, you are rather sorry for yourself. What you want is a few whiz-bangs over the Savoy. I know all about it, old man. This leave business is a ghastly dull affair. What you really want is—ah, well—you're a padre, eh? No—that won't do. Don't you ever drink? No? Pity—You know, when I came home a bit knocked about" (he had only lost a leg "and a section of his belly," as he said) "I didn't care whether I lived or snuffed out. Fact is, I was just desperately tired and sick at heart. I hadn't a real friend in London. I am originally a Scot though I avoid the accent, and I didn't care a damn what happened to anybody."

"Pretty bad, eh?" I said. "I know exactly how you felt."

"Worse than all, my girl had married a War Office hero who couldn't be spared for the front line. I think that cured me. She came to see me. She was tenderly sympathetic, she promised to send me books and all that. I told her I was awfully glad she had found another man, because as a matter of fact I had picked up a really dandy little girl in France, a front-line ambulance driver. My only trouble was she was in France and I couldn't see her. That held her a bit. I've never seen her since.

"And your little girl ambulance driver?"

"Oh! still in France. I'd never really seen her, you see. You got a girl in Canada?"

"Six, and their mother." I then gave him my pen name.

"Sorry! What a damn fool I am!"

It was pleasant to find that he had read my books.

He proceeded to explain that all I needed was rest.

"Don't worry about London. She's a great old burg. She is not frivoling. She is just carrying on. These English folk are great folk. They may get a bit of a licking, but they'll never let anyone know. They'll just carry on. All this gaiety stuff is mere smoke screen. Get a good long rest. Don't try to eat too much—don't try shows—yet. I'll look in later tonight— Say! Go to the House tomorrow! Go and hear those old boys. Every man has a son or two in France—a lot of them will stay there. Go to the House!"

He was a splendid chap. I felt immensely bucked up. His words — "Don't worry about London, she's a great old burg. She is not frivoling. She's just carrying on"—did me a world of good.

Next day I went to the House. I had been introduced in 1913 by Mr. Joseph Allen Baker to John Burns, once the great Labor champion of "Dockyard Strike" fame. I sent in my card. At once he came out and gave me a wonderful welcome.

"I remember you, major," he said. "And I have heard all sorts of things about you. Now what can I do for you? By the way, do you know this House? No? Come along."

I was afterwards told that no man living knew Westminster as did John Burns. I don't believe I have ever spent an hour so filled with fascinating historic lore. Then he took me to lunch and—this was characteristic of him—only after a good lunch did he ask about the war.

"How is it going?" he asked. "I always want firsthand impressions."

"We are winning," I said. "We are just getting our second wind.

The boys all think so." And I told him about the Ypres salient.

His big blue eyes burned into mine.

"God grant you are right. Our War Council has made one long terrific mess of things. You know they should have made me minister of war."

I grinned at him, remembering his pacifist attitude at the beginning of the war.

"I know what you are thinking about. I won't bother you with explanations. But no man in Europe knows so much about the armies of Europe as I. For twelve years I have attended the maneuvers of every great European army. I have studied war strategy. Yes, if I had been minister of war there would have been no Mons retreat."

For an hour I listened to the most amazing dissertation on the strategy of war spiced with anecdotes about international figures. "King Edward—knew him well—a great personal friend of mine— called me John. The Kaiser—I know him well, brilliant fool. It is God's mercy old Blood and Iron isn't at the head of things in Germany today. They have no great general left since Bismarck. And their Kaiser! Their Kaiser will be their ruin someday. Let me tell you a story about him and Edward. You remember the Kaiser's last visit to England." I said I had heard about that visit. "Well, after they had taken him all about the place and shown him all our works —I told Edward he was making a mistake, but he only grinned. 'Don't worry, John—' he always called me John—'we are showing him only what we want him to see.' Well, there was a great ball at Windsor. I was there and as I was loafing about, Arthur Balfour came along and greeted me—I know him well—and asked— 'Have you met the Kaiser? Come along, I'll introduce you.' By and by, whom should we meet but Edward; 'Hello, John,' he said, 'have you met my nephew?' 'No,' I said, 'not yet.' 'Come along, and I'll introduce you.' Well, it was rather awkward. I explained that I had just agreed to go with Arthur Balfour.

" 'Oh,' said Edward. He was a little huffed I could see, but I couldn't let Balfour down. 'Oh! Come along, we will both introduce you.' So he took one arm, Balfour the other, and away we went. I was duly presented to the Kaiser, who received me in a lordly and indifferent manner—he was an awful snob, you know.

"'Oh,' I said, after he had given me a distant nod. 'I have never had the honor of meeting His Majesty, but I have seen him many times at maneuvers. He very nearly killed me once.'

"'Ah!' said the Kaiser, wakening up. 'When was that?'

"'At the last army maneuvers at Berlin, when you led that great cavalry charge you almost ran me down.'

"'Ah!' He was rather confused because he had got quite a wigging for that particular charge, a perfectly fool maneuver it was—a charge right across the front of a whole battalion of infantry which would have wiped out his cavalry to a man. But he recovered himself quickly and said:

"'Well, what do you think of my army, Mr. Burns?'

"It was an awkward question, for in my opinion his whole army was out of date, but I could hardly say so.

"'A very fine body of men,' I said without much enthusiasm.

"'Oh! What's the matter with them?' he asked sharply.

"Fortunately at that moment his chief of staff came along.

"'Here!' he cried, calling him by name, 'Come here and listen to this. Mr. Burns is critical of our army—now then, Mr. Burns.'

"His manner annoyed me. I didn't mind what I said to his chief of staff, so I replied:

"'Well, you have a magnificent army, but in modern warfare I doubt if they would last long.'

"Well, you ought to have seen his face. He was purple with fury.

"'And why, may I ask?' said his chief of staff, with a supercilious smile on his face.

"His smile nettled me, so I proceeded to show them that in modern warfare massed troops, either cavalry or infantry—and especially infantry—in the face of well-directed artillery would be wiped out of existence in a few minutes.

"They both came at me, hammer and tongs, but I stood up to them. You see, I knew more about army maneuvers than either of them. At last the chief of staff turned away from me with a contemptuous smile.

"'Oh, I know what you are thinking, your Excellency,' I said. 'You are thinking of the millions of men you have at your disposal.

But let me tell you that the day is past when emperors and generals can think of men simply as cannon fodder. The people will attend to that!" The Kaiser and his chief walked off with their noses in the air, but Edward put his arm through mine and drew me away chuckling, vastly delighted.

"'Splendid, John! You scored that time! Come, let's have a drink.'"

As I was bidding Mr. John Burns good-bye at the door of the Parliament Buildings I said, "I hear you have a wonderful library, Mr. Burns."

He glanced at his watch. "Can you spare half an hour?"

"If you mean, to see your library, I am quite sure I can."

As the cab which he had whistled was coming up he asked:

"Do you know London?"

"Only as tourists do."

"Well, I think I can say that no man in England knows London better than I do. There is only one really great book on London, and of that book there are only three copies in existence, one was owned by Edward, one by the Czar of Russia, the third is in my own possession. Do you see that building across the street, with the corner tower —well, that is—" and during our drive to his home in Battersea, which went at walking pace, he kept up a running comment on the various buildings which we were passing. His intimate historical knowledge was astounding.

I cannot begin to describe the library. It made one marvel. The section on economics seemed to hold literally every book I had seen or heard of on the subject. One room was furnished with drawers, which were filled with rolls of parchment gorgeously got up. These were a series of illuminated addresses given him by various public bodies, learned associations, universities, etc. One, by the government of South Africa, he was very proud of.

"The government of South Africa gave me this for my services in writing their national constitution," he said. "Lord Milner got the credit, but as a matter of fact I wrote it."

Never in my life have I met a more interesting, better informed man. Egotistical, self-assured to an amazing degree, but with an experience quite unparalleled among all men that I have known. Yet in spite of his extraordinary egotism and self-appreciation he was simple as a child, so that one could not think of him in the least as a conceited bounder. He was simply unique, with quite extraordinary mental powers, with a human heart, and with immense powers of achievement in any line he might choose. He was an effective tonic. He left me amazed, almost gasping. Certainly he had helped to cure me of my nostalgia and physical collapse.

PART FOUR
Two Nations

CHAPTER XXVIII

War Politics in Canada

THE DEATH of our colonel made an important change in my life. Shortly after that sad event advices from home in relation to the colonel's estate, which unfortunately had become involved with my affairs, seemed to make my presence in Winnipeg necessary. The colonel's executors refused to act without consultation with me, so on the advice of our new O.C., Colonel Grassie, General Lipsett and other officers I determined to make a hurried visit to Canada.

Upon my arrival I proceeded at once to Ottawa and reported to General Sam Hughes. He received me with bluff kindness.

"Tell me!" he said. "What about that damned Regina Trench?"

Without comment I gave him the story of our battalion's tragic loss and of the colonel's death. Under promise of silence I told of General Gough's interview with our divisional commander, General Lipsett. Sam Hughes was regarded by many as a rough-tongued, blustering bully. But that day I saw a man with a big, warm Irish heart, passionately loyal to his friends and intensely devoted to his country's good. He listened to my story with tears of rage and grief running down his face. It would not be fair to give a verbatim report of his comments on the High Command of the British army. The vigor and variety of his expletives would tend to obscure the shrewdness and insight of his criticism of some of the operations and of much of the general administration of the war. Sam Hughes was no fool.

I asked him about recruiting in Canada and repeated to him the conversations between our O.C. and the British colonel from whom we took over at Neuville-Saint-Vaast.

"Two hundred and fifty?"

"Two hundred and fifty-seven."

"Major, I have a job for you," he said, thumping the table. "I'll have a talk with the Premier."

The same afternoon when I called on the Premier he placed before me a proposition to address a public meeting in Ottawa on the general subject of front-line experiences, with specific reference to the absolute necessity of strengthening the front line.

I suggested that my first duty called me to Winnipeg where I must consult with the executors of my late colonel's estate. The Premier agreed heartily, suggesting that I take a couple of weeks to visit my family and friends and rest up a bit.

I was conscious of a shock of surprise, indeed of indignation.

"Two weeks?" I exclaimed. "Two days will be enough."

The Premier, in his courteous and deliberate manner, made no reply for some moments, then he said quietly:

"Major, wire me when you are ready and we shall arrange a meeting for you here in Ottawa."

On my train journey home I read every newspaper I could get hold of, and I talked with men in the smoking room. I could hardly believe the evidence of my eyes and ears. What had come over the Canadian people? These men I talked with, mostly business executives, were evidently of the opinion that the war was going along quite nicely. The press was filled with stuff that made my heart hot. There was criticism of the slackness of the government in pushing on the war, but evidently from a purely partisan point of view. There were charges of graft in connection with the manufacture of munitions, with the purchase of food and other war necessities interlarded with mean and contemptible personalities. Worse than all, I was horrified to observe that there was growing the old bitter racial and religious strife between rampant Orangeism in Ontario against bigoted Roman Catholicism in Quebec. I remembered that early glorious unanimity among the French and English crowds that had filled the streets of Montreal and Quebec with loyal Canadians singing now "La Marseillaise" and again "Rule, Britannia." I remembered how my heart had been filled with a new hope for a new national unity that would wipe out forever from true Canadian hearts all the racial and religious jealousy and hate that had darkened the future of our Canadian life. Now all was back again, and in a more disgraceful and dangerous form. Small wonder that recruiting of men had grown slack. Where was all that first wild enthusiasm that had blocked the recruiting offices with men of all ranks, of all nationalities fighting for a place in the ranks of first and second contingents? I was shocked to find that there was talk of conscription! Conscription? Actually, conscription in Canada!

My mind went back to the front line. What would be happening in France today? The first German rush had been checked and the Allied lines were moving, slowly it is true, with desperate fighting, but still moving steadily toward the German frontier. But who could say what a single day might bring forth? Germany had poured a million men into the western front during this last year. On every front the Allied fighting line was swaying forward and back.

Then there came to me the memory of the new dread on the high seas. The submarine menace was daily growing more deadly, neutralizing to a large extent the splendid guarding of the trade routes of the Allies by the British fleet.

I arrived at home sick to my soul's depths. My interviews with the executors of the colonel's estate revealed a grave state of affairs. I gave what information and assistance I could and after a few days wired the Premier that I awaited his orders. A reply wire announced a public meeting in Ottawa three days later. I said good-bye to my family and hurried to Ottawa. The meeting took the form of a public dinner by special invitation to members of Parliament, public officials, representatives of churches of all denominations, of the press of all shades of opinion, and was held in the great dining hall of the Château Laurier, Ottawa.

In the meanwhile I had had time to estimate the state of public opinion in Canada, and my whole soul was filled with grief and burning indignation. These people of Canada were taking the war quite easily. There was a settled and calm conviction that, while desperate fighting was going on, still on the whole the Allies were winning the war.

With a kind of mad rage I looked down upon that company of secure, fat-faced fools! What could I do to "stab them broad-awake"? How could my single futile voice make any impact upon their calm sense of security and well-being?

In his introduction the Prime Minister told them how I had received his suggestion that I take a couple of weeks' rest.

I began with a few sentences, expressive of the feeling of grave uncertainty as to the outcome of the war in the minds of those who were close to the heart of things in England. "Everything depends upon the answer to two questions. First, can the British navy check the new submarine activity of the thousand submarines of the German navy? Second, can that superb Allied front line be kept full? There is no doubt as to the strength and fighting quality of the British navy. England never had so good a navy as she has today. But can it meet this new and deadly instrument of death, the submarine? That question is keeping the men of the Admiralty awake at nights."

There was no question as to the fighting quality of the Allied armies. Mons had demonstrated that for the British. Ypres had proved the Canadian soldiers' steady valor in the face of overwhelming superior artillery and under the new experience of the hellish, deadly poison gas. It was not a question of valor or military skill, but solely of numbers. I told them of the 43rd battalion at Regina Trench and now holding the line with 257 men where there should be a thousand.

"You are proud of your Canadian army. You have a right to be. Even in comparison with the British regulars, the greatest fighting men in the world, they stood equal."

I gave them firsthand stories. I told them many of the things recorded in these reminiscences.

Occasionally I would pause to express my surprise and amazement at the condition of things in Canada, but very briefly and with few words of blame.

"Why do these men keep going back into that burning hell of the front line? I can never cease to wonder at them. They draw a dollar-ten a day. Is there a gentleman here in this room making legitimate profits out of munitions?—I would not insult Canadians with suggestion of graft—when he receives his next check I beg him to look at its color. Red! Our front-line men are glad to get these shells. So glad that they pay for them with blood. Red on the checks! I wish the gentleman joy of it. Let him buy comforts with it for his women and children. It is the blood of a brother Canadian."

I referred to their partisan political strife, party strife dividing our home guard into fighting sections one against another. "What we need in Ottawa is to hear over this magnificent hotel the whine of a few German shells. I almost pray they could reach this far. Just a few shells would do to transform this structure into the likeness of the Ypres Cloth Hall or the Library of Louvain, or a thousand towns and villages in Belgium and in France. Party strife? God forgive these men who divert the Canadian mind from the appalling scenes daily witnessed in the area of the war.

For an hour after I had finished they hurled questions at me. Bitter questions, scornful questions, political questions, questions of war administration. I refused to argue, but fortunately every question gave me a chance to tell another story.

"Should Canada not have a Union government?"

It was on the tip of my tongue to answer, "Oh, to hell with your silly party politics," but instead I said:

"I am for the government that will do one thing and one thing only. I am for the government that, at all costs, will keep that front line full with plenty of artillery behind it. That government will win the war. No other can."

The yell that came back did me more good than anything I had experienced since coming home.

Next day the Premier sent for me. He urged me to tour the chief cities of Canada and repeat word for word, as nearly as I could, the speech of the previous night. I was not to argue, but simply tell the people what I had seen and heard.

"Give them those stories," he said. "I've never heard such stories."

"Sir Robert, I must first see Sir Wilfrid Laurier. I have always believed in his wisdom and his integrity."

"Go, by all means! I deeply regret that he and I cannot see eye to eye. But he is of his people, I of mine."

That afternoon I met the great French-Canadian Liberal leader. No living Canadian had a more loyal heart toward his country and the Empire. But he found himself in an impossible position. He deplored the slackness of the government in the conduct of the war. He was indignant with the profiteers, he was disgusted with the place hunters, he was grieved with the cleavages in the ranks of his own party. But chiefly he was distressed with the change that had come over the spirit of his own people of Quebec. "They are misunderstood by their English and Protestant fellow Canadians. They are neither cowards nor traitors."

"We know they are no cowards, Sir Wilfrid," I answered warmly. "The Twenty-second Battalion at Courcelette taught us that."

"No, they are neither cowards nor traitors, but they are terribly misled. It is Bourassa!"

At the mention of that name his soul seemed to burst into flame. "Ah! That man! Well he knows the French habitant! None better! He plays upon his ignorance, his racial prejudices, his religious convictions! Ah! That Bourassa! He is a dangerous man! I am afraid of him. I fear he will destroy my lifework among my people and in the Dominion."

"No man and no power can destroy that, Sir Wilfrid. But you think I should go on this speaking tour?"

"It will do nothing but good. But you will be generous and forbearing with my people. Remember, they are but children in world affairs. They are a brave people, a noble people, a generous people, but they are a simple people and a sensitive and proud people. They hate to be called traitors and cowards." His voice was trembling, his eyes were bright with tears.

"I know them, Sir Wilfrid. I was born up the Ottawa. My old nurse sang me to sleep with habitant songs. Besides, I have seen them in the war. No! Nothing that I shall ever say will wound the heart of any honest French Canadian."

"Go then! Tell them stories as to children." In spite of his fine self-control, his voice failed him.

He was utterly right. The French-Canadian problem in Canada could be solved only by mutual respect, patience and brotherly love. The Bonne Entente organization under the leadership of Mr. J. M. Godfrey backed me strongly in my campaign.

I came away from that interview filled with indignation and grief. It was such a wicked and cruel shame that so great a Canadian, so loyal to Canada and to the Empire, so wise and so able a counselor, so necessary to the best, the most effective, the most united effort of the nation, should by forces he could not control, and especially by the unscrupulous petty party politicians who were seeking his elimination from public life, be thwarted, checked, bedeviled in his loyal efforts to serve his country and the Empire in their hour of desperate need.

My most difficult meeting was in Toronto, the center of Tory partisanship in its most virulent form. I made the mistake of turning myself loose on the party politicians and pouring upon them the deluge of my most bitter contempt and wrath. At once I was conscious that, though I had gained the wild applause of the most rabid opponents of the government, I had divided my audience. For some moments I tried to beat down both applause and opposition. I failed with both. Fortunately I recovered myself and remembered that their party dissension was the very thing I was combating. I was neither Tory nor Liberal, I was simply a Canadian trying to show Canadians the supreme peril of the hour in those front-line trenches. I frankly acknowledged my error.

"In my anxiety for my comrades in the front line I have forgotten that it is no part of my mission to force my opinion upon my fellow Canadians. Partisan jealousy is easy to arouse. Only one thing can cure it. A look at the front line."

Then I told them a story of an experience I had had of jealousy and rivalry between two regiments in the early days of the war. "You will observe, gentlemen," I said, "that I wear the kilt. Our first British camp in England was on St. Martin's Plain. There the Forty-third Camerons had the ill luck to be placed between two ordinary line battalions, who had the misfortune to be wearing the trews. Steeped as we were in all the glorious history of the Highland Scots of Britain's wars, we had for all other types of soldiers a quiet but deep-seated pity, if not of contempt. The result was that wherever our men came in touch with those of ordinary battalions, in our games, at the canteen—especially at the canteen, there was trouble which resulted in unhappy interviews next day with our O.C. in the orderly room. These difficulties became more and more acute as the days went on. The most grievous penalties could not suppress these outbreaks of racial jealousy. A day came when we were all together at Camp E within the sound, and at times under the impact, of enemy shells. It happened that one of our rival battalions was sent up first to the front where they had an experience of an enemy attack, which they beat back with great gallantry. After ten days of heavy fighting the news came that this battalion had been relieved and was returning to Camp E for a rest. Immediately our O.C. ordered out our pipe band, which marched up to receive our returning comrades. Our men and those of other battalions in camp lined the road on either side and waited. Soon we heard our pipes and down between these lines of their quondam rivals, headed by our pipe band, who with chests out and kilts swinging were blowing their heads off, came the returning remnant. They presented a moving appearance. Unshaven, unkempt, gray of face, and with a kind of proud indifference to the mad welcome of their comrades, that band of heroes marched between the madly cheering, weeping lines into camp. That day all rivalry between kilts and trews died its last death.

"It is my privilege and my duty today simply to remind you that your fellow Canadians in the front line have no other enemy than their country's enemies. All Canadian soldiers in the front line are brothers, willing to give all they have for one another and ready to forget minor jealousies and differences for the cause to which they had pledged their lives."

The effect of this appeal was immediate. All causes of dispute and bitterness were forgotten.

I had a somewhat similar experience in a great meeting held in the Château Frontenac, Quebec, largely under the auspices of the Bonne Entente. The audience was composed for the most part of French Canadians, members of the legislature, representatives of the learned professions and high dignitaries of the church. Naturally and properly I recalled with pride and gratitude the splendid enthusiasm of the people of Quebec in the first days of the war; their eagerness to enlist, the generous gifts of their wealthy men, the marvelous spirit of unity between the two races. I told them of the superb achievements of the French-Canadian soldiers in the front line, of the dash and daring courage of the 22nd Battalion at Courcelette. At the close of my address a Nationalist enthusiast rose and asked why it was that the English majority in Canada persisted in denying to their French fellow citizens their rights in the matter of education and religion. A new spirit of hostility at once flamed up in my audience.

There flashed into my mind the face of the dying Roman Catholic, Donnelly, to whom I have already referred. Vividly I saw his pale face illumined with its radiant smile as I held up before his dying eyes the little cross of two sticks tied together with binder twine.

"I carry with me, and shall to the day of my death, a beautiful silver cross blessed by His Holiness the Pope, sent me by a devout Roman Catholic lady in gratitude for my service that day to that dying Roman Catholic lad. I am a Presbyterian minister, a stanch Protestant, but before God I believe there is not a man in this audience but will echo and endorse the words of the lady who sent me the cross: 'I am a Roman Catholic,' she said, 'this cross is the dearest of all my possessions, but I send it to you in gratitude for your help to that fellow Roman Catholic of mine in his last moments.' I think I did right. Would any man here say I did wrong?"

There was no reply in words, but in their tense silence, in their deeply moved faces there was an eloquence that no words could have expressed.

The story of the change in the spirit of the people of Quebec during the last years of the war is the saddest in all Canadian history. I shall refer to this again, but here I speak out of my personal knowledge and experience what I believe is the simple and solemn truth that the shame of Quebec in their attitude to the Great War is not the shame of Quebec alone. It is the shame of narrow-minded bigots, of mean and self-seeking party politicians, of shameless place seekers in whose hearts personal, racial and religious considerations had distorted and destroyed their nobler emotions and loftier principles.

CHAPTER XXIX

The World's Greatest Neutral

I TOOK a week off at Christmas, arriving home on Christmas Eve.
What a night! What a welcome! A woman with courage of the front-
line type, a boy of sixteen, already in training for the war, and six
girls from fourteen to a babe of eighteen months, receiving now the
answer to their morning and evening prayers, "God bless Daddy and
keep him safe."

And yet with all the wonder and joy of that Christmastime, I
was conscious of an undercurrent of unrest and anxiety. I would
often be startled broad awake from sleep by the sound of a shell,
to realize first how safe I was, but with the next breath to listen
through the dead stillness for the sounds of war. But there were
none, only the soft beating of the snow upon the window, the quiet
breathing of my wife at my side or a happy grunt from the baby in
her cot.

I actually welcomed a summons by wire from the Premier,
shortly after the New Year. He had been approached by the British
government with the proposal that a Canadian should be sent from
the British and Canadian governments to the United States to present the Allied view of war, especially the point of view of Canada
in regard to the war, and that my name had been suggested. I told
Sir Robert that I had one strong objection to going.

"What is that?" he asked.

"The Americans have actually made billions of dollars—eight
billions, I think—by this war, and all from the Allies. Why should
they be anxious to end the war? In the past I have lectured to thousands of them and they have made me welcome. I liked them and they

294

apparently liked me. But now, I can't stand the American people."

"But they have been most generous in their loans."

"Sir Robert, you have reminded me of the most shameless, most contemptible bit of business practiced by any nation in the war. They have loaned us billions—four billions, I think—but they have asked good interest, and every dollar of those billions has been invested in American munitions and supplies, at prices from fifty to one hundred per cent higher than the prewar price. No, I couldn't speak to an American without insulting him. Don't ask me to go."

"Major, every man to whom I have spoken says you are the one to go. Your work in the recent campaign in Canada has convinced us that you have the material, the point of approach, the personality, and from your popularity as a writer you have the entree to the hearts of the common people of America—the people we want to reach. We think you are the man."

"Sir Robert, I am not the man. For instance, how could I approach President Wilson with his sickening, disgustingly rotten notes? I couldn't bear to look at him. I despise him so."

He paused a few moments and then said quietly:

"Major, you have been telling us that in this war there is no place for personal feelings or prejudices. Only one thing matters—the front line. One thing is certain. The man who helps to bring in America on the side of the Allies will help win the war. You have been rather hard on some of us in Canada because we have not put the war first—before everything in life, except honor."

I had a sinking feeling that he had me.

"Sir Robert, I don't think I'm the man; but if you make it an order, I'm a soldier."

He smiled.

"Well then, major, we make it an order."

If ever a man hated a job I was the man and this was the job.

I wrote George Doran. No man I knew in America had better powers of organization. His ability amounted to genius. I found he knew all about it. He had been in touch with the American government and he was deeply involved with the pro-Ally interests in America. He was enthusiastic. At once he organized a committee of some of the ablest Americans who were pro-Ally in their sympathies. The chairman was Frank Vanderlip, one of America's leading financiers. With him were associated such men as Theodore Roosevelt, Henry Clay Pierce, Elihu Root and others of like caliber.

After a rush home for a day or two, I found myself in Doran's office listening to his plan of campaign.

"You will enter every door that will open to you, the big financial organizations, the New York Chamber of Commerce, the New York Merchants Association, the universities, the churches, the service clubs. Surely they are interested in international justice and right. We will get you into Presbyterian synods, women's associations. You will have all the best people with you."

"Oh, yes." I said laughing. "The American Women's Association for Peace, eh? Jane Addams will help! So will Henry Ford and Oscar Straus and W. J. Bryan and LaFollette."

"Well, Jane Addams is a woman, a fine woman, a great social worker, a friend of the oppressed, but she knows nothing about international affairs. Bryan, of course, is an ass. Oscar Straus? Well, don't be too sure about him. But don't make any mistake, you will be in the greatest campaign, outside a presidential election, ever seen in America."

"All right, when do I begin?"

Doran hesitated. "Well, at present we are having a little difficulty."

"What do you mean, difficulty?"

"Well, the New York Chamber of Commerce declined to have you. So also the Merchants Association of New York. But—"

"That's a start, eh! The two greatest business associations in the United States. What about churches?"

"Well, next Sunday Charles H. Stewart wants you in the North Reformed Church, Newark."

"Charley Stewart is a great boy. We have been through blood and fire together in Winnipeg. What of the universities?"

"Nothing doing there either, I am afraid."

"George, you can't swing these Americans. The war is paying them altogether too well. The longer it lasts the better. Look at your rotten President!"

"Forget him, major! Forget him please! Let's talk about skunks!" Doran was quite furious. "But never fear, major, give us a little time; we will swing this country all right."

I have a vivid recollection of poor Doran's face. One of the most genial souls in the world, a tremendous Canadian although now an American citizen, and a man who could not bear to be beaten.

"Give me a month, major, and your program will be full."

I gravely doubted him.

"Well, first I must present my credentials to your blessed President," I said.

"How will you arrange that?"

"Easily. Sir Cecil Spring-Rice is our ambassador. I have a letter for him from our prime minister."

But here too I had a check that quite annoyed me. Sir Cecil was gracious, but rather dubious of the wisdom of my mission.

"Come to lunch tomorrow and we shall talk it over," he said.

Next day the ambassador was eager to help but not very keen about my direct proposal. I felt that he was not enthusiastic about sponsoring me to President Wilson.

"On the whole I think you will do much better if you go on your own. As a matter of fact I am *persona non grata* with Mr. Wilson. You say you have met him?"

"Yes, at his inauguration. He was most cordial. Had me to lunch and all the rest of it. But frankly I have no use for him. In my opinion he is waiting to see the way the cat jumps."

"Ah! something in that. But he does not regard me with any great affection. We have not been able to see eye to eye."

"Well, I'd be sorry for you if you had."

"But really, I feel you will do better without any introduction from me. Send him a note. He will certainly see you."

I was disgusted. I have never quite forgiven the ambassador for his attitude. However, I went to my hotel and wrote President Wilson a formal but polite note asking for an interview. Within half an hour a reply came and next day I presented myself at the White House. I was received by the secretary, Mr. Tumulty, whom I had known before, since he was a great friend of George Doran's.

"Major," he said, "the President is much pressed for time. Don't make your visit long. Say ten or fifteen minutes."

"Five will do for me," I said.

"Oh, take ten. But the President is a tired man."

I went in no very pleasant frame of mind. But I received a shock.

The President came to me with both hands outstretched. He remembered me well, he talked of my books.

"Now what can I do for you?"

Without a word I handed him Sir Robert Borden's letter of introduction. He read the letter twice.

"Yes. Now, just what can I do for you, major?"

"I am asking only the privilege of presenting our case in this war to the people of America."

"Ah! Yes! Why, certainly. That can do nothing but good."

"Thank you, Mr. President." I rose to go.

"But sit down, major. I am delighted to see you and to talk with you. Now tell me, just what do you Canadians think of us Americans?"

Well! That knocked the wind out of me. What did we think of him and his people and his "notes"? I had no trouble recalling in what words my fellow officers in the trenches had described him as we read from time to time those same notes. What should I reply? For a moment or two my brain went whirling. Should I be polite and say smooth things, or should I tell him in plain Anglo-Saxon just how my comrades at the front, my friends in the British House of Commons and in Canada had described him. If I insulted him he might kill my whole mission then and there. I was so filled with rage and contempt that I threw every thought of policy to the wind.

"Mr. President," I said, and I was vexed that my voice was thick and trembling, "do you want me to tell you the simple truth?"

"I want the truth, major. I was delighted when I received your note, for I said to myself you would surely tell me the truth. I find it difficult to get the simple and unvarnished truth."

"Mr. President, it may be bad diplomacy for me but I will tell God's truth as I see it. And this is the simple truth, that as for your people, we hate and despise you."

He sat back sharply in his chair and stared at me for a few moments.

"Hate and despise us? Now, just what do you mean? You must tell me just what you mean."

"I will, Mr. President. Over three hundred thousand of my fellow Canadians from the Yukon to Halifax have gone to war, and are today in the various front-line trenches, dying by hundreds. Why are they dying? Do you know? I am only hoping you don't know, for if I thought you understood I could not remain in your presence. Why should my two brothers and my friends, why do you think more than three hundred of my church members in St. Stephen's, Winnipeg, with two of my elders and three of my managers have left their wives, mothers, families, to plunge into that hell in France? Why? Honor? Fame? Political or financial gain? National pride, or any such folly? Are we all fools and madmen? Am I, a Presbyterian minister, hating war, a madman? How can the American people who hold the same religious faith, who cherish the same Christian ideals, stand on the side lines unmoved and watch our men die for these ideals?"

His face was gray, his fingers trembling.

"But—but—my dear major—what—?"

"No! You can't answer. You have lived beside us, you have done business with us. I have preached in the pulpits of your greatest churches. How do you justify your cool, grasping attitude to us? You are making billions of dollars out of our agonies, out of the blood of our men, the tears of women and children.

"Then, too, Mr. President, we can't understand your speeches and your notes. Our men read them in the trenches and consign you and your notes to hell."

He caught at my words.

"My notes. What specifically do you refer to?"

"They are too many, Mr. President, and too terrible."

"Specify please," he insisted, leaning across the table to me.

"Well, first, there is that appeal of yours to your people, imploring them to be neutral in thought and feeling in regard to the immediate cause of this war. Are you neutral in thought and feeling in regard to the desolation of Belgium? I have seen those ruined villages, those wretched women and children combing our refuse heaps for crusts and bones. Can your people be neutral in thought in regard to the horrible agonizing barbarity of poison gas? Did you protest? You have sent generous help to Belgian women and children. How can you be neutral in feeling, Mr. President?"

"Now, major, let me explain. I feel as you do about these atrocities in Belgium."

"Did you ever say so? Did you people protest? Did Congress make any move?"

"What I meant, major, was this: we are not belligerents, we are really neutral. We must therefore refuse to allow ourselves to become prejudiced in favor of either side. We must maintain our neutrality. You see that?"

"Mr. President, I am quite unable to see that. If I see a man behaving like a beast to helpless women and children, my whole soul is revolted. Yours apparently is not."

"Well, let us go on. What else?"

"You said in one of your notes that the aims and motives of all the belligerents were the same, and you invited all belligerents to state definitely just what they must have rather than peace. Mr. President, you are of our stock. You are Anglo-Keltic in your blood. You are a Presbyterian. I had always considered you a God-fearing Christian. Can you say to me today, as one Christian man to another, that you consider the aims and motives of Germany in this war to be those of Britain or Canada?"

"No, never, and I did not say so."

"I have the document in my room in the hotel, Mr. President."

"I am quite familiar with the document. If you compare Article Nineteen with Article Seven [I am not sure of these numbers now] you will get my point. I was amazed that so many people have missed my point. Even my friend Lord Bryce failed to get it. Wait a moment, please. What I meant was this—that on their own showing all the belligerents are fighting against aggression, all are desirous that justice should govern in international affairs. They all profess the same aims and motives."

"Mr. President, pardon me, I am not quite a child."

"That is my statement. On their own showing they all seek noble ends and profess noble motives. What I wanted was a definite statement as to what they demand rather than peace."

I made no reply.

"What else?"

"Well, in one of your declarations you announce your conviction that the peace which will end this war will be a peace without victory! Think of a great neutral state announcing its conviction that peace will not come by way of victory. Now, Mr. President, please listen to me, I do not know every battle front in this war, but I know the Canadian front."

"You mean you have been in the fighting zone, actually in the fighting line?"

"Once only was I unable to go up with my battalion."

"But, major, you are not a combatant?"

"No, but my men are. They meet wounds and death. They need me, don't they? Many of them are of my congregation."

"Major, I never thought that you a chaplain would be in the fighting line!" His hand moved toward me. I took no notice.

"As I was saying, I know the minds of our Canadian soldiers. On my way through London I spoke to a group of members of Parliament, I know the feeling among the British people, and I know how the Canadians feel. And let me tell you, Mr. President, that the British and Canadian peoples will never cease fighting till the German military machine is utterly smashed. Peace without victory? In the hour of our desperate need you, the President of a great kindred people, with the same moral and religious ideals, you encourage us by expressing your conviction that we are not going to win. But let me tell you we are going to win. We are pushing that vast German army slowly but steadily toward their own frontier. We are moving to victory, Mr. President, in spite of you and your people."

I was enraged to find my voice breaking, but the President came back quickly.

"Again, major, you completely misunderstood me—no, don't rise—listen." He seemed deeply moved. "I believe the Allies will win."

"What?" I shouted. "You think we are going to win?"

"I believe the Allies will win. But I also believe that peace will not come to the world by way of victory, but by way of negotiation and mutual concession."

It amazed me to hear him express his confidence of the Allied victory.

"Then why didn't you say so? That was a wicked and cruel thing you said. You used the weight of your position and of your reputation as a great thinker to discourage in us the hope of victory."

"I had no such intention. Now what else?"

By this time much of my heat had gone. He really had treated me with great courtesy and forbearance.

"Well, Mr. President, I think I shall say no more."

"I cannot tell you, major, how grateful I am for your coming to me. It is extremely difficult to get firsthand information and impressions. Germany is certainly becoming difficult. What is before us in America I cannot tell, but I want to say to you that my main purpose during these last five months has been to unite my people behind me."

When I told this to my committee in New York, Frank Vanderlip smashed his fist down upon the table. "Did the President really say that?" he said. "By God, that means war!"

"Those are his very words, for after the interview I went to my room and wrote the whole thing down as I remembered it."

To return to our interview. The President was most kind to me in saying good-bye. His face was that of a worn and weary man. He came with me to the door with his arm through mine. He gave me the impression that in spite of his equivocal and uncertain notes and public utterance his sympathies were wholly with the Allies.

"Now, major, is there anything I can do for you to help your campaign?" he asked as he was saying good-bye.

"You give me permission to say what I like?"

"Yes, but I trust you to be judicious. You have many enemies in this country."

"May I wear my uniform?"

"Why, certainly. And if I can do anything to help you let me know."

His tone and manner immensely surprised me. He certainly went as far as I had any right to expect a neutral to go. I came away with a lighter heart than I had know for many a day.

CHAPTER XXX

An American Welcome

MEMORIAL TO A GREAT AMERICAN — PROGRESS
ON MISSION — FIRST SPEECH IN NEW YORK —
CHANGE OF AMERICAN VIEWPOINT — OYSTER BAY
— T. R. IN ACTION

As ONE walks eastward along the north shore of Lake Geneva with
the great Cathedral of Saint-Pierre, Calvin's church and the smaller
church in which John Knox preached on the left hand and across
the blue waters of the lake the great glittering peak of Mont Blanc and
the glorious mass of the Dent-du-Midi, one finds himself walking on
what is known as Quai Wilson. Toward the very end of this street on
the left there is placed a marble tablet with the following inscription:

A la mémoire
de
Woodrow Wilson
Président des Etats-Unis
Fondateur de la Société
des Nations.

The day will come when that marble will crumble into dust,
but the work that President Wilson did in connection with the
founding of the League of Nations will abide in the international
life of the kingdoms and democracies of the world. At present there
are many to be found, especially in his own country, who place a
low estimate on the service rendered by Mr. Wilson in connection with
the founding of the League, but as the centuries roll on the worth
of this work to the world will become increasingly evident. The
League of Nations is no perfect organization. It has grave defects
in its constitution. But it gave visibility to the great principle of in-

ternational government by collective agreement that the world will appreciate more and more.

There are those who criticize Woodrow Wilson on the ground that his attitude during the first three years of war was due almost entirely to his overweening self-assurance and his personal ambition. It is obvious that I shared this opinion during the early part of the war, but my later experience of President Wilson and a closer study of his policy have convinced me that the delay in entering the war cannot be traced solely to those elements in the character of the President. I have come to feel that he saw more clearly than most that an earlier entry into the war might have rent his people into two factions and thus have made the contribution of the United States to the Allied cause one of doubtful value.

As I left his presence on the day of my interview with him that most significant statement of his, "and I have been trying these last five months to unite my people behind me," awakened in my mind deep questioning. I confess I was completely mystified, for I regarded him at that moment as a pure opportunist who kept his eye steadily upon the wind. Frank Vanderlip's words kept repeating themselves: "Did the President really say that? By God, that means war!"

Actually, however, although the President's words had surprised and encouraged me, I did not hope for much help from him for the Allied cause.

The day following, while waiting in the Waldorf-Astoria for some word from George Doran, the telephone rang. It was Henry Pierce, the president of one of the great insurance companies of the United States and a warm personal friend of former days. The weight of his influence in financial affairs in America may be estimated from the fact that shortly before my arrival in New York he had placed an insurance of two million dollars upon the life of Mr. J. P. Morgan, the chief financial representative of Britain in America, and a million and a half insurance upon Mr. Morgan's second-in-command.

After mutual greetings and felicitations, he said: "I want you to come to a dinner of Yale graduates of my own year at the Biltmore Hotel tonight."

"Thank you, Mr. Pierce," I replied, "but I have no interest in any social function in this city just at present."

"But I want you to come and address that group of Yale men.

They represent some of the largest and most important business interests in this country."

"No," I said. "I am here to speak on one subject and on no other. I am here to speak on the war."

"That is exactly what I want. I want you to speak to these men on the war and given them the Canadian point of view."

It seemed to me an utterly futile proposition. So I excused myself: "I have already a kind of dinner engagement and I would like you to excuse me. I do not believe it would serve any good purpose that I should address these university men upon the subject of the war."

Mr. Pierce was very insistent and strongly urged me to put in an appearance. "Come late," he said. "It doesn't matter how late."

"Well," I replied. "I cannot get there till ten o'clock."

"Ten o'clock will do, but be sure and come."

Finally I accepted his invitation.

At ten o'clock I entered their dining room in the Biltmore Hotel and took my seat beside the door. A young undergradute was making a speech, in which with passionate enthusiasm he was urging these graduates of the university to extend some financial assistance to some college scheme or other. He took himself and his theme seriously. His very earnestness awakened my contempt. Here were these men, leaders of thought in this great republic, actually giving serious consideration to these trivialities while hundreds and thousands of men were fighting for world justice and world freedom across the sea. How remote their fussy little function seemed from real life.

Then followed a young professor of history. He was presenting a new view of the causes and results of the American Revolution, which had issued in the establishment of the United States. From his point of view the American Revolution was only an echo of a greater revolution in the homeland of Britain. "The fight for American freedom," he said, "was fought, not in America alone, but chiefly in England, and especially in the House of Commons. It was a fight between the Liberal party, in which were to be found the greatest statesmen of the Empire, against King George and his Tory Ministers. The great body of the best people in England were wholly in favor of the claims of the American people to their rights in free trade and for constitutional government.

"The Boston Tea Party, too," the professor continued, "was brought about originally not by the American revolutionists. As a matter of fact, the tea tax had been paid by America for years with little complaint. The tea conflict originated with a body of Bristol tea merchants who stirred up the trouble in the United States and not the American people.

"Finally," continued the professor, "the treaty that established the United States of America as an independent government was arranged by the Liberal party, and the terms granted were far more liberal than had been expected by the American plenipotentiaries." A good deal of this was new to me, but nothing could have served better for an introduction for what I had to say.

At the close of his address the chairman, Starling W. Childs, who had been chairman of the Yale *Daily News* and a prince of good fellows, sent a messenger to bring me to the head table. I was wearing my Cameron uniform with the kilt. Immediately as I rose from my chair and proceeded toward the head of the table the company burst into enthusiastic applause, which continued in growing volume and violence till I had finished shaking hands with the chairman and taken my seat beside him. I had expected merely a polite reception, but this enthusiastic volume of applause quite knocked me off my balance.

The chairman then undertook to introduce me to the company. And certainly I was in for a surprise. His speech was a eulogy of the Allied cause and of the magnificent military and naval achievements of the British people. But when he came to speak of the Canadian contingent and of the part it had played in the war, his burning words really overwhelmed me.

My whole speech, prepared for an audience steeped in indifference, if not hostility, suddenly had to be reconstructed. My attitude toward this group and the people they stood for had to be abandoned. During the few minutes of the introductory speech I was furiously engaged in reconstructing my whole case, and what was more difficult, in readjusting the whole temper and tone of my mind toward them. The chairman referred to me as a British and Canadian officer who had seen front-line service and had distinguished himself in the fighting line, and as one whom they delighted to honor.

When I rose to speak, my audience once more gave me a welcome that grew in volume and enthusiasm until, rising from their chairs, they broke into loud cheers, waving their napkins. For the first time since the outbreak of the war I was conscious of a new feeling of friendliness toward the whole American people. It took me some time to get into my stride. I began by telling them stories of scenes I had witnessed at the Canadian enlistment offices. I told them of the crowds fighting for a chance to secure registration—old men, young men, boys. I told them of the men from the far Yukon, four thousand miles away, dropping their gold mining and taking the earliest boat for Vancouver; of the men of the ranches who, unable to enlist in the regular way, hired a cattle train, loaded their own horses and supplies and equipment and made their way to Ottawa demanding a place in the First Contingent. I then concentrated upon my personal experiences in the front line with my comrades, wounded and dying and dead. Later I told them of my return to Canada and of the five hundred women meeting me in a great gathering in my church to listen to my report as to the conduct and service and suffering, wounds and death of their husbands and sons. I said little at first about the political aspects of the war, but I did touch briefly, somewhat bitterly, upon our inability as Canadians to understand the attitude of the American people, our friends and neighbors, largely of the same racial stock and holding the same ethical and religious ideals in regard to the rights of our common humanity.

The hour was late, so I had to content myself with a thirty-minute address. When I sat down, my whole audience again rose to their feet and demanded more. I said, "If I turn myself loose on war matters I shall keep you here all the night."

They came back with shouts: "Go on! . . . We'll stay with you! . . . We've got all night for it!"

Actually for another whole hour I talked to those Yale men in regard to the issues of the war. I was desperately in earnest. So apparently were they. They were utterly committed to the Allied cause. They were full of indignation at their own government. Then for half an hour questions were put to me, which I answered as best I could, each question giving me an opportunity for a fresh presentation of our cause. At the close of the question period a young man rose and proposed a resolution condemning the action of a United States senator, a member of this class, who had voted recently against the suggestion that America take a new attitude toward Germany in this war. The resolution declared that this senator no longer represented his university or the people who had elected him, and demanded his immediate resignation.

This was carried unanimously.

A second proposition was then presented, which deplored the attitude of the United States toward the cause of the Allies and demanded that the President should immediately announce a state of war between the United States and the Central Powers. This, too, passed without a single word of protest. Needless to say, I was overwhelmed. This response was so completely unexpected.

Thereupon we adjourned to another room where supper was served. There again they gathered round a table, while I with a few others to keep me in countenance, proceeded to have some refreshment. Every minute of that half hour was filled with questions and answers. The amazing unanimity and enthusiasm of their support for my cause was so unexpected and so full of warm personal emotion.

The next morning George Doran called me up for a report. I gave him a brief account of my experience. He was delighted.

"Of course," he said, "these are important men in the business life of New York, but they are only a small group and we must not expect too much. But it is all to the good and will undoubtedly help us to get our campaign going."

In the afternoon he called me again. A considerable number of Yale men had been telephoning him. He was quite stirred up.

"I assure you, major," he said, "you are really getting somewhere. I have been hearing all morning about your speech, and have been getting inquiries in regard to your engagements. Also," he continued, "Roosevelt has got word of it and we are going out to Oyster Bay to lunch with him the day after tomorrow."

All this was good hearing. It looked as though some doors which had been closed might now be open to me.

Two days later we drove out to the little seashore town of Oyster Bay to ex-President Roosevelt's home. Mr. Roosevelt was out somewhere on his farm when we arrived, but after a few minutes he made his appearance. In rough tweeds, wearing a wide cowboy hat, stocky, sturdy and red-faced he appeared in the doorway with a lovely little girl perched on his shoulders, his grand-daughter. The two made a beautiful picture. I saw Roosevelt, a rough, forceful, almost ruthless politician in quite a new and different light. He greeted us with great cordiality. He was intensely interested in my campaign, he would do his very best to make it a success, but meantime he had something in hand upon which he was anxious to secure the opinion of Mr. Doran and myself. "You are a publisher, Doran, and you a preacher, doctor, and I shall get two important points of view on what I have to offer you.

"You have seen, Doran, the challenge of that pacifist secretary of ours, Bryan, challenging me to debate with him in a public meeting the propriety of the United States' entering the war on the side of the Allies. Here is my answer. I have declined his proposition, telling him that there were certain subjects a gentleman refused to discuss with any man. For instance, his wife's honor."

He then proceeded to read his reply to Mr. Bryan's letter. It was full of shrewd, biting invective and sound reasoning.

When he had finished he turned to Doran and said, "What do you think of that?"

"Splendid!" said Doran. "You could not have done better. That will certainly get him."

He then turned to me, "What do you think, major?"

"Very fine! Very effective!" I said. "But there is a certain phrase in regard to which I am in some doubt. It is that quotation of yours from Scripture."

"What is that?" he asked abruptly. "I know my Scripture."

"The quotation is, 'like priest, like people.' The suggestion is that the priest is responsible for guiding the thinking of his people. I have a feeling that the quotation should read the other way, 'like people, like priest,' with the suggestion that the priest represents the sycophant official as the creation of a sycophant and timeserving populace."

"You are wrong," he said. "I know my Book. That quotation is all right."

"It may be," I said, "but it struck me at the time that it might be wrong."

"Have you a *Concordance* here?" asked Doran. "We will look it up."

"Sure," said Roosevelt.

He went to his library shelves, found a *Concordance,* looked up

the reference and discovered he was wrong. You never saw a man
more badly taken aback.

"Well," he said, "I couldn't have believed that I would have made
a mistake in quoting Scripture, but what a lucky thing you were here.
I wouldn't have that pusillanimous polecat catch me out in a quotation
of Scripture for a thousand dollars. You know he capitalizes his religious attitude and activities. He is a great saint, and nothing would
have pleased him so completely as to catch me on a Scriptural quotation."

At lunch we met his wife and family and a friend or two. There
was only one subject of conversation—the war and the part that
America should play. Mr. Roosevelt was furious in his denunciation
of President Wilson's attitude. His description of the President was
vivid, indeed lurid at times. "We should have gone in immediately
after the *Lusitania* affair," he declared. "We had abundant justification and we had a great and overwhelming outburst of passionate
indignation on the part of the nation to help us on. Now he has let
that go by and it is doubtful if we will ever again have so outstanding and so unequivocal a cause for war."

He was particularly indignant at the President's notes to the
British government on the matter of the the freedom of the seas.
He quite lost his temper. He rose from the table and strode up and
down the room cursing the President for his political obliquities and
cowardice.

"We must have a public meeting," he said. "I will get Root and
Lodge and Putnam and Vanderlip and a lot of first-class men for a
platform. I shall speak myself, and the major here will speak and
we shall have one of the greatest meetings ever held in Madison
Square Garden."

About three days later the meeting was actually held and in spite
of the brief period of time for advertising, Madison Square Garden
was packed to the rafters. Roosevelt had secured a platform of distinguished men. Lodge was unable to be present, but Root was there
and George Haven Putnam and a large group of outstanding citizens
of New York. I had a place on the platform, but declined to speak.

"This is not my meeting," I said to Mr. Roosevelt. "This is a
meeting of Americans. I am not here to tell the Americans what to

do or how to do it. I am telling them what we are trying to do and why."

George Doran quite agreed with me.

That evening I had the great delight of watching Roosevelt, who was indeed one of America's most forceful orators, sway the vast audience of Americans with every mood and tense of his passionate address. At the close of the meeting a resolution was carried demanding that the President take steps immediately to invite Congress to express itself as in favor of entering the war on the side of the Allies.

CHAPTER XXXI

The Rising Tide

PROGRAM OF SPEECHES—RESPONSIBILITY FOR THE WAR—COLLAPSE OF RUSSIA—THE STORY OF MONS—AMERICAN RESPONSE—ISOLATION VS. INTERNATIONALISM—AMERICA DECLARES WAR

DURING the week following my Yale dinner in the Biltmore Hotel, my program of addresses rapidly filled up till it became necessary and advisable to make a selection of only such engagements as would most effectively further my mission. I strongly urged that my campaign should begin with my personal friends and most enthusiastic supporters. Of these one of the most prominent and pronounced was the Rev. Dr. Charles H. Stewart, minister of the North Reformed Church of Newark, N. J. As a student in Manitoba College, Charley Stewart had been a member of my congregation of St. Stephen's; later he became a fellow presbyter, the pastor of a young and vigorous congregation, and still later an enthusiastic comrade in arms in our long fight against a corrupt government in Manitoba, in the interests of temperance and morality. From him and his congregation came a warm invitation to preach in the North Reformed.

A full church greeted me. For an hour I set forth the cause of the Allies in this great war. It was an extraordinary pulpit experience for me. Again and again that congregation, mainly composed of descendants of stolid Reformed Dutch Presbyterian stock, broke out in cheering, the whole service closing with the hearty singing of the British national anthem and of "My Country, 'Tis of Thee" to the same noble music. The sight of that old-fashioned body of orthodox Presbyterians breaking through the ancient traditions of decorum and dignity in the house of God did most amazingly hearten me at the outset of my campaign. I have never ceased to remember gratefully the hearty support given me that day by this fine old congregation and their minister.

The following Sunday I preached in the Fifth Avenue Presbyterian Church, which was probably the most conservative and powerful of the Presbyterian churches in America. In this service I fully expected a dignified and at best mildly sympathetic hearing. I was amazed to find my Newark experience repeated, and in spite of its traditions of dignity, the congregation cheered again and again. When I reported this to George Doran he could hardly credit it.

"Doran," I said, "I am coming to the conviction that this American people is far more sympathetic with our cause and much nearer to war than you and your friends imagine."

"It may be," he replied thoughtfully. "It may quite well be that we have been far too much influenced by the subsidized pro-German propaganda carried on in this country. However, we shall soon see."

Certainly my campaign committee were bucked up in their minds and proceeded with great enthusiasm to complete the arrangements for my program. Thenceforth there was never a Sunday during my stay in America that I did not have two and often three opportunities to speak from the pulpits of the various Christian churches. And why not? To me the cause of the Allies was then a sacred cause, in complete harmony as I felt with the tenets and principles of the religion I professed. It was the cause of human freedom and justice toward weak and defenseless people against the tyranny of grasping national ambition and military aggression. Twenty years have passed since those days and my study of international affairs since that time has not changed my opinion. I freely confess that today I see with clearer vision the inequities and wrongs practiced by all nations toward one another in their economic policies. Nonetheless, I retain the conviction that while the nations forming the Triple Entente cannot escape their own measure of responsibility for the outbreak of the Great War, the chief and dominant cause of the conflict, in the main, must be discovered in the blind, militaristic spirit of the Prussian Junta which cowed and forced the great German people, fully half of whom were thoroughly socialistic and antimilitaristic in their modes of thought, into that criminal adventure for the conquest of the world. Even in those days of war, however, I am now glad to think that never was I conscious of any feeling of personal hatred for the German people and rarely did I find, among the rank and file of our soldiers, feelings of hate and an implacable desire for vengeance upon the soldiers whom they were meeting in the battle line from day to day.

At this point I venture a slight digression to illustrate my conviction. Among the officers of our battalion the only champion of the hate motif was our second-in-command, the big warmhearted Scot, Major Grassie, whose supposedly vengeful spirit I always suspected to be more or less on the surface.

"I'd like to make those devils suffer as they made Belgium suffer," he would say at the mess table. "We treat our prisoners far too kindly. Bread and water I would give them and make them earn their keep too."

One day in the trenches on the Somme, I saw emerge from a deep trench one of our sergeants, his rifle slung carelessly over his shoulder, nonchalantly conducting a long line of German prisoners to our rear. They were a broken-spirited lot. The line halted at the order of the second-in-command who happened to be the officer in charge. With a look of contempt and wrath in his eye he stood for some moments regarding the wretched prisoners. Suddenly he bellowed in English at the poor wretch nearest him:

"What is your name?"

There was a trembling, mumbled reply in German.

"What is your battalion?"

Again a mumbled reply. Our officers' extremely limited knowledge of the German speech made the interrogation difficult.

"What part of Germany do you come from?"

Still there was no intelligible reply. Long, contemptuously and wrathfully our major regarded the enemy. Suddenly he reached for his cigarette case:

"Here, you poor devil, have one."

A snicker ran through the circle of officers. Never again at mess table did we hear from our second-in-command any comment, any hint of a bloodthirsty desire for vengeance upon our foes.

No! Our hatred and wrath we kept for those classes among our enemies which were responsible for the origin of the war and for the ruthless brutality of the soldiers toward the defenseless noncombatants of Belgium and France.

Very early in the campaign I was invited to address a meeting of the Yale Alumni Association in New Haven. I approached my audience with a certain degree of anxiety. I was warned to expect a large amount of heckling, inasmuch as my audience would be composed of the keenest minds among the American people and would also, in many cases, be of German extraction. The chairman of the meeting was openly and hotly pro-Ally and in his anxiety to be absolutely impartial leaned quite considerably backward in his words of introduction. Looking back upon my experience at that meeting I can see now that his attitude of strict and cold impartiality, in the long run, best served my cause. In my address, however, I made the mistake of taking some time to analyze characteristics of German thought and the principles of German government, tracing German history from the days of the German Revolution and dwelling with some degree of severity on the character of the Hohenzollerns.

I made the tactical error of suggesting that before such an assembly as this I should, welcome, at any moment, the request for further elucidation on any point that might not be quite clear. It happened that in my audience were a number of graduates and professors of German extraction and with German education. Very soon they had me on the grill. What about the atrocity stories? I told them what I had seen in Belgian towns and villages, what I had heard from front-line war correspondents. I gave them a little of the war philosophy of "Schrechlichkeit." They quoted examples of alleged "frightfulness" in the War for Independence and the Indian Wars in which British generals had been involved. I made it quite clear that I justified no atrocity, whether in Connecticut or in Wyoming Valley.

"Finally," I said, "it is hardly necessary to recall the fact that the military practices of the eighteenth century cannot be regarded as justification for those of the twentieth century.

At this point there was a quick burst of applause from these dons and professors such as one might have expected from a group of undergraduates. The chairman interjected a word: "I think it might be better for all of us to allow Major Gordon to continue his address without further interruption," he said with grave severity.

"It sure would," was the emphatic remark of an American professor of middle age, whose comment was received with an outburst of laughter, which relieved me from my more formal method of address assumed for the occasion.

I thereupon proceeded to tell them stories based upon my own experiences. I began with some moving tales of the early recruiting in Canada.

"It is difficult for me as a Canadian to speak in cool language of these things. I shall never be able to wipe from my memory the scenes of those first recruiting days in Canada. For instance, I think of a young Highlander, a member of my congregation, who could not be persuaded to wait for the First Contingent to be organized in Canada, but set off to join the first battalion of the Black Watch in Scotland, in which famous regiment his father and his grandfather were officers. I was there the day he left home. I stood beside his mother and sisters who were watching from the open door his departure. As he approached the corner of the street, the mother was about to re-enter the house. 'Wait, mother,' said one of the girls, 'he will turn to wave good-bye at the next street corner.' We waited for this last farewell, but it never came. The boy turned the street corner and with never a backward look was lost forever to view. Within a month word came that he was killed in his first battle."

From that moment these learned gentlemen, ceased to be critical representatives of Yale University and became simple human beings with human hearts. But most of my time had already been exhausted and I was forced to conclude my address with the unhappy feeling that I had missed my opportunity.

Before the close of the meeting, however, a gray-haired and bespectacled professor rose and said something like this:

"Mr. Chairman, it seems to me that it is quite essential that Major Gordon should have an opportunity of presenting to the whole body of our students a full statement of his experiences in this war. We as American citizens owe it to ourselves and to our country to become intelligent in regard to this tremendous upheaval in the world at this time. I, therefore, move that Major Gordon be invited to address a mass meeting of the students of Yale University and be given a full opportunity to set before them the facts that have come within his experience."

The motion was seconded and unanimously carried.

The date of the meeting was arranged to fit in with my program and set for the following Sunday evening. The great public Assembly Hall of the university, comfortably seating two thousand, on this occasion was packed to its last available foot with an audience that numbered, according to reports, some three thousand students.

"Tell them stories," said my chairman. "Let us do the argumentative part."

Remembering my experience in Canada, I knew how right he was. From the very moment of my introduction and for more than an hour I told these young men and women stories of my own experiences in the war, in Belgium and in the valley of the Somme. I was especially keyed up for the occasion. My former comparative failure stimulated me to my highest effort. Never in my life have I addressed a meeting held in such tense interest and thrilled with such deep emotion. Over and over again that body of youthful students burst into applause.

At the close of my address a young man arose and presented a motion, which expressed in the first place complete approval of the cause of the Allies and then called upon the President of the United States at once to declare the United States of America to be at war with the Central Powers in alliance with the forces of the British and Canadian armies. Some minor changes were suggested and accepted by the mover and seconder and the resolution was thereafter carried by a standing vote, which as far as I could see was practically unanimous.

The next few weeks were strenuous enough. My itinerary covered New York and cities of the eastern states. In Boston I joined eight hundred bankers in their annual dinner. I spent some time in Philadelphia and the small towns in its neighborhood. I went as far west as Chicago. There I received a welcome of extraordinary warmth and enthusiasm. The businessmen invited me to a luncheon and gave me an earnest and sympathetic hearing. The men of the university, both faculty and students, packed their splendid hall. I had been warned that the Middle West was distinctly antiwar and strongly pro-German and would either boycott me entirely or howl me down. My experience was altogether different. I was quite overwhelmed with the warmth of my reception at every meeting held in Chicago. I had the advantage of being a western man myself, which gave me an understanding of the psychology of Westerners and of their point of view. Whatever the reason, I received a cordial welcome from every class of citizen, from the businessmen, from the churchfolk, from the university people and, to my surprise, even from the highest social circles. Never have I had from any body of women a more cordial reception than that given me by the Evanston Women's Literary Club. One reason for this warm reception may have been the fact that Mr. Fleming H. Revell, the publisher of *Black Rock* and *Sky Pilot* and George Doran, his sales manager, were citizens of that beautiful little suburb of Chicago at the time these novels were published fifteen years before.

Of all the meetings held during this campaign of mine in the eastern and midwestern states two stand out in my memory with vividness: one, a meeting of businessmen; the other, a meeting of university students.

The first of these was the luncheon given me by the New York Merchants Association. In the early part of my campaign, it will be remembered, my committee had been unable to secure a date with that powerfully influential body of New York businessmen, but there came a day when the Waldorf-Astoria dining room was packed with twelve hundred guests, whose women friends filled the alcoves on the second floor above to listen to what I had to say in regard to the war situation, which for America as well as for the Allies was daily becoming more gravely serious.

That was one of the blackest days of the war. The morning papers carried the appalling news of the political upheaval in Russia. Even today as I write, I can feel again the weight of dread lest this day might mark for us the beginning of the end. I well knew that the Russian debacle would release an army of a million men, possibly a million and a half, for service against the Allies on the western and other battle fronts.

The reports, too, of the quite remarkable German successes in their submarine warfare were ominous enough. It was a black day for the Allies. As I sat at lunch watching the cheerful, prosperous group of American people about me, thoroughly enjoying their food, my heart grew hot and bitter. The contrast between this body of secure Americans and that desperately swaying fighting line on every battle front was almost more than I could endure. In the Far East, in Mesopotamia, in Persia, Eastern Turkey, the Allied forces were desperately striving to hold their ground. In the Central European area Rumania was almost out, Italy was gallantly holding on, but making little real headway. Gallipoli was shrouded in black uncertainty. Along the Somme valley for more than fifty miles the Allies were slowly driving the enemy toward their own boundary line, but with issues that no man could certainly foretell. There had been disquieting rumors of French war weariness in the Verdun sector. I could make little response to the kindly and courteous efforts of my friends at conversation. The big black letters of the morning papers "Russia in Collapse"—"Germany Jubilant"—"Perilous Position of the Allies" —were before my eyes.

Suddenly I became aware that the chairman was introducing me to this cheerful company. He was frankly sympathetic with the Allied cause. He dwelt with foreboding upon the Russian collapse. He referred anxiously to the German submarine victories. Britain had been putting up a magnificent fight, France was gallantly pouring out blood and treasure. But the question was, how long could the Allies maintain the dreadful drain of men and material in this war? No one could predict what the next few weeks might bring forth; in fact, there were those who were fearful that the Allies might be forced to accept a German victory. At this point quite unconsciously I burst out into a loud laugh. I could have cursed the fool. German victory! I could hardly wait till he should conclude his silly chatter.

I rose with a smile on my face but fury in my heart. I had come with the intention of seeking to win these Americans to our way of thinking, but at this moment I did not care a hoot what Americans did, we would still fight on and we would win.

"A German victory?" I hurled the words at them with a laugh of scorn. It was rude and undoubtedly not good policy, but I was helpless in the grip of the forces of rage that possessed me. "An agreement with Germany? Can you imagine Britons taking orders from Germany? British sailors obeying the commands of German admirals? They have not done so for a thousand years. They will never do so. Americans may sail their ships under orders from the German High Command, British people laugh at such preposterous nonsense. True, Russia has abandoned the fighting line and thus millions of Germans will be free to increase their pressure upon their western front. That is an ominous possibility. But, gentlemen, I have seen Ypres. I stood on the front line where Canadians, green, untrained soldiers who had never fired a gun in wrath, held at bay the finest and best equipped battalions of Germany's army. I was not present at that desperate fight, but I have heard the story of it from those who were there, when the Canadians had that new, brutal and terrible method of war by poison gas first tried upon them. I have been told how the frenzied Algerian troops, thinking that the devil had fallen on them, fled choking from their lines leaving a gap of four miles wide on the Canadian left flank. The Canadians, too, got the gas, it choked scores of them to death—yes, hundreds of them—but their comrades lying on the open plain in front of their trenches which were full of gas, continued firing their rifles till they died. The remainder who could walk met with volleys of rifle fire the advancing lines of jubilant Germans, and finally with the bayonet drove them back in flight, fiercely snatching from them the victory they thought they had already won. A night, a day and another night, the Canadians lay fighting back new hordes of the advancing enemy. A troop of British cavalry, hurriedly dispatched from the rear, leaped from their horses, marched into that fatal gap and held the line to allow the remnant of staggering Canadians to retire from that deadly gap. Again fresh troops of the enemy attacked, and again they were driven back. The pressure of enemy troops finally became so intense—they would not bear to have their first gas attack turn out a failure— that the British general in command asked the Canadian remnant to go in again. Without a moment's hesitation they went back into that hell and held the line for another day and another night, till a French battalion coming up on their left flank had filled the gap and made the line safe. From eyewitnesses I have learned that when that poor, worn and battered remnant of Canadians finally staggered back into reserve the British regiments there received them with full military honors, cheering madly as they marched back to rest quarters.

"A German victory? What nonsense is this? Have you ever read the story of Mons? Never were soldiers more certain of easy victory than were those Germans of the Second and Third Army Corps who jauntily marched forward to encircle that little army of 'Contemptibles' at Mons. Seventy-five thousand British regulars were holding the line on that Sabbath morning against two hundred thousand, yes, at times three and finally four hundred thousand, of the pick of the Germany army. Realizing the desperate character of the situation the

British officer commanding the division gave orders to retire. As a first move in giving effect to these orders General Smith-Dorrien made a fierce attack upon the enemy before him. So terrible was this attack and so fiercely pushed home that the German command imagined this little army must have received heavy reinforcements.

"Immediately after that attack the British troops began their desperate retreat, the fame of which will never die. Throughout Monday they fought a rear-guard action. Monday night they snatched a few hours sleep, Tuesday they fought all day, and Tuesday night snatched again a few hours sleep, Friday and Friday night, Saturday and Saturday night they fought and marched and fought again, till with unbroken ranks though sorely decimated they came to the Marne and there stood.

"A final German victory? Absurd! If any man talks to you of final German victory tell him to read the story of Ypres and the story of that glorious anabasis from Mons to the Marne.

"Let me remind you that during the first year of this war the British forces were woefully lacking in artillery. The guns they had were as good as any but were terribly outmatched in weight, in range and numbers. Well do I remember a day when after a heavy bombardment my O.C. telephoned back to headquarters begging for retaliation. I heard the reply 'We can only give you four rounds of retaliation.'"

Not a word of all this had I prepared for my address. I spoke with headlong, breathless passion, often with voice breaking and tears running down my cheeks. Even today I am not ashamed of such weak emotion. But that day when my tears were flowing I was not alone. On all sides of me men were weeping, openly weeping. At a table immediately before me a white-haired gentleman put his head down upon the table and sobbed aloud. I had not thought of making a speech, I had no thought of striving for effect, I was simply proclaiming in my own way the deathless resolve of the British people and of their allies that never would they take orders from Germany, or from any race of kindred spirit and purpose. My speech, contrary to my custom, was a short one.

Before I closed I could not forbear, for the first time in my campaign, a word of direct appeal to the American people. "I am here trying to make you Americans see why it is that three hundred thousand Canadians, on their own motion, without a single request or appeal from the motherland, are now in the war zone. They are not there for any national ambition or purpose of aggrandizement, they are not there from any hate of any people in the world. They are there because they believe that the future of all free peoples, that their own future, is bound up with victory over the imperialistic, mad ambition of a people determined to enslave the rest of mankind. Americans have asked me how Canadians can support such a drain upon their manhood, and whether Canadians are not growing weary of the conflict. I have just returned from a journey across Canada, from Victoria on the Pacific to Halifax on the Atlantic. I have yet to find a single Canadian who thinks or dreams of anything but final victory. They have sent three hundred thousand men across the seas, they are planning, now as I speak to you, how best they can equip and send another three hundred thousand or five hundred thousand or more, if such be the need of the Empire and or its allies. What Americans will do I know not, I had almost said I care not. But let me close my word to you with this solemn declaration: Canadians know right well that that Allied line in France is Canada's last line of defense, and with solemn conviction, as in the presence of God, let me say to you that that Allied line is America's last line of defense as well. I am not telling you your duty, but I am not afraid to tell you that when that front line breaks your front line will meet you, not in France or in Flanders, but on the free soil of this great American people."

I make no apology for recalling, as nearly as I can, the words of my address to the merchants of New York. I spoke without brief, and without a note. That terrible, overwhelming news of the morning gave me my message and gave me the passion with which to deliver it. After I had closed there was no resolution one way or the other, but when the meeting broke up more than a score of the men at the head table, great merchants and financial magnates of New York, crowded about me eager to give me their hands and eager to pledge their support. It was Frank Vanderlip himself, I think, who said: "Major, there are fifty men here who would gladly subscribe to a fund to send you across this American continent delivering, wherever you go, this message that you have given us today."

"I am under orders," I said. "I came under the direction of the

Canadian and British governments. Where they tell me to go I will go. But I should dearly love the opportunity of saying what I have said today to Americans in all parts of this country, for I believe it is God's solemn truth."

I am come to the climax of my American campaign and, in relation to my political thinking, one of the supreme moments in my life.

From the outbreak of war my mind had been torn between the ideas of national independence and international responsibility. I held firmly to the idea that every nation has the inherent right to hold and to realize its ideal of national development, but I had not worked out the implications involved in a universal internationalism in which each nation must come to its highest and fullest development. World peace as a result of balanced world powers seemed the only possible condition of world peace and co-operation. Like the vast majority of Britishers, I had come to regard the international policy of Edward VII as a veritable triumph of British diplomacy and as the only possible policy for Britain to follow. The Great War, however, made quite clear the utter unwisdom of such a policy for world development. How a great Empire could at once be utterly true to itself and its own development and at the same time do justly by all other nations I had not thought out. The world was wholly committed to the doctrine of world peace as conditional solely upon world power.

To the American people the isolation theory of international existence seemed the adequate and, for America, the only possible theory of international relationship. During these days America was struggling, and vainly struggling, to justify and to enforce her policy of international isolation. She was about to discover how impossible such a doctrine was in the modern world, and also to discover her responsibility to the peace and security of the whole world.

Under the auspices of the Yale Alumni Association a meeting had been arranged for April 2nd, which I was asked to address on the general subject of Nationalism and Internationalism. During the preceding weeks the relations between the American and German governments had become acutely strained in regard to the new doctrine of Germany as to the freedom of the seas in time of war. After the second inauguration of President Wilson on March 5th events crowded rapidly upon one another. During one month of war six American vessels flying the American flag had been torpedoed without warning. On the 9th of March orders were issued for the arming of merchant vessels and contracts let for new cruisers and battleships amounting to $136,000,000. The attitude of Germany became increasingly arrogant, as its submarine policy became less effective. My experience of American audiences had convinced me that the President had vastly underestimated the extent and intensity of the spirit of resentment against German aggressive insolence in the matter of American sailing rights as well as the feeling of abhorrence of Germany's war methods in general. President Wilson's last note had definitely rejected Germany's demand that American trade shipping should be confined within certain sea lanes and carried on in ships bearing certain markings and subject to search by German vessels of war. Indeed, the American government had given the German ambassador, the unspeakable von Bernstorff, his walking papers.

The atmosphere was oppressively charged with explosive material and a break might come any day. I was conscious of an intense strain of anxiety lest Germany be able to find a formula that might make it possible for America to resume friendly relations with her. But during the last few months the British navy had discovered ways and means to largely overcome the German submarine warfare. The loss of German submarines was becoming increasingly heavy, the British shipbuilding industry had made enormous strides in overtaking her losses at sea, and worst of all for Germany, the heavy loss of personnel in crews from her submarines was being acutely felt. Both in numbers and in morale the crews of the submarine navy were steadily and rapidly reduced. In addition to all this, the naval blockade had brought about an almost intolerable scarcity in the means of living for the German people. Germany could not for a moment accept any suggestion that would tend to lessen the effectiveness of her most powerful weapon of war.

Through personal friends in the Cabinet, the committee in charge of the Yale meeting had come to know that that very evening it was possible that President Wilson would make an announcement to Congress, meeting in joint session, of more than ordinary importance.

I have no remembrance of the line of thought taken in my address but at the close an event occurred which stamped the moment, from one point of view, as the greatest in my life.

Immediately after the applause following my address had died down, the secretary of the association rose and said:

"Mr. Chairman, I have just received a wire from Washington announcing the President has declared to Congress meeting in joint session that in his opinion Congress should immediately declare the existence of a state of war between the United States of America and the German government."

As the sound of his voice died away that company sat in rigid silence. For some seconds all eyes were fixed on the chairman. Gradually I became conscious that all eyes were turned upon me.

Somehow an inspiration came to me. I slowly rose, lifted my glass high and said:

"Mr. Chairman, I have the very great honor to propose the health of His Excellency Woodrow Wilson, the President of the United States of America, our latest and greatest ally."

The reaction came with the suddenness and violence of an explosion. Men leaped to their feet, drank the toast, climbed on their chairs and wildly waving their napkins they rocked the room with their vociferous cheering. I was conscious of an overwhelming tide of emotion. The final issue of the war was already decided.

CHAPTER XXXII

"Now Cracks a Noble Heart"

A VIOLENT shock awaited me on my return to Canada about the middle of the summer of 1917. Fresh from my experiences among the people of our neighboring republic, now eager to express in deeds their devotion to the cause of the Allies, the situation in Canada filled me with amazement and horror. After such a magnificent entry into the war Canada was now torn by factions, political, religious and racial. It was a bitter experience for me. In reply to a communication to Premier Borden telling him of the completion of my work in the United States, a wire from him summoned me to Ottawa.

From reports in the press of the Premier's utterances since his return from Britain and the front line, I fully expected to discover in him certain changes, but I had not expected to find in Premier Borden a completely new man. His eleven weeks in Great Britain had transformed him. He had received a new viewpoint from which to study the methods and threatening consequences of the war. During his visit to Britain he had been feted by distinguished personages from royalty down. He had addressed the House of Commons, he had taken part in the newly constituted Imperial War Cabinet. All this had produced an effect which nothing but personal contact with those who represented British life could have achieved. But I was convinced that even this would not fully account for the change that had taken place in the spirit and temper of the man.

He had seen what was going on in the war zone. He had been given a close view of the war. He had visited the trenches where Canadians were fighting day and night. He had spent some hours at the Canadian headquarters, at the British headquarters and the headquarters of the French High Command. He had seen the men actually going up the line, and he had seen them come back. He had visited every Canadian hospital in Britain and had noted there the dreadful ravages of war upon Canadian soldiers. He had spent some hours with the maimed and blind and demented. All these experiences had wrought in him a profound transformation. He returned to his native land filled with one single determination which became a ruling passion with him: by every means available, Canada should continue to take her full share of the war. He was ready to accept any and every possible suggestion that could be offered, the continuing of government without an election by the extension of the life of the Parliament to 1918. He had at first opposed conscription, but after his experience of the failure of recruiting in Canada and after his experiences in the war zone he finally came to a settled conviction upon two matters: first, the Canadian ranks at the front could be kept strong and full only by a policy of conscription; second, there must be a Union government representing the best and most able men available. Later he came to accept the proposition that an immediate election was necessary.

It was after he had arrived at these convictions that I first met him on my return. He invited me once more to enter upon a campaign to stimulate recruiting. I asked for time to consider the matter. I found my mind in a state of confusion. I believed in a Union government but only in a Union government representing the best minds in the country, and among these should be the veteran leader of the Liberal party, Sir Wilfred Laurier. A little later a committee was formed representing a body of men not only eager to continue the war under the most hopeful and most favorable conditions, but anxious to save the country from the disaster of racial cleavage and religious conflict. In that committee were representatives of those who had been striving to carry on the Bonne Entente campaign so as to neutralize the Nationalist movement among French Canadians headed by Bourassa, which was sweeping like a raging fire through the whole province of Quebec. I found myself unable to make up my mind immediately.

"If you are asking me to enter upon a recruiting campaign with things as I find them in Canada, I refuse point-blank. It seems to me that the first thing to be done is to secure co-operation and cohesion among the leaders of all parties, political, racial and religious, in a single unified body with a united policy to present to the people. Next there must be a cleaning out from public life of this mass of money-making and place-seeking Canadians who disgrace the name of their country. The present government cannot escape responsibility for a most shameful condition of affairs in Canada."

After a few days I met the committee again. They had come to learn my decision. I told them that I had come to a definite decision upon certain points. First, there must be a Union government composed of sincere and honest men, free from party, racial and religious bitterness. Second, this government should announce definitely the policy of conscription for service in the war. Third, there must be a complete house cleaning from public life of all profiteers, an eradication of patronage in contracts for munitions and material for war, and a clean sweep from government and military offices of mere figureheads. And, fourth there must be a new election at the earliest possible date. Gradually I had come to accept these four planks as absolutely necessary to a successful war campaign in Canada.

The committee then asked me to see Sir Wilfrid Laurier.

"You know Sir Wilfrid well," said the chairman. "You respect him and believe in him, and he knows you."

"That is true," I said, "and—Sir Wilfrid Laurier must be a member of the Union government."

"You believe that without him Quebec cannot be brought into line with the other provinces?"

"I believe that most emphatically," I said.

"You believe also that conscription is necessary as a policy for recruiting?"

"I have come to believe that," I replied. "But if you wish me to go to Sir Wilfrid Laurier, give me a definite proposition that I may lay before him. Make it a proposition which he, as a great Canadian statesman and the leader of a great political party, as the most completely representative French Canadian can honorably accept."

They thereupon gave me authority to offer Sir Wilfrid Laurier second place in a Union government. To make up a slate that would include only honorable men of all parties who were prepared to give first place to the war, to eliminate from the government every man who had made a fortune in this war, every religious bigot, every racial maniac, choose only Canadians determined to do everything, to sacrifice everything, to win this war.

With a doubtful and uncertain mind I went to see Sir Wilfrid Laurier.

His cordial reception touched me deeply. He seemed to me a disappointed and lonely man.

"I have followed your war work," he said, "not only in the front line, but in Canada and in the United States, with interest and with pride."

"You are having a hard time, Sir Wilfrid," I said.

"I have done my utmost to serve my country in this war from the first," he replied. "I have been thwarted, checked and halted on every hand."

"Sir Wilfrid," I said, "I know something of what you have been suffering during these months. I am sure you will believe that you have my complete sympathy. I am deeply grieved that in the present situation you find it impossible to do your best for Canada, but I am still hopeful that a way can be found by which you can still greatly serve, and indeed save, your country, as you have done in similar circumstances before now."

"I fear it is too late," he said. "I have lost many of my dearest friends, of my most loyal supporters. I have made many bitter enemies; worse than all, I have lost hold of the vast majority of my people in Quebec."

"I do not believe it, Sir Wilfrid," I said. "I am convinced that most Canadians consider you a loyal and honorable Canadian seeking to serve your country. May I ask you, are you irrevocably opposed to conscription?"

"Not to conscription as such, but I believe conscription should be preceded by an appeal to the people through referendum."

"But, Sir Wilfrid," I interposed. "Suppose the answer is in the negative, what would follow then? Are you prepared to abandon the war altogether?"

"No! Never!" he said with great emphasis. "But I am confident that if the matter of conscription be put fairly before the people by way of referendum a favorable answer will be returned. Even if the answer were unfavorable, we should be no worse off than we are now."

"Sir Wilfrid, I am not here to discuss that," I said. "I have no right to offer an opinion on that matter. Failure in a referendum would hopelessly split Canada into fragments. But let me ask you another question. What of Union government?"

"Months ago," he replied quietly, "I was heartily in favor of Union government. I am still in favor of Union government, if not attached to the policy of conscription. Furthermore, I was opposed to the proposition of a war election. Now, however, I can see that it is too late for anything else."

"Sir Wilfrid," I said, "will you answer this question? Is it now too late to hope for a Union government in Canada with you as a member of that government?"

He was silent for a few moments and then said sadly, "It is too late. Bourassa has made that impossible now."

"Sir Wilfrid," I replied, "I cannot believe that. Let me now tell you the purpose of my visit. I came at the instance of a strong committee, representative of all shades of opinion in Canada, and came to ask you whether you will consider a place still in the Union government before going to the country in an election."

"It is too late," he said sadly. "It is too late! Were I to accept a place in a Union government on the platform of conscription my people would stone me in the streets of Quebec."

"Sir Wilfrid, you cannot make me believe that," I remonstrated. "I feel strongly, and men who know much better than I feel strongly, that your offer to join a Union government and accept the policy of conscription would be regarded as a noble and a patriotic and magnanimous gesture and would make a mighty appeal to your own people of Quebec."

"It is too late!" he repeated. "It is too late! It is impossible. At one time I was opposed neither to conscription nor to Union government, but my enemies have made any other course than opposition impossible to me. Bourassa has stolen away the hearts of my former friends in Quebec, and many of my former supporters have turned from me."

"Again let me say, Sir Wilfrid, that I cannot accept this opinion as being correct."

"It is too late," he said with bitter emphasis. "My enemies have alienated my people from me—and will you answer this?" he exclaimed passionately. "What thing could this government have done that they have not done to turn the hearts of the French-Canadian people against this war? I am speaking very frankly to you. I believe in you as a loyal Canadian and as sympathetic with my people of French Canada. You have already proved that in your last campaign. I shall never forget your generous references to the people of Quebec in your speeches. But consider the circumstances which have surrounded me. You remember, at the beginning of the war, the loyal and enthusiastic response of the French Canadians all through Quebec, rich and poor alike?"

"I remember," I said. "And I remember well my pride in the French-Canadian people's response."

"Then will you answer this question? What is it that has made it difficult, if not impossible for my people to continue in their first splendid enthusiasm for the war? I will tell you. Remember my people are French and Roman Catholic. Who was the Minister of Militia, controlling all the military activity in Canada? General Sam Hughes. Now personally I have nothing against General Sam Hughes, I am just asking you to look at that fact through the eyes of the French Canadian. Who is the leader of the whole war movement? Is he not a rabid Protestant? Is he not the editor of the *Orange Sentinel* and one of the hottest of the Orange order in Canada? Remember, I am finding no fault with him for his opinions, but I am asking you to consider the effect of these facts upon my French-Canadian people. The chief organizer of the war to them is a man associated with the most bitter, the most relentless, the most bigoted opponent of the religion of my people, which is to them their life. Again let me say, I am making no charge at this moment against General Hughes. I am simply stating a fact that must be considered.

"Second: when war broke out the government asked me to assist in an educational and recruiting campaign throughout the Province of Quebec. I assented gladly and for six weeks to the very best of my ability I gave myself to this work, and indeed with marked success. Then what happened? Whom did this government send with me as coadjutors in this recruiting campaign? Armande Lavergne, Savigny, Marcil and their political confreres. Who are these men? These are men who in the last election were elected on the Nationalist platform, but sold themselves to this government for a place in the Cabinet.

"Third: then when the campaign for the recruiting for the overseas contingent was inaugurated, who was chosen to be the chief recruiting officer? Will you believe it? A Methodist minister, an Orangeman from the North of Ireland, the home of the most bitter antagonists of the Roman Catholic religion in all the world. This was the man sent to co-operate with me and with the Roman Catholic clergy to win the French-Canadian habitant for war service. Can you imagine a folly more supreme?

"Fourth: when some of my friends in Quebec, gentlemen of the most distinguished families in the province—my friend Colonel Panet, for instance, one of the oldest and most respected names in Quebec— when these gentlemen approached the government with offers to raise battalions for service in France, what response did they receive? General Sam Hughes's answer was that he did not want any damned papists in command of his soldiers in this war. This was his answer to my friend Colonel Panet. Will you think of that? Now will you tell me what it is they have not done which they could have done to antagonize my French-Canadian fellow citizens or to render futile any attempt I or any other loyal French Canadian could make to gain recruits for this war?"

His face was pale, his voice trembling with passionate grief. I was utterly amazed and shocked by this story of the stupidity, the folly, the wicked and shameful ineptitude of those responsible for this appalling and cruel folly.

"Sir Wilfrid," I said, "you amaze me and overwhelm me. You will believe me that I most deeply sympathize with you and with your people. But I have one question which I must ask you and which I know you will not resent. Where is the Church in all this business?"

"Ah!" he said, "I will answer you frankly. When the war broke out you will remember that the archbishop and almost all the bishops and almost all the great leaders of the Roman Catholic Church were openly and wholeheartedly in sympathy with the war, as indeed most of them are to this day. I can give you their names. I have copies of their public declarations and instructions to the people."

"Yes, it is true, Sir Wilfrid," I said, "But what of the curé who has the people under his immediate care?"

"Ah," he replied, "there you have made a point, an important point. Now consider who is the curé? He is a son of a peasant, he is of the common people, he comes from the village over the hill, he is educated in the parish school and in the seminary. What does he know of the great international questions involved? He is of the people, he conceives it to be his duty to protect his people from harm. Why should he ask his people to go and fight for a cause he knows nothing of? But tell me what was done to educate the curé? What steps were taken to explain to him the reasons for this war and to make him see his duty in regard to the war? Nothing! Absolutely nothing!"

I confess his case seemed to me incontrovertible.

"Sir Wilfrid," I said, "I think I am forced to agree with you in almost all you have said. But can we not forget the past. Cannot something be done, even yet?"

"No! It is too late," he replied in a voice of infinite sadness. "Their minds have now been poisoned by men for whom a narrow racial nationalism is everything. Bourassa, Armande Lavergne and their confreres have done their work only too well. It is too late."

"Sir Wilfrid," I said in a voice which I could not for the life of me keep steady, "I earnestly beseech you to think again. I speak in the interest of the man at the front. I have seen that front line. I know it. I know that good men are dying there, that our Canadian men are dying for a great cause, that their women and children are suffering here at home. Russia is out of the war. This will release a million and a half men for Germany on the western front. Rumania is practically out of the war. The submarine menace has reached a terrible height of efficiency. True, America has come in, but America will be able to do little for many months. France is almost wavering. A terrific crisis is impending for our cause. If it could be announced that Canada had overcome all her difficulties—which are well known, mark you, in Germany—and that she is now preparing a great effort, the effect upon the Allied lines would be enormous. Can nothing be done? It lies with you, Sir Wilfrid, more than with any other Canadian, to speak the word."

He sat for some moments in silence. At length he replied in a voice tremulous with emotion: "You know, major, I am heart and soul with the Allies in this war. I would do anything, make any sacrifice, endure any humiliation to bring Quebec strongly into the fighting line. I may have made mistakes, but I have done my best. I have failed! It is too late!" He repeated the words: "I have failed! It is too late!" His voice, his manner, his whole attitude was one of profound grief and despair.

With all my powers of heart and mind I made one last appeal.

"Sir Wilfrid, it is not too late. I believe there is yet a chance to win Quebec, to save Canada's name from shame and to help greatly our cause. Now let me tell you something. If you will accept the invitation of this committee whom I represent, if you will join Premier Borden in forming a Union government and go to the country upon a common election platform, if you will unite with him in an appeal to Canada for a great new forward movement in pushing the war—"

He interrupted me quickly.

"Have you the authority definitely to give me this invitation?"

"I have," I replied, and I gave him some of the names of the committee for whom I was acting.

"Alas! Alas!" he said. "Bourassa has done his work well. I fear it is too late."

"Sir Wilfrid, the situation is desperate, but not hopeless. Supposing we were to bring back from the front line men who have fought and suffered in the war like the heroes in the 22nd battalion with their glorious record. Supposing we bring them some priests from France now fighting in the Allied cause—you know, there are twenty-five thousand priests in the French fighting line—supposing we were to bring these to Quebec. We will sow this country knee-deep with literature for the common people to read. We will instruct the curés in the issues involved. I believe that with Sir Robert Borden and Sir Wilfrid Laurier heading this campaign we can save this country from unspeakable shame and bring immense help at this moment of crisis, and may indeed help to turn the scale for victory."

Sir Wilfrid rose from his chair, walked up and down the room. He was obviously deeply stirred. Suddenly he wheeled upon me: "And who would be the head of this Union government?" he asked.

"Sir Wilfrid," I replied, "it is not for me to say, but I would remind you that the present head of the government is Sir Robert Borden, and the Sir Robert Borden of today is not the man he was six months ago. He would naturally be the head of the government to begin with. If a change is found necessary, the Cabinet itself would take the necessary steps, and Sir Robert Borden would not be the man to raise objection."

Sir Wilfrid nodded his head in agreement. "That is so," he said.

I rose. "Sir Wilfrid, you know my regard for you. There are millions of men in Canada who would rejoice greatly to see you in a Union government. You can do for your country what no other man can do. Will you not try?"

He stood looking at me with great intensity, his face set, his mind obviously far away. How long he remained so I cannot say. Finally he offered me his hand. "If Sir Robert Borden invites me, I will do it."

"You authorize me to say that to him, Sir Wilfrid?"

"I do," he replied.

Without further speech I left him. I was too deeply moved for words. I went immediately to Sir Robert and told him as much of the interview as I thought was necessary. When I gave him Sir Wilfrid's promise he could hardly believe me. "You mean to say that Sir Wilfrid authorizes you to say this to me?"

"I am giving you his very words," I replied.

"I cannot tell you how glad and how relieved I am to hear this," he said. "Now I want you to go to Mr. R. B. Bennett and tell him what you have told me."

I went to Mr. Bennett and found him in an office filled with clerks and buzzing with industry. Mr. Bennett received me cordially. He was astonished at my message, but immediately went into an explanation of the working of the National Service Board, which he had been operating for some months. He handed me an information card by means of which the government would discover from Canadian men what kind of work they were prepared to do for their country. I had already examined the card and had made up my mind that as a method of recruiting it was hopeless.

"Mr. Bennett," I said, "this seems to me an excellent scheme to enable Canadians to indicate how they can serve their country in every way but fighting. Now what my battalion wants is seven hundred and fifty fighting men to line up beside the two hundred and fifty-seven who are now struggling to hold the front line at Arras. Will this get you a single recruit, for instance, from the Province of Quebec?"

"This is only a first step," he replied. "There will be follow-up cards."

"Mr. Bennett, from my point of view, I can't see how this kind of thing will get the French Canadian of Quebec a step nearer the front line."

I left in a depressed state of mind. What I had considered a noble and self-abnegating gesture on the part of Sir Wilfrid Laurier did not seem to have impressed Mr. Bennett in the least. I may have been mistaken, but I feared for the fate of the truly magnificent offer of the great Liberal leader.

CHAPTER XXXIII

"Vale Laurier!"

WHAT WRETCHED and fatal influence intervened to prevent the consummation of Sir Wilfrid Laurier and Sir Robert Borden's desire for co-operation in a Union government, I have never discovered. I reported to Sir Robert and to my committee the result of my interview with Sir Wilfrid and thereupon went on with my campaign for a replenished and refitted front line. There were apparently plenty of sinister political, racial, and religious influences at work against the old Liberal leader to make co-operation between him and the Premier impossible.

In a short time the Premier announced the members of his Union government, whose personnel was a splendid tribute to his sagacity, generosity of spirit, and political wisdom, proclaimed his policy of conscription and of an immediate election.

While I greatly deplored the failure of the proposal to include the Liberal leader in the new Union government and while I hated to find myself working against him, I accepted the Premier's policy and went on with my campaign with new heart and enthusiasm. Personal loyalties and friendships were comparatively nothing. A full front line alone mattered just now. Indeed, I found that my well-known friendship for and my admiration for Sir Wilfrid Laurier gave an additional punch to my advocacy of the cause which now claimed my support.

A very brief campaign in Western Canada took me as far as Regina and Saskatoon. At the latter place I addressed the Synod of Saskatchewan which to my surprise and satisfaction passed a unanimous resolution in favor of Union government and conscription.

Immediately thereafter I was asked to devote myself chiefly to Eastern Canada and especially to the Maritime Provinces. The people of the Maritimes with their Scottish and United Empire Loyalist heredity and convictions, take their politics as they do their religion. With them the two are akin, in many cases identical. Furthermore I had the immense advantage of a warm place in their affection as the author of *Black Rock, Sky Pilot* and the Glengarry tales. It almost broke the hearts of some lifelong Liberals to find me opposing their great old chief in this election. Other lesser breeds of Canadians can't understand the loyalty of a clansman for his chief. But I was careful not to insult them or wound them by uttering one single word of personal criticism of Sir Wilfrid. He was acting according to his conscience, he was true to his deepest convictions, and for these things I honored him. But my conscience forced me to oppose him. I knew what the men at the front felt about Canada's letting them down. He knew nothing of this by experience. He had adopted a mistaken policy; hence for the sake of our men at the front and for the sake of the sacred cause which they stood for, I must oppose him. It was the only argument that could shake those Maritime folk in their allegiance.

It was quite a wonderful experience. The stories I could tell of my talks, far into the night, with old lifelong Liberals, men and women, especially the women, would make a thrilling book. I had, moreover, the immense advantage of knowing those Maritime people by the heart, the only way to know them. Was I not born and bred among their stock in old Glengarry? I knew every quirk and turn of their theology and their consciences.

I have had experience of strenuous campaigns in my time, evangelistic, church union, political, but never did I go through such a whirlwind of speechmaking and interviewing as I did during those last nine weeks preceding the election day on December 17th.

Perhaps I can best give an idea of the breathless character of my campaign by an extract from a letter written to my wife at this time.

> I don't suppose I have ever had any more strenuous days than those through which I have passed during the last three weeks. Interviews with individuals and groups of men—speeches— church gatherings—interviews with newspapermen—political groups—all these journeyings longer than those of old St. Paul.

Poor St. Paul! He never knew the mingled delights of Pullman cars and diners, but on the other hand he never knew reporters or writers of leading articles. The rush has been tremendous, for instance—Halifax on Sunday morning, in the ancient Anglican St. Paul's Cathedral—Archdeacon Armitage, poor chap, an old varsity comrade, got a member of his church after him for allowing a nonconformist to preach from his pulpit in a political campaign! A great crowd crammed the church to the doors —a great service. At night in St. Matthew's Presbyterian Church —and fancy in that old staid church—bursts of applause punctuating my sermon. Such a thing never had been heard before. Next night, the Canadian Club—a packed hall—tremendous interest and enthusiasm—a supper meeting following—politicians of all stripes present—but only of one opinion—one policy—the approval of my platform. Next day, Rotary lunch— enthusiasm even more intense—lots of hide-bound Liberals but unanimously resolved to organize for Union government. The day following at New Glasgow, meeting of the Presbyterian Synod of the Maritimes—remember these people are fierce party politicians—spoke for an hour and a half—adjourned for lunch —spoke again for an hour—unanimous vote of thanks—the brethren standing and applauding—questions followed. Then the Moderator in thanking me said, "Never has the Synod been so thrilled as today. Never have we listened to so moving an address." Met afterwards the Synod's Committee—appointed to prepare a Resolution, which was unanimously and enthusiastically adopted. The Resolution unanimously and enthusiastically approved Union government—and fancy! Government control of Dominion resources, men, women, and materials for the war. Just think this Resolution goes down to every Presbyterian Congregation in the Maritime Provinces. Drove forty miles that night—caught a night train for St. John. Had meeting there the following night. Next night at St. Andrew's—Night train to Montreal where I spent the week end.—Three goes on Sunday. The day following off to Toronto.—Two days later Ottawa for a dinner with the Premier and his new Union government—had a glorious time and a great reception from the members."

My experiences with the Highland Scottish Roman Catholic folk of the St. Francis Xavier University at Antigonish were unique. No type of Roman Catholics that I know are so utterly devoted to their faith as are those of the Scottish nationality. Leave them alone and they will leave you alone. Attack their religious tenets and you will have a war on your hands that you will not soon forget. In arranging my program, my Halifax committee decided that a visit to Antigonish would be quite useless. To a man they would certainly back Laurier and their French Roman Catholic coreligionists. But the elements intervened. A violent snowstorm blocked the railways, a not-infrequent event in Nova Scotia, and I found on the following day that I could not go beyond Antigonish. I wired my committee to arrange a meeting for me at Antigonish. The arrangement was made and I found myself the following afternoon in a little hotel in that university town. The streets were piled with snow, level with the fences.

"Not much of a meeting here," I said to myself.

As I was sitting at supper, a young man came in, introduced himself as James Tomkins, a priest and the financial agent of the University of St. Francis Xavier.

"I know you," he said. "My cousin is the Roman Catholic padre in your battalion."

"What? Father Tomkins? A splendid chap he is too."

I was delighted to meet him. As senior chaplain of the Canadian 3rd Division, I had been able to be of some service to Padre Tomkins.

"Yes," Father Tomkins said, "you got a horse for him after the commanding officer had refused to get him one."

I remembered the incident and Padre Tomkins's gratitude for the service I had done him. The young priest then proceeded to explain that he had done everything he could to get a meeting for me. But the storm would prevent the country people from coming in, so that he feared my audience would consist chiefly of the university students and professors and a few people from the town. Expecting a small audience, I was surprised to find the hall packed, not only with university folk but with townspeople as well.

The Rector of the university, who I think was in the chair, introduced me in a brief and rather formal manner. My reception was politely chilly. The fact that I feared I had a bad hour before me, no doubt put me on my mettle. I went at them with the best I could give. In the front seat some professors sat in a polite but unresponsive row. It was the hardest hour I had experienced during my whole campaign. They simply would not take fire. The applause was almost nil. At the close I invited questions. To my amazement not a word was said about the Quebec situation. Not a word as to racial and religious question. The progress of the war, the strength of Germany, the eastern front, recruiting in Ontario, the effect of conscription, these questions were brought up. There was nothing to stir emotion or to suggest religious controversy. I left the meeting with a feeling of complete failure.

Next morning, the railroad still being blocked, I was having a nice long rest, with the luxury of breakfast in bed, when word came up that Father Tompkins was below and was anxious to see me.

"Send him up," I said, wondering what this early morning call might mean. To my amazement he began with enthusiastic praise of my address. He had been delighted. The professors and students were all delighted.

"Then why the deuce didn't they let me know?" I exclaimed. "I never spoke to such a cold-blooded audience."

"Oh, that is our custom. We are trained to self-restraint."

"Well, you are a hard lot to speak to," I said. "You nearly killed me."

He seemed amused.

"Never mind," he said, "you put it across. We are all for you."

"What? For Union government?"

"Of course! What do you think we are?"

"Well, I expected to find you pledged to Laurier."

"Don't forget we are Scots. Our boys have relations in almost every Highland battalion in the British army."

What a dolt I had been not to think of that. What a chance, I with my Highland blood, had missed! To my amazement the young priest began to pour out his soul to me on the war, its causes, its issues, the present prospects. He was for the war to the last man and the last dollar. He had called to find out how he could serve me. He had his cutter outside. Wouldn't I like to see the college? There were no classes that day. I would be delighted. Would I like to call on Bishop Macdonnell? I certainly would.

We visited the university buildings. We went to call upon His

Grace, who received me cordially. He regretted that a cold had kept him from my meeting, but he had had most enthusiastic reports of my address. We talked of the war. I told him of some of my experiences. His warm Highland heart took fire. He was heart and soul for the Empire and its cause. As to the Canadian situation, he was thoroughly indignant at the foolish and wicked strife that had grown up between Quebec and the rest of Canada. He criticized Sir Wilfrid Laurier's handling of the campaign. I warmly defended Sir Wilfrid, explaining the situation created by Bourassa in Quebec and the religious bigots on both sides. Much of what I told him seemed quite new to him.

At this point, Father Tomkins, with a sudden burst of passion, made a remark which surprised one greatly at the time, and which I have never forgotten.

"I believe, bishop, that the time has come when we Scottish Catholics should no longer be dragged at the carttail of French Quebec."

The bishop raised his eyebrows slightly.

"Further, I believe it is our mission, rather than that of the French Catholics, to interpret our religion to our fellow Canadians of the Protestant faith."

"It may indeed be so," said the bishop with a little smile.

In bidding me good-bye Bishop Macdonnell was good enough to wish me luck in my campaign.

"Would you come to visit our girls' school carried on by the sisters?" Father Tomkins asked me as we left the palace.

"I should be delighted," I declared.

We were received with charming grace by the lady superior of the nunnery. By her side stood a tall, dark, handsome woman, who introduced herself to me as "the woman from Glengarry," and she proceeded to explain to the superior who Ralph Connor was. After seeing through the buildings, the superior whispered something to Father Tomkins, who asked me:

"Would you like to speak to the young ladies?"

I assured him that nothing would give me greater pleasure. This was a new experience for me, and as I faced that gathering of shy and charming young ladies I was for a few moments puzzled to know just what to say. None of my usual addresses on the war seemed suitable. Suddenly there flashed into my mind a scene I had witnessed in a French hospital that was filled with wounded soldiers, ministered to by English and Canadian nurses. I had never spoken upon this theme before, but as I tried to picture those hospital wards with their rows of white faces and broken bodies, and those clever cheery young ladies from Canada and Britain attending them, I quite unexpectedly found myself struggling to keep my voice steady and my tears from flowing. Nothing in all my long experience had I found so overpowering, so deeply moving, as the memory of my few visits to the base hospitals in France. Needless to say, the effect upon those young ladies and upon their teachers was quite overwhelming. They listened with tears flowing down their cheeks, some of them audibly sobbing. I was ashamed of myself. It took every atom of will power I had to regain my self-control and to continue my story in some sort of decent form. At the close of my address I was presented to the group of nuns who had gathered in the Assembly Hall, after which I hurried away.

As we were driving along through the snowdrifts, I tried to apologize to my friend for the exhibition I had made of myself.

"Believe me," I said, "I never did such a thing in my life before. I loathe seeing a speaker act like a baby."

"You will never make a better speech in your life," he said with emphasis. "You had me by the short hair, all right. I wonder could you dine with us at the college tonight and give that speech to the students?"

"Not if I am quite sober at the time," I replied. "But I would be glad to dine with you and speak to your men."

That night I had dinner with a hundred or so wild and rugged young men, mostly gathered from the farms of Nova Scotia, with a sprinkling of youths from the other provinces of Canada and from the United States. The fame of St. Francis Xavier University as a training school for young farmers, mechanics and businessmen has gone far and wide. I had had no time for preparation. I did not care to talk politics to these young men of the Roman Catholic faith, some of them in training for the priesthood while I was a regularly ordained Presbyterian minister, probably the first of the kind they had ever listened to. Now, if my war experience had taught me anything it had taught me how relatively trivial are the denominational distinctions that divide Christian people into sects. When a boy is looking with dimming eyes into the Great Unknown Land no decent human being, let alone minister or priest, thinks of any theological refinements. A brief prayer to the Heavenly Father, a word about the loving Saviour and Friend of all men and of all kinds of men, the feel of the warm grip of a brother's hand, that is what men want in supreme moments.

I stood before that company of young men and said quietly, "I am going to talk to you about religion."

They rather gasped at that.

"The religion of the front line. I am a Presbyterian minister, have been for twenty-seven years. You are of the Roman Catholic faith. I know the theology of my church and of yours. Yet I had to go to the front line to learn what religion means. I learned this: religion is the supreme thing in life, and for this reason religion is the thing that makes a man act decently toward God and toward his fellow humans. Why go to the front line to find this out? Because the front line faces you up to reality. The whine of a shell suggests a terrific reality, the grim reality of death—death perhaps next minute.

"Religion makes men reverent, clean, brave, human, kind. I never knew how kind was the human heart till I saw a man desperately wounded try to help another man a little more desperately wounded. These things humbled me, purged me of many false and foolish notions about religion."

Then I told them the story of Donnelly and his last prayer with his eyes fixed upon the little cross made of two sticks tied with binder twine. That story I rarely repeat.

"We forget our religious differences in the front line. We are too keen to help one another to fool with these comparatively unimportant things. Ask Padre Tomkins when you see him, the cousin of my friend here, Father Tomkins. We never hesitated to do each other's work at the front. We tried to help every man, Catholic or Protestant. They were all our brothers."

I am not going to preach a sermon in this writing, but my story got those young fellows where they lived. At the close of my address a young man, in beautiful and simple English with a touch of literary flavor, moved a vote of thanks, which was seconded and carried with a quite unexpected and tremendous roar of applause, which subsided and broke out again and again. Then one of the professors spoke; to my amazement, he echoed my sentiments in regard to the relative unimportance of mere formularies in religion and the vital importance of right thought and feeling toward God and toward man.

"Those boys will never forget that, major," said Father Tomkins, as he drove me to the train. "Never while they live, nor will I. It is a pity we need to go to the front line to learn that stuff about religion."

I heartily agreed with him. Later I came to know what fine work he was doing in Nova Scotia in the way of co-operative industry.

As he shook hands with me at the train, he said, "Major, this was a lucky storm for us."

"For me too," I said heartily. "I haven't enjoyed anything like this for a long time."

"And let me tell you too," he added in a lower tone, "stay with us a week and we will sweep this country for Union government."

"That's your job," I said.

"You bet it is. And I'll attend to it."

The polls showed that the Highlanders were not tied altogether to the Quebec carttail. But it also showed that without the vote of the soldiers, the hold of the great old Liberal leader upon the hearts of his followers in the Maritimes was still unbroken. The roots of loyalty run deep into the Scottish heart.

The story of Laurier's last fight is a saga of gallant adventure, indomitable courage, loyalty to the highest ideals, fidelity to conscience. The story also of a fatal misreading of the mind and spirit of the people of the country, which he had so nobly served for half a century and more.

The final issue was not Canada's attitude to the Great War and its objectives, the issue was one of method and means to be employed for the consummation of victory. Laurier chose one method, Canada chose another. In the face of overwhelming odds, the Liberal leader —the greatest Canada ever knew—went down to defeat, not, however, with ignominy or contempt, but with flag flying at the masthead, with the vociferous and heart-filling plaudits of partisans and political opponents alike ringing in his ears from Winnipeg to Victoria. In the last moment of his last fight, to the last drop of his heart's blood, in the face of desertion by lifelong friends, against the narrow bigotry of his coreligionists, against the narrow nationalism of his racial affinities, he kept his conscience in regard to his duty to country, to Empire and to the cause of world freedom unspotted to the end. It was the clouding of his vision alone that made him choose the wrong path, for which he paid the price in defeat, but defeat with personal honor unstained and with character untarnished.

An analysis of the hostile forces marshaled against the Liberal leader awakens chiefly wonder at the narrow margin of victory against him. His policy lost him the support of the great majority of his former lieutenants in party conflicts. Every provincial premier except Sir Lomer Gouin of Quebec was ranged with his opponents. The sentiment of all political parties in Canada except in Quebec was without doubt overwhelmingly in favor of the vigorous prosecution of the war. The fact that the Province of Quebec, which under Henri Bourassa's leadership was wholly Nationalistic, opposed to Canadian and Empire solidarity and furthermore opposed to the vigorous prosecution of the war, was also solidly united in its support of Sir Wilfrid Laurier intensified the feeling against him in the other provinces of the Dominion.

In Canada west of the lakes the element of personal loyalty to party leaders was much less highly developed than in the older provinces. They were Canadians rather than Canadian politicians. They gave an extraordinarily enthusiastic welcome to the Liberal leader, but they voted against him. I happened to be in Winnipeg on the occasion of his first meeting in Western Canada. It was a truly astonishing meeting. Eight thousand people crowded to welcome him and do him honor. Eagerly they listened to his address, couched in beautiful and mellifluous English. Rapturously they cheered him wherever he gave them the slightest opportunity. At the close of his oration they stood cheering and wildly waving at him. After the campaign was finished Sir Wilfrid, referring to his Winnipeg experience, said to a friend, with a touch of sardonic humor, "They gave me everything but their votes." The Western Canadians thoroughly appreciated his gallant courage, his lofty personal character, his long and honorable service to his country, but they resolutely rejected his policy for Canada in the war.

The vote throughout Canada revealed some interesting facts. Of the total vote, Laurier received over 41 per cent, of the total Liberal seats over 67 per cent, but of the soldier vote only 7.9 per cent. That soldier vote flooded the whole situation with a clear light. The front-line men alone saw clearly that their country's desperate need was for front-line men without delay. The soldier vote for Laurier even from his own province also made this startlingly plain, for it registered only 17 per cent. The red light from blazing guns and bursting shells is the only light that reveals the stark and terrible truth in war. It was that light also that cleared from Sir Robert Borden's eyes the misty twilight in which he and his government had been carrying on for the past twelve months. It was the front-line experience of Canada's Premier that brought him that clear vision and that resolute determination to organize his country into a fighting unit, which enabled Canada to do its full duty in this terrific war for world freedom and world right.

CHAPTER XXXIV

Slow Daybreak

CONSCRIPTION IN THE UNITED STATES—BRITISH
AND FRENCH MISSIONS—NORTHCLIFFE IN
AMERICA—ARMISTICE—HOPE FOR WORLD PEACE

THE MORAL effect of the entry of America into the war was such as practically to determine the final issue. It is nevertheless true that Germany heavily discounted the striking power of America as a military organization. A nation without a standing army, without the machinery to produce an efficient military organization could not be prepared to make its full power felt in the fighting line before a year had gone. In this opinion Germany proved to be entirely correct but not for the reason she adduced.

Nothing in the history of the Great War was so astonishing as the ease with which President Wilson put into effect legislation by which the whole manhood of America was conscripted for service of war. With practical unanimity, without riot, almost without protest, the whole nation accepted the legislation and moved as a united body into war.

President Wilson has been bitterly arraigned for his cunctatory methods in preparing for war in contrast to the vigorous, driving passionate energy of Theodore Roosevelt, who has been cited as the only type demanded by the desperate needs of the Allies. For instance, immediately upon the declaration of war Roosevelt was continually urging the president to "put the American flag at once in the firing line in France and keep it there." As a demonstration of what that wholehearted and energetically directed organizing power could effect in war preparation, Mr. Roosevelt, by the first of May, was able to announce that he had 180,000 men enlisted and ready to follow him immediately to France, and furthermore that he was able to offer to the government for immediate service two fully equipped military divisions. This achievement was a sufficient proof of the amazing energy and organizing ability of this great American. Wilson and Roosevelt represented two types of Americans, each with his own qualities fitting him for his own peculiar service. Both types combined in a single leader undoubtedly would have produced results impossible in each alone. The passionate energy of Theodore Roosevelt would undoubtedly have strengthened the Allied line during the terrible years 1917-1918 with men and with munitions to such a degree as to have broken the strength and the spirit of the Central Powers and would have shortened the war by many months and saved thousands of valuable lives. On the other hand, Woodrow Wilson's methods confirmed in the German High Command their contempt for the striking power of America and thus stimulated them in that last terrific drive for victory which came so near to bringing disaster to the Allies. At the same time, however, all will agree that President Wilson achieved a magnificent result in getting his people united into one compact body which carried them through the war with great power for victory. Thus undoubtedly, while prolonging the war, the policy of President Wilson finally broke the heart of Germany and forced her to sue for peace. The work of the President in effecting the conscription for war service of the total man power and the total material resources of his people was an achievement that stamped him as a man of extraordinary foresight and political ability.

* * * *

In the summer of 1917 there took place the synchronizing visits of official missions from the governments of France and Great Britain. To most Americans the war was still far away from their actual experience. The leader of the British Mission was the Right Honorable A. J. Balfour, British Foreign Secretary. The French Mission was headed by Marshal Joffre and M. René Viviani, ex-Premier and Minister of Justice, a lineal descendant of Lafayette, whose name has ever exerted so potent an influence over the American people. It was my good fortune to be present at a dinner given in honor of both missions at the Waldorf-Astoria on May 12th. One thousand of New York's distinguished citizens gave a rousing welcome to these representatives of the Allied governments. Among the notable guests was Joseph H. Choate. I remember his closing words after the brilliant address by M. Viviani:

"If I had to make reply in a single sentence to this truly great address to which we have listened my word would be this: I am glad that at last our people have seen their duty in this war, but for God's sake, America, hurry up!"

Almost like a peal of thunder came back the response in varying tones and phrases:

"You bet we will! We'll be there!"

The effect upon me was overpowering. I believe I could hardly have spoken a word to save my life. After nearly three years of agonizing struggle a day with the promise of victory was at length in sight.

But before that day came there were times of dark despair. In January of 1918 an urgent wire from George Doran brought me to New York. Next day I found myself identified with the Northcliffe Mission one of the chief objectives of which was to assist in the mighty task of speeding up America's active participation in the war. I was still engaged in this work when the news began to break of the big German push, toward the end of March. I was due to preach in Fifth Avenue Presbyterian Church on March 29th and was sick with anxiety over the broken front line. On Saturday night I wrote home:

> Fifth Avenue pulpit tomorrow. These are great and terrible days. The papers are of course making as light as possible of the situation at the front. But anyone who does not feel that we have reached a great crisis and that grave possibilities of loss are before us is ignorant of the situation or is criminally indifferent. We have checked the advance so far, but that a great and wonderful achievement must be credited to Germany we must freely and ought freely to admit. Further, we do not know just what may be in store for us yet. But we shall hold and we shall win in the long run. If only this people would get into the thing.

How I got through my sermon I don't know. I know I cast all thought of consideration for American sensitiveness to the winds. Joseph Choate's cry to this people of a year ago was ringing through my heart: "For God's sake, America, hurry up!"

* * * *

A phone call from my friend Doran told me that New York was

fast becoming delirious over a newspaper report just received that the war was over, that an armistice had been signed, and that he was throwing a lunch party in the Waldorf about two. Immediately the connection was cut and I was left dazed and gasping. The war was over? No more need for campaigning? Thank goodness! And no need for rejoining my battalion. The boys would be coming home. A new world had been born. Never again would the great nations indulge themselves in the mad folly of war.

I arrived in New York to find the Pennsylvania Station packed with a seething mob of "jollificators" trying to make their way out. I did my best to secure a taxi. Taxis there were, plenty of them, hundreds of them, thousands of them, but all quite useless. The great traffic avenues of New York were blocked with lines of cars, trucks, taxis, and every horn honking. The officers had long ago abandoned all hope of traffic movement and were doing what they could to keep the people steady. Strange to say, though every man at every wheel was frantic to get on his way, there was no one fighting. They were long past fighting. The war was over. This was no day for fighting. Indeed, but for the chauffeurs, all cars were empty. Every New Yorker was slowly, steadily, but cheerily following the crowd as best he could to wherever he desired to go.

I should like to have seen lower Broadway and Wall Street that day. The immense tunnels of masonry were apparently in the grip of a blizzard, the air thick with falling snow. From thousands, millions, of windows tons of paper torn into fragments were fluttering into the streets below. It cost New York, next day, some hundreds of thousands to sweep up the mess. Who cared? The war was over!

Finally I reached Fifth Avenue. The street was solid with lines of cars headed in both directions but immobile. The sidewalks were packed with slowly moving columns of men, women, children, shouting, singing, dancing, cheering, all in a state of emotional delirium. The war was over! Wildly crowding, shoving, dancing, groups of the hoi polloi got tangled up with well-dressed groups of New York's Four Hundred, gaily, hilariously exchanging greetings, all in their own peculiar style of address.

My Highland uniform, with bonnet and kilt, brought me more than my share of trouble. A group of young bloods, escorting their lady friends to luncheon, held me up with a shout.

"Say! Boy!" cried one of them who was a bit elevated, reaching for me with one hand and for his flask with the other. "What have we here? Ladies and gentlemen, my friend and old comrade in arms, Lord Ronald Macdonald." They all crowded about me, flasks everywhere.

"Try mine! His is rotgut."

"Here! The war is over! Here's to the Fifty-first," said a tall young chap.

"What, you know the Fifty-first?" I said, taking his flask in my hand.

"Do I know Colonel Malcolm MacKay?" he said. "Haven't I fished the Tummel with him?"

We shook hands all round.

"Armistice Day!" said the young man who had presented me as Lord Ronald Macdonald. "Too bad! Too dashed bad! War all gone flooey! On my way this week with my own plane—a bird! A blessed bird! And now—!" his voice broke.

"Never mind, old warhawk! There'll be another war soon," his friend consoled him.

"Never!" he said tragically. "Never with the Huns! Little Willie is all bust up!"

I broke away with difficulty, feeling quite unable to sympathize with him in his bitter disappointment. A little farther on a group of schoolgirls were strenuously struggling to execute a snake dance. Immediately they had me within their circle.

"Hello, Jock! Be a sport! Isn't he just lovely?" said one.

"What a dear little bonnet!" said another. "And my dear, what a sweet little skirt! I wonder if—"

"Hush, Pat! You shock me," said her friend.

They were quite mad. They besought me to go with them. They were going to dance! They were delightfully frank and frantic. I explained that only an official engagement made me deny myself their company.

It had taken me quite an hour of heavy work to make the Waldorf-Astoria. There fresh trouble awaited me. It was almost impossible to move through the packed crowd.

I explained my business to the clerk, whom I knew quite well.

"Awfully sorry, major, I can't possibly go with you. Can't leave my desk. Mr. Doran has gone in. If he can get out he will come for you—but I suggest you'd better make a try for it."

"But how in the world—?"

"Bore in, major! Bayonet exercise! Charge!"

I did my best and got within ten feet of the main door of the dining room. There I was hopelessly stuck. There was no room inside —absolutely no room.

Vainly I signaled and shouted to the official at the door that my place was waiting me.

He shook his head. Impossible!

At this juncture, at the official's side, appeared a tall broad-shouldered man in the Highland uniform of the Lochiel Camerons which I recognized at once. There he stood, his eyes searching the crowd. I gave him the war cry of his clan in the ancient tongue.

Instantly he spotted me.

"I say! What does this mean? What do you mean by keeping out one of His Majesty's officers? And a Queen's Own Cameron Highlander at that? Make way there! Come along, colonel, we are waiting for you!"

Immediately, at the cost of terrific squeezing, the company good-naturedly made way for me. He reached out, grabbed me by the arm and had me safe through the door in a minute's time.

As I was expressing my gratitude and exchanging cards with him, Oscar, the famous chief of staff, in the dining room, caught sight of me and hurried to my help. I said good-bye to my clansman and went off to my table. I never saw him again.

As the crowd which packed the great dining room caught sight of my uniform they burst into loud cheers of welcome. At that moment I represented to them the entire Allied forces in the front line. They were quite mad anyway, and welcomed the opportunity to yell.

We were a happy group about that luncheon table that day. The reaction from the terrific strain under which we had been living for the past four years was almost beyond endurance. Every few moments Doran would call my attention to friends about us who were signaling their desire to join our celebration in a drink. As my drinks were quite harmless I was able to retain my senses, but it took all Mrs. Doran's watchful care to see that her husband's loyalty did not overcome his powers of resistance.

As we were finishing our second course, a friend of Mr. Doran's came and whispered something in his ear.

"Certainly! Quite all right!" said Doran. "Major, Mr. Curtis would like you to visit his table and exchange courtesies with his guests."

Off I went with Mr. Curtis. As I reached his table, his whole company, some twenty or more, rose and received me with loud cheers.

"Ladies and gentlemen, allow me to present Colonel Gordon of His Majesty's Highlanders," with a fine disregard of rank or regiment.

They would have me take a place at their table, which I declined. They filled up a glass, which I held in my hand.

"Ladies and gentlemen," I said, "I have the honor to give you 'The officers and men of the American contingents on the front line, the latest and most gallant of our Allies.'"

With loud shouts they drank the toast. As they were drinking my friend said, "Say a few words to them."

"Not on your life," I said. "I must go back to my friends."

"All right, colonel," he said, "we won't keep you, but before you go we will have another toast. Fill up, ladies and gentlemen! I have the honor to give you 'Our Canadian comrades in France, the best of the best.'"

The toast was received with wild acclaim, during which my friend conducted me back to my table.

"Say, Doran," I said, "these people are all crazy."

"Not a bit of it, major. They have just come to their senses." For all his American citizenship, Doran was a Britisher to the marrow of his bones.

It was certainly a weird and wild company, and none too sober. As we came to our ices a gentleman came to my host and whispered something. I had an uneasy sinking of the heart that it boded some ill to me.

"Major," said Doran, "there is a general request that you say a few words to this company."

"In heaven's name, what about?" I gasped.

"Oh, anything! Talk to them about the weather in France, eh?"

I made my way to a little speaker's balcony overlooking the dining room and stood looking down over that company of Americans.

It was a great moment not only in my life, but in the history of the world. I don't remember just what I said, but it was something like the following:

"Ladies and gentlemen, a friend of mine suggests that I say a few words to you about the weather—the weather in France. I am glad to tell you that in France this is a perfect day. Such a day as they have not seen for a thousand days and more. The sun is shining and the whole country—yes, the whole world—is bathed in a heavenly stillness. When I last saw it the whole country was rocking with the roar of cannon and the clash of arms, with the fiendish yells of men going out and over the top, and with the groans of dying men. Today all is quiet. The men in the trenches are lolling about on sunny parapets, their rifles stacked in their dugouts underground. For this day we thank you Americans. But for you we should have been forced to wait a little longer for this glorious day. The guns would still be roaring and all the horrible sounds of war still filling the air. What a day! What a day! What a day for the hundreds and thousands of mothers in little homes in America, in Canada, and throughout the Allied lands. And now, please God, we must address ourselves to the great business of making a new world in which war shall be no more.

"For my comrades of Canada, for all who have suffered for these four terrible years, I say thank God for America and America's sons who have helped to bring about the dawn of peace."

There was but a ripple of cheers. A hush had fallen upon that mad crowd, but when I came down from the balcony and entered the room again and made my way to my table, the room rocked with wild yells such as Americans alone know how to give.

"Fine, major!" said my friend Doran.

"Was it? I don't know what I said—but you gave me my text and God my sermon. At any rate it was not mine."

When I reached my room that night I tried to remember what I had said but was not quite sure of the words. But that was the meaning of my speech.

* * * * *

Nearly twenty years have gone, and God pity us and forgive us mortals, for still the mad notion holds us that only war can end war, and that world peace can be secured only by world armament. Must we again mass our men to kill other men? When I think of the millions of men who Sunday after Sunday bow in their Holy Places in reverence before Him who said, "Blessed are the peacemakers: they shall be called the children of God," and who then march forth to war, I ask myself, do they think they are fooling Him or are they simply fooling themselves? There is a path to peace for men, but it is not by the way of war. When the followers of the Prince of Peace in the world stand in the path of men who march to war and say "Kill us first!" then war will cease.

That was the end of my various campaigns in the United States of America. For me, I shall never cease to be grateful that they gave me so warm, so generous a welcome before they entered the war. Also I have come to believe that never will the nations of the world cease to make war till America stands side by side with the British Empire and says to the nations, "Let us reason together. Let us have peace."

PART FIVE

They Strive for Peace

CHAPTER XXXV

Toward Peace in Industry

CANADIAN DEMOBILIZATION — GENERAL STRIKE
— COUNCIL OF INDUSTRY FOR MANITOBA
FORMED — EXAMPLES OF ARBITRATION — PRINCI-
PLES GOVERNING INDUSTRIAL HARMONY

THE AFTERMATH of war is more war.

The soldier's life is regimented. It is largely a life without personal initiative. Life is planned for him. His keep is assured, he is fed, dressed, doctored, kept clean, his hair cut, by the one that pays him, the government.

His discharge from the army ends all that. He must now be on his own. He has still his compensation money in his pocket but a soldier acquires the free spending habit and soon his money is gone, an unpleasant situation. His own boss? He soon tires of that boss. He is looking for another. Who wants a returned soldier? He was formerly a carpenter, but now there is no building going on. Or a skilled mechanic, but shops are closed. The war is over, and the old jobs are in the hands of youngsters who never could get to the war or of old boys who had flat feet.

He begins to fret. He is a decent chap. All he wants is a way to live decently. He is lonely. He joins a union. There he meets old comrades. He compares experiences. He grows bitter. A few months ago he came home a hero. They all wanted to give him a drink, to show their respect for him, their appreciation of his noble service to his country. Now they hate to see him come round. And in the shop the foreman, himself a returned man, is sorry but can't possibly make a job for him. He grows more and more bitter. What's the matter with this country? "I'll tell you what's the matter with this country," says the soapbox orator, "the gang that stayed home got all the booty, we, who went to war, now get the boot."

One day there is trouble at the shop. The cause? It's a question of the union. The head of the plant is a bullheaded Englishman, a decent enough fellow but he runs his own shop and no union can tell him what to do. He can hire and fire as he dashed well pleases. "He can, eh?" says the union boss. "We'll show him." They do. They close his shop up tight. Ha ha! It is the old game. The game they played in France for four years. They know all about this game and they know no fear. Soon all the shops are closed up tight.

They parade the streets. The police are ordered to stop them. The police?

"Why, Mack old chap, glad to see you!" So is Mack glad to see him. It was at Sanctuary Wood they last met.

"You helped to carry me down the trench," says Mack.

"Why, sure thing! Them were the days, eh, Mack? Give me the bloody old war back again."

Will Mack arrest this old comrade? Nothing doing. He knows the kind of soldier Jim was. Let the City Hall go to hell!

The police are out, the firemen, the streetcar men, the telegraph and telephone men are all out.

Every train brings recruits. Orators appear on the street corners, silver-tongued chaps with a wealth of passionate oratory. They know what they want and they are going to get it.

The city authorities are powerless. The mayor asks for a conference. Sure! The Strike Committee file into the Council Chamber and sit with their hats on, smoking cigarettes. The Mayor rises to open the meeting.

"Shut up and sit down," orders the chairman of the Strike Committee. "Who told you to speak?"

The mayor shuts up and sits down. He'd better and he knows it.

The strike chairman is in command of the meeting—yes, and of the city too. He dictates the terms of settlement of this industrial trouble.

"Impossible!" says the mayor.

"Then get to hell out of this," says the strike chairman.

He gets.

For six weeks the Strike Committee tells the city what to do. And the city does it. Order is maintained. Not a streetcar moves, not a telephone rings, not a telegram is sent, except by order of the Strike Committee. Not a light bulb shines. No bread, no milk, no water, for 260,000 Winnipeg citizens, except by order of the committee. The picture houses, the dance halls, are run by order of committee.

A Committee on Public Order, consisting of one thousand men, mostly young, is organized, army officers most of them.

The Manitoba government steps in and calls out the Mounties. The Mounties ride up and down, carbines in their holsters, pistols in their belts. What next?

Ah, what next? The Strike Committee don't know. They are divided in their councils. Their money is running out. Their orators hesitate. No money? What's the matter with the money in the banks?

Ah! That's different. These strikers are not bank robbers. They are decent chaps who want only their rights. They want no more. Their rights they will have. But how to get them, that's the question.

The Manitoba government finally finds a way. There is a conference in the Legislative Buildings. The Premier is a "wise guy." He sympathizes with the returned men. He had suffered by the war. So have the members of the government. Their sons are lying face up in those graveyards in France with densely packed little crosses. The government guarantees that every workingman will get his rights. No industrial boss, no big-moneyed magnate will be allowed to bully the returned soldier or deprive him of his rights.

A joint committee is formed. They talk together. Rights are guaranteed. The strike is off! But it was a near thing—near, very near to blood, fire and riot. For these strikers knew the game and were ready to play it.

The provincial government learned their lesson. They call into council the best men representing all classes interested. The result is the creation of the *Council of Industry for Manitoba,* constituted of two representatives of labor, two of the Employers' Association. Then they came and asked me to accept the position of chairman of the Council of Industry for Manitoba.

"Why ask me? I am a minister."

"That's partly why. You stand outside of all interested parties. You have been preaching justice and fair play in industrial affairs for years. You have had some experience in the arbitration of industrial disputes. The government of Manitoba wants you to be chairman."

It was true that as convener of the Social Service Committee of the General Assembly of the Presbyterian Church I had studied with the best men of the church the problems of industry.

Our convictions had been embodied in a *Manifesto* issued by our Assembly's Social Service Committee and approved by the General Assembly. The *Manifesto* was the first of its kind issued by any Christian church in the world. Besides this, I had acted for the Dominion government as arbitrator in a number of rather big strikes.

I consulted my congregation. My joint boards urged the acceptance of the position as my duty. I secured an assistant for whose salary I became responsible, and took the job.

For four years the council carried on its work. Under its jurisdiction came everything that had to do with the interests of the working people of the province. Their work and working conditions, their housing, their health, the constitution of their labor organization, everything, in short, that had to do with the life and work of the people of Manitoba came within the purview of the Council of Industry. The record of the council is unparalleled by that of any other like organization in the world, which is saying a good deal. For four years the council carried on dealings with all kinds of disputes between capital and labor, between companies and unions, between company and company, between union and union, between unions and their members. During those four years the Council of Industry dealt with 107 cases without registering a single failure.

A member of Parliament from Australia once called on me to inquire as to the organization and work of our council. I explained our constitution and our methods, showed him our records, graphs, reports and other materials collected. After a half day of investigation he said to me:

"Dr. Gordon, I have had much to do with industrial affairs in Australia. I have had a good deal to do with labor legislation. I have sat with arbitration boards of different kinds, but never have I seen anything like this. It is to me a miracle, a perfect miracle! How have you achieved such marvelous results?"

"The answer is simple enough. I had four quite remarkable men working with me in the council, two representing the workers and—"

"How were they chosen? By the unions?"

"No, and this is important. The four were appointed by government. They represented the whole body of the people of Manitoba. Of course, the government, like wise men, consulted with the interested parties but the members of council received their appointment at the hands of the government, they represented the government and to the government they reported. This fact is of the highest importance."

"That is interesting. Our boards of arbitration are chosen by the parties interested."

"Which is a fatal mistake," I pointed out. "This is a government institution, representative of the two parties in industry, but responsible only to the government. That is where the primary and fatal mistake is made in the constitution of most boards of arbitration."

"Who were your men on the Labor side?"

"The secretary of the Trades and Labor Council and a city alderman, elected by the Labor vote of the city."

"And the other two?"

"Two men representing the Employers' Association. But, remember, chosen and appointed by government."

"Wonderful!"

"They were men of high character, of large experience and loyal to this council."

"But how could you come to agreement? Did you go by majority report?"

"Never! I would have considered a mere majority report a failure. During my four years of office, we had a hundred and seven cases. We came to a hundred and seven unanimous decisions."

"Amazing! How could that possibly be achieved?"

"By first of all getting them to see that our objective was to find out, for our clients, a way of working together. Not at all to discover who was right and who was wrong, that was only a part of our main objective. We must get the two parties to agree upon a plan of working together. Anything else would be failure."

"What an achievement!" he exclaimed. "It would seem to me impossible."

"Not so. You see, when a case came before us it was the privilege and the duty of, say, the labor representatives on the council, to act as advocates to get that case before the council in the best possible light for their labor friends. Similarly with the representatives of the employers. They, too, acted first as advocates doing all they could for their clients. But once the case was fully before the council and the parties excluded, the whole structure of the council was changed. These four men ceased to be advocates and became at once judges. Their business now was to discover a way of agreement for both parties. It took me about three months' hard and patient work to get this principle accepted and established, but once that was done the main difficulty was over. Five honest men, set on discovering the path of right and fair dealing, and that alone, can hardly fail to discover a way of agreement."

I must resist the temptation to dilate upon my experience in the Council of Industry. But considering the current world-wide importance of these problems, some observations may be permissible as to certain immediate causes of industrial strife under our present economic and industrial system without reference to the more fundamental causes inherent in the system itself.

The Council of Industry was established to prevent industrial strife. The quite remarkable success in all of its operations seems to justify the recounting, in some detail, the history of specific cases. The following excerpts from my notes may be interesting as illustrating the Council of Industry's methods of dealing with industrial trouble:

Very frequently the causes are almost entirely personal. For instance, one morning an angry man announced through my telephone that he wanted to see me right off. He was a warehouseman whom the foreman had dismissed that morning for carelessness, impertinence and insubordination.

"Come along," I said. I called the foreman and invited him to come also.

The warehouseman—Burton, we shall call him, told his tale.

"This morning I was trucking stuff from the warehouse to a car. I was in a hurry to get the car filled and had piled an extra big load on my car. Two boxes fell off. Just at that moment the foreman came into the warehouse. He flew off the handle, yelled out, 'Why the devil do you pile up a load like that on the truck?' I tried to explain I was in a hurry to fill the car. He wouldn't listen. He cursed me and called me names. I told him what I thought of him. He fired me."

The foreman's story was quite different.

"This man is clumsy at his work," he said. "When I remonstrated he became impertinent. Indeed, he had threatened to attack me. I fired him, and he'll stay fired."

Both men were hot. Burton would carry it to his union. The foreman told him to go as far as he liked. I did not summon the council. We talked together for two hours. Finally I said:

"If you wish it I shall bring this before the council, but really I feel sure you will both feel and look rather silly. You both lost your tempers. Be honest now."

Yes, they agreed, they had.

"You can carry this to your union, Mr. Burton, and make a good case of it, but if you won out, would you go back to your present job?"

"No, certainly not. I wouldn't work for this man for no price."

"And you would make a poor showing before your chief," I said to the foreman. "You lost your temper and called this man names, a thing no foreman should do. Why not both call it off, act like sensible men?"

They looked at each other rather foolishly.

Finally the foreman said, "Burton, I confess I was up late last night at a big dinner the wife was giving for some friends of ours. She had plum pudding—I took two large slices—I guess that's what did the trick."

"Well, I wouldn't mind if I had one of the slices," said Burton with a grin.

"Sure thing, you'd both be better off with one slice each," I said. "Shall we call the whole thing off?"

They called it off, the foreman taking Burton home with him for a slice of plum pudding.

I cite this extremely simple case as an illustration of a large proportion of industrial troubles. Personal eccentricities, jealousies, ill-tempers, are responsible for a good deal of the strife.

But there are cases where great principles are at stake, with large interests involved.

One day the secretary of the Iron Workers' Union called me, full of righteous indignation. A new manager in one of Winnipeg's largest ironworking industries, without consulting his workmen, much less their union, had simply posted a notice that at the beginning of the next month, wages would be cut from one dollar per hour to ninety cents. Now the Iron Workers are the aristocrats of organized labor. They are not accustomed to this kind of cavalier treatment. The secretary wrote an indignant letter of protest. They were working under an agreement and the agreement must be lived up to. The new manager was not accustomed to dealing with unions. He ran his own shop according to his own ideas, as he told the secretary in no uncertain words. The secretary was furious, so were the men. He promptly threatened to strike and appealed to the Council of Industry.

This was not a simple matter of personalities. It was a case that concerned the very existence of the union and, as the manager thought, the existence of the company.

It will be remembered that the Big Strike of 1919 originated with the Iron Workers, and the hang-over, in the way of mutual dislike and suspicion, was quite definite.

After due notice both parties appeared before the council. The secretary of the union, Ryan by name, a shrewd but hotheaded Irishman, brought with him his full committee of fifteen or twenty men. The manager appeared with his "official family" to back him up. It was a full-dress affair, not so much of personalities as of principles.

I asked Mr. Stevenson, the new manager of the Winnipeg Iron Works, to state his case. He had got two sentences out when Ryan came back with a heated exclamation: "That's a lie—a damned lie."

I immediately halted proceedings.

"Mr. Ryan, you have already been before this council and you know that you cannot insult this council or the government it represents, with profanity."

"I apologize, Mr. Chairman, but it's a lie all the same."

"I accept your apology, Mr. Ryan, but I want you to know that if the official representative of the Iron Workers' Union cannot conduct their case without insulting this council, they might consider the advisability of finding another secretary. I have accepted your apology, but I must ask you to withdraw your statement as to Mr. Stevenson's remark."

"But it is a lie, and I can prove it."

"The council will not allow you or anyone else to use that statement."

"But what he said ain't true."

"You have a right to say you don't believe that the statement is true, but you cannot say that Mr. Stevenson made a statement which not only was not true but which he knew was not true. You can't say that. How do you know what Mr. Stevenson is thinking?"

"Well, I take it back, but it ain't true all the same."

"You mean you think it is not true, Mr. Ryan," said Mr. Baker one of the representatives of the Employers' Association, who had a quiet sense of humor.

"I know it isn't true."

"You mean you are quite sure about it. But there is a possibility that you may be mistaken."

"I'm telling you, I know and I can prove it."

"That's just what I am saying, Mr. Ryan. You are convinced you know it isn't true. But all the same—"

"Go on, Mr. Ryan, we all know Mr. Baker is a philosopher of sorts—" I said.

"Philosopher or fool, but he can't tell me what I know and don't know."

"Just what I've been trying to tell you, Mr. Ryan, that you think you know that what Mr. Stevenson thinks he knows is true may not be or may be true after all. I hope that's quite clear."

Mr. Ryan stood gaping at him for a few moments in dazed silence.

The whole assembly burst into a shout of laughter at his blank face, in which Mr. Ryan at last himself joined.

"Well, gentlemen," I said, "since we have all come to a perfectly clear understanding of the point at issue, perhaps Mr. Stevenson will now go on."

Again the whole company indulged in a laugh, after which Mr. Stevenson proceeded with his case. Here again may I insert the observation that a laugh is a most valuable emollient of all sore spots.

Mr. Stevenson's case was quite simple. He had received word from his chief customers that—

"May I ask who they are?" asked Mr. Robinson, secretary of the Trades and Labor Council.

"Not necessary, Mr. Stevenson," I said.

"Oh, I don't mind. The Canadian Pacific Railway is doing a lot of bridge construction. They have been our best customers, especially since this depression in the building trade has set in. They tell me they cannot pay last year's prices."

"They'll have to pay what others pay," said Ryan.

"They have this advantage over others in the way of buying. They can get the stuff made in Montreal where men get eighty cents an hour. Their freights are low. Their freight cars are coming west empty these days. Our competitors are in Eastern Canada. Gentlemen, we simply can't compete with Montreal with wages at a dollar an hour. I thought it best to tell you the simple truth."

After some discussion in which Mr. Ryan took no part—indeed, he seemed quite unconcerned about the whole matter—I said to Mr. Ryan:

"You have heard Mr. Stevenson's statement, Mr. Ryan, have you anything to suggest?"

"Yes," said Ryan promptly, "I suggest Mr. Stevenson take a look at this paper. I showed it to him before. He refused to look at it."

"What is that paper, Mr. Ryan?" asked one of the employers' representatives.

Ryan took it up. "'Agreement between the Winnipeg Iron Works of the First Part and the Union of the Iron Workers' of Winnipeg of the Second Part.' In that agreement there is clause number eight, which stipulates that the wages for iron workers of the first class shall be one dollar per hour. The figure had been the previous year one dollar and ten cents. Further, clause number nine stipulates that no change can be made in this agreement without two months' notice."

"Is that in that agreement? Let me look at it," said Mr. Stevenson. "To tell the truth, gentlemen, I don't take much stock in agreements. I have always made my own agreements with my men. I propose to continue the policy."

"You mean to repudiate an agreement?" said Ryan, rising to his feet. "All right. There is no use for us to stay here talking any more.

I understand Mr. Stevenson to say he does not stick to agreements."

"Sit down, Mr. Ryan. This council is still in session and we have not yet come to a decision."

"You listen to me," said Mr. Stevenson. "I never worked on an agreement before. That agreement still stands. There will be no immediate change in rates, but I give you notice now that in two months' time that agreement will terminate. But, gentlemen, I want also to tell you that with conditions as they are and if the Canadian Pacific Railway stands by its present prices, it may be necessary for us to close down our shops indefinitely. I would not like these men to regard this as a threat. I simply think it fair to warn them of possibilities. It would pay us to close down. I am speaking quite sincerely. I hope Mr. Ryan and his friends will believe me."

The whole atmosphere was changed. Mr. Stevenson's evident sincerity made a profound impression. After a half hour's further talk in which Mr. Stevenson frankly quoted figures that revealed a serious situation in the iron business, Mr. Robinson suggested that we now adjourn and that a small committee, representative of both parties, should study the whole situation with the chairman of the council for two weeks, when there should be another meeting of this body of men. This was unanimously agreed to. Before adjournment Mr. Ryan asked permission to say a few words.

"Go on, Mr. Ryan," I said, fearing further recriminations.

"I want to say first that I appreciate Mr. Stevenson's readiness to stick to our agreement. It was his unwillingness to do so that annoyed us."

"I tell you I never looked at the thing. I never worked under an agreement like that before."

"You see," said Robinson, "you never worked under a Council of Industry."

"Quite right," said Stevenson.

"But really what I want to say," continued Ryan, "is this. I want to apologize to Mr. Stevenson for what I said at the beginning of this meeting."

"Oh, that's all right, Ryan," said Stevenson heartily. "I guess we were both a bit to blame."

"And the next thing I want to say is that I thought I had a hard job keeping this gang of mine in order—"

"You bet you have, Mike," said a voice from his crowd, raising a general laugh.

"But," went on Ryan seriously, "I believe Mr. Stevenson has a harder job than I have and I'm willing to go as far as I can to meet him in a just and fair settlement."

Mr. Stevenson looked at Ryan steadily for a few moments, then said:

"Ryan, I believe you're a right fellow. I believe we can fix it so that there will be no shutdown. I'd hate to shut down on fellows like you."

There was no shutdown. After two weeks' study a new agreement was signed. The men, of their own accord, offered to cut their wages immediately to ninety cents, for conditions in the iron trade were deplorable, and to sign a new agreement at eighty-five cents. Mr. Stevenson agreed that in three months he would meet the council again, and if business warranted it he would go as far as he could to restore the old rate of wages.

The important feature in this case was, of course, the fact that an element other than the two parties entered into the situation, namely, the Canadian Pacific Railway, whose attitude was influenced by circumstances partly beyond their control. The change in the postwar scale of wages had a decided bearing upon the question.

That is but a sample of how the council carried on. Out of the 107 cases, the settlements effected showed about 55 per cent in favor of the workers, and 45 per cent in favor of the employers.

Our toughest case was one with the Winnipeg Street Railway Company, which cost us interminable discussions. The character and personality of certain workers was involved, but the main difficulty lay in the fact that the local management was hampered by absentee ownership. The council could get into actual grips neither with the shareholders nor with the actual heads of the company. This factor of absentee control constitutes, in a big company, one of the main grounds of industrial trouble. The fatal fact that it is impossible to bring to bear purely financial consideration upon a nebulous entity consisting of a multitude of stockholders whose contact with the workers is purely financial, a weekly pay check or a semiannual dividend, tends to remove the human element from the case.

But even this difficulty is not insuperable, where the conditions of co-operative effort as already set forth in this writing are honestly fulfilled.

In the month of November, the T. Eaton Company of Winnipeg decided to rush the erection of a large building to take care of the extension of their mail-order department. A large force was put on, representing every building trade in Winnipeg.

On a certain Thursday morning I noticed in the paper a head-line announcing trouble between the Iron Workers' Union and a structural iron foundry, and that if the foundry did not come to terms a strike would be called on Saturday morning and that the strike would involve every union in the building trade. The paper called attention to the fact that the parties immediately involved were those who had been responsible for the Big Strike of 1919. Every worker in Winnipeg would be on edge and ready for war. It was an exceedingly grave situation.

I called up the secretary of the labor union involved and asked why he had not brought his grievance to the council.

"No use. It is a question of closed or open shop. We don't want a strike, especially this time of the year, but we have no choice. We won't let that company put this open-shop proposition over us if we have to pull every workingman in Winnipeg off his job."

He was quiet but there was no mistaking his determination.

I tried the president of the iron foundry. He was indignant.

"Those union fellows want a fight? Well, we'll give them one they won't forget. It won't be like the 'nineteen strike either. We weren't ready for them last time but we are ready this time, and what's more the city of Winnipeg is ready also."

"What is the exact issue?"

"We made the iron stairs for the new Eaton Building. The installing is part of our contract. It is expert work and we can't entrust it to novices. We sent our men in with the stairs. Our men, of course, are open-shop men. We won't employ any others. The foreman ordered them off the building. The Eaton people want us to complete our contract. The union will call off every workman on the building if we insist on our rights."

The issue was well defined. The collision was head on. Nothing but a fight seemed possible. The union were keen to have another go at their old enemy, besides, with them it was a matter of principle.

The ironworking company made their position a matter of principle as well. They could not retire.

I called both parties to a conference with the Council of Industry. As yet we had handled no big case. This was one with over half a million dollars involved and with a strike already called, which might issue in serious trouble. Both parties were unwilling to come.

"What's the use?" said the manager of the foundry. "The strike is called for Saturday."

I had our Mr. Robinson, the secretary of the Trades and Labor Council see the union officials. With great difficulty he got the union to postpone the strike till Monday. Furthermore, we called a meeting of the Council of Industry for Friday morning and summoned both parties to appear.

The council had a long conference with the parties without result. Both parties were set and bitter. The issue of the closed or open shop was clear and was still, in Canada, one to be fought out to a finish. Also there were, as is always the case, a number of minor grievances piled up on either side intensifying the war spirit. I spent the whole of Saturday with the two parties, going into private conference with each in turn, the members of the council also doing the same and reporting to me from time to time. No progress was made. Finally I set down these two questions for each to answer:

First: Is it more important to the citizens of Winnipeg that this question of closed or open shop should be fought out now, or would it be better for all parties to allow the work on the Eaton Building to proceed to such a point as will furnish work to hundreds of workers in all the trades, indoors, during the winter months and postpone the fight on closed or open shop?

Second: The important question of closed or open shop must be settled sooner or later, somewhere. Do the interests of the citizens of Winnipeg demand that the arena for this fight should be in Winnipeg?

I took these questions personally to each party in turn, and asked for a signed answer to each question, which I might publish if I thought it necessary.

The manager of the iron foundry at once replied that he wanted no fight on the question of closed or open shop. It was simply a matter of completing his contract with expert workmen who would ensure sound work. He would willingly give the union a letter stating that the matter of closed and open shop would be left *in statu quo*.

The secretary of the Iron Workers' Union, upon the advice of the labor representatives on the council, agreed to accept such a statement as satisfactory, on the further condition that the men on the job should be paid union wages and should be under direction of the union foreman on the building. This was at once accepted by the council and agreed to by the manager of the foundry.

The other points at issue were adjusted during the week. No definite statement was made to the public as to the specific terms of agreement except that the question of the closed or open shop did not enter into the basis of the settlement.

In industrial disputes the tendency with disputants is to extend the area of controversy as widely as possible for bargaining purposes. The defect in these tactics is that they lack sincerity. In every case, settlement is most easily effected by narrowing the field of strife and by coming to agreement upon minor points as speedily as possible. Every point agreed upon adds an element to the general basis of goodwill.

Very early in the history of the council, a house famine with consequent increase in rentals created in the public mind a suspicion of profiteering on the part of rental agencies. The widespread unrest stimulated the council to action. A general announcement that the council was prepared to deal with the matter of rental charges brought a large number of complainants. There followed a period of intensive study of the whole question of *home values* and *rentals*. I knew nothing whatever about the subject. We called to our aid the best accountants in the city. I was astonished to discover how completely the majority of renting agents simply followed the trail that pioneers had broken long ago. Indeed, with one or two exceptions, rental agencies fixed their charges by the rule of *use* and *wont,* modified by the principle governing business in general, that the charges for goods and services should be generally "all the traffic would bear."

The most perplexing question which arose, and which revealed the astonishing practice in the rental business, was that of depreciation of building values and how to deal with it. After extensive inquiry from Canadian, American and British authorities, the general principle was agreed upon that the rate charged for depreciation should be the amount annually set aside necessary to recover the original investment during the lifetime of the asset, the rate to be calculated on the original investment.

It was decided that the rate for Winnipeg, in good residential districts and on apartments soundly built, should not exceed 1½ per cent per annum. Tables and charts were furnished, which justified the council's decisions but astounded the local agencies, whose rates for depreciation varied from 5 to 10 per cent on the original investment.

It was to me a great satisfaction to receive from a friend, Sir Evan Spicer, a prominent London financial authority, a confirmation of the council's decision backed by the authority of his son, a chartered accountant for the Bank of England.

Comparison of the council's operations with those of industrial courts in Britain, New Zealand, Australia and America revealed the fact that while these Courts of Industrial Relations registered success in effecting settlement of disputes at 40, 50, 60 per cent, the Manitoba Council of Industry practically showed a 100 per cent successful settlement.

The following paragraph may be skipped by all not specially interested in this matter of Labor troubles.

The general principles, here set down as being useful under the present industrial and economic system but *mutatis mutandis,* are also applicable under an economic and industrial system controlled by the state.

GENERAL PRINCIPLES GOVERNING INDUSTRIAL HARMONY

I. Industry is defined as the co-operative application of energy to raw material for the service of the whole community.

II. The Factors in Industry, under any system, are Capital, however owned or controlled, Labor, Management, and the Community.

III. Co-operation of all four Factors is necessary to success in all Industrial enterprises.

IV. Co-operation is achieved when each Factor is secured in its Rights and assumes its Responsibilities.

V. The Rights of all Factors can be expressed in identical
terms. They are: 1. Security
2. Freedom
3. A fair return
4. Growth.

VI. The Responsibility of each Factor is the granting of each of
the other Factors its Rights.

The denial of Rights to any Factor, or the refusal of Responsibility by any Factor, will render impossible the
highest success in industry.

Resolute insistence upon these principles will eliminate industrial strife and will ensure to industry its highest
success.

After four years of operation, the necessity for the Council of
Industry seemed almost entirely to disappear. I resigned my position
as chairman and for the last dozen years the council has not been
called upon to exercise its functions. Indeed, in Manitoba, with minor
exceptions, there has been no industrial trouble. The practice of settlement by conference, as under the Council of Industry, has been
found to be all that is necessary.

CHAPTER XXXVI

The Hope of Geneva

CHEQUERS—RAMSAY MACDONALD—JOAN'S WEDDING—LEAGUE OF NATIONS—THE ASSEMBLY IN SESSION—LORD ROBERT CECIL—EAST AND WEST—IRAQ ENTERS THE LEAGUE—LIBERIA—A LEAGUE EXPERT—DISARMAMENT CONFERENCE—REARMAMENT

In the early Autumn of 1932 I was invited to preach the sermon with which the League of Nations opened its deliberations.

On my way from Canada to Geneva I had the good luck to have for a fellow traveler, Mr. Malcolm MacDonald, the son of the British Prime Minister, Mr. Ramsay MacDonald. My son King and Malcolm had been collegemates in Oxford, and Malcolm had just been spending a few weeks with us at Birkencraig, our summer home at the Lake of the Woods in Western Canada.

We arrived in London on a Saturday morning on our way to Chequers, whither the family had gone for the celebration of the marriage of the second daughter, Dr. Joan.

I secured a copy of the London *Times* and was shocked by a flaring headline announcing Germany's refusal to attend the Disarmament Conference and her bold challenge of the equity of the Treaty of Versailles. I remember well the look of dismay upon the Prime Minister's face as he read the announcement and exclaimed,

"Ah, the fools! What madness!"

"But, sir," I ventured, "surely Germany has a right to equality of status with the other members of the League."

"Yes," he said slowly as if to himself, "yes, Germany was a member of the League and had a right to equality of status with all other members, but her time was coming, and besides what folly to challenge the Treaty!"

"But the Allies, while not actually agreeing to reduce armaments, did virtually lead Germany to believe that gradual disarmament was to be their policy."

"Yes, true enough, and that was coming. But 'at this particular time, when America was considering the whole matter of armaments, war debts, and reparations! It is most inept! Germany can be trusted to do the inept thing politically."

That evening he spent an hour on the telephone and next morning the *Times* editorial was a masterpiece of diplomatic writing. A slap on the wrist for Germany for challenging the Treaty, a stern reminder that the Treaty must be held inviolate—this for France's benefit—but also a quiet statement that no one wanted to keep Germany in a position of inferiority.

But here let me finish my story of Chequers. Chequers is a godsend to the prime ministers of Great Britain. It often stands between a British premier and a nervous breakdown. It is a veritable haven of rest. A lovely old country place which has remained in the hands of one family for a thousand years, set in a charming old English countryside, Hampden's country and Cromwell's. But I must not indulge my desire to tell you all about that beautiful manor house and its rare treasures. Nor can I pause to reproduce the charming picture of the Prime Minister in the midst of his family of boys and girls, grown to be young men and women but in that home still boys and girls. You never really know a man till you see him at home.

One touch I will venture to give. On the morning of the wedding day when we were passing in to breakfast, the Prime Minister came to me and said:

"When you say grace this morning perhaps you will remember the little girl who leaves her home today."

"Thank you," I said, "I shall count it a privilege to do so."

I knew well that on that wedding morning they would all be acutely conscious of the vacant place in the family circle, once filled by that rare and lovely woman who had been its uniting bond, the mother.

The wedding was quite what Scots would call "a grand wedding."

It said much for the place the Prime Minister held in the hearts of the people that along the roads leading to the little village church where the ceremony was performed the whole populace lined up in their Sunday best to do honor to their own laird as well as to the Prime Minister and to send away the young lady to her new home laden with their blessings. '

One little touch of a personal nature I must record. I was specially delighted, as were the members of the family, that the young lady sent by the London society paper should be Miss Corinne Irwin, the dearest friend and chum of my daughter Ruth, who had spent a part of every summer holiday with us at Birkencraig.

A very special honor was mine, not only to have a part in the ceremony but to have the privilege of proposing the health of the bride at the wedding feast.

But I am on my way to Geneva and must no longer delay.

The church service at the opening of a League Assembly is made one of official ceremonial solemnity. The national, civic and ecclesiastical dignitaries were present as well as League officials and representatives from member nations. The service was a full-dress affair, the officiating clergymen being:

The Rev. David F. McCready, rural dean of Switzerland;

The Rev. Dr. Everett P. Smith, rector of the American Episcopal Church of Geneva;

The Rev. Dr. T. M. Watt, chaplain of the Church of Scotland in Geneva;

The Rev. Jean de Saussure, pastor of the National Protestant Church of Geneva.

The lesson was read by Lord Robert Cecil.

At the organ M. Otto Barblan presided, rendering the Prelude to Act I of Wagner's *Parsifal,* while the procession made its entry.

The service was marked by simplicity, sincerity and warm religious fervor. The sermon might have been better. The officiating clergymen, however, were good enough to express appreciation, and what really gratified me most of all, the American newspaper reporter took it down word for word, and came next day to tell me that the sermon kept him wide awake from start to finish, adding the cheering comment, "It takes some sermon to do that for me."

The preacher stood in the lofty pulpit of the ancient Cathedral of Saint-Pierre, whence the great reformer, scholar, and statesman,

John Calvin, was wont to thunder forth his messages to the people of Geneva.

Next day, when I went to the opening meeting of the Assembly of the League, a number of members greeted me as if I had been an old friend. This proved a most useful introduction to various League functions.

Looking back over twenty years of League history, I find in my heart a deep disappointment that the spirit of united Christian fellowship that permeated that opening service has not found expression in the practical activities of the League.

Before I pass from this opening service I wish to note the profound significance of the fact that in that formal religious function of the League of Nations a layman representing one of England's oldest and most distinguished families should have considered it an honor to take part. There is a very real significance in the fact that the official heads of the League should consider it appropriate that the League formally open its business with a public recognition of the Christian religion.

The whole world is familiar with the structure and procedure of the League of Nations. Without preliminary I shall try to picture my first view of the Assembly at work.

As an instrument of world peace, the League has made an enormous contribution to the harmony of international relations. Unhappily, critics of hasty and faulty judgment, who allow their social, political or economic proclivities to determine their thinking, consider the League a sentimental absurdity, a conspicuous failure. But nineteen years of experimentation with the League of Nations has convinced the world of the necessity for some such institution for collective counseling in international affairs, collective application of the principles of international justice, as well as for the carrying on of those multitudinous services to humanity which have made for the League an enduring place in the world.

There is a sound basis for the opinion that perhaps the prime cause of failure, where the League of Nations has failed, is found in the fact that the League as conceived by Woodrow Wilson was so tragically abandoned by his own country. And this is rendered all the more tragic by the demonstration of success by the League in all those many social, moral, and economic services in which the

United States has co-operated so heartily. The League, however, has so completely justified its existence that, in spite of two conspicuous failures, the world will earnestly set itself to remedy its defects and restore it to the confidence of those nations who are resolutely set upon the establishing of *world peace* upon a basis of *world justice* and *world goodwill*.

My first experience with the Assembly was disappointing. The great glass-enclosed structure is unimpressive and does not lend itself to satisfactory audition. The necessary practice of translating every speech into either French or English is tedious. The program, too, was quite uninteresting. It consisted of a sort of "free-for-all" canter around the oratorical parade ground, the members all striving to establish a more or less perfunctory justification of the existence of the League, with explanations, justifications and palliations *ad nauseam*. I was disappointed, the whole thing was so commonplace, so deplorably lacking in idealism, in spiritual quality. M. Herriot, the fiery orator from France, however, galvanized the audience into something like life, but when Lord Robert Cecil walked up to the bema with a bit of paper in his hand the whole audience came alive. All chatter, all lounging, all moving about, ceased. I shall not attempt a résumé of the speech, I merely say this: it differed from all the other speeches in that it made no defense for the League. The speaker frankly justified the criticism poured upon it.

"But there is nothing really wrong with the construction of the League," said Lord Robert. "Some changes in constitution and procedure will doubtless need to be made. But the trouble is not with the League as a whole. The trouble is with you, the members of the League, who fail to live up to your obligations."

He thereupon, with the utmost frankness, specified instances of failure. There was not the slightest striving after oratorical effect. He was far too earnest for oratory. The interests represented in the League were far too important for anything but the most serious and most conscientious consideration. The world was in a troubled condition, economically, socially, politically, and only the utmost wisdom and sincerity, under guidance of Almighty God, would enable the League to justify its existence.

I was never prouder of my British heritage than at that moment.

The simplicity, the sincerity, the high moral tone, the intense and passionate conviction behind his appeal swept that company of hard-boiled political agents off their feet. Again and again they broke into applause. The moral quality of his appeal found a response in their deepest and finest convictions and emotions.

And that is a characteristic of the Assembly. They are diplomatic agents, obsessed by national prejudices and passions, but they do rise to the appeal of great world interests when presented with moral passion.

After the close of the Assembly I met Lord Robert in the ante-room. I ventured to thank him for his address. He was kind enough to thank me for my sermon the day before.

"Lord Robert," I said, "this is my first touch of the League. I am fearfully disappointed. Yours, if I may say so, was the only speech that touched the moral and spiritual aspects of World War problems."

He was apologetic for his confreres. The first day was always more or less perfunctory, he said.

"Do you know, Sir Robert," I ventured, "what I think the League wants? Don't think me impertinent."

"No fear of that. The matter is serious."

"I believe that what the League needs is a rebirth of that moral passion that brought it into being."

"You are right. You are undoubtedly right," he said with emphasis. "Moral passion is what we need. But how can that be secured?"

"I have wondered if a League of the great Christian churches of the world, backing the League of Nations, might be of some use."

"Undoubtedly it would. It is a great idea. But can such a League be secured?" He was doubtful.

Following up this idea, let me add that later I approached M. Benes, the distinguished delegate from Czechoslovakia. He threw up his hands and exclaimed, "Ah! If we could only have that!" I approached other delegates on the matter. Everywhere the idea was received with enthusiasm but with doubt as to its feasibility.

There came a day when reports from commissions were being received. The delegate from China, Dr. Yen, rose. A few days earlier I had heard him hold spellbound for an hour a great gathering at a luncheon in the International Club, as he told us the story of China for some five thousand years—a masterpiece of literary art and of condensed historic lore.

Today, however, in the Assembly, he was bringing the gratitude of over three hundred millions of his people for the League's achievement in taming the Yangtze Kiang within dikes erected on both banks for two thousand miles inland from the sea, under the direction of a League committee of international experts, employing the labor of a million Chinese workers for six months. He also conveyed the grateful appreciation of his people for the League's service to China by means of a commission of experts on education, which had introduced a new system of national education. He spoke in beautiful English, under deep emotion, and received the enthusiastic applause of the Assembly when he took his seat.

The League does one thing for Occidental people of quite ordinary intelligence, it cures them of their silly sense of superiority over the peoples of the Orient.

On another day a quite dramatic incident was staged. There was a knock on the door of the Assembly. A League official, sent to inquire, returned with the announcement that the country of Iraq, under mandate to Great Britain for the last thirteen years, was at the door seeking entry to the League of Nations. The whole Assembly rose to receive Great Britain and her protégé, little Iraq— "the oldest people in the world," as Sir John Simon said a few minutes later.

A formal document from the League's Committee on Mandates reported that Iraq had successfully passed its examinations before the eight committees in charge of this matter and had given guarantees of her fitness to hold a place among the nations of the world. The necessary resolution was moved and seconded and passed. Speeches of welcome were spoken by M. Herriot for France; he made a graceful reference to Great Britain, which had set up a standard by which all future mandates would be tried, by the manner in which she had guided to full status of nationhood this Kingdom of Iraq.

Then followed an ornate flourish by the delegate from Turkey, the age-long and bloody oppressor of poor little Iraq, in which he welcomed, almost with tears in his voice, "Turkey's oldest friend and neighbor" to fellowship in the League. This, the other delegates received with tongue in cheek.

Sir John Simon made acknowledgments for Great Britain. It took him about six minutes to express in a perfect gem of English speech the appreciation by his country of Iraq's loyal co-operation through these thirteen years, in building up into a modern state, worthy of a place in this Assembly, "this Kingdom of Iraq, the oldest people, the youngest nation in the world, the very names of whose ancient cities sound like bugle calls down the corridors of time."

It is in the Council, however, that the real work of the League is done. It was my immense good fortune to be present during the presentation of the report of the Special Commission of Council, appointed two years earlier to extricate the Republic of Liberia, that conglomerate mass of American Negroes, descendants of liberated slaves, from the financial, social and political morass into which it had sunk during the last hundred years. The story, were it not for the tragic human horror of it, might furnish material for one of Gilbert and Sullivan's comic operas. A commission of three men had been appointed to this work. A year later they presented a report of an amazing bit of constructive nation building, which I cannot here take time to set forth. This year, however, another report was presented of an even more amazing character. The Republic of Liberia is a purely coastal country. In the hinterland, however, there are some twenty-five tribes of Negro peoples, the Kru, a high-spirited, independent and warlike race of magnificent physique and quite superior intelligence. These had been placed under the administrative care of the Republic of Liberia, whose mission it was to instruct them in the arts and practices of civilized life. The story of Liberia's civilizing of these tribes is one long tale of ruthless exploitation, of savage and bloody wars, in which a "frontier force" of those civilized American Negroes armed with machine guns and rifles decimated these naked warriors, armed with clubs, bows and arrows, ancient guns and muskets sold them by their civilizing overlords, and drove them from their homes into the back wilds.

The report of the previous year, which had recorded a fine bit of government reorganization and financial rehabilitation had, however, called the attention of the Council to the deplorable condition of the unhappy Kru tribes, harried and oppressed by their overlord, the Republic of Liberia. The Council invited Dr. MacKenzie, one of the first commissioners, to take over the medical supervision of these tribes of the hinterland and to do what he could to win them to peace. It was a task of great delicacy and of enormous difficulty. Dr. MacKenzie agreed to accept the task.

"How many men will you require with you?" asked the Council, with a vision of at least a half company of soldiers to act as a bodyguard.

"Oh, one man will be enough, if you get me the man I want."

"And who is that?"

"The sergeant major of the London Royal Scots."

A British gunboat landed these two intrepid souls at Monrovia, the capital of Liberia, and left them there to work out their task.

The report of the work of these two amazing Scots was presented that day. Without heroics, in the barest forms of speech, the report told of medical treatment for disease, of dispensaries established among these savage tribes with trained natives to administer the remedies. The most astonishing part was that which dealt with the pacification of the Kru warriors. By his medical services and by the influence of his personality, this Scottish medical officer had persuaded the chiefs to sign a treaty of peace for one year with Liberia, and as a guarantee of good faith to actually deliver their weapons of war to Dr. MacKenzie. These weapons were carefully labeled with the names of their owners, carried to Monrovia and there deposited for safekeeping under lock and key. The report was formally received and passed, and that was all about it.

One member of Council—Lord Robert Cecil, if I mistake not—was dissatisfied with this casual disposal of what he considered a marvelous bit of work. He rose and asked if some further details in regard to this remarkable achievement could not be supplied by Dr. MacKenzie. Much embarrassed, the doctor rose, assured them that all the necessary data could be found in the report, and sat down. After some further demands for details had met with meager response, there rose a tall handsome Negro, as black in face as his own quite elegant morning coat, a member of the Liberian Parliament. In rolling periods of sonorous English he gave us details of Dr. MacKenzie's toilsome and dangerous journeys up sweltering rivers and through fetid jungles, of his power of winning the admiration and affection of the Kru tribes and their chiefs, a great tale worth the telling. Dr. MacKenzie sat the while in abject misery.

The same evening I had the rare privilege of dining with Dr. Mac-

Kenzie and his Royal Scots sergeant major. It was a great evening. We dined simply, Dr. MacKenzie giving us learned, valuable and interesting information as to the ethnological origin of the Kru, their form of tribal government, their carefully guarded domestic relations, their system of education in schools for boys and for girls under the care of their priests, their rigid civic regulations, their magnificent physical powers; in short, everything about the Krus except the one thing I wanted most of all, the story of his own achievement in winning their trust and affection, in persuading them to cease their wars of retribution upon their tyrannous overlords, the corrupt and morally rotten government officials of the Republic of Liberia. I failed to get his story, but my failure was almost atoned for when he and his sergeant major brought forth their bagpipes. What a night! The room was only some fifteen by twenty feet, but what of that? The doctor, by his own confession, was a mere tyro in the ancient Highland art of playing the pipes, but the sergeant major was a master. They played in solo, they played in unison. They began with lighter numbers, reels and strathspeys and marches, but they soon passed into the higher reaches of their art, and marching round that narrow space instead of through the glens and over the hills of Scotland, they poured forth the heart-moving strains of the ancient pibrochs and laments of their clans, with chests expanded, with grave faces, with eyes seeing things to me unseen. It was a great night. It recalled one of the soul-stirring performances of my father's in the Harrington manse.

These two men represented the high quality of the experts in their various departments to whom the League of Nations entrusts its varied and delicate services to humanity, of which the world knows nothing. Liberia stands a monument to the League, with its million human beings, set free from the financial slavery into which the foolish and wicked vagaries of its government had plunged it, its administration transformed from the fantastic folly of an opéra bouffe into a sound and sane system of ordered control and that noble race of free, though savage, people delivered from tyranny. Liberia reconstituted and redeemed is one of the many justifications of the existence of the League of Nations.

It was my good fortune to sit in the Assembly of the League throughout the whole period of the preliminary deliberations and also throughout the encounter between those intellectual gladiators, Dr.

Wellington Koo, representing China, and Mr. Matsuoka, representing Japan. My experience during these two debates put the final touches to my complete emancipation from the Occidental sense of the intellectual and cultural superiority of my race over the peoples of the Orient. Seldom have I heard equaled, never surpassed, the clear logic, the sustained eloquence and controlled passion of Dr. Wellington Koo during his three days' presentation of China's case. In Mr. Matsuoka he had a foeman worthy of his steel.

I shall not enter into the merits of the dispute between China and Japan. The report of the League commission under Lord Lytton was in the hands of the League and formed the basis of its decision. That decision condemned the action of Japan in setting up the puppet state of Manchukuo, demanded a withdrawal of her forces, and proposed a new administration of Manchuria consistent with the sovereignty of China and the rights of all interested nations.

Japan replied by walking out of the League. Action by the League against her would have meant war. And for war the League was morally and physically unprepared.

The judgment of the world is that the League failed to justify the world's hope of World Peace by Collective Action. Under that judgment the League of Nations still rests.

The Disarmament Conference was the offspring of the League of Nations. Great hopes were built upon that institution for the peace of the world, largely because of the active co-operation of the United States. I confess I was never able to work up any violent enthusiasm over it. The conference met in Geneva in an interval between sessions of the League.

The action of Germany in leaving the Disarmament Conference paralyzed for a time the whole activity of the conference. Obviously, discussion and agreement as to disarmament would be futile if Germany were not a party to any agreement arrived at.

The situation was complicated still further by the publishing at this particular time of crisis of the French Plan which had been in process of incubation for some weeks. I can clearly recall the consternation created by its publication in almost all circles except that of the Little Entente which, of course, would back up France's proposal. The

French Plan was, briefly, the creation of an elaborate system of international police and the setting up of a rigid system of supervision in the
different countries which might be expected to express practically the
mind of France.

The announcement was made that Sir John Simon was to appear
before the conference in order to set forth the attitude of Great Britain
in the present situation. Sir John arrived by plane. The conference was
crowded, every delegate was in his place and everyone was on the
alert for the British announcement. Sir John Simon has been subjected
to severe criticism on many occasions for his attitudes and acts in the
conduct of his office but on this particular occasion he received universal
approval. Mr. Arthur Henderson was in the chair, and immediately
announced that Sir John Simon, representing the British government,
was present to bring to the conference an important communication
from that government.

Sir John rose in his place among the British members of the conference to make his announcement. The chairman invited him to speak
from the bema. Immaculately turned out, perfectly at ease, yet finely
courteous, he began his address with a reference to the extreme gravity
of the world situation at that moment. This crisis would be regarded by
all of them as a sufficient justification for the unusual action of his
government in sending a special message to the Disarmament Conference which represented the important nations of the world. Before
delivering his message, however, he must refer to an event of special
significance to the world. He then referred to the French Plan, which
must receive and would receive the most careful study by the conference. But important as was that plan and important as were other matters before the conference, the opinion of his government was that there
was another matter which must take precedence over all these questions.
This was the opinion not only of the British government, but of the
British House of Commons as well. The matter which must receive
the immediate attention of the League of Nations and of this conference was to discover a method by which Germany should be brought
back to her proper place in the League and at the table of this conference. Any plan of disarmament that did not carry the approval of Germany would be futile. In one second the atmosphere surrounding the
conference was completely changed. It was as if a window had been
opened and a breath of cool air from the snow-clad slopes of Mont Blanc

had poured into the room. Everyone immediately saw clearly how right he was. At that moment, one might say, the French Plan elaborated with such care passed into limbo.

After careful consideration steps were taken which were finally successful in bringing Germany back to the conference.

I spent some days in the meeting of the Disarmament Conference. Although it was intensely interesting as an assemblage of trained pleaders and although one could not but sympathize with the high motives of the members, I could not escape the feeling that the whole basis of the conference was unsound. The limitation of weapons of destruction in their death-dealing powers, the eliminating of certain instruments or means of destruction in war, seemed to me for the most part utter futility. An American friend put the whole thing in a sentence.

"What difference will it make to the dead man whether the shell that killed him came from a six-inch or a sixteen-inch gun?" I asked this young American secretary.

"Well, you can make war less horrible, can't you?" was his reply.

"Can you make it anything but utterly horrible?" I asked.

"By jinks, he's dead right," said his friend. "I've always had the feeling that we are monkeying with a lot of darn-fool nonsense. The long purse and the big battalion will win in the end. And after all, once the war starts, what use are covenants? The first gun will blow all covenants to blazes."

I soon lost all interest in the Disarmament Conference. So, though many of the reasons for it may seem valid, I gave up attending its meetings. Nor have I ever been able to revive any interest in this aspect of the question of peace and war.

The League of Nations continued in session earnestly and anxiously, considering the problem of the Sino-Japanese conflict. China, of course, accepted the decision of the League, but Japan in abandoning the League rejected its decisions and pursued her course of absorption of Chinese territory.

I have but one observation to make in this connection and that is that if the League of Nations failed to implement its covenant, the signatory nations to the Kellogg Pact failed more definitely and more culpably. We may leave the matter there, but the Sino-Japanese tragedy has made definitely and unmistakably evident to the world that any international instrument of world peace, so far as Japan and China are concerned, which does not include the wholehearted commitment not only of the League members, but of the signatories to the Kellogg Pact, will be futile. And as a further corollary, the world is convinced that any international covenant pledged to the maintenance of world peace that does not include the greatest trading nation in the world, the United States of America, is doomed to failure. The nations who truly love peace founded on international right and human goodwill are the only nations who can secure world peace for humanity.

I am no expert in international affairs, but it has been my privilege to have somewhat intimate relations with those who have had to do with world affairs. Furthermore, within the communion of a great Canadian church I have been charged with the responsibilities of leadership in those various departments of Christian activity that impinge definitely upon such matters as world goodwill, world right and world peace. Hence without being guilty of presumption and without offense, I perhaps may be permitted to point out what I consider the crucial defect in League organization and League procedure. *It is the failure to organize for the promotion of world peace, the goodwill of humanity.* Not *big guns,* but *goodwill,* can curb the ambitions, the greed, the pride of inflamed nationalisms and build for the world a path of peace. This will be received with loud jeers of derision by the political experts and realists. But five thousand years of experimentation with their war methods might have taught them modesty and might surely have wrought in them a willingness to allow an honest, wise and resolute experiment of another way. One thing we can confidently assert: the results to humanity cannot be more cruelly disastrous, more bitterly disappointing than those which their methods have made humanity suffer. The five continents are strewn with the wreckage of mighty empires, eloquent of the futility of the "Big Gun Method." Why not adopt the modern scientific law of rejection of methods that have failed and experiment with the new?

For instance, as I write this every great nation is planning vast expenditures in war preparation. Great Britain, proclaiming herself the great protagonist of world peace, has a budget beginning with $750,000-000, and it may run to $2,000,000,000. If one-tenth of these war budgets were expended in the culture of mutual understanding and mutual goodwill among the peoples of the world, war would soon be considered an anachronism and a ghastly failure.

CHAPTER XXXVII

The New Spanish Republic

GRAPE HARVEST IN THE RHONE VALLEY—FRENCH-
SPANISH CUSTOMS—SPAIN PAST AND PRESENT—
SAFFRON PICKING—MADRID—EDUCATION—PEOPLE
OR PRINCES—ROMAN REMAINS

BY AN EXTRAORDINARY piece of good luck I was invited to accompany the Governing Body of the International Labour Office of the League of Nations on a visit to Spain as a guest of the government of the year-old Spanish Republic. Would I go? To Spain, the last remaining home in the world of medieval romance, the newest experiment in Socialist government in the modern world? I was one of a party of three, with Dr. Walter Riddell, the permanent representative of Canada at the League, and his wife, my niece, in their car.

Our route took us over the Jura Range within sight of whose peaks we traveled southward through the Rhone valley, the most glorious valley in all France, a land of cultivated farms, of orchards and vineyards, now in the full purple splendor of the grape harvest. Everywhere the vineyards were filled with women and children gathering the huge purple clusters in great baskets to be carted off to the presses. Often we paused to gaze upon the grapegatherers at their work. We offered to buy, they loaded us down with huge bunches the size of my head, and cheerfully refused payment. We paused at a winepress, not as in the old days when women with empurpled feet trod out the clusters, but by a huge press operated by a donkey. Outside the building the debris, stalks and skins, was piled high.

"What will they do with all this mess?" I asked Walter Riddell. "Make manure of it for the fields?"

"Ask them," he said.

I did. The man in charge was horrified at the mere suggestion of such waste.

"You will see at the next village," he replied.

In the next village we saw huge heaps outside a large building; inside we discovered immense vats packed with this refuse. Live steam was turned into these vats and from them issued an innocent-looking colorless liquid.

"Pour boire?" I asked.

"Ah, oui," said the young girl attendant. She filled a glass and tossed it off with evident relish, then handed one to me. I swallowed a generous mouthful. Instantly my hat flew off my head, my shoes were off my feet. At least, so it seemed to me.

"Try it, Walter," I said, recovering my breath. "It is wonderful."

"Not me. I shall take your reaction as quite sufficient."

I took a bottle home with me. If I wish to avenge myself upon an enemy I shall treat him to a glass of Rhone valley "eau de vie."

We now began to climb and continue for two or three hours. Then from the top we catch a glimpse of one of the world's most exquisite scenes. Over wooded mountaintops our eyes flit and rest entranced upon an expanse of shimmering blue.

"The Mediterranean!" Dr. Walter informs us, and in silence we feast our souls upon the scene. There are no adjectives in my vocabulary to describe this blue shimmering panorama of rounded mountain ranges, of variegated green, then far away a plain of ineffable azure meeting at the horizon a canopy of fainter blue. How maddeningly defective is language for the great moments of life! I have no feeling just yet for the throbbing pulses of history. I am saturating my senses with this blue. Thank God, no one bursts into ecstatic attempts at description.

In silence we turn inland some thirty miles to present ourselves to the frontier officials, first the French, slovenly in dress and manner, then to the Spanish customs officials, natty, polite, efficient, our first touch of the New Republic.

Something had gone wrong with our advance notifications. Walter is busy with the customs officials. I see a handsome young fellow in a mountaineer's dress with a jaunty feather in his cap cleaning a gun.

"Hunting?" I say.

"Sure!"

"What? American?"

"Sure thing."

"I am from Canada, shake." We shake like long-parted friends.

"From Canada," he says. "Montreal? Toronto? Ottawa?"

"No, Winnipeg," I say proudly. "Western Canada."

"Ah-h-h!" A note of envy in his voice. "Never saw the West."

He had spent a few years in America. He was delighted to see Americans again. They were a kind people and "awful smart."

Our new friend relieves us of all linguistic difficulties, explaining to the customs' officials Dr. Riddell's high position in the League of Nations and our distinction of being guests of the Republic. They were proud to serve us. They would have given us their customhouse if we had asked for it. With warm mutual farewell, we are away down the southern slopes of the Pyrenees and are really in Spain.

Spain! Spain? Mingled emotions. Land of vanished races, Iberians, Goths, Visigoths, for three hundred years, the Moors, fierce warriors but with scientific culture for four hundred years, the great empire of Ferdinand and Isabella, with Christopher Columbus plowing his adventurous furrow through unknown seas to a new world. Ah, that new world of the Spanish Americas and of Mexico, doomed to tragic horrors of conquest, reeking with bloody rapine! Spain! Home of great artists, poets, scholars, and now the New Spain of the Republic.

On perfect roads, through cork-tree forests, vineyards, olive and walnut groves, then out again to the blue Mediterranean, we pause at the great coast city of Barcelona, Spain's financial capital. A glance at the great masses of Roman foundations, a look at the cathedral and then away, touching such great cities as Saragossa and Lerida and out onto the plains of Aragon. Aragon! What a name! Once proud, haughty, but now poor, with its brown burnt plains and wretched little villages of adobe or red and yellow brick. The village streets are so narrow that we must drive carefully lest we run over the children at the doors. What wretched rabbit warrens for little children to be born in, with little holes for windows looking into dark burrows behind.

This road, splendidly surfaced, near to Barcelona, is crowded with transport. But what a mingling of the centuries! Donkey carts, and goat carts; donkeys lost to view under their loads, women with heavy loads on their heads. Sturdy and squat they are. Alas! for my dreams of dark-eyed señoras and señoritas. All are alert to dodge the American and European motorcars, honking their way on to Madrid. Half a day of the rich lands of eastern Aragon, then desert, poverty-stricken desert, with poor patches of green where a little stream, struggling for life, makes its way.

Now and then we see a lonely peasant at work in the fields. We pause to watch one plowing with a span of rickety mules hitched to an ancient plow.

"Let us go over and see him plow," I suggest to Walter.

"Go on! I've often seen them."

What an outfit! Five hundred, perhaps a thousand years ago that plow was invented. It consists of a three-cornered piece of iron with a single wooden handle, thrust into a socket. A boy drives the mules, and the man by hard leaning on his plow handle strives to keep its nose in the ground.

It is lunch hour. The man takes from his pocket a long cylinder of crusty bread, cuts off a chunk for himself and for his boy. He lifts a small leather bag from the hames of the harness, unscrews the cork, tilts back his head, opens his mouth to receive a stream of wine which gurgles down his open throat. He graciously offers me a drink and in return I offer to plow a furrow. I soon desist, I can't possibly keep this iron thing in the sun-baked earth.

Poverty! Abject and hopeless poverty. At the far horizon are ranges of hills through which great rivers flow. Along the sides of the hills we can trace the lines of abandoned irrigation ditches of Alfonso's time. He began well, but the great cavaliers needed money for their palaces and the irrigation ditches had to go.

Near the little villages we see now and then a patch of purple flowers with yellow hearts. We do not know what they are. At one of the villages we pause to watch an interesting scene set in the open street. In a tiny courtyard before a little house we observe a group of men standing about. It is just after the noon hour. Beside the open door a little table is set and seated at it are a tiny tot, a dark and wrinkled little lady and two toothless ancients. On the table lies a bunch of purple flowers. We make our way to them and find that with meticulous care they are picking out of the hearts of these purple flowers, the stamens and pistils, and depositing them carefully in a dish. What does this mean? After vainly struggling with our meager Spanish we try French. At once a man steps from the crowd and explains. They are picking "saffron," to be exported to America for dyeing and for flavoring foods.

We wonder and pity. One by one, stamen by stamen, the saffron is picked. I shake my head and say "Très tard," the nearest I could come to "Slow work." My tone of pity seemed to stir the little lady. She jumped up, ran into the house and returned with a little parcel of dried saffron, wrapped it in a paper and gave it to me. I made the fatal mistake of offering her a few pesetas. With a superb wave of the hand she refused my money. This was a gift from a lady to a gentleman. I took her hand and bowed low over it. A ripple of laughter ran round the circle. The little old lady picked up her skirt with a dainty finger and thumb, swept me a bow and smiled.

I place the pesetas upon the table beside the little lass, stoop and kiss her and we are off, I do confess with a hot choke in my throat. Poor! Terribly poor! But what courage! And a bit of the chivalry of old Spain! Heaven grant the New Republic will not kill that. I often think of the little group in that tiny courtyard, too young and too old for the day's work, sitting in the sun, gossiping and laughing, picking saffron that American ladies may dress in golden colors and flavor their sauces. Ah verily, they work for their lives, sending their poor little toll of pesetas to Madrid that a great Spanish grandee may drink his canary at ease. "God save the Republic!"

As we approached Madrid we enter a new world. Irrigation ditches mean fields of grain, herds of cattle, flocks of sheep, vineyards, olive trees, dates, better villages, happier homes. Madrid, an old city quaintly medieval, with lovely old dwellings within high-walled gardens, lofty cathedrals, great museums. New Madrid, splendid in a way, with good streets, banks, department stores, rather baroque and vulgar but apparently busy and prosperous.

We see a bit of the modern world jostle the old. They are making a new street. An American grader is tearing up the pavement. Women are carrying the debris in baskets on their heads and dumping it into donkey carts.

We are here in Madrid to attend the sixtieth meeting of the Governing Body of the International Labour Office but there are other things we cannot neglect. Cathedrals we must see, and plazas, museums, and art galleries—El Prado, for instance. El Prado! That you may not neglect. Here many of the world's art treasures arrest you, hold you breathless. We cannot enumerate, but two great masterpieces you dare not pass. Raphael's *Cardinal* and Velazquez's *Cristo Crucificado*.

My first look at the *Cristo Crucificado* holds me. I go back for a second look and for a third. You must give time to this. You must let the touching serenity of the *Cristo Crucificado* enter your soul. That naked, pallid figure, not gruesome or repulsive but penetratingly pathetic, pierces your heart. Give time to it. You will be the better for it. Love victorious over hate. Life over death, poignantly pathetic. But it is a strong man hanging there. You dare not pity. Jesús Crucificado! Before I am aware, the tears are streaming down my face.

Spain is proud of her three great painters, Goya, El Greco and Velazquez, and well may she be proud. Parts of three days I spent wandering amid these masterpieces of Spain's great artists.

I cannot tell you of the meeting of the Governing Body. They are an important section of the League doing great work for the world, representative of the three great classes of the world's toilers—employers, laborers and government representatives—keen, clearheaded, reasonable, solving the labor problems of the world. They are Radicals and Conservatives, working for world peace and world unity. Co-ordinated world workers make for world peace. Nationally-minded rival workers make for war. I listen, watch them, admire them, salute them! They are worthy and none among them more worthy than our own Tom Moore and Walter Riddell, representing Canadian workers.

These men work strenuously but they can play as well. This government of the New Republic knew how to be generous in its courtesies, dinners, concerts, receptions, visitations to art galleries and museums of wonderful art treasures in tapestries, gold, silver, bronze, marble statuary. This New Spanish Republic was no assemblage of "roughnecks." Tradesmen and mechanics there are in the government whose hands are eloquent of their tasks, but scholars, artists, lawyers, inventors, builders as well.

The Grand Presidential Dinner in the royal palace is quite beyond my powers of telling. These Spanish cooks know their job. The meats, the pasties, the roast guinea fowls and partridge, the puddings and sauces, the ices, are beyond speech. And the wines! A presidential dinner in the Grand Royal in Madrid is no place for a teetotaler, especially if he is of Scottish ancestry. The glorious splendor of the palace, with its art treasures, its furniture, its priceless Goya tapestries and paintings, all just as Alfonso, poor chap, left it. I could not but pity him, but the memories of those squalid villages, of the arid plains of

Aragon, of the horrible hovels in Spain's great cities, the millions of children growing up in barbaric ignorance, the victims of the ruthless rapacity of the great grandees of Spain, fill me with a pity more poignant. Alfonso and his princes and his prelates and his landowners and merchants had their chance. They failed. Let the New Republic have its chance to build this ancient empire into a state where the first consideration of its rulers will be the happiness and the security and the moral worth of its people.

There is but one reason why any government should endure: it is care for its people. And that the new government is seeking to do. At least so do they protest.

After the dinner there was a formal reception. This is rugged democracy with a vengeance. If anyone wishes to greet the President he just pushes through the crowd. Jack and his master stand on the same level.

After the reception, a dance. First the modern crude, formless jiggles. It makes me think of a western hoedown. But wait! The band, some forty guitars great and small and mandolins, zithers and some weird stringed instruments I know nothing of; the band, a group of dark-skinned, dark-eyed desperadoes, I am sure they carried knives in their girdles. The band strikes up a weird, tortuous, bewitching melody. There is a loud cheer. The jigglers cease their silly jiggles and begin to move in swaying curves of exquisitely sinuous grace, sensuous and bewitching. For the first time in my life I yearned to dance. My eye singles out one pair of dancers. The gentleman, a man of middle age, iron-gray hair, but with all the easy grace of youth, and with him a lady in flowing draperies, grace in every movement of her lovely body. Ah! This is old Spain! This is dancing. For the first time I understand how it came that Herod offered the dancing harlot, the daughter of Herodias, the head of John Baptist! Gradually the floor is cleared and the two have the floor to themselves. The lady, her face of pale ivory framed in soft masses of dark hair, her eyes lustrous, languorous, flash their luring witchery upon her cavalier. He advances, she retreats. He follows, she sways toward him, she is in his arms. Together they sway in a long embrace. She breaks away, he pursues. The wild music urges, summons, maddens. How lovely she is! How bewitching! The dancers come to rest at a table near me, upon the table a glaring lamp, brutally revealing. I shall always regret that nearer view. But she can dance!

We were taken to see the magnificent new University City in a suburb of Madrid. Hundreds of acres of magnificent forest carefully laid out with drives, playing fields, lawns and gardens. The new buildings dedicated to science, agriculture, engineering, architecture, are really impressive. In a single year twelve thousand schools have been opened. Old Spain registered eighty-five per cent illiteracy! A loan of five hundred million pesetas has been floated for schools alone. In addition to schools, pedagogical missions are organized to tour the villages with cinemas, equipped with radios, gramophones, a week's visit to each village. Theaters, too, portray history, art and practical science, with a touch of humor here and there. Charlie Chaplin is a tremendous favorite. Money is flowing like water from the confiscation of great estates and taxation of great fortunes. The church is made to release its millions, stored up in the great cathedrals and religious houses. There is danger here. Does the Republic realize how great is the danger? The events of 1937 seem to indicate they did not.

The Governing Body completes its work and we are off on our return journey. Toledo! What a city! What a history! What priceless art relics of ancient days! And the cathedral! Ah, how tragic the futility of mere words. I attended a service in that great ancient fane on a high saint's day. We are certainly fortunate. The Toledo choir of men and boys is famous throughout Spain. The anthem is new to me. Never have I heard such strange, wild harmonies. They told me later that as in the cathedral structure there are touches of Gothic, Visigothic and Moorish architecture, so in their church music there is a touch now and then of the Visigoth. This is great music soaring up into the arched dome overhead. The anthem moves onward and upward in a succession of mighty crescendos.

"There," I said to myself after a great climax, "that is your limit. You can't beat that."

But once more the choir begins its onward and upward march. Up and still up, deeper, fuller, stronger, the mighty strains soar till at length in the final crescendo the whole lofty nave seems to rock with a mighty blast of brazen trumpets, carrying the voices upward to hitherto untouched heights.

"How did they do that?" I ask myself.

I glance up at the organ. There protruding at right angles to the pipes I see a series of brazen-mouthed trumpets. Ah! now I understand the tremendous overwhelming climax of that glorious final crescendo. I found myself with fingers deep into my palm and my breath coming quick. It was that final brazen touch of the barbaric Visigoth that did it.

But the people? Where are they with such a service going on? Twenty-three old women, six old men and about the doors a throng of wretched, ragged, blear-eyed beggars. The mass of the people show little interest in this great religious service. It is quite remote from them.

Now we are away again. Rich country, orchards, vineyards, grain fields and gardens. How is this? The water is on the land. Through numberless little ditches it carries its touch of life.

The irrigation system wakens my curiosity. Every farm has its own. I see a mule plodding his weary eternal round beside a well. A deep well, an endless chain of buckets, the mule turns a wheel and the water flows.

The farmer explains volubly. He is proud of his vegetables, pulls up onions, carrots for us. We offer to pay. Not at all. This is from one gentleman to another. We offer a package of cigarettes. With a sweeping bow, it might have been from an ancient cavalier, he accepts.

This irrigation problem is the problem of agricultural Spain. Give Spain water and the products of its soil will go over the world. Small wonder the new government is spending millions on the study of irrigation systems, even in America and Canada. But when all the money from the confiscated estates of the gentry is gone, what then? I wonder.

They are honestly, earnestly trying to solve Spain's agricultural, educational, industrial problems. But all at once. Are they too ambitious? Time will tell.

I ask quietly here and there about the King. There is no hatred of him, only of his entourage of military officers, great landed gentry, great merchants, and the church with its vast wealth, more loyal to the great princes and lords than to the masses of toiling peoples, struggling desperately to live. This eternal tendency of all great churches is their eternal undoing. This is the story of the Christian church in all its branches for two thousand years. They forget the common people, their needs, their problems, their wrongs and the people forget them.

The King had begun well. He was modern in his thinking and eager to serve his people following in his father's steps. He inaugurated great schemes, roads, public utilities, agriculture, tourist travel. The revenues of the country rose in fifteen years from fifty million pounds to almost a hundred million. But alas! for him, he had not the training in democratic institutions and form of government which his father had known in England and which found noble expression in his first manifesto written from Sandhurst to his people. Here is a fragment:

"In the early days of the monarchy, Spanish princes set nothing of first-class importance in hand without first consulting the Cortes. I shall not forget this—and when the time arrives for action, agreement will be easy for a loyal prince and a free people."

His son forgot this thing, that for centuries in the common people of Spain there had been a strain of passionate liberalism. Read this oath of allegiance administered in 1187 to Alfonso I:

"We, who are as good as you, swear to you, who are no better than ourselves, to accept you as our Sovereign Lord, provided you observe all our statutes and laws, but not if you fail to do so."

This from Spanish people in the twelfth century!

Alfonso XIII made one fatal mistake. He forgot that he was king for his people's good, not for his own greater glory. He made the mistake of linking his fate with the nobles, the church, the army, rather than with the common people. He had not learned the lesson so often forgotten by rulers, that to rule a people a king must first serve them.

But Walter is driving hard. He sees the piles of correspondence in the Canadian office of the League, and he hears the low steady grind of the mills of the International Labour Organization. But his democratic spirit halts him at Tarragona.

Tarragona! The reverberations of the centuries roll through it. Tarragona, Rome's western outport of defense against barbarians nineteen hundred years ago. Let us visit the necropolis where their bones lie in the dust. It is partly built over by a factory where millions of cigarettes are manufactured every day. Could a decadent age express more fittingly its contempt of its mighty dead? We descend to view their tombs which still taunt the tooth of time. Christian and pre-

Christian tombs, invoking in their inscription Jesus and Jupiter alike. Their symbols chiseled in the marble recall their deeds, their faith, their triumphs. These symbols—the fish, the rising sun, the entwined initials of the Sacred Name—speak of the triumph of Christian faith over life's last enemy, Death. But pause here. Ah, what a poignant stab! A tiny alabaster coffin holding a tiny skeleton and beside it, in exquisitely carved ivory, a little doll. Two thousand years ago a mother's tears fell fast as she laid the little doll in the waxen hands of her dead baby.

About us everywhere are the remains of mighty Rome, mistress of the world from China to the Pillars of Hercules, from Germanic forests to the sands of the Arabian desert. But not mistress of herself. Her wealth besotted her. Power made her heartless. Sixty million slaves sweated blood that Rome might gratify her lusts. She forgot her people, her lusts dragged her down to destruction. When will the nations learn this eternal lesson of the ages?

With humbled hearts we turn from that necropolis to the noblest of all tasks—the service of God, which is the service of humanity.

CHAPTER XXXVIII

For Peace and Democracy

RISE OF FASCISM—PLACE OF THE CHURCH IN RE-
BUILDING THE WORLD—INTERNATIONAL ARBITRA-
TION—WAY TO PEACE

(Note: It was not originally intended that this letter should be part of the book. The letter answered a request for my father's comments on a statement by the moderator of the United Church of Canada expressing horror at the desolation and suffering in China. The letter is my father's last public statement. It is at once a confession of faith and a desperate call to action—the action necessary if peace and democracy are to be saved. It comes fittingly at the close of this record and is included in its original form.—J. K. G.)

FIRST let me express my satisfaction at the existence of the League for Peace and Democracy. The name of the organization indicates its line of approach to the subject of world peace. A few months ago I could not have linked into a unity the two ideas of peace and democracy. The threat of fascism had appeared to me as fantastic folly which, however seriously it might be taken by such pitiably neurotic peoples as Germany and Italy, would never be taken seriously by sane peoples such as those of Great Britain and those composing the young nations of the British Commonwealth. The fantastic caperings of Sir Oswald Mosley and the young bloods that largely constitute his following in England seemed worthy only of the contempt of sane folk. But recent world events have changed my mind. I have come to feel that fascism constitutes a very real threat to the democratic peoples of the world. So long as fascism was confined to Germany and Italy, both of whom have apparently been bitten by the bug of world imperialism, I was content to let them work out to a finish their own madness. But the tragedies enacted in Abyssinia and in Spain have forced me to consider this threat of fascism as grave enough to force democratic peoples to take it seriously. So long as fascism seemed to express itself in wild mobs of parading youths, garbed in shirts of many colors and expressing their various allegiances in fantastic salutes to their superior officers, I was content to regard it with mild contempt. But Ethiopia and Spain have changed all that. The alliances of these two fascist nations in an obvious policy to impose upon European peoples a government of autocratic absolutism must awaken grave concern in the minds of all who believe in free government for free people.

The recent outrage of Japan upon China serves only to intensify the gravity of this new world madness in its relation even to such a country as Canada. It is significant, too, that in initiating this last outrage upon China, Japan should formally proclaim a fascist government.

You enclose a copy of the utterance of the Rev. Dr. Peter Bryce, moderator of the United Church of Canada, under the caption, "I can no longer keep silent." You describe this as a "moving appeal," and rightly so. It is a moving appeal. My first reaction to this breaking of silence on the part of the distinguished Christian minister was one of surprise that the head of a great church like the United Church of Canada and a former moderator could succeed in keeping silent so long.

Indeed, the amazing phenomenon in the whole vast area of world politics during the last nineteen years is the deadly silence of the Christian churches of the world in regard to the moral implication of the International happenings. The magnificent gesture of President Woodrow Wilson in the direction of world government in the interests of justice and goodwill was an expression of the fundamental basic faith of the Christian religion in a Kingdom of God whose primary and essential principles are Righteousness, Peace and Goodwill.

The League of Nations was declared by many distinguished Christian leaders to be an authentic expression of this Kingdom of God. But the Treaty of Versailles, whose creation it was, gave the lie to this declaration, for in some of its essential articles the Treaty was the negation of righteousness, peace and goodwill. In its very terms it incorporated injustice, it made peace impossible, and it sowed the seeds of permanent national hatreds.

Why did the Christian churches of the world, whose very reason for existence is the Kingdom of God, make no protest, offer no suggestion, make no appeal? How could they have kept silent?

The League of Nations is the first and noblest world attempt to express in concrete form the foundation principles of the Christian church. For long I believed in the League of Nations, but as I saw it in action during some six weeks in 1932, I was conscious of a certain uneasiness. There were great and noble men there. Men of high character and honest purpose, such as M. Herriott and Paul Boncour for France, M. Beneš for Czechoslovakia, Dr. W. W. Yen for China, Birger Braadland for Norway, M. Madariaga for Spain, Lord Robert Cecil for Great Britain, Cahan and Dr. Riddell for Canada. Yet, as I listened to their debating, as I watched their diplomatic maneuverings, I could not help a feeling of dismay. They were supposed to be there to promote world right and world peace, to guard the rights of weak peoples, to eradicate social evils from the world and above all, to promote goodwill among nations. I was conscious of a great lack at that point in all their deliberations. They were intent, mainly, it seemed, to preserve the peace of the world by maintaining so far as possible the world status quo.

In conversation with Lord Robert Cecil, a great statesman and a great Christian, I ventured to refer to what I considered a great lack in the working of the League. I had come into somewhat intimate relations with Lord Robert. It was he who had read the lesson in the service in the old Cathedral of Saint-Pierre where I had the honor and privilege of preaching the League Sermon from John Calvin's old pulpit.

"Yes," he said, "what is that?"

"It is the absence of that moral passion which at the first brought the League into being. In conversation with President Wilson himself I came to the conviction that in his heart there burned a fervent desire to awaken among the nations of the world a passion for international justice and goodwill long before he proposed his plan for a League of Nations."

He paused a few moments and said gravely, "I believe you are entirely right. I fear that moral fervor in the League is dying out." Then he added, "But how can that moral passion be rekindled?"

"I have been wondering what would happen if the Christian churches in the world were banded together to promote and to back up the purpose of the League in establishing goodwill among the nations. If they should constitute themselves into a Department of Goodwill."

"Ah!" he said with great emphasis, "if we only could have that!"

To M. Beneš I made the same remark. He threw up his hands and exclaimed, "Ah, if that could be realized? A League of Christian Churches behind the League! It is a noble idea. That might transform the whole spirit of the League."

I spoke to other leading men. Everywhere the idea was received with enthusiasm. Professor Adolf Keller, a wise Christian internationalist, was also keen for it, but doubtful of its possibility.

On my return to London I was invited to address a committee of the Alliance of Free Churches of Britain. I urged the idea of a League of Christian Churches to support the League of Nations, to pour into its organism the moral and spiritual fervor of Christian faith and practice. The whole committee was eager in its support of the idea and promised to do what they could in the matter. On my return to Canada I met a group of leading United Church laymen and laid the proposal before them. They were in fullest sympathy with the idea. I spoke to prominent officials of the church on the matter. Nothing came of it.

At two successive meetings of the Conference of Manitoba, strong resolutions were unanimously passed in support of the idea and sent on to the General Council. By the General Council they were given decent interment in the archives of that august body.

All this is in support of my statement that the Christian churches have conspicuously failed in pouring the passionate fervor of their life into the support of the sacred cause of world right and world peace.

True, resolutions have been passed, addresses have been delivered, sermons have been preached, but no definite movement pulsing with the fervid passion of Christian love for humanity and for the rights of the weak, secondary peoples of the world. There has been no ringing denunciation by the Christian churches of the world against the cynical robbery of China by Japan in 1932, the ruthless rape of Ethiopia by Italy, the shameless aiding and abetting of fascist brigands in their attempt to choke the life out of the new government of Spain, which is striving to free its people from the tyrannous, corrupt and shameless oppression and ruthless robbery by the united forces of the most oppressive aristocracy and the most corrupt Christian church that Europe has ever known. Yet in the face of all this Crucifixion of the Christ, His church has taken no united action, has expressed no horror, has offered no suggestion.

Yet when the funds of the church ran low in the days of the depression its officials organized a campaign, went out after the money, got it, and saved the church from what they called collapse. Now when the streets of Shanghai are running "rivers of blood" from the torn bodies of peace-loving and peace-seeking Chinese, the moderator of the United Church cannot any longer "keep silent." He makes a noble appeal. "Rivers of blood!" "Fragments of human bodies!" "Heaps of mangled women and children!" Whence came these rivers of blood? Whose bodies are these whose fragments shock the moderator? What cruelly massacred women and children are these? God's—the Christian God's. Why do these bloody rivers run? Why? That fascist Japan may build a world empire to join in the world threat of Germany and Italy against the liberties, the lives of free peoples like those of Canada. Why the silence of the Christian churches of the world? Was not all this their concern?

What is to be done now? Protests? Resolutions? No! Demands! Demands by such Christian churches of the world as still think more of the blood of slain men than they do of ceremonial rites, glorious cathedral structures, numbers of faithful devotees, or wealth in vested interests. The noble words of the ancient Hebrew prophet come echoing down the corridors of time, "Precious shall their blood be in his sight." Demands that the governments, whom they have helped to elect, will have no art nor part in the activities, political, economic, industrial or social, of governments whose policies demand "rivers of blood," "fragments of human bodies" and "heaps of mangled women and children." Dangerous? Yes, very dangerous. But not so dangerous as becoming partners in these bloody activities and in the results, political, economic, industrial or social, that follow. Let the governments who still wish to rule free peoples, who stand for right and goodwill between nations, come out clean from fellowship with these governments whose policies inevitably issue in "rivers of blood." That may mean war and Christian churches do not believe in war. Then let them suffer for their former infidelities to their faith and with their own blood purge their skirts from the blood of the innocent whom they did not lift a finger to save. For it is God's way of administering justice that those whose policy it is to lay the foundations of their empire in blood will themselves see their empire laid low in bloody ruin. Is any lover of peace so deaf to the message of human history that he will not understand that empires built at the cost of human blood will not shrink from the shedding of blood in their defense? Is there any student of history so dull as to imagine that the triumph of fascism in Germany and Italy will not involve the extension of fascism throughout Europe? Or is anyone dull enough to imagine that democratic Britain and the democratic commonwealth of British peoples can purchase their democratic freedom without putting down the price of peace in blood when dealing with fascist and triumphant Europe and Japan?

Will a fascist Japanese Empire, dominating the Orient, make terms on a basis of international justice with Australia? Will a fascist Germany and Italy, heading a great European coalition of fascist states, heed any remonstrance from Belgium, from the Netherlands, yes, even from France herself? All this is madness, some people will say. Yes, but this is the lesson written plain in the history of the great empires from Sumer to Rome. Rivers of Blood! The runways of history run full with blood. And unless the spirit of the Kingdom of God, which is right and peace and goodwill, and which is supposed to be the spirit of the church of Christ, is to overcome that spirit of Antichrist which is dictating the policies of the great fascist empires today, history will repeat itself in our day and in that of our children.

Is it too late? No. The moral and spiritual forces that exist in the Living Body of the Living Christ are still invincible because they are of the Lord God Almighty and because righteousness is the only enduring foundation of enduring peace. But these forces are found only in the Living Body of the Living Christ. What is that Living Body of the Living Christ? The massed church membership of our Christian churches. "He beheld the city, and wept over it, 'Oh Jerusalem! Jerusalem!'" A church of God once crucified the Christ of God. Will history repeat that tragic story? Let the moderator of the United Church and the members of that church ponder that question. And all of us.

But I hear two questions with a note of impatience in them. First, what definite thing could the Christian church do in the interests of right and goodwill and peace in the world? Second, is there the remotest possibility of anything like united opinion or action among the Christian churches of the world?

Let us deal first with the second. I do confess to some dismay when I ask myself under what possible conditions could we secure anything like unity of opinion and action in regard to any single international question of first-class importance? But let us fall back upon the foundation principles of the Christian faith. And I select only three.

First: The Founder of our Christian faith believed in unity of His church. For this, in his last prayer with them, he made earnest petition to His Heavenly Father. But practical men will answer by a single gesture of contempt, "Look at your Christian churches of this twentieth century. Unity? What absurdity!" Before this appalling fact of disunity we may well stand humiliated. Yet in the Living Christian church the desire of its Founder cannot be ignored. In spite of tragic failure in the past, I hold to the faith of our religion that the thing desired by the Head of the church, His church can achieve.

Second: The objective of the Kingdom of God, to establish which His Christ came to earth, consists of righteousness, peace and goodwill. The failure of the Christian church to achieve this great objective is a serious failure, but the refusal to seek this as an ideal is a negation of the Christian religion. The church accepting this failure with content has ceased to be a Christian church.

Third: It is of the Christian faith that the hope of humanity to realize its noblest destiny lies in the establishing among the nations the reign of right, goodwill and peace.

Let us revive our faith. The history of the Christian church in spite of its present lassitude and infidelity is radiant with achievements no less difficult and glorious than the establishing of peace among the nations upon a basis of right and goodwill today.

Let us not be too pessimistic over the League's failures. The story of the services of the League itself to humanity, in spite of these lamentable failures, is a stimulus to the hope that world peace may yet be attained. Anyone who has followed the history of the League's services to humanity in the areas of peacemaking, social service, economic cooperation, humanitarian achievement, national reorganization, cannot fail to be inspired with a profound conviction that in a League properly constituted and resolutely backed by all people loving right and goodwill, there lie immense possibilities of service to the world. On the other hand, without some such institution all that is left is chaos.

During the first seven years of its history, the League prevented twenty-seven threatened wars. Its achievements in the suppression of slavery, the checking of the trade in narcotics, of the white slave trade, its championing of the causes of oppressed minorities, its financial rehabilitation of nations threatened with bankruptcy, its reorganization, for instance, of the bankrupt and disintegrated Republic of Liberia and in that connection the putting an end to the ruthless outrages by that republic upon the twenty-five tribes of Kru natives in the Liberian hinterland, all these works of goodwill give promise of what is possible through a League backed resolutely by a united and organized Christian church, for all these are Christian services of humanity.

Had there been an organized department of the League representing the spirit of the Christian Church who raison d'être was the promotion of goodwill by a sympathetic study of the causes of strife, economic, racial, yes, and political, and by patient and wise effort in the removal of these causes, there need not have been the first outrage of Japan upon China. With a Department of Goodwill expressing and promoting the spirit and practice of the Christian church actively operating in the League, Japan need not have walked out of the League. Indeed, there was an open door for sympathetic study of Japan's claims, Japan's needs, incorporated in a clause in the Lytton Report. I was amazed that there was no reference to that clause. A Department of Goodwill would have seized upon the suggestion in that clause and might have averted that international calamity. Similarly, with a Goodwill Department actively operating in the League, the Ethiopia outrage might have been averted.

Nations have hearts that can be deeply stirred by deeds of kindness. I can never forget the effect upon the Assembly of the League, composed as it is of shrewd diplomats, of a speech by Dr. Yen of China, conveying to the League the gratitude of over three hundred millions of his people for the League's magnificent engineering achievement in rendering secure against floods, two thousand miles of the Yangtse River on both banks, under the direction of a committee of expert engineers selected by the League. As a brilliant Chinese gentleman told his story, with tears in his voice expressing his nation's gratitude in eloquent words, even that Assembly of hard-boiled diplomats was deeply moved.

I believe in the fundamental basis of the League of Nations. It is a gesture in the direction of justice and goodwill. It has not altogether failed, not by any means, but it has not fulfilled the hopes it kindled in the hearts of hundreds of millions of right-thinking people through-out the world, sick of war and convinced of its futility as an instrument of peace. But the League as at present constituted will never succeed in bringing the nations together in an atmosphere of kindly goodwill. The League as at present constituted is not the League of President Wilson's dream. I know, because in the White House before his people decided to enter the Great War he gave me a hint of what was in his mind. He had no idea of a League of World Powers, organized to give ex-pression to the idea of peace by force.

The League will fail so long as its final hope lies in force. What it needs is a Department of Goodwill behind which will be organized the massed convictions and the united and sacrificial energies of all those millions of loyal Christian hearts who truly believe in a Kingdom of Heaven, which is right and peace and goodwill and who sincerely pray to Him they adore, and whose Kingdom it is, "Thy Kingdom Come."

To the practical churchman, the man to whom the church stands as a symbol and guarantee of well-ordered, kindly, honest and successful living, all this concern for other than our own people may seem fanci-ful and idealistic if well-meaning folly. "Look at your world," he says. "Can you imagine that any sort of goodwill activities by such Christian churches as could be mobilized for such a purpose would turn fascist Germany, with her world ambitions, her theory of absolutism in govern-ment, her idea of a totalitarian state absorbing all authorities and pow-ers, into any other than she is today?"

The answer is "Yes."

We all remember the Germany of 1913, bristling with military equipment, beating the big war drum, challenging, threatening the whole of Europe. One day in August of that year—note the date—I was in Premier Asquith's office in No. 10 Downing Street, in company with that wise, enthusiastic, unwearied champion of peace, Mr. Joe Allen Baker, M.P. We were talking about the possibilities of war.

"Mr. Asquith," I said, "I should greatly like to carry back with me to Canada a definite answer from you to this question, "What is your judgment as to the prospects of war with Germany in the immediate future?"

The Premier remained silent for a few moments and then made a deliberate answer. "Had you asked me that question six months ago I should have been forced to answer that I considered the possibilities of war with Germany in the very near future as very grave indeed. But within these six months a remarkable change has taken place in German public opinion. You have read of the exchange visits of the great Peace Missions between Germany and Britain, organized largely by the untiring efforts of my friend here, Mr. Joe Allen Baker. They were church deputations mainly. The results of these exchanges of visitations, of frank conference in an atmosphere of goodwill between great church leaders, have been perfectly amazing. For these and other reasons I can authorize you to tell your people that in my judgment the danger of immediate war with Germany has largely passed away."

Within a year, owing to the mad act of a crazed pressman, the Austrian guns were blazing into Belgrade. But that fact does not weaken the validity of Mr. Asquith's judgment as to the value of patient and wise conference in an atmosphere of goodwill in the alleviating of the causes of strife between nations.

I have tested this plan in my four years' experience as chairman of the Council of Industry for Manitoba for the composing of industrial disputes than which there are none more bitter, more savage, more unreasonable that I know. Yet out of one hundred and seven cases of industrial strife of all kinds, one hundred and seven were composed, and the contending parties who entered our council rooms in furious enmity went out in the most friendly relations. The principles are the same whether in small things or great. Human nature is the same in great statesmen and petty factory bosses. I believe that, given an honest desire for peace, all matters of dispute between nations can be composed by patient, wise and understanding conference, in an atmosphere of sympathy and goodwill, by men of understanding who are earnestly seeking a way of peace.

A department of Goodwill in the structure of the League, backed by the Christian churches of the world, would go far to remove causes of conflict and compose international jealousies and hatreds in the interests of world peace.

But the method and plan upon which the Christian churches might operate in the interests of world peace are matters for discovery by men of wisdom, experience, courage and Christian loyalty. The one motive behind this writing is the earnest desire that some Christian leader or leaders may not only refuse to any longer "keep silent" but may be moved to action such as will mobilize the Christian churches of the world for united effort in the interest of world peace upon foundation of right and goodwill, so that Christian churches everywhere may pray truly and not in mumbling mockery, "Thy Kingdom Come," and "rivers of blood" shall cease to run down the streets of cities where people, after all, do most earnestly desire to live in peace.

CHAPTER XXXIX

Two Women

THIS WRITING began, as did my life, with a woman, and it ends with a woman. More than all other influences, these two women inspired me and determined all that is best in me. The first woman came into my life in a Presbyterian manse in that part of Glengarry County known as the Indian Lands. A wild new land it was, peopled by emigrants from the Highlands of Scotland who, driven forth by their overlords from their little crofts among the hills, gallantly gave themselves to the high adventure of taming the dark Canadian forest into fruitful farms and happy homes for themselves and their children, carrying in their hearts the fear of God but knowing no other fear. To that high adventure my father, a young and fiery Highland minister, brought with him a young woman from her cultured home in the town of Sherbrooke where an earlier migration from Scotland had settled among the French habitants of Quebec in what was known as the Eastern Townships. Into the wilds of the dark pine forest my father brought this valiant, delicate, intellectual young lady who, while still a girl of twenty-three, declining the principalship of Mount Holyoke Ladies' Seminary, at that time the finest educational institution of its kind in the United States, set forth with the soul of the saints of old to give herself mind and heart and body to this high enterprise of Christian service.

There for eighteen years, remote from all that beautiful and cultured environment in which she had been born and bred, she lived bearing her children, six boys and one girl, making for them and her husband a home as like as was possible in spirit and intellectual atmosphere to that home in which she had been reared. She rode the forest trails on her little French-Canadian pony, helping the women to make their homes something like her own, bringing to them and their daughters the beauty and fragrance of her own Christian spirit, all without the faintest suggestion of sacrifice but with the gay courage of God's true saints in all ages.

Later her home was, for twenty years, in another Scottish community, West Zorra in Oxford County. Her environment had more of culture and larger opportunity, but her life and her service till the end breathed the same lofty spirit of devotion.

In the midst of her busy working, young as any of us at her three score years, God called her. In gladness of spirit and serenity of faith, pledging her seven children to the service of God and humanity, she closed her eyes in peace taking with her the dearest and loveliest thing I had known in life.

Her six sons carried her to her grave and covered her with God's kindly earth, but never could one of them speak of her without a quickening of the heartbeat.

Even yet in my highest moods, when my memory wanders back over the years and rests awhile amid my misty memories of old Glengarry days, I find my heartbeat quicken with a dull ache just for sheer longing for her, my mother.

The other woman I saw first when I was a young man at college. She came romping into her mother's drawing room with her young brother and coming to me, a stranger, greeted me with frank and fearless camaraderie. A wee girl, not beautiful except for her eyes, blue as a bit of sky and as clear. We had a game which ended in her sitting on my knee.

My brother Gib and I were members of her father's church through university and college days and were frequent visitors in Dr. King's home.

After my experiences among the mountain and foothill country in Western Canada as a missionary, I became the minister in a city mission in Winnipeg. Dr. King, who had left his church in Toronto to become first principal of Manitoba College, was my leading elder and his daughter, a schoolgirl preparing for university, was a loyal and enthusiastic worker in the mission. Loyalty, a cheery, enthusiastic loyalty, was her striking characteristic. Her smile was like a sunburst. It still is and she has handed it on to her six daughters. She became a university student, not brilliant, but again her loyalty to her duty won her a good place in the class lists, bringing her a scholarship in German. The young people of my church were a jolly lot, Christians of a wholesome type, fond of clean sports and keen for all sorts of social activities. I made large demands on their time and their energies. They responded, most of them, with a wholehearted devotion that made my work among St. Stephen's young people the very joy of my life. There were, of course, those among them who needed constant watchful care and checking up. But never Helen King. Anything she undertook she carried through to a perfect finish. She brought to her work a conscience that never failed. Throughout the forty-three years of my ministry not one single instance can I remember where she failed to carry through whatever she undertook.

She lost her mother, a high-souled lady, in her early girlhood. Her father's sister came to take charge of the household and faithfully did her duty by the two motherless children. Her young brother also died in early life, one of the most attractive lads I ever knew and this left her as the light of her father's eyes and the comfort of his heart. She graduated from Manitoba University and began to assume larger responsibility in her home. She passed out of her girlhood and became a young lady. Her home became a second home to me. Young men began to hover about her. I assumed a big brother's responsibility for her. I undertook to choose her friends for her, but that she quietly but effectually put an end to. She let me see that she felt quite competent to order her own life. This greatly disturbed me. However, I accepted her decision and allowed her to attend to her own affairs while I attended to mine. It annoyed me, I confess, to discover in her a new competence, a new efficiency, and a new independence that made my care quite unnecessary. An example of this I remember well.

One night in my big-brother role, I had treated somewhat lightly an engagement to meet her at a certain place and time. I failed to meet her. I had what I considered a perfectly satisfactory reason, some duty I had to perform which I thought should take precedence over a social engagement with a little girl. I came to the place of meeting. She was not there. I was quite annoyed and somewhat anxious. I found her at home, quite placidly engaged in a bit of work which apparently she considered a matter of some importance. In answer to my annoyed remonstrance she said:

"You were not there. I waited a quarter of an hour, then I came home." Her voice was quite pleasant but there was a tone of offended dignity. I explained the situation. She listened quite unmoved, then with a pleasant smile she replied:

"I understand. Your other engagement was quite important. I did not matter."

"Good night," I said crossly and turned toward the door.

With a swift movement she stood with her back to the door, barring my exit.

"No! You can't go away like that," she said as if speaking to a bad little boy. Her quiet dignity, the utter rightness of her attitude showed her to me in a new light. This young woman could no longer be treated as a child, and I, her minister, must carry myself as a minister and a gentleman should. With apology and regrets I acknowledged my fault, when with her old flashing, radiant smile, she held out her hand.

"Now that is quite all right. Good night. You are coming to tennis tomorrow at two remember."

I went away, humbled and rather dazed. So far as Helen King was concerned, my whole life had changed. Apparently she could get along quite satisfactorily without me, but without her my life would hold a blank that nothing else could fill. I sat down to some work. I could not make it go. I went about putting some finishing touches to my sermon, but between my eyes and the paper there was ever and anon the trim, taut figure, the serene, self-confident face and the radiant smile of a young woman quite competent to order her own life as she thought best. But to me she had suddenly become important. Important? No, absolutely essential. The child was gone. The big-brother and little-sister notion became absurd. This was an entirely new situation to me. Of all the girls I had known, charming, attractive, never had I treated one of them as other than a good comrade and friend. This was something new. This girl was different from all others. I wanted her for myself. I began to count the years between us. Alas, she was far too young for me. The thing was absurd. I determined to turn this page down and attend to my business. Next morning I telephoned to call the tennis off.

"Oh, why? It's such a lovely day and I have the lawn all cut." It was the voice of a little girl frankly disappointed and a little hurt.

I could not bear that hurt tone.

"Oh—well—let's see—perhaps—oh, hang it all, I guess I can come."

"Oh, good!" came the joyous response and then, "Besides, it *was* an engagement, you know."

"I'll be there," I said, but I was quite resolved not to make an ass of myself. I would carry on as before but with a strict supervision of my heart reactions.

This is an old old story, as old as Eden and as new as today. I became absorbed in my work. I gave up tennis à deux. I arranged our sports in groups. Helen King went serenely on her way. I have since asked her if she knew how carefully I began to plan my engagements so as to avoid tête-à-tête combinations. She knew nothing of all this. Now it all seemed rather foolish to her. She was too simple, too sincere, too modest to plan meetings by accident.

Then her father took a hand. It was my custom to dine every Sunday at the principal's house. This I put an end to. I found that the preparation for my men's class took every spare minute of my Sunday afternoon. There was a strange mingling of pain and a secret satisfaction as I noted the dismay in her face when I announced my inability to continue my Sunday dinner engagements. Soon after this the principal had a serious conversation with me on the matter. I told him frankly how it was with me. He pointed out the absurdity of it all owing to the disparity in our ages. I entirely agreed with him. I would be more careful in the future. I was too careful. In making an elaborate explanation of the situation I spoiled it all. My secret escaped me. I have never forgotten the quick flash of rapture in her eyes as I told her that for her father's sake and for my own sake I must keep away from her. The joy in her voice amazed me. Nothing mattered but the fact that it was because I loved her that I must keep away from her.

"Keep away from me?" She laughed aloud. "Don't be silly. Everything will come out all right." Her high courage made her scorn difficulties. Everything would come right. She was content to wait events.

Her father sent her for a winter to Edinburgh. No letters passed.

Then an important event forced her father's hand. A call from a young and promising congregation in a Montreal suburb came to me.

This offered me a respite from the intolerable situation in which I found myself. My session and my congregation, however, would not consider any change in our relations as minister and people. Dr. King himself urged me to remain in St. Stephen's. I pointed out the intolerable nature of my position. I felt sorry for him.

"Give me time," he begged.

I declined the call. His daughter returned unchanged as, of course, I knew she would. Nothing under heaven would change that girl's heart. Loyal to her father, she made no plan to further our desires. "Everything will come out all right" was her word. Her courage, her serene faith, her wise, wise heart taught her patience.

Then unexpectedly her father became seriously ill. I visited him daily. He was very good to me. He treated me as if I were his son as well as his minister. As he neared the end he called me to his bedside.

"I don't want you to think I have anything against you," he said. "I feel very happy that Helen will be in your care. She would be happy with no one else. I am content."

"You will be good to her," he said in our last talk together. "She has a very loyal and a very tender heart."

"Don't I know it?" I said.

We were married in Toronto. My father was still alive though retired from active service and would, of course, expect to officiate at the ceremony. There was one grave difficulty in the matter, and that was his tendency to sermonize. An address of half an hour, or indeed of three-quarters of an hour, might easily be expected. This I resolved must be avoided at all costs. Yet to pass him over would wound him terribly. Very cleverly, as I thought, I avoided the difficulty by asking Mac Hamilton, first bass in the Student Quintet and one of my closest college friends, to take the service, assigning to my father the actual putting of the vows and the tying of the knot, which could not possibly take more than five minutes.

I ought to have known my father better. With his utter disregard for all ordinary forms and customs he proceeded to make the most of what was a really great occasion in his life and mine. I was his son, the only son who had become a minister, the last unmarried of six. The bride was the daughter, the only daughter, of a distinguished churchman, a principal of a college, a moderator of the General Assembly. This was one of the great moments of his life, and the last and only opportunity of functioning at so important an event. To put him off with five minutes? This would be a desecration of a holy ordinance of the church, and a mere trifling with one of the events in the history of the Gordon Clan.

It took him just thirty-five minutes to "put the vows" with an appropriate elaboration of the nature of marriage, its symbolic representation of the bond between Christ and His church, its functions in the life of a people and other cognate subjects. My agonized facial contortions made not the slightest impression on him, only to stir him up to further elaborations.

"Ah!" he exclaimed in answer to my uplifted eyebrows, "a very important doctrine! And one too often forgotten by young people upon such an occasion as this!" And away he went along a new line of argumentation. He might have heard the grinding of my teeth in my fury, though that would have only stimulated him to further flights. The prayer that followed took twenty-five minutes.

I must confess that at the close I was in no mood for felicitations. It did not help my mood that my men friends were in paroxysms of delight at the huge joke of which I was the subject. Nor later when in response to my furious ravings in the train to my new-made wife, over what I called an outrage, she took it lightly, rather sympathizing with my father's evident determination to make of the event an occasion. Indeed, she was much amused at my making so much of a mere eccentricity of an old gentleman's desire to do special honor to his son and his son's new wife.

Forty years of experience of her gentle heart have only emphasized my amazement at her capacity to make little of other people's faults and failings.

Our welcome home was the occasion of a great congregational meeting. It was a welcome to her father's daughter as well as to the minister's wife.

Every young married man yearns to be thought a hero by his wife, and every young preacher eagerly waits for a word of commendation of his sermon from his wife, especially during the early days. Her sensitive nature shrank from anything savoring of flattery. I firmly believe she thought I was a good preacher and at times preached quite a decent sermon. But would she utter a single word of praise? I could not drag it out of her.

"Fine congregation!" I would say as we walked home together.

"Yes, a splendid congregation." A pause.

"And didn't they sing heartily?"

"Yes, indeed, the singing was fine." And then another pause.

"A great subject that."

"Yes, a really fine theme." Silence.

"And they listened well too!"

"Yes. Of course, I couldn't see their faces from my seat." A longer silence.

"Well, dash it all! Wasn't it a good sermon?"

"Oh, yes. A very good sermon indeed. I liked it."

She has heard hundreds of sermons from me, some of them in my moments of inspiration, which I considered quite good. But never once can I remember her volunteering a word of praise of even my best efforts. She emphatically denies this but such is my remembrance. There was in her a shy modesty that made impossible anything like flattery or even sincere praise.

The congregation were carefully considerate of her. It was difficult for her to take the place of the minister's wife in a congregation where she had been a child. The young people remained her comrades and friends but somehow, though so young, she held their respect. The older women mothered her and took her under their care, and when it became known that she was to have a baby their tender consideration was most beautiful to see. Many a time also did they venture to instruct and admonish their minister as to the care he should give his wife, under the special circumstances.

The arrival of a baby in a home is so commonplace an incident that I had never estimated the tremendous significance of the event, nor the possibility of tragedy in connection with it. But when with blushing timidity—she was old-fashioned enough to be shy, thank God —she told me that she was actually to produce a baby I began to think new thoughts, to fear new terrors. It did not help in the least that millions of babies were born every year or that in almost every home in my congregation the thing was a common event. It was my wife who was facing a woman's most terrible hazard. In the new situation I made new discoveries as to my wife. She laughed at my fears, she made nothing of her peril. I have often thought that God must provide a special endowment of courage for the event. My wife cannot sing.

She can distinguish between "God Save the King" and "Old Hundred" but beyond that her musical knowledge is hazy. But in those days I could hear her going about her household tasks singing softly to herself. She amazed me.

One night a nurse arrived in the house. I waited with my wife in her bedroom trying "to keep her mind occupied." She laughed at me and turned me out.

"Go out and make a few calls," she said. She was ever keeping me up to my pastoral duties.

"What! Leave the house?" I was shocked at her heartlessness.

"Well, go down cellar and fix up the furnace. Get some kindling split." I used to tend my own furnace in those days.

"There is plenty of kindling," I answered.

"Well, go away and stay away. I'm going to be busy."

"You heartless creature," I cried.

"Well, why make all the fuss? It's not you that's going to have the baby."

"Quite right," said the nurse, "you are much better out of the way."

I went down to the cellar and began at the kindling. As I was piling up a good stock there came to me the thought, "Is the house warm enough for a new baby?" I hastened upstairs. I stood listening. The clock was ticking loudly. Agnes, my wife's old nurse, was in the kitchen.

"Do you think the house is warm enough for—I mean—it's a desperately cold night. Do you think the house is warm enough, Agnes?"

"I just opened the door a little ago," she said. "It was too hot."

"Oh, too hot, eh? Do you think I'd better check the furnace?"

"No, sir. It's cooler now."

"Oh, all right. By the way, is the doctor come?"

"Oh, no, sir. There is no need for the doctor just now."

"No need for—"

"I mean the nurse will call him when he is needed." Agnes spoke rather severely as if I had suggested some failure in duty in someone.

"Oh, of course. The nurse will attend to that, all right. I just wondered. He might be out, you know."

"He has been warned, sir. The nurse has instructions in case he's needed."

"Oh, of course," I said with a careless air.

"By the way, what is the time?" I then asked glancing at the kitchen clock. "What's the matter with the clock? It's only nine."

"The clock was correct at noon today, sir," said Agnes. "I always sort it at noon if it need anything."

"Oh, of course. It's all right," I replied, glancing at my watch.

"There is no need for anxiety, sir," said Agnes in a pitying tone. "The nurse is upstairs and I am staying here."

"Oh, certainly. I only thought—" But what I thought I never revealed as at that moment the doorbell rang.

"The doctor," I said. "I'll answer it, Agnes."

"It'll no be the doctor," said Agnes reprovingly. "He'll come when he is sent for."

"Oh! Yes! Well, I'll see no one. I'm busy."

"Busy? It might be better if ye were busy," said Agnes, with the liberty of one who had been on duty the night my wife arrived in the world.

The memory of that night is still a nightmare to me. Before midnight the doctor arrived. I went in with him to the bedroom. My wife greeted him with a cheery smile. I was amazed at her. We chatted together, all of us in quite a jolly humor and my wife the gayest of us all.

During that night the doctor allowed me to see her two or three times. Each time she greeted me with cheerful courage, but would wave me away with a smile when her moment of agony approached. The hours dragged on. I never knew how long an hour was till that night. Toward morning the doctor came with a message. Things were not going well.

"She says you must go to bed. And you had better go. It will ease her mind."

"Sure, I will. Tell her I shall go at once. May I say good night?"

"Just run in for a single minute," said the doctor, "but for heaven's sake don't carry a face like that."

"I'll dance a jig, if you think it might help her. But, doctor, you must tell me the truth. I am no child. Is there any danger?"

"Danger? Well, I wouldn't say danger. But complications have arisen. Go in quietly, say good night and come away."

The doctor said afterwards that I behaved exactly as I should. But the sight of her wan and sunken eyes was worse to me than any battlefield I have seen since.

"I'm quite all right," she said and smiled at me. But her smile almost shattered my resolve to be calm and cheerful.

All that night and all next day the long-drawn agony went on. Late at night the doctor found me in the furnace room.

"We can save the mother," he said, "but I hardly think both."

"Then for God's sake save the mother, doctor," I said. "Nothing else matters."

But when he left I knelt and prayed.

The doctor came back in an hour.

"Everything's all right," he announced. "A fine boy!"

What I did I don't know. The doctor remained with me.

"You might see her for just a minute," he said.

I could have put my arms round him but I said nothing.

When I entered the room she looked up, smiled her old smile.

"Well, daddy! What do you think of him?"

"I don't care a hoot for him, if only you are all right."

"Oh, what a shame! Poor baby! Go and see him," she ordered.

"He looks all right, the little beggar," I said as the nurse held up a red and wrinkled little old man for me to admire.

As I left her the smile was still on her wan face. Courage! Smiling courage! That is her characteristic in times of stress. We have met many trials together. There have been times when I might have weakened in the face of threatening danger.

Duty. Right. Conscience. These were the regnant words in her vocabulary, and these words she has passed on to her family. She gave herself first of all to her home and family as she conceived to be her duty. Next came duties as a minister's wife. As to her record in that capacity ask any of the thousands who have known her work. The larger interests of the church, and especially the mission enterprises of the church, have taken first place with her in all her more public work. From her mother and her aunt, Mrs. Watt, both women of high devotion in all the women's missionary activities, she received her first missionary inspiration and training. All her life from early girlhood she has poured the full religious energy of her heart into that work till this present day, filling the most important and responsible offices in these organizations in congregation, presbytery and province with devotion and efficiency and with self-effacing modesty that have won the love and respect of all her fellow workers.

In the sphere of social duty she has made her home a place of rendezvous for young people homeless in a great city. She has in an especial degree the rare gift of winning and holding the trust and affection of young men whose homes are far away. To her they come with their problems and their difficulties and without their knowing she helps to keep them in ways that their mothers would approve.

I write these words in our island summer home at Birkencraig. Our home is full of young people all summer long as it has been for thirty years. She is easily the center and soul of all our summer sports and goings-on. No picnic, no game is perfect without her. She is the youngest and the gayest of all our routs. Her hair is gray and wrinkles line the smooth cheeks of her girlhood and she is now a grandmother, yet her spirit is as bright, her heart as young as that of the best of us, and on her shoulders still lies the burden of the household management. They all love her with a tender devotion and respect that is her chief reward. She never rebukes; rather, she excuses and palliates any little shortcoming in courtesy, or any break in temper that may befall and at the dock, when they take their departure, it is for her they keep their tenderest farewell.

What the end will be only God knows, but whenever and however it may come she will meet it with the same loyal love that has made her the light and joy of our home these happy golden years since that day forty-one years ago when in answer to my anxious question, "Do you really love me, Helen?" she answered, "Yes, I do. You know I do."

Yes, I know it well. When I doubt that I shall doubt God Himself. But never will that day come, please God, while life is mine.

L'ENVOI

Winnipeg, Canada, October 31, 1937

After this it was noised abroad that Mr. Valiant-for-truth was taken with a summons, by the same post as the other, and had this for a token that the summons was true: "That his pitcher was broken at the fountain." When he understood it, he called for his friends and told them of it. Then said he, I am going to my fathers, and though with great difficulty I am got hither, yet now I do not repent me of all the trouble I have been at to arrive where I am. My sword I give to him that shall succeed me in my pilgrimage, and my courage and skill to him that can get it. My marks and scars I carry with me, to be a witness for me that I have fought His battles who now will be my rewarder. When the day that he must go hence was come, many accompanied him to the river-side, into which as he went he said, "Death, where is thy sting?" And as he went down deeper, he said, "Grave, where is thy victory?" So he passed over, and all the trumpets sounded for him on the other side.

INDEX

425

Books by Rev. Charles William Gordon (1860-1937)

THE ARM OF GOLD. 1932

BEYOND THE MARSHES. 1898

BLACK ROCK. 1898

BREAKING THE RECORD. 1904

CORPORAL CAMERON OF THE
  NORTH WEST MOUNTED POLICE. 1912

THE DOCTOR. 1906

THE FOREIGNER. 1909

THE FRIENDLY FOUR, AND OTHER STORIES. 1926

THE GASPARDS OF PINE CROFT. 1923

THE GAY CRUSADER. 1936

THE GIRL FROM GLENGARRY. 1933

GLENGARRY SCHOOL DAYS. 1902

GWEN. 1904

GWEN'S CANYON. 1898

HE DWELT AMONG US. 1936

THE MAJOR. 1917

THE MAN FROM GLENGARRY. 1901

MICHAEL McGRATH, POSTMASTER. 1900

THE PATROL OF THE SUN DANCE TRAIL. 1914

THE PILOT AT SWAN CREEK. 1905

THE PROSPECTOR. 1904

THE REBEL LOYALIST. 1935

THE ROCK AND THE RIVER. 1931

THE RUNNER. 1929

THE SKY PILOT. 1899

THE SKY PILOT IN NO MAN'S LAND. 1919

THE SWAN CREEK BLIZZARD. 1904

TO HIM THAT HATH. 1921

TORCHES THROUGH THE BUSH. 1934

TREADING THE WINEPRESS. 1925

THE LIFE OF JAMES ROBERTSON. 1908

POSTSCRIPT TO ADVENTURE. 1938

HERITAGE BOOKS

From the beginning, the experience of Canada has been recorded and illuminated by our writers—not only by the novelists and poets whom we think of as the prime makers of Canadian literature, but also by scores of biographers, diarists, travellers, clergymen, and parliamentarians. In the preface to *The Man from Glengarry*, Ralph Connor wrote: "The solid forests of Glengarry have vanished, and with the forests the men who conquered them. The manner of life and the type of character to be seen in those early days have gone too, and forever. It is part of the purpose of this book to so picture these men and their times that they may not drop quite out of mind. The men are worth remembering."

Heritage Books propose to recover from the past the lives and works of such men and women. Their lives are indeed worth remembering. More than that, their works are good to read. The records they have left testify to the energy and optimism of all the generations of Canadians—and each unique work is its own monument to the vigour, humour, and endurance of the man or woman who wrote it.

Clara Thomas
Professor, Department of English
York University